5/96

Sixties Radicals, Then and Now

Sixties Radicals, Then and Now

CANDID CONVERSATIONS WITH THOSE WHO SHAPED THE ERA

by Ron Chepesiuk

McFarland & Company, Inc., Publishers
Jefferson, North Carolina, and London

British Library Cataloguing-in-Publication data are available

Library of Congress Cataloguing-in-Publication Data

Chepesiuk, Ronald.
    Sixties radicals, then and now : candid conversations with
those who shaped the era / by Ron Chepesiuk.
        p.   cm.
    Includes bibliographical references and index. ∞
    ISBN 0-89950-778-6 (lib. bdg. : 50# alk. paper)
    1. Radicals—United States—Interviews.   2. Radicalism—United
States—History—20th century.   3. United States—Civilization—
1945–   4. United States—Social conditions—1960–1980.
5. United States—Social conditions—1980–   I. Title.
HN90.R3C48   1995
306'.0973'09046—dc20   94-37664
                                                             CIP

Manufactured in the United States of America

McFarland & Company, Inc., Publishers
  Box 611, Jefferson, North Carolina 28640

For my wife and my mother,
the two people who make my life

Acknowledgments

I would like to thank the following individuals and organizations for helping me to complete the project:

Dr. Gerald Fish, Gloria Kelley, and Gina Price, my colleagues at Winthrop University, for taking the time to read the manuscript and for offering valuable suggestions on how it could be improved.

The Winthrop University Library's Management Team, which gave me time off to complete the project. Special thanks to Dr. DuBois, dean of the Winthrop University Library and head of the Management Team, who provided encouragement and support throughout the project.

Anne Thomas, Lois Walker, Zackary Maddox, and Genie Poag of the Winthrop University Library; Linda Kelter, formerly of the library; Greg Ellis of the Winthrop University Archives; Oscar Aranda, researcher; and Mary Mallaney of the York County Library for helping me to locate information and hard-to-find books and articles for the project.

Larry Mitlin for helping to keep my computer and printer functioning until I completed this project.

Joel Nichols for duplicating most of the photographs used to illustrate this book.

The Southern Regional Education Board and the Winthrop Research Council for providing grants in support of the project.

And the interviewees who took the time to sit down and talk about their experiences, then and now, and without whom this book would not exist.

Ron Chepesiuk
Summer 1994

As long as the world shall last there will be wrongs, and if no man objected and no man rebelled, those wrongs would last forever. —CLARENCE DARROW, speech to jury, 1920

The right to revolt has sources deep in our history. —WILLIAM O. DOUGLAS, *An Almanac of Liberty*, 1954

There is a time when the operation of the machine becomes so odious, makes you sick at heart that you can't take part; you can't even tacitly take part, and you've got to put your bodies upon the levers, upon all the apparatus and you've got to make it stop. And you've got to indicate to the people who run it, to the people who own it, that unless you're free the machine will be prevented from working at all. —MARIO SAVIO, University of California at Berkeley, 1964

Contents

Acknowledgments   vii

Introduction   1

A Chronology: 1960–1973   7

1 PAUL KRASSNER
    Father of the Underground Press   25

2 CLEVELAND SELLERS
    From Black Revolutionary to Educator and Community Worker   41

3 JANE ADAMS
    From Grassroots Organizer to University Professor   56

4 DAVE DELLINGER
    Radical for Peace   74

5 BILL AYERS
    Radical Educator   92

6 WARREN HINCKLE
    Unreconstructed Radical   107

7 PETER BERG
    From Digger to Environmental Activist   118

8 NOAM CHOMSKY
    Radical Intellectual   133

9 TIM LEARY
    From High Priest of LSD to Guru of High Tech   147

10 PHILIP BERRIGAN
    Radical for Christ   158

11 ANITA HOFFMAN
    Reluctant Radical   169

12 JERRY RUBIN
    A Man for All Seasons   182

13 ERICKA HUGGINS
    From Black Panther to AIDS Activist   198

14 JIM FOURATT
    Gay Rights Activist   211

15 BERNARDINE DOHRN
    From Revolutionary to Children's Rights Advocate   223

16 BARRY MELTON
    From Rock Musician to Activist Lawyer   240

17 PETER COYOTE
    Hollywood Radical   254

18 ABBIE HOFFMAN
    An American Rebel   272

    Notes   285

    Bibliography   297

    A Select Glossary   303

    Index   313

Introduction

The decade known as the sixties was one of the most radical periods in American history. It was a time when thousands of citizens, many of them young, participated in shaping what became an era of protest and challenge to the American system.

Sixties radicals were scornful of a political system that talked about representative democracy and consensus politics and then locked out millions of its citizens from any real participation. The radicals rejected the consumer society, distrusted capitalist technocracy, and rebelled against the prevailing hierarchies of power. They challenged the vested interests and dominant "straight" life-style of American culture. Radicals stunned mainstream America by shutting down campuses, confronting and battling police, marching on the White House and Congress, laying siege to the 1968 Democratic Convention in Chicago, and eventually resorting to violence to prod the establishment to change.

Ironically, for many who eventually adopted a radical viewpoint and rejected the American system and what it stood for, the sixties had begun optimistically and in sharp contrast to the conformist and apathetic fifties, a decade dominated by what later became known as the "silent generation."

As one writer described the fifties, "On the campuses, there were no radical organizations, and the vast majority of students displayed little interest in politics. Student energy and aggression were vented on sports and fraternities. A few professors spoke out against the apathy of their students and wondered what would become of America when their spiritless group of young people, later called the silent generation, assumed power."[1]

Yet even before the fifties had become history, signs were evident that a vibrant political and social militancy was emerging in the country. The civil rights struggle had already started in the South. Rosa Parks, a black woman, had refused to give up her seat in the front of a Montgomery, Alabama, bus to a white man and to move to the rear, the area designated for blacks. Parks's heroic action led to a boycott of the Montgomery bus system, and, when the federal courts ruled that racial laws applied to bus transportation were illegal, blacks saw the power they had to make change.

Meanwhile, with the formation of SLATE at the University of California

1

at Berkeley in 1957, new militant and politically oriented student groups were forming at very large universities.[2] A foreshadowing of the militancy that was to characterize student activism in the sixties came in 1960 when SLATE organized demonstrations against the House Un-American Activities Committee (HUAC), which had come to San Francisco to hold hearings to investigate "subversive" activity in the Bay area. Protesters were beaten and hosed, but it was the first time that the powerful HUAC had been so openly challenged.

The sit-ins of the early sixties and the example set by the freedom riders and the Student Nonviolent Coordinating Committee (SNCC), which began registering voters in Mississippi, inspired many young people, both black and white, all over the country to get involved and work to change the system. There was a feeling that reform was possible and that it could be brought about by working within the system.

Thousands of students flocked south to Mississippi to participate in Freedom Summer. The experience transformed them. As Jane Adams, then a young student at Antioch College in Ohio, recalled, "I very quickly came to see the world through black eyes. That perspective permanently changed how I saw the world. When I tried to understand myself as a woman later on . . . I drew direct parallels between what I learned in Mississippi and my experiences as a woman."[3]

The nascent civil rights movement lit the fire to a loosely knit political movement that became known as the "New Left." But unlike what it was to become, the New Left of the early sixties was moderate and cautious. Its leaders did not propose a radical critique of the American capitalist system, nor did they offer radical alternatives. The communist model offered by the Soviet Union had appealed to millions of Americans during the poverty-stricken thirties, but it had been largely discredited by the revelations about the brutal dictatorship of Joseph Stalin that surfaced after his death in 1954.

Meanwhile, the American Communist Party, with its old guard, rigid orthodoxy, and slavish devotion to "Mother Russia," had little appeal to the young idealistic activist. As James L. Wood explained, "The discrediting of communism left a radical vacuum, which members of the early New Left tried to fill with reformist solutions."[4]

Another impetus to the growth of the New Left came in 1962 when 47 students gathered at Port Huron, Michigan. After four days of marathon brainstorming, the young group produced a remarkable 64-page document that led to the formation of the Students for a Democratic Society (SDS) and offered many young people an exciting vision of how to transform American society.

At first, SDS still believed in the inherent reformability of the American system. It championed participatory democracy and the right of every American to determine his or her own life and political direction. Members of SDS expressed optimism about the potential power of young people and predicted that they would rebel against a system that considered them politically unimportant. The group worked hard to create an "interracial movement of the poor" by launching the Economic Research Action Project (ERAP), a project that reached out to poor and racially mixed communities in ten American cities. But only a small number of participants joined ERAP, and the project failed.

By 1965, SDS had already begun to shift its focus and energy in response to the growing U.S. presence in Vietnam. On April 17, 1965, more than 25,000 people responded to the call of SDS and poured into Washington, D.C., to voice their opposition to the Vietnam War. By this time SDS became part of a broad-based coalition of organizations dedicated to getting the United States out of Vietnam.

Opposition to U.S. involvement in Vietnam spread quickly when the body count of U.S. casualties rose and the war affected more and more Americans as family and friends were killed and wounded. Many Americans grew frustrated as the number of American troops in Vietnam rose steadily from 20,000 to 250,000. By 1969, many Americans were abandoning their moderate views and were beginning to believe that America was a dangerous, racist, and imperialistic country.

The antiwar movement dominated the lives of young radicals in the late sixties, but other forms of radicalism began to take shape as well. "Working in these movements, we began to identify as members of a growing community of radicals," recalled Annie Popkin, sixties activist and feminist. "Being part of 'The Movement' was not just a matter of political opposition but criticism and withdrawal from the dominant culture as well."[5]

Supporters of "black power," led by SNCC and the Black Panthers, condemned the mainstream civil rights movement on the grounds that its goals were too moderate. "We asked: Who could do the best job determining the destiny of African American people?" explained Cleveland Sellers, a program secretary for SNCC in the mid-sixties. "We concluded that African Americans could do the best job. We also concluded that we could not be strong enough to build a coalition with whites until we were strong enough in our communities."[6]

Other ethnic groups were also becoming more militant and willing to lay their bodies on the line for their rights. On November 20, 1969, 78 Indians seized Alcatraz Island in San Francisco Bay and demanded that it be turned over to the Indian community. The following year, a radical Puerto Rican group called the Young Lords issued a 13-point platform of liberation demands.

Meanwhile, many women were being radicalized by the sexism in the movement. They formed women's groups such as Bread and Roses and Cell 16 and called for the overthrow of male-dominated institutions. On July 27, 1969, over 2,000 people protested a police raid on a gay bar called Stonewall in the heart of Greenwich Village, New York City, and ignited the Gay

Liberation Movement. Many young people took high priest of LSD Tim Leary's advice to "tune in, turn on, and drop out" and joined the counterculture where they crowded together in communes and participated in the drug subculture.

By 1970, the Vietnam War and America's social, economic, and political problems had made the country far different from what it was in 1960. Given the U.S. government's intransigence in the face of a growing awareness that the majority of Americans wanted out of Vietnam and of the tension and divisions existing in American society, many radicals thought the country might be moving toward a revolution. Widespread protests broke out at campuses across the country when President Richard Nixon announced that the United States had spread the war in Indochina by invading Cambodia. At Kent State University in Ohio, National Guardsmen shot and killed four students on a grassy meadow. Ten days later, police killed two black demonstrators at Jackson State College in Mississippi. More than 400 colleges and universities were shut down in protest, and nearly 100,000 demonstrators converged on Washington.

A violent response, some angry radicals concluded, was the only thing that the American war machine understood. "By 1968 and '69, frustration was beginning to set in," recalled Bill Ayers, a member of the Weather Underground, which in the early seventies conducted a campaign of bombings in protest against the U.S. government. "We began to feel that no matter what we did, they would escalate the war and we couldn't stop that escalation. So we began to think the best tactic was to inflict on them the kind of pain that would make them draw back."[7]

On March 6, less than two months before Kent State, three members of the radical Weather Underground blew themselves up in a Greenwich Village townhouse when a bomb they were making accidentally exploded. Later, in the year, a University of Wisconsin Reserve Officers Training Corps (ROTC) building was firebombed, beginning a wave of 500 bombings and incidents of arson on university campuses. The decade that had begun nonviolently with so much hope and optimism had ended on a bloody note with the nation bitterly divided.

This book is the story of 18 radicals who participated in the seminal events that dominated the sixties, from the sit-in at the Greensboro lunch counter on February 1, 1960, to the violent opposition against the U.S. government that took shape in the late sixties and early seventies. In the following pages, the radicals talk about the politics, life-style, civil rights, counterculture, music, activism, race relations, drug scene, education, and relations of the sexes in the sixties, among other subjects.

The book examines the following questions: What motivated the radicals to do what they did in the sixties? What role did they play in one of the most turbulent periods of American history? In retrospect how do they feel about their actions? What is the legacy of sixties radicalism?

This book is as much about today as it is about the sixties. As Edward P. Morgan wrote, "The struggles and issues that came to a head during the decade haven't gone away; nor, thankfully, has the commitment to democracy that compelled so many to be active. For the most part, we still need to learn the lessons the sixties can teach us."[8] So the book also addresses the following questions: What impact did the interviewees' sixties radicalism have on their activities today? What are the interviewees' views on the major issues and problems facing America today? How is their thinking on these issues shaped by their sixties experience?

The sixties remains one of the most controversial periods in American history, the subject of a plethora of books that either disparage its shortcomings or laud its virtues. It is hoped that this contribution to the literature about the sixties will help to put the era in perspective and perhaps reveal something about America and the modern era. In the spirit of the sixties, *let the reader decide*.

A Chronology: 1960–1973

1960

January 3 Senator John F. Kennedy announced his candidacy for the Democratic presidential nomination.

January 9 Vice President Richard Nixon announced his candidacy for the Republican presidential nomination.

February 1 Four black students staged a sit-in at a lunch counter in Greensboro, N.C., to protest "white only" serving policy.

March 15 Ten nations, including the United States, USSR, Great Britain, and France, attended the Geneva disarmament conference.

March 25 U.S. Circuit Court of Appeals in New York ruled that the unexpurgated version of D.H. Lawrence's *Lady Chatterly's Lover* was obscene.

April 15–17 The Student Nonviolent Coordinating Committee (SNCC) was formed in Raleigh, N.C. The group became national liaison for sit-in demonstrations that would spread across the South.

May 3 Caryl Chessman was executed. Protests followed.

May 6 Civil Rights Act of 1960 was signed by President John F. Kennedy.

May 9 The U.S. government approved the first birth control pill, Enovid, as safe for use.

May 19 Alan Freed, radio disk jockey and originator of the term *rock and roll*, arrested on charges of commercial bribery in payola scandal.

June 6 The United States accused the Cuban government of undertaking a campaign of slander.

July 6 The United States cut Cuban sugar imports by 95 percent due to poor relations.

July 12 Democratic National Convention adopted a civil rights plank supporting sit-ins and school integration.

July 27 Republication National Convention nominated Vice President Richard M. Nixon for President and Henry Cabot Lodge of Massachusetts for Vice President.

September 26 First of four television debates between presidential candidates Kennedy and Nixon was held.

7

November 8 John F. Kennedy elected President, Lyndon B. Johnson elected Vice President.

November 30 Anti-integration riots in New Orleans led to 200 arrests.

Also in 1960 University of San Francisco students were hosed and gassed as they protested House Un-American Activities Committee (HUAC) hearing in San Francisco.

1961

January 3 United States broke diplomatic relations with Cuba.

January 17 President Dwight Eisenhower, in his farewell speech, warned of increasing power of the military industrial complex.

January 20 John F. Kennedy was inaugurated President, Lyndon B. Johnson inaugurated Vice President.

February 22–23 Birth control as means of family limitation was endorsed by National Council of Churches.

March 1 Peace Corps was established by executive order of President Kennedy.

April 17 CIA-trained Cuban exiles invaded Cuba at Bay of Pigs and were defeated within 24 hours.

May 4 Congress of Racial Equality (CORE) sponsored the "Freedom Riders," interracial groups that sought to end segregation on interstate bus routes in the South.

June 19 Supreme Court ruled against use of illegal evidence in prosecuting state court cases.

September 8 *Journal of American Medical Association* reported link between smoking and heart disease.

September 15 United States began underground nuclear testing.

October 10 Joseph Heller's *Catch 22* was published.

December 11 Kennedy sent 400 U.S. troops to South Vietnam.

Also in 1961 Black voter-registration worker Herbert Lee was murdered in Mississippi; Student vigils protested resumption of nuclear testing.

1962

January 3 U.S. Communist Party members were denied U.S. passports under new regulations.

February 1 Ken Kesey's *One Flew Over the Cuckoo's Nest* was published.

February 3 President Kennedy ordered trade ban with Cuba.

February 20 Astronaut John Glenn was first American to orbit earth, circling three times in Mercury space capsule.

February 22 Attorney General Robert Kennedy denounced Berlin Wall during meeting with West German Mayor Willy Brandt.

February 26 U.S. Supreme Court ruled that segregation laws in interstate and intrastate transportation facilities were unconstitutional.

April 10 United States and Great Britain appealed to Soviet Union to agree to international nuclear test ban.

April 25 United States resumed atmospheric nuclear tests after three-year moratorium.

May 6 First submarine-launched nuclear detonation exploded near Christmas Island in the South Pacific.

May 12 United States sent naval and ground forces to Laos to support anti–Communist troops.

June 11–15 Students for a Democratic Society (SDS) held first national convention in Port Huron, Michigan.

June 25 In *Engel v. Vitale,* the U.S. Supreme Court declared reading of prayers in New York public schools unconstitutional.

August 5 Film star Marilyn Monroe died.

September 12 Thurgood Marshall was confirmed as a member of Second United States Circuit Court of Appeals after one-year delay by Southern opposition in U.S. Senate.

September 30 Black student James Meredith was admitted to the University of Mississippi against angry opposition.

October 22 Cuban Missile Crisis developed when Kennedy revealed that U.S. had photographic evidence of construction of Soviet missile bases in Cuba and demanded removal of all missiles and dismantling of bases. He requested UN Security Council and Organization of American Unity support and ordered naval blockade around Cuba.

October 28 Soviet Premier Nikita Khrushchev announced that missiles and bases would be removed from Cuba.

November 20 U.S. announced intention to end naval blockade of Cuba; Kennedy signed executive order prohibiting racial discrimination in federally funded housing.

November 23 Cuba announced release of 1,013 prisoners from the 1961 Bay of Pigs invasion in return for $62 million worth of medical supplies, food, and farming equipment.

December 31 Eleven thousand U.S. military personnel were helping South Vietnam.

Also in 1962 U.S. troops on training mission in Vietnam were ordered to fire if fired upon by enemy troops; The "Twist" was born in The Peppermint Lounge nightclub in New York City; Rachel Carson's *Silent Spring* was published; Bob Dylan released song "Blowin' in the Wind."

1963

February 19 Betty Friedan published *The Feminine Mystique.*

April 12 Rev. Martin Luther King, Jr., arrested in Birmingham, Alabama, after participating in civil rights march.

May 10 Attorney General Robert Kennedy ordered halt to police action directed against civil rights demonstrators in Birmingham, Alabama.

June 8 American Heart Association began anticigarette campaign.

June 11 University of Alabama desegregated after President Kennedy federalized Alabama National Guard; two black students enrolled.

June 12 Civil rights leader Medgar Evers was murdered in Jackson, Mississippi. Riots broke out in protest.

June 17 U.S. Supreme Court declared Bible reading in public schools unconstitutional.

July 8 U.S. banned virtually all financial dealings with Cuba.

August 5 U.S., USSR, and Great Britain signed comprehensive nuclear test ban treaty.

August 28 Freedom march on Washington, D.C., drew more than 200,000 participants, as Dr. King delivered his famous "I Have a Dream" speech.

September 15 Racial tensions heightened when four small black girls died in bombing of Sixteenth Street Baptist Church in Birmingham, Alabama.

October 10 Senate ratified Nuclear Test Ban Treaty.

November 2 South Vietnamese President Ngo Dinh Diem was killed in a coup. U.S. government recognized South Vietnamese provisional government following overthrow of Ngo Dinh Diem's government.

November 22 President Kennedy was assassinated in Dallas, Texas; Vice President Lyndon B. Johnson was sworn in as President.

November 24 Alleged assassin Lee Harvey Oswald was shot and killed by nightclub owner Jack Ruby.

December 17 President Johnson addressed UN and called for "peaceful revolution" to eliminate hunger, disease, and poverty.

Also in 1963 Civil rights demonstrations occurred throughout the country; U.S. continued aid to South Vietnam; Michael Harrington's *The Other America* was published; Harvard terminated the contracts of Timothy Leary and Richard Alpert (today known as Baba Ram Dass) for experiments with LSD; The Commission on the Status of Women reported that there is discrimination against women in the U.S.; SDS began the Economic Research Action Project (ERAP), organizing poor communities in ten northern cities.

1964

January 8 President Johnson delivered State of the Union message on national War on Poverty.

January 11 Surgeon General announced proof that cigarette smoke causes cancer.

February 25 Cassius Marcellus Clay (Muhammad Ali) defeated Sonny Liston in World Heavyweight Boxing Championship.

January 23 The Twenty-fourth Amendment to the Constitution, prohibiting the denial of right to vote by "reason of failure to pay any poll tax or other tax," was adopted.

March 31 U.S. Supreme Court set aside contempt citation of African-American Mary Hamilton, who declined to answer in Alabama Court when addressed as "Mary."

June 22 U.S. Supreme Court ruled that provisions of Internal Security Act of 1950 denying U.S. passports to Communists were unconstitutional.

June 23 Three civil rights workers (James Chaney, Andrew Goodman, and Michael Schwerner), who were participating in Mississippi summer project, were reported missing.

July 3 Civil Rights Act of 1964 was passed and signed into law. It was the most far-reaching civil rights legislation since the post Civil War amendments.

July 7 Race riots broke out in Rochester, N.Y.

July 19 Race riots broke out in Harlem, N.Y.

July 23 Senate passed antipoverty bill providing for $947 million in aid for measures to combat poverty.

August 2–5 Two U.S. destroyers patrolling Gulf of Tonkin off North Vietnam were allegedly attacked by North Vietnamese P.T. boats. U.S. sank two P.T. boats and bombed bases.

August 5 Bodies of Goodman, Schwerner, and Chaney were found in newly built earthen dam near Philadelphia, Mississippi.

August 10 Gulf of Tonkin resolution was passed in U.S. Congress. It gave the President power to take necessary measures to defend U.S. forces and to prevent further "aggression." In the Senate, only senators Wayne Morse and Ernest Gruening voted no.

August 17–18 Race riots broke out in South Chicago.

August 20 President Johnson signed Equal Opportunity Act.

August 29–30 Race riots broke out in Philadelphia, Pennsylvania.

September 24 Warren Commission released its report, concluding that there was no conspiracy in the assassination of President Kennedy and that Oswald was the lone assassin.

October 15 Rev. Martin Luther King, Jr., won Nobel Peace Prize.

November 3 Lyndon B. Johnson was elected President in landslide. Hubert Humphrey was elected Vice President.

December The U.S. Supreme Court confirmed the constitutionality of that section of the 1964 Civil Rights Act prohibiting discrimination in public accommodations.

December 4 FBI arrested three Mississippians on charges of conspiracy to kill Chaney, Goodman, and Schwerner.

Also in 1964 SNCC launched the Mississippi Freedom Summer Project and thousands of students flocked from northern campuses to Mississippi for the summer voter-registration drive; During 1964, the civil rights struggle in Mississippi resulted in three killed, 80 beaten, three wounded by gunfire, more than 1,000 arrested, and 35 churches bombed; Beatles appeared on Ed Sullivan Show; Stanley Kubrick's film *Dr. Strangelove* was released; University of California at Berkeley banned political activity on campus.

1965

January 4 In State of the Union message, President Johnson described goals for the "Great Society."

January 20 Lyndon B. Johnson was inaugurated for his first elective term. Hubert Humphrey was inaugurated Vice President.

February 6 Vietcong guerrillas attacked U.S. military base in Pleiku, killing eight and wounding 126.

February 7 President Johnson ordered bombing of North Vietnamese bases.

February 21 Malcolm X assassinated by rival Black Muslims in New York City.

March 7 State troopers attacked 525 civil rights demonstrators in Selma, Alabama, as they prepared to march to Montgomery to protest voting-rights discrimination.

March 8–9 U.S. marines landed in South Vietnam to protect air force base at Danang.

March 8 U.S. Supreme Court ruled that a person holding belief in a supreme being may be exempt from military combat training and service.

March 21 Three thousand two hundred civil rights marchers, led by Dr. Martin Luther King, Jr., began a trip from Selma to Montgomery, Alabama. They were protected by over 2,200 U.S. troops; 25,000 gathered in Montgomery.

March 25 Civil rights worker Viola Liuzzo was shot and killed in Alabama by KKK.

April 2 President Johnson committed to increasing military and economic aid to South Vietnam.

April 7 President Johnson announced that U.S. was willing to participate in "unconditional" talks with Hanoi to end war.

April 28 First contingent of marines was sent to Dominican Republic during that country's civil war.

April 29 U.S. Commissioner of Education Francis Keppel announced that all public school districts were to desegregate their schools by autumn of 1967.

May 9 Government announced total U.S. fighting force of 42,000 in Vietnam.

May 17 First mass bombing raid in Vietnam War was conducted.

May 26 President Johnson signed the 1965 Voting Rights Act, which was passed by the U.S. Congress and provided for the registration by federal examiners of those black voters turned away by state officials.

June 26 U.S. government announced a deployment of an additional 21,000 U.S. soldiers to Vietnam.

July 10 The rock band Rolling Stones established themselves as a major rock group when their record "Satisfaction" hit number one.

July 26 President Johnson announced decision to increase presence in Vietnam to 125,000 men.

August 4 President Johnson requested $1.7 billion for war effort.

August 11–16 Major race riots in Watts (black section of Los Angeles) left 35 dead and hundreds injured.

September 9 U.S. Department of Housing and Urban Development (HUD) was established.

October 1 Antipollution bill empowered U.S. Secretary of Health, Education, and Welfare (HEW) to set emission standards on toxic pollutants in new diesel- and gasoline-powered automobiles.

October 15–16 Nationwide antiwar demonstrations were followed by rallies and petitions supporting U.S. policy.

November 8 *Autobiography of Malcolm X* was published.

November 15 Mandatory federal registration by members of Communist Party was ruled unconstitutional by Supreme Court.

November 27 Ken Kesey and Merry Pranksters held first "acid" test open to public.

Also in 1965 Miniskirts became popular; Color TV swept the nation; The first campus teach-in on the Vietnam War was held at the University of Michigan; Three thousand joined a SANE antiwar rally at the United Nations; Over 20,000 attended the SDS-sponsored Washington rally against Vietnam War; The largest draft call since Korean War was issued; The first draft-card burning occurred at New York protest organized by War Resisters League; Berkeley activists tried to stop train enroute to Vietnam; Bob Dylan went electric at Newport Folk Festival.

1966

January 10 Julian Bond was denied his new seat in Georgia State Legislature because of his opposition to U.S. involvement in Vietnam War.

January 12 In a State of the Union message, President Johnson pledged to continue the Great Society program while maintaining commitment to South Vietnam.

January 13 President Johnson announced resumption of U.S. bombing raids over North Vietnam, after 37-day pause.

January 21–22 San Francisco Trip Festival (first Hippy enclave) was held.

February 8 President Johnson concluded three-day conference with South Vietnam Premier Nguyen Cao Ky.

March 2 U.S. troop strength in Vietnam reached 215,000.

March 3 Cold War GI Bill of Rights granted special education, housing, health, and job benefits to veterans who had spent at least 180 days in service since January 31, 1955.

March 7 U.S. Supreme Court upheld Voting Rights Act of 1965.

March 24 Dr. Martin Luther King, Jr., announced that he would take a stand against Vietnam War because it was a major obstacle to the civil rights movement.

March 25–26 Antiwar demonstrations were held in San Francisco, Chicago, Boston, Philadelphia, and Washington, D.C.

April 3 Walt Disney died.

May 15 Antiwar demonstration in Washington, D.C., attended by 10,000 people.

June 6 James Meredith began 200-mile civil rights march from Memphis, Tennessee, to Jackson, Mississippi, to encourage voter registration among blacks in South.

June 7 Meredith was ambushed near Hernando, Mississippi.

July Riots in Cleveland and Chicago ghettos and 14 other cities occurred.

July 1 The national convention of CORE endorsed the "Black Power" concept.

July 4 NAACP dissociated itself from "Black Power" concept.

July 10 Martin Luther King, Jr., addressed a predominantly black crowd of 45,000 in Chicago and launched drive to rid the nation's third largest city of discrimination.

July 28 President Johnson appointed 11-member committee, headed by Governor Otto Kerner of Illinois and Mayor John Lindsay of New York City, to study causes and propose solutions to race riots of previous July.

August 7 Tim Leary urged people to use LSD and to "tune in, turn on, and drop out."

August 7 Lenny Bruce died of heroin overdose in California.

August 8 First successful artificial heart pump was installed; *Time* magazine asked: "Is God dead?"

September U.S. Senate confirmed appointment of Thurgood Marshall as first black Associate Justice of U.S. Supreme Court.

October Black Panther Party was organized.

October 6 California banned use of LSD.

November 3 Truth-in-Packaging bill required accurate labeling of supermarket items.

November 8 Edward Brooke of Massachusetts became first black elected to U.S. Senate since Reconstruction; Republicans gained three seats in Senate and 47 in house; Ronald Reagan, former movie actor, became Republican governor of California.

Also in 1966 SNCC denounced Vietnam War and announced support for draft resistance; Young people flocked into Haight-Ashbury district of San Francisco with increasing frequency; Stokeley Carmichael was elected chairman of SNCC and urged "Black Power"; The National Organization of Women (NOW) was organized; The SDS council condemned the Vietnam War and antidemocratic draft.

1967

January 5 U.S. State Department announced 5,008 Americans killed and 30,093 wounded in Vietnam since 1966. Current troop strength reached 380,000 soldiers.

January 8–19 In Operation Cedar Falls, 16,000 U.S. and 14,000 South Vietnamese soldiers participated in offensive against North Vietnamese positions 25 miles northeast of Saigon.

January 16 First black Southern sheriff since Reconstruction, Lucius Amerson, sworn in at Tuskegee, Alabama.

January 27 Space demilitarization treaty prohibited orbiting of nuclear weapons and forbade territorial claims on celestial bodies was signed by U.S., USSR, and 60 other nations.

January 8 Following a decision by U.S. Supreme Court, Julian Bond was seated in the Georgia General Assembly.

January 14 San Francisco Human Be-In took place.

April 15 Up to 400,000 attended antiwar demonstration in New York.

April 17 Pro–Vietnam demonstration in New York City drew 70,000.

April 28 Muhammad Ali was stripped of his world heavyweight boxing title because of his refusal to be inducted into the U.S. armed forces.

May U.S. launched first strike on central Hanoi, North Vietnam.

May 1–October 1 The worst period of racial disturbances in U.S. history occurred. There were more than 140 incidents in New York City, Chicago, Washington, Atlanta, and other cities.

June 12 U.S. Supreme Court ruled state laws forbidding interracial marriages were unconstitutional.

June–August Summer of Love took place.

July 16–18 Monterey Pop Festival took place.

July 23–30 Worst race riot in U.S. history erupted in Detroit, Michigan, following police raids on after-hours drinking club. Forty-one were killed; 2,000 injured; 5,000 left homeless; and some $200 million in property damage. Federal troops were summoned.

July 26 H. Rap Brown, Chairman of Student Nonviolent Coordinating Committee (SNCC), was arrested on charges of inciting a riot following outbreak of racial violence in Cambridge, Maryland.

October 21–22 March on Pentagon occurred.

August 30 Thurgood Marshall became first black justice of U.S. Supreme Court.

July 1 The Beatles album "Sergeant Pepper's Lonely Hearts Club Band" topped pop album charts.

October 3 Folk singer Woody Guthrie died.

October 6 Diggers and hundreds of Haight-Ashbury flower folk celebrated last hippy event, "the Death of Hippy."

October 20 Seven Ku Klux Klan members were convicted of conspiracy in 1964 murders of Chaney, Schwerner, and Goodman in Mississippi.

October 20–21 Antiwar demonstrations in Washington, D.C., involved 35,000 protesters, 647 were arrested.

October 26 Order was issued for cancellation of draft deferments of college students who violate draft laws and interfere with recruiting.

October 31 President Johnson reiterated U.S. commitment to South Vietnam.

November 9 *Rolling Stone* published first issue.

November 14 Air Quality Control Act provided about $428 million to fight air pollution.

December Nationwide "Stop the draft" movement was organized by 40 antiwar groups. Protesters were arrested in Cincinnati, Ohio; New Haven, Connecticut; Manchester, New Hampshire; and Madison, Wisconsin.

December 5 More than 1,000 antiwar protesters attempted to close down the New York induction center; five hundred eighty five people were arrested, including Dr. Benjamin Spock and poet Allen Ginsberg.

Also in 1967 The musical *Hair* was produced; *Ramparts* exposed CIA funding of National Student Association; The Doors song "Light My Fire" was hot on pop charts; Easter Be-In, a celebration of counterculture in New York City's Central Park occurred; The International War Crimes Tribunal, sponsored by the Bertrand Russell Peace Foundation, began an investigation of U.S. role in Vietnam; The first national Black Power conference was held in Newark, New Jersey; Che Guevara was killed in Bolivia; The CIA, FBI, and Army Intelligence began surveillance of the antiwar movement; The Reverend Philip Berrigan and three others raided a Baltimore draft office and poured blood on draft files.

1968

January 30–February 24 Tet offensive, involving massive assault by North Vietnamese throughout South Vietnam, took place.

February 8 At South Carolina State College in Orangeburg, three black students died and several others were wounded by South Carolina law enforcement officials; Governor of Alabama George Wallace announced candidacy for president as third-party candidate on law and order platform; Eldridge Cleaver's book *Soul on Ice* (McGraw-Hill, 1968) was published.

March 2 The President's National Advisory Commission on Civil Disorders (the Kerner Commission) reported on causes of social unrest in summer of 1967. Commission said "white racism" was primary cause.

March 12 Senator Eugene McCarthy of Minnesota, campaigning on an antiwar platform, won 42 percent of the vote in the Democratic primary in New Hampshire.

March 30 Black separatists met in Detroit to set up independent black government.

March 31 President Johnson announced cessation of Vietnam bombing north of twenty-first parallel and his decision not to run for reelection.

April 4 Rev. Martin Luther King, Jr., was assassinated by a sniper in Memphis, Tennessee.

April 8 Operation Complete Victory offensive, involving 100,000 troops, began in Vietnam; Bureau of Narcotics and Dangerous Drugs was established.

April 23 SDS led seizure of buildings on Columbia University in New York City to protest university involvement in research connected with Vietnam War.

April 24 Some 300 black students occupied administration building at Boston University and demanded stronger emphasis on black history in curriculum and increased financial aid for blacks.

April 29 *Hair* premiered on Broadway.

May 10 Peace talks began in Paris between U.S. and North Vietnam.

May 11 Dr. Ralph Abernathy, successor of Dr. Martin Luther King, Jr., and head of SCLC, led a march for "a poor people's campaign" in Washington, D.C.

June 5 Robert F. Kennedy was shot in Los Angeles while campaigning for presidency.

June 6 Robert Kennedy died, and Jordanian immigrant Sirhan Sirhan was charged with his murder.

June 8 Exconvict James Earl Ray was arrested in London for murder of Martin Luther King, Jr.

June 14 Dr. Benjamin Spock was convicted of conspiracy to abet draft evasion.

July 1 Nuclear nonproliferation treaty was signed by U.S., USSR, and 51 other nations.

August 7 Rioting erupted in Miami, Florida.

August 8 Republican National Convention nominated Richard Nixon for President and Spiro Agnew for Vice President.

August 10 Senator George McGovern announced candidacy for Democratic presidential nomination.

August 26 National Student Association reported that during the first six months of the year, there were 221 major demonstrations at 101 colleges and universities.

August 26–29 Democratic National Convention nominated Vice President Hubert Humphrey for President and Senator Edmund Muskie of Maine for Vice President; Antiwar protesters clashed with police and national guardsmen outside Democratic National Convention in Chicago. Police beat protesters, bystanders, and reporters.

September 8 Black Panther leader Huey Newton convicted of manslaugher in California.

October 16 Two black athletes at Olympic Games in Mexico City, Tommy Smith and John Carlos, used victory ceremony in the 200-meter dash as vehicle for Black Power.

October 31 President ordered end to U.S. bombing of North Vietnam.

November 5 Shirley Chisolm became first black woman elected to U.S. House of Representatives.

November 6 Nixon was elected President.

November 6 Student strike began at San Francisco State College.

December 21–27 Apollo Eight orbited moon ten times and yielded spectacular photographs of earth and moon.

Also in 1968 Simon and Garfunkel's song "Mrs. Robinson" was released; Student revolts erupted in Germany, Italy, and France; The Revs. Philip and Daniel Berrigan and seven others raided the Catonsville, Maryland, draft board and destroyed draft files with homemade naphalm; Black Panther Party leader Eldridge Cleaver was chosen as presidential candidate of the Peace and Freedom Party; Women's liberation activists protested the Miss America pageant; The first liberation conference was held in Chicago.

1969

January 20 Richard Nixon was inaugurated President of the United States; Spiro Agnew, Vice President.

March 10 James Earl Ray sentenced to 99 years for murder of Martin Luther King, Jr.

April 3 Combat deaths in Vietnam since 1961 reached 33,641.

April 4 First artificial heart transplant was done.

April 7 U.S. Supreme Court ruled laws that attempted to prohibit reading or viewing of obscene material in privacy of one's home unconstitutional.

April 9 Group of 300 students, mainly SDS members, took over Harvard University's main administration building and evicted eight deans.

April 10 Some 400 local police cleared Harvard administration building.

April 23 Sirhan Sirhan was sentenced to death for murder of Senator Robert Kennedy.

April 24 U.S. B-52s dropped nearly 3,000 bombs in an area near Cambodia border, northwest of Saigon.

May 15 Squatters were evicted forcibly from "People's Park" in Berkeley, California.

May 20 U.S. and South Vietnamese forces captured Hamburger Hill after ten-day bloody battle.

June 6 Court testimony revealed that FBI had tapped phones of Martin Luther King, Jr.

June 8 President Nixon met South Vietnamese President Nguyen Van Thieu on Midway to discuss Vietnam War. The meeting led to U.S. troop reduction of 25,000 troops.

July 8 President Nixon announced withdrawal of U.S. troops from Vietnam, but U.S. B-52s intensified bombings of Communist sanctuaries in Cambodia.

July 14 Movie *Easy Rider,* starring Peter Fonda, Dennis Hopper, and Jack Nicholson, was released.

July 20 Astronaut Neil Armstrong was first man on the moon; Several traditionally all-male colleges, including Yale, Bowdoin, and Colgate, admitted women students for the first time.

July 27 Stonewall uprising erupted. Over 410 police battled with over 2,000 people protesting police raid on gay bar, located on Christopher Street in heart of Greenwich Village, New York City. Incident sparked Gay Liberation Movement.

August 9 Tate–LaBianca murders in Los Angeles were committed by Charles Manson and his "family."

August 15–17 Woodstock Music and Arts Festival took place near White Lake, New York. More than 300,000 attended.

September 16 U.S. troop reduction of 35,000 was announced.

September 24 Federal trial began of seven antiwar protesters (Jerry Rubin, Abbie Hoffman, Dave Dellinger, and others) who were indicted for conspiracy to incite riot at 1968 Democratic National Convention in Chicago and who were known as the Chicago Seven began.

October 8–11 The violent "Days of Rage" by Weather Underground faction of SDS took place in Chicago.

October 15 First Vietnam Moratorium Day was observed by millions; National Audubon Society began a national campaign to ban DDT because the chemical was killing bald eagles.

October 29 U.S. Supreme Court ordered immediate desegregation of 33 Mississippi school districts.

November 11 Pro–America demonstrations in support of U.S. policy in Vietnam were held.

November 14 Second Vietnam Moratorium Day began with "March Against Death" in Washington, D.C.

November 15 Largest antiwar rally in history of U.S. occurred in Washington, D.C., as 250,000 protested involvement in Vietnam War.

November 17 First round of Strategic Arms Limitation Talks between U.S. and USSR opened in Helsinki, Finland.

November 20 Use of pesticide DDT banned in residential districts; Some 78

Indians seized Alcatraz Island in San Francisco Bay and demanded that it be turned over to the Indian community.

November 24 Lt. William Calley charged with murders of civilians in massacre of 102 civilians at My Lai, Vietnam.

December 1 First draft lottery since World War II held in New York City.

December 2 At a huge Rolling Stone concert at Altamont Speedway in California during the 1969 tour, a gun-wielding black man was stabbed to death by Hells Angels who had been hired for security; Student strike at Harvard to end ROTC and in support of black student demands started.

December 8 Raid on Black Panther headquarters in Los Angeles led to shootout and suspicious deaths of Fed Hampton and Mark Clark.

Also in 1969 Pantsuits became acceptable for everyday wear by women; Kenneth Tynan's musical *Oh! Calcutta!* made debut; A Gallop poll showed 58 percent of Americans opposed Vietnam War; A conference of the Underground Press Syndicate adopted a series of resolutions condemning male supremacy in the ranks of underground newspapers; The Russell War Crimes Tribunal issued its report, condemning U.S. war crimes in Vietnam.

1970

January 2 FBI director J. Edgar Hoover claimed that black militant groups were "encouraged and infiltrated from without" in their violent attacks upon U.S. government.

January 5 Black children were enrolled in formerly all-white public schools in the districts of Mississippi under watchful eye of federal marshals.

January 21 Coroner's jury in Chicago, Illinois, concluded that deaths of Black Panther leaders Fred Hampton and Mark Clark, slain by police in a raid on December 4, 1969, were justifiable.

February 1 Southern school officials in 20 districts in Alabama, Georgia, and Mississippi defied federal order calling for total school desegregation.

February 4 Environmental cleanup program was proposed by President Nixon.

February 18 Jury acquitted seven of Chicago Eight of conspiracy charges, but convicted five of individual acts of incitement to riot.

February 26 Army announced it would discontinue surveillance of civilian demonstrators and maintenance of files on civilians possibly involved in civil disturbances.

March 6 Greenwich Village townhouse demolished by explosion of Weather Underground bomb factory.

April 1 Cigarette advertising was banned from television and radio.

April 16 Second round of SALT talks opened in Vienna, Austria.

April 20 U.S. troop reduction of 15,000 from Vietnam by end of the year was announced.

April 22 First Earth Day was observed across country.

May Thirty ROTC buildings were burned or bombed during the first week in May.

May 1 President Nixon announced incursion of American combat troops into Cambodia.

May 4 Four students at Kent State were killed by National Guard gunfire; four hundred forty-eight colleges and universities around the country closed in protest.

May 5 Nuclear nonproliferation treaty went into effect.

May 8 Construction workers attacked antiwar demonstrators at Wall Street, New York City.

May 9 More than 100,000 gathered in Washington to protest Cambodian incursion.

May 14 Two black students at Jackson State College in Jackson, Mississippi, were killed and 12 injured during protests.

May 29 Conviction of Black Panther leader Huey Newton of manslaughter was reversed by California Court of Appeals.

June 15 Conscientious objector status on moral grounds was found constitutional by U.S. Supreme Court.

June 18 Voting age was lowered to 18.

July 1 New York State abortion law left decision to woman during first 24 weeks of pregnancy.

July 7–31 Racial rioting occurred in several northern cities.

August More than 200 school districts across the South that had resisted school desegregation since U.S. Supreme Court order in 1954 responded peacefully with newly desegregated classrooms; Black Panther Huey Newton released on $50,000 bond after serving more than two years in a California prison for manslaughter conviction.

August 17 A judge and three kidnappers were killed in escape attempt by black militants from San Rafael, California, courthouse. A warrant was issued for Angela Davis's arrest.

September 1–7 Members of Black Panthers and women and gay liberation movements held first session of the Revolutionary People's Constitutional Convention in Philadelphia.

September 13 Eldridge Cleaver presided over the opening of the Black Panther Party's first international section in Algiers, Algeria.

September 18 Rock guitarist Jimi Hendrix died of drug overdose in London.

September 26 President's Commission on Campus Unrest called gap between youth culture and established society a threat to American stability.

September 28 Cleveland Sellers convicted of participating in riot on the campus of South Carolina State College in Orangeburg.

October 4 Rock singer Janis Joplin died.

October 7 Nixon's five-point peace plan for Indochina was rejected by North Vietnam.

October 12 U.S. Commission on Civil Rights reported a major breakdown in the enforcement of the nation's legal mandates prohibiting racial discrimination.

November 2 Third round of SALT talks opened in Helsinki.

November 12 Courtmartial of Lt. William Calley, Jr. began.

November 21 U.S. raid on Sontay, North Vietnam, in an attempt to free U.S. prisoners of war occurred.

December 2 U.S. Environmental Protection Agency (EPA) was activated.

December 31 National Air Quality Control Act tightened air pollution standards.

Also in 1970 Kate Millet's book *Sexual Politics* was published; The film *Catch-22* was released; A University of Wisconsin ROTC building was firebombed, beginning a wave of 500 bombings and arsons on university campuses; Militant Puerto Rican group, the Young Lords, issued a 13-point platform of liberation demands; Students burned down a Bank of America branch in Santa Barbara, California.

1971

January 5 Angela Davis was arraigned on charges of murder, kidnapping, and criminal conspiracy in a Marin County, California, court for her alleged participation in the August 7, 1970, incident at the San Rafael courthouse, which resulted in the death of four men.

January 12 Rev. Philip Berrigan and five others were indicted for conspiracy to kidnap presidential advisor Henry Kissinger and to bomb heating systems of federal buildings in Washington, D.C.

January 25 U.S. Supreme Court made first decision on sex discrimination in hiring practices, ruling that businesses cannot deny employment to women with preschool children unless they apply the same criteria to men.

March 1 Licensing of commercial whale hunters was halted; Capitol was bombed by Weather Underground.

March 29 Lt. William Calley, Jr., was convicted of 1968 murder of 22 South Vietnamese civilians at My Lai; Charles Manson and three others were sentenced to death for 1969 Tate–La Bianca murders.

April 20 School busing as a means of desegregation was upheld by U.S. Supreme Court.

April 24 Some 200,000 people attended antiwar demonstration in Washington, D.C.

May 3 May Day antiwar protest was held in Washington, D.C.

May 25 Bobby Seale and Ericka Huggin were acquitted of charges that they murdered a Black Panther member in May 1969.

June 13 *New York Times* began publishing classified Pentagon Papers about U.S. involvement in Vietnam. Supreme Court upheld right of *New York Times* and *Washington Post* to publish papers.

August 15 The National Black Feminist Organization (NBFO) was formed in New York City with chapters in other cities.

December 15 Huey Newton was declared free after manslaughter charges against him for 1967 death of Oakland police officer were dismissed. He had spent two years in jail.

December 26–30 Massive air bombardment of military installations in North Vietnam took place.

1972

January 13 U.S. announced withdrawal of 70,000 American soldiers from Vietnam.

March 22 Senate approved Equal Rights Amendment, sending it to 49 states for ratification.

April 5 "Harrisburg 7" were acquitted of conspiracy to kidnap Henry Kissinger.

April 10 Treaty banning biological warfare was signed by U.S. and 120 other nations.

May 2 FBI director J. Edgar Hoover died.

May 26 U.S. and USSR signed pact pledging nuclear freeze at current levels.

June 4 Angela Davis was acquitted by all-white jury of murder, kidnapping, and conspiracy charges.

June 14 DDT ban was announced by EPA.

June 17 Five men were arrested for breaking into the Democratic Party Headquarters in Watergate office complex in Washington, D.C.

October 18 Water Pollution Control Act was passed by Congress over President's veto.

November 17 President Richard Nixon was reelected in landslide victory over George McGovern, taking 49 states.

December 11–30 Paris peace talks broke down, and U.S. resumed bombing of North Vietnam.

December 31 EPA-ordered ban on DDT pesticide went into effect.

1973

January 27 U.S. and South Vietnam signed cease-fire with both Vietnam and Vietcong, ending Vietnam War; U.S. ended military draft.

January 28 Wounded Knee, South Dakota, was occupied by militant members of the American Indian Movement.

February 7 Senate Select Committee on Presidential Campaign Activities established to investigate Watergate Conspiracy.

May 11 Charges against Daniel Ellsberg and Anthony J. Russo for theft and circulation of Pentagon Papers were dismissed.

August 14 Bombing raids into Cambodian territory were halted.

September 1 New York State enacted nation's toughest drug law.

November 7 War Powers Act, which required Congressional approval for commitment of U.S. troops to combat abroad for longer than 60 days, passed by Congress over President Nixon's veto.

1

Paul Krassner
Father of the Underground Press

> There is a difference ... between the alternative press of today
> and the one in the sixties. In the sixties, to work for alternative
> press meant you were making a revolutionary commitment. To-
> day, it's more like a career move. But that's okay. The alternative
> press still comes up with angles you don't get in the mainstream
> press.

Paul Krassner, perhaps as much as any other sixties radical, shaped the thinking of the sixties counterculture. He did it through his satirical magazine *The Realist*, which he launched in 1958 at the tender age of 25 with a three-dollar subscription from comedian Steve Allen.[1] A decade later, at the height of the counterculture, *The Realist* had 100,000 avid readers who delighted in Krassner's provocative columns, which casually mixed fact and fiction.

Nothing was sacred to Krassner—neither motherhood, the pope, pop-culture icons like Walt Disney, nor the American presidency. As Krassner explained, "I wanted to write the most outrageous thing possible and make it sound true." *The Realist*'s 1967 "Disneyland Memorial Orgy" issue depicted Walt Disney's characters in various modes of copulation. In one of his best known columns, Krassner wrote that Lyndon Johnson had sexually violated John F. Kennedy's corpse on the flight back from Dallas after the President's assassination. The establishment accused Krassner of bad taste at the least and of sacrilege at the most. Noted journalist Harry Reasoner wrote in his memoirs that Krassner not only attacked established values, he attacked decency in general.[2]

Born in Brooklyn in 1932 and raised in Queens, Krassner honed his satirical skills in the fifties, first as an editor for *Mad* magazine and then as a comedy writer for Steve Allen's television show. He could easily have had a comfortable life as a comedy writer for the Hollywood establishment, but he became increasingly frustrated by the taboos placed on him and launched *The Realist*.

The Realist propelled Krassner into prominence as "the king of the outrageous," and during the sixties he hung out with some of the most famous

Paul Krassner (photo by Lynn Kushel).

and interesting personalities, including Bob Dylan, Allen Ginsberg, Lenny Bruce, John Lennon, and many prominent leaders and activists in the counterculture, such as Abbie Hoffman and Jerry Rubin.[3] He married Norman Mailer's adopted daughter and dropped acid with Groucho Marx. After watching President Lyndon Baines Johnson on television, Krassner thought it was time for the counterculture to march on the 1968 Democratic Convention. He coined the name "Yippie" to describe the politically motivated hippies who descended on Chicago.

Krassner knew that the counterculture would make great media copy and believed that the so-called "straight society" would believe any absurd statement, so long as it was presented in convincing fashion. Jokingly, he claimed that the Yippies were going to drop LSD into Chicago's water supply. A frightened Richard Daley, Chicago's mayor, surrounded the city's reservoirs with National Guard troops, even though quick calculation would have revealed that all the LSD in the world—and more—would not have been able to do the job.

But by the early seventies, Krassner's frenetic life-style began to unravel. The FBI bugged and harassed him. He went broke and had to close down *The Realist* in 1974. The counterculture fragmented, and Krassner drifted through the seventies, working as a part-time comedian, gag writer, and freelance writer. In 1977, a financially strapped Krassner took pornographer Larry Flynt's offer of a $90,000-a-year salary to work as publisher of *Hustler* magazine. But six months later, Krassner was fired after a bullet paralyzed Flynt and the management of *Hustler* was taken over by Flynt's wife.

In 1985, Krassner revived *The Realist* in newspaper format on a quarterly basis, more as a hobby than as a money-maker. Today, he lives in Venice, California, and makes a living by performing as a kind of "alternative" comedian in small clubs where middle-aged freaks come with the curious young to see the sixties legend. Krassner is generally credited with being the father of what has become known as the "underground press," a form that was copied and mimicked throughout the sixties and by the hundreds of alternative publications of the far left and the far out that have sprung up since the sixties.

In summing up the legacy of Krassner's *The Realist*, novelist Terry Southern wrote that the magazine was "the first American publication to really tell the truth . . . externally and figuratively—by ignored outlandish fact, by parable, by image, by creative hook or crook, whatever it took. *The Realist* lit the way for the counterculture and the periodicals that followed."[4]

*   *   *

It's interesting to learn that the "father of the underground press" and a major figure of the sixties counterculture is living in Venice, California, a city known for its beaches, suntan, and good times.

Actually, Venice has a lot to do with the sixties. Ken Kesey used to live here.[5] Furthermore, it's an open-minded community, and a lot of the sixties spirit flourishes here. But that is not the reason I'm here. I lived in New York until 1971 when I moved to San Francisco. I lived there for about fifteen years or so. I'm a political satirist; but I don't do comedy clubs, so I have to find other venues.

A producer named Scott Kelman was starting a theater out here in downtown L.A. called the Wallenboyd, and he had me open it for him in 1984. He let me stay in his apartment. I'm still here. My apartment is a block away from the beach, and I can see the ocean from my kitchen window as I talk to you. So I love living on the edge of the country, literally and figuratively. There's always vignettes going on. It's like a minicircus, with a variety of interesting people here.

I can imagine that the Venice scene gives you a lot of satirical material.

That's true. And it's very therapeutic to walk barefoot on the beach. I don't own a car, so Venice Beach is like my desert island and Los Angeles is the mainland.

You don't drive a car by choice?

By circumstance, really. I was brought up in New York where I always caught cabs, trains, and buses. When I moved out to San Francisco, I bought a car—a Volkswagen convertible—but I never learned to drive it because there were other priorities. That was the time I was heavily into conspiracy research, and I would have felt guilty if I took the time to learn to drive.

You say you don't do comedy clubs. Why is that?

It's a different rhythm. I do a show that's an hour and a half long, and the comedy clubs are like conveyor belts where the humor consists of easy humor reference jokes—for example, Tammy Bakker's makeup.[6] It's hard to establish a real relationship with an audience. Besides, I don't like the cigarette smoke, and there is usually a two-drink minimum. It's not like the audience is coming to hear what I have to say. They came to see a little comedy and get drunker as the evening goes on. I think a lot of what happens in comedy clubs perpetuates stereotypes instead of liberating the audience. It divides people instead of uniting them.

What kind of people come out to see your comedy act?

People who know my work and people who have heard of it. People who come because other people have recommended it. In my last show, there were parents who brought their kids and vice versa. What my audience and I have in common is the realization that the emperor has no clothes, and, when they come to hear me, they also learn that he has a hard on. [Laughs]

[Laughs] What are some of the subjects your satirical comedy act takes on?

Lately, it has been the topics of the day: the [presidential] campaign, Supreme Court decisions. . .

Is hitting on the topics of the day as interesting as it was in the sixties?

More so, in a way, because everything is escalating. I was involved in an abortion referral service when it was illegal in the sixties and all underground. But today, the abortion issue has escalated and intensified and is much more in the public's eye.

When you do your comedy routine, does the audience expect you to touch on the sixties and make a nostalgia trip?

I don't think so, but sometimes I do. For a while, I would tell anecdotes about the sixties, but I try to stay away from that now. Recently, I was invited to appear on a television show, but refused because it was only for six minutes and I didn't want to be frozen in the sixties.

Yes, I guess there is danger of becoming a relic.
   A psychedelic relic.

[Laughs] Most people would be surprised to learn that you are sixty years of age.
   I'm the most surprised of all. [Laughs]

[Laughs] Was it traumatic when you turned sixty? Did you say, "Hey, it's time to slow down?"
   No, no. I can understand how it can be very depressing and demoralizing for people [to turn sixty], depending on where their life is at. Sure you miss certain things about your youth and have certain fears about the future. But then I think about the young generation today. Many of them have died from AIDS or from drive-by shootings. Many of them probably have a life span that consists of less than the number of years I have left in my life. That gives me perspective.
   Anyway, my philosophy is very existential. I live in the present, which is all you can really do. I believe anything can happen. I can get hit by a bus tomorrow. The ultimate credo of the sixties was to live in the present. It would make a lie of that credo to be in the nineties and still be living in the sixties. Besides, I believe there is a counterculture emerging today like the one in the sixties, except this one will have a loss of innocence.

Where is this counterculture forming?
   All over ... internationally at all levels. I think there's a momentum building, which is going to pull the wool from people's eyes.

About the issues?
   Yes, about the issues.

Do you see any kind of commitment to social change that is like the commitment many people had in the sixties?
   Well, as we speak, Clinton and Gore are ahead of Bush and Quayle by the largest percentage maybe in polling history. This means something. More people seem to be voting for Clinton rather than against Bush. Gore is strongly associated with the environment, even though he voted for the war in Iraq, which led to the worst environmental disaster in history. One of life's ironies. [Laughs]

Is there an analogy here? Are the nineties like the late fifties and early sixties when we moved from the age of Eisenhower into the age of Kennedy?
   The sixties counterculture exploded out of the blandness and repression of the Eisenhower-Nixon period. Today, there's a counterculture exploding out of the blandness of the Reagan-Bush era.

So are your sixties going to be an exciting period?

Yes! We have a lot of things coming out: Spike Lee's movie *Malcolm X*, my autobiography, the recent biography of Abbie Hoffman.[7] All these things combined are going to wake up people in the growing counterculture more and more and get them involved with what's happening in mainstream culture.

Is there much difference between the youth of today and youth of the sixties?

Sure. In 1959, I wrote an editorial from a completely idealistic point of view that said there should be no separation of male and female categories in the help wanted ads. I thought it was cockeyed optimism to believe it would happen in my lifetime. But in '64, it became illegal to discriminate like that. Now young people take it so much for granted.

They don't even realize that such male-female distinctions ever existed. Women fought hard so they could wear slacks to school. Now people don't even know it was once forbidden. So there are things we struggled for that young people take for granted. But, on the other hand, there are issues like the economy, censorship, abortion, and ecology that we didn't really have to face. The sixties counterculture was in a more affluent context. It was easier to drop out when you had parents sending you a stipend every month.

I guess, if the counterculture is forming again, you're not nostalgic for the sixties?

I don't know if I ever was. If there is one thing to be missed, it would be the sense of community we had in the sixties. All the people who had been the only martians on the block found out that there had been a martian invasion. They saw the connection between putting people in this country in jail for smoking marijuana and dropping napalm on the other side of the world.

But today, it's exciting to hear a nine-year-old girl talk about the dangers of styrofoam. I remember watching an episode of the TV series *Married with Children*, and this nine-year-old girl saying, "That is so sexist!" When we were nine years old, we didn't even know how to spell *sexist*. And she said that while she was playing Nintendo! That's what gives me hope. You are interviewing people from the sixties who have names that are recognizable, but there were a lot of people from the sixties who were on the front lines of the struggle and didn't get any publicity for it. I meet these people while I travel. They have kept their values from the sixties as much as possible.

That's interesting because many critics of the sixties counterculture assume that the counterculture disintegrated and [that] there is hardly a trace of it left.

The critics are in their ivory towers. They don't know what's going on. People from every walk of life—education, religion, I'm sure even from the Justice Department—have come out of the sixties with the sensibility that there must be a better way and it's possible to change the system. The blueprint in life is not set in stone.

Paul Krassner (photo by Jay Green).

Earlier, you alluded to the camaraderie that existed in the sixties counterculture. You must have had a hell of a lot of fun in the sixties running around with some of the great characters of the period—Jerry Rubin, [Abbie] Hoffman, [Allen] Ginsberg.

Jerry Rubin came to my performance recently. I saw Anita Hoffman [Abbie Hoffman's ex-wife] the other day. I recently spoke with Ken Kesey on the phone. The friendships developed organically. You didn't say, "The decade is over. Goodbye." It's not just rhetoric when I say we are truly an extended family.

So most of the people you ran with in the sixties are still your friends?

I'll probably see Tim Leary next week. All of these people have not been frozen in time. They have developed, although they have gone through a lot of changes.

You sound like a very tolerant guy because a lot of your fellow sixties activists seemed to have moved in the opposite direction from you. Take Rubin, for example. He ate up the age of Reagan and is involved with a lot of things you seemed opposed to, including making a lot of money.

Yeah, he may be a pyramid schemer, but at least he's not selling missiles. He's not a warmonger and not an evil person. He's a workaholic in terms of running his business. He's using a lot of skills he developed in the antiwar movement. People have to survive, you know. A lot of people have had to take jobs they didn't want. There is an old saying: a liberal is a radical with a family. People responsible for their families have had to make certain compromises.

My goal has been to compromise as little as possible. Even when I was broke in the seventies, I turned down an audition for a part in *The New Mary Tyler Moore Show* because the script called for me to play a character who kills his cable TV repairman when he couldn't get a good picture. I didn't want to contribute to the idea that casual violence is the way to deal with problems. I do that so I can live with myself. But I'm not going to get self-righteous and put down other people because they might not have taken my path.

One of your friends from the sixties who never seemed to change was Abbie Hoffman. What kind of relationship did you have with Abbie?

An intimate and stormy one. We were very good friends, like brothers, but when I took acid during the Chicago conspiracy trial (the trial of the Chicago Seven in 1968), he stopped talking to me.

Why did he do that?

He thought it was irresponsible to take acid before I testified.

Were you shocked by Abbie's death?

Oh, sure!

Suspicious?

Well, I'm an old conspiracy nut, but I checked his death out, and I'm convinced it was suicide. Abbie was clinically diagnosed as a manic-depressive. There are some people I know, though, who are convinced Abbie's death is a conspiracy.

Didn't Dave Dellinger believe it was a conspiracy on the part of the CIA?

At the very beginning he did, but more and more information came out and he changed his mind.[8]

So it's settled that Abbie's death was a suicide?

In my mind and his family's [minds], I know it is.

How would you assess Abbie's place in history?

He will hold a legendary place in history. There are three books being written about him, and I'm sure there will be a movie. He was unique. I think he will serve as a role model for people who want to learn how to fight City Hall . . . creatively.

I read an article that said you were contacted by two different producers to write a script about Abbie's life.

Oh, yeah, they called right after his death. I treated them like vultures who circle around a carcass. I know what movies can do. I remember what they did to Lenny Bruce. A writer doesn't have much control over a script. I retain 100 percent of the movie rights to my autobiography. It's bad enough what Hollywood can do to a novel, but I don't want them to fuck up my life.

Does your magazine The Realist *provide you with a living?*

The Realist isn't really a business for me. It's art. The only reason I charge for it is to limit the audience. [Laughs] I have not been able to depend on it for a living. It's been pretty much in the red.

[Laughs] But I believe at one time in the sixties, The Realist *had a readership of over 100,000.*

Back then it was published in a real magazine format and sold in bookstores. I also had no competition. There was no *Spy*, no *Utne Reader*, no *National Lampoon*, no *Saturday Night Live*, and no *Doonesbury*. There was a hunger for a magazine like *The Realist*. Now, a lot of the stuff I would have published I now see in other magazines. The taboos have changed so much. Today, *The Realist* is in newsletter format and it's sold in a few select bookstands and newsstands. A lot of people aren't aware that *The Realist* is still being published. I get a lot of mail from people who write, "I didn't know you were still around."

[Laughs] To show how low key your publication is, when I mentioned to someone that I was going to interview you, he said, "There is a rumor that The Realist *is starting up." [Laughs]*

[Laughs] My autobiography[9] will let people know of *The Realist's* continued existence, and I'm sure there will be a surge in subscriptions.

You don't seem to mind being out of the limelight?

It's tricky. Sometimes it can be frustrating because I feel I have things to say and would like a larger audience. Any artist wants to reach out to as many people as he can without compromising, but it's not an ego thing with me.

Besides, the format, is the new Realist *really that much different than the old* Realist.

At times, when publishing the old *Realist*, I would get self-righteous. Now, I guess I'm more tolerant. Again, the taboos have changed so much. Lenny Bruce was arrested for saying "cocksucker" in San Francisco. Twenty years later, [actress] Meryl Streep got an Oscar for saying the same thing in *Sophie's Choice*.[10] I now have a lot more avenues to go down, so to speak.

Weren't you credited with introducing four-letter words into journalism?

Oh, yeah, at the time, they were using asterisks for four-letter words. Norman Mailer told me *The Realist* served as a role model for other publications. When I think of the thing I'm most proud of, the introduction of four-letter words doesn't come to mind. I did add two words to the English language, though: Yippie and soft-core pornography.

I know you introduced the word Yippie, *but I didn't know about soft-core pornography.*

Anyone could have done it. It [Krassner's use of soft-core pornography] was a takeoff of the Supreme Court designation of hard-core pornography . . . it just gives you a soft-on. [Laughs]

[Laughs] Looking back to the sixties and The Realist, *what impact did it really have on the times? How influential were you?*

The feedback I get from people is that *The Realist* woke them up and made them see the bullshit that they were taking for granted. It also made them laugh at things that were held sacred and made them question their own conditioning. I still get correspondence from old readers. Let me read you a letter I got recently: "Dear Paul: Enclosed is a check for twelve dollars to cover a six-issue subscription. . . . Incidently, I would like to thank you for the big influence you had on my life. In 1965, when I was thirteen, I became a subscriber to *The Realist*. Initially, I subscribed to read an interview with Jean Shepherd, but I loved all the other stuff. Through an article in *The Realist* I met Larry and Michele Cole. I became the first volunteer of their Lower East Side Action Project. They became my surrogate hip parents, and, for thirty years, we have stayed friends. I am currently working on an interactive video project about the sixties. It's come full circle. . . .'

So you get a lot of letters like that?

Oh, yeah. A lot of the people who subscribe say they were influenced by *The Realist* in the sixties or that their parents were influenced. At Abbie's memorial service, I met Jackson Browne who told me his mother used to read *The Realist*.[11]

But you had your detractors, too. I ran across an article in Regardie's *[magazine] in which Harry Reasoner attacked you for "a lack of decency."*

He said not only did Krassner attack establishment values, he attacked decency in general.

Did criticism like that ever get under your skin?

It's fair comment, but what bothered me is that TV voted him "the most respectable journalist" or who "looked like the most respected journalist," yet he missed a lot of what I was saying. But when the FBI sent a letter to *Life* magazine calling *The Realist* "a smutty, unimportant little rag" and me "a raving, unconfined nut," that bothered me. At least Harry Reasoner signed his name to what he said. The FBI letter was signed by "Howard Rasmussen, Brooklyn College, School of Graduate Studies," which was a phony name. The FBI was using taxpayer money to do character assassination. That was fascistic.

How did you find out about the FBI dirty trick?

Through a Freedom of Information request, which gave me my FBI file. Also, Yippie archivist Sam Leff brought to my attention another FBI dirty trick—the FBI's attempt to create a rift between Jews and Blacks.

But you did write a lot of shocking things in The Realist. *One of the most famous was having Lyndon Johnson violate the corpse of John F. Kennedy on the flight back to Washington after JFK's assassination. What were you trying to do with that bit of satire?*

It worked. People believed it, if only for an instant. That was because of the context. It took an act of necrophilia, not dropping napalm on Vietnam, to get readers to realize that President Johnson was nuts.

Did you ever fall flat on your face and write something in The Realist *that didn't turn out the way you wanted it to?*

I can't think of anything offhand, but I'm sure there was. I'm my own severest critic; so I assume that because it makes me laugh, it will make my readers laugh. If they don't it's just a failure to communicate.

Were you ever sued for libel?

No, I was threatened. But I did get sued for something I wrote in *Rolling Stone* when I was investigating the [Charles] Manson case.[12] I accused somebody of being in navy intelligence and posing as a hippy artist. It was a false lead. But I did find out a lot of interesting things.

Like what?

That the L.A. police had seized porno films from Sharon Tate's house and sold them, and that somebody from a cocaine ring had dropped by the place before the murders tooks place.

What is your opinion of the alternative press today?

People magazine wrote that I was "father of the underground press." I wrote back to them, demanding a blood test. [Laughs] But I think today's alternative press is in good shape. It serves as a nice antidote to what the mainstream press gives us.

There is a difference, though, between the alternative press of today and the one of the sixties. In the sixties, to work for the alternative press meant you were making a revolutionary commitment. Today, it's more like a career move. But that's okay. The alternative press still publishes stuff and comes up with angles you don't get in the mainstream press. Today, the mainstream press reads the alternative press and gets many ideas from it.

But today, many alternative publications look like the mainstream press with their advertising and slick layout and the fact that they deal with a lot of mainstream issues.

Yeah, and you wonder if the advertising sometimes affects content. It's all relative, though. I remember the wonderful work done by a reporter named Murray Waas in the *Village Voice* when the war against Iraq was breaking out. He was investigating the U.S.'s relationship with Iraq before the war. I now see his stuff in the *Los Angeles Times,* which, along with the other media, are now investigating the U.S.'s relationship with Iraq before the war. The fact that angle on the Iraq story went from the *Village Voice* to the *L.A. Times* to the network news shows that alternative press is playing its role.

Are you still an activist? Do you still go out on marches and protest the issues?

In my own way. I just did a benefit for The Alliance for Survival, which is an antinuke group. I also did a benefit for Americans Before Columbus and spoke out at a pro-choice rally. But I don't go running wild in the streets anymore.

Like you used to. [Laughs] Earlier, I asked if you had a lot of fun in the sixties. Did you get involved with some of the zany tactics, such as levitating the Pentagon and dropping dollar bills on the floor of the Stock Exchange?

Yeah. In fact I remember speaking at a literary conference at the University of Iowa, and Abbie asking me to bring some cornmeal back to sprinkle around the Pentagon in a prelevitation rite.

[Laughs] Humor was an important part of the counterculture, wasn't it?

Yeah, it was like being in school. You gravitate toward the teacher who makes you laugh. When you laugh, your defenses are down and you can listen better.

How did you see your role in the counterculture as it evolved?

Part chronicler, part court jester. I was like the Bob Hope of the counterculture.

[Laughs] Were you heavy into the drug scene?

There were periods when I was taking acid every week and smoking marijuana every day.

How did it affect the way you looked at the world?

Sometimes, I got an idea when I was tripping or stoned and couldn't tell if I would have gotten that idea if I hadn't been tripping or stoned. Acid and grass are not like heroin and speed, which can either slow you down or speed you up. But drugs helped me understand what was going on. I know there are some who would disagree.

Do you still take drugs?

Sure, but not at the same level as I did in the sixties. I take Ecstasy occasionally and marijuana. They are the only drugs I do today. But I make sure I don't do any legal drugs.

[Laughs] Given the antidrug climate in the country today, do you have much fun doing drugs today?

The fun is in the process, not in the breaking of the law.

Do you think the drug subculture had a positive or negative effect on sixties activism and the counterculture?

Drugs were inextricably tied in with the counterculture because they served as a catalyst for people to get in touch with the values they really wanted to live by and to relate to other people in a more intimate manner. It allowed us to talk about things that really mattered, not just the superficial stuff the mainstream culture was feeding us.

You were actively involved in the Yippie Party. What was its significance in terms of the sixties legacy?

The emergence of the Yippies forced people to see a police state in action. A lot of people weren't aware of that until the 1968 Democratic Convention.

The Yippie Party was short-lived, wasn't it?

It was a myth to begin with. I came up with the name so it could serve as a label for a phenomenon that already existed; namely, a coalition between the psychedelic dropouts and the New Left activists, which had organized around the Vietnam War.

Could there have been a counterculture without the war?

I think so. As I said before, the counterculture showed that we couldn't separate the politics from the culture; so the war was just an extension of the kind of injustices that were going on inside America.

There was much talk of revolution, especially after the 1968 Chicago Democratic Convention. Did the radicals really believe a revolution was possible, or was it just rhetoric?

I remember asking somebody, "Do you really believe a revolution is going to take place in your lifetime?" and getting the reply, "I would crawl up into a corner and die if I didn't believe it." It depends on how you define *revolution*. There were certainly a lot of personal revolutions taking place.

Have you read Peter Collier and David Horowitz's book about the sixties?[13]

No, but I've read articles about their book, and I've heard them on the radio.

In their book, they write that "the [sixties] decade ended with a big bang that made society into a collection of splinter groups, social interest groups, and newly minted minorities whose common belief was that America was guilty and untrustworthy." What's your response to that interpretation of the sixties legacy?

That's how they raise money for their conversative causes. They need to propagate that point of view because they've probably hypnotized themselves into believing it. It's just a stinky generalization. They were ideologues in the sixties, who were against the hippies because they were having fun.

Maoists in disguise. [Laughs]

[Laughs] Something like that. They weren't really part of the counterculture.

Collier and Horowitz might ask you then, "Okay, Krassner, did anything positive come out of the sixties?" How would you answer them?

People involved in the sixties counterculture started to act responsibly

towards their value systems. They began to substitute nonviolence for violence, caring and sharing for selfishness. They really tried to live their alternative life-style, instead of just being theoretical. And the way they brought
up their children . . . the counterculture legacy is one of respect for children
and the belief that one should learn from kids, rather than try to avoid them
and make them feel inferior. The children of the counterculture are continuing the legacy and living up to the credo of change. When my daughter had
a punk hairstyle, I welcomed it. She was free to exercise her sense of individuality.

You stopped publishing The Realist *in 1974. What was the reason? Were you
burned out?*
    Yes, I was. I went nuts from information overload. I was publishing infor-
mation about the JFK assassination, the Manson case, and Watergate while it
was still being called "a burglary." It was more than I could handle. I freaked
out. I have written my autobiography in part to learn how that happened to
me because I've always been sane.

You must smile with all the talk today of conspiracy theories.
    People come up to me and say, "You were crazy, but you were right."

So how does a counterculture hero come to write for Hustler? *[Laughs]*
    I took a lot of heat working for *Hustler.* I think it's snobbery not wanting
to communicate with an audience just because they jerk off to a magazine. I
was working at *Hustler* when Larry Flynt got shot. If I tried to write a novel
about a porno publisher who became a born-again Christian, having been converted by an evangelist who was the President's sister, and then got shot and
ended up in a wheelchair, wearing American-flag-style diapers, and then went
to the Supreme Court that way and called the Justices "the eight assholes and
a cunt" . . . it might seem farfetched. [Laughs]

[Laughs] You got a short bang for your buck, so to speak, because your tenure at
Hustler *lasted six months.*
    I was brought in to work for the magazine because I offered redeeming
social value. It was too absurd an offer to resist. At that point in my life, I had
to borrow money to buy a pair of blue jeans. Suddenly, I was making $90,000
a year, which I had to use to pay off my debts. In fact, when I left *Hustler,* I
had less money than when I started.

Why did you leave Hustler?
    Larry Flynt got shot. Althea Flynt (his wife) took over, and she fired me.
There were cash flow problems at the magazine, and I guess she thought I was
superfluous.

*How about your old friends from your activist days? Did they make any judg-
ments about your working at* Hustler?
    Not those who really knew and trusted me. There were some feminists

who thought I had sold out. But I was able to get some articles on abortion and other important social issues into *Hustler.*

Have you reconciled with your feminist critics?

Yes. One had called me a pig and a fascist, but later apologized to me.

How did you get out of the financial mess you were in?

I'm still in it. I'm depending on my autobiography to get me out of it.

God, you've been in a financial mess from 1974 to 1992?

Well, there have been jobs in between, but I don't have any money for next month's rent. I'm borrowing money based on the fourth installment of my advance from Simon and Shuster. Magazine and foreign rights sales will help. I've begun to feel a little more secure about money. Jobs have come along every once and a while . . . like the "Wilton North Report" on the Fox Network. I was a writer for that program. I was a head writer for a 1980 HBO special satirizing the election; and, ten years later, I was a writer on the "Ron Reagan Show."

Don't you sometimes wish you were back working for the "Steve Allen Show?" You could have been rich with a home in Bel-Air.[14]

I consider myself extraordinarily fortune to have been able to exercise total freedom of expression throughout my life. You can't measure that in terms of money. So I don't think I've sacrificed anything.

In addition to your friends in the counterculture, you've had a lot of great relationships and have been friends with some of the most interesting people of the twentieth century.

Yes, I've been in the right places at the right times.

Didn't Lenny Bruce call you his closest friend?

I don't know if I was his closest friend, but we were pretty tight. He was a big influence on me as a performer. He and Mort Sahl were my role models.[15]

Was Bruce in tune with the counterculture?

When I went to the Diggers garage in Haight Ashbury, I saw a picture of Lenny Bruce. The Diggers knew Lenny was articulating their consciousness.

What about Groucho Marx and your experience dropping acid with him?

It was very surrealistic. Groucho was very human in contrast to the image the public had of him. He didn't make a big thing of the experience, although he did open up, and [he] talked about what was going on in America. He didn't like what was going on politically. At one point, he did a hilarious imitation of his walk. He was funny.

Was Groucho in tune with the counterculture?

He was aware of it and approved of a lot of things that were going on.

What's going to happen after your autobiography comes out? I would guess the royalties will not be enough money to retire on.

I will be able to live month to month until the paperback comes out and then I will be able to live some more.

But you've only got one life to write about?

I'm already thinking about some projects; for example, I'm thinking of putting together an anthology of investigative satire. A novel has been evolving for some time now about a controversial comedian. The idea was inspired by Lenny Bruce. Actually, I've been retired since I was six years old.

[Laughs] From the straight life?

Yeah. One definition of *happiness* is "having as little separation between your work and play as possible." So if I retired, I would retire to what I'm doing now anyway. If I were independently wealthy, I don't think anything would change in my life. I might buy an extra pair of jeans, or perhaps start a radical think tank. Maybe I would take taxis a little more often.

So you are happy?

As happy as I can be in a world with so much suffering.

When it's time to go to that great counterculture in the sky, how would you like history to remember you?

My epitaph might read "Wait, I'm not finished!" or "You're alive and I'm not," or "If I were made of styrofoam, I would still be around." I hope my work will have served as a catalyst to wake people up and to bring them closer to themselves or [will have] inspired them in some way or made them laugh.

2

Cleveland Sellers

From Black Revolutionary to Educator and Community Worker

> SNCC was on the cutting edge and acted as a gadfly and catalyst. It forced the civil rights movement to take notice and to move in a much more progressive direction more quickly than it would have if SNCC wasn't around... SNCC didn't take on any powder puff issues. It took on issues that had an impact.
>
> That's the role we played, but you can't play it forever. Either you become institutionalized or you go off the scene. SNCC just ran out of the energy and life blood it needed to sustain itself.

In April 1960, the Student Nonviolent Coordinating Committee (SNCC) was organized in Raleigh, North Carolina, to serve as the liaison for the sit-ins that had sprung up across the South following the Greensboro, North Carolina, sit-in on February 1 of that year. The SNCC quickly assumed a leadership role in the civil rights movement. Staff members and volunteers got involved with the Freedom Riders the following year and later organized voter registration drives in Mississippi. The SNCC was one of several African American civil rights organizations that led the 1963 March on Washington to demand jobs and an end to employment discrimination.

Cleveland Sellers was a 19-year-old student at Howard University when he dropped out in 1963 to become a SNCC volunteer. The following year, SNCC selected Sellers to be its program secretary, and, as the battle for racial justice raged across the South in the sixties, he became an insider privy to the strategies, conflicts, and struggles within the civil rights movement. He was best friends with charismatic SNCC leader Stokely Carmichael and talked and debated with the sixties' most prominent African American leaders, including Malcolm X and Martin Luther King, Jr. In 1964 he participated in Freedom Summer, a seminal event that historians credit with leading to the passage of the 1965 Voting Rights Act and later paving the way for federally funded health care clinics and Head Start programs.

Sellers was also at the Democratic National Convention in 1964 when SNCC tried to break the domination of the regular Democratic Party in

41

Mississippi by organizing the Mississippi Freedom Democratic Party (MFDP). Acting on President Lyndon Baines Johnson's orders, Vice President Hubert Humphrey tried to arrange a compromise that would have given MFDP delegates representation at the convention, but no voice or vote. SNCC rejected the plan, and Sellers, like other of the organization's militant leaders, concluded that the Democratic Party could not be trusted to hasten the liberation of African Americans.

They came to embrace *Black Power,* a concept that split the civil rights movement and angered many of its supporters, especially after SNCC expelled white volunteers from the organization. SNCC chairman Stokely Carmichael defined *Black Power* as "a call for black people in this country to unite, to recognize their heritage and (to) build a sense of community"; but the press began to interpret the slogan as meaning black violence against whites.[1]

By the late sixties, SNCC influence on the civil rights movement had begun to wane. As historians point out, SNCC lacked unity, strategy, and discipline, and, to function, it relied more on key personalities than it did on organization. The SNCC, moreover, became, like the Black Panthers and other civil rights organizations, the object of the FBI's COINTELPRO program, which was designed to sow confusion and chaos within civil rights groups that FBI director J. Edgar Hoover deemed subversive.

Sellers's life changed dramatically in February 1968 when a group of students from South Carolina State College marched on a local bowling alley in an attempt to integrate it. Some students got in, but the bowling alley was closed. When students returned the following night in larger numbers, law enforcement officials were waiting. Some of the students, including coeds, were beaten. The next day, the angry students said they would boycott local businesses unless their demands were met.

As tension increased, South Carolina Governor Robert E. McNair called in the National Guard to reinforce police already on the scene. The police fired on the students after they mistakenly thought one of the officers had been shot. Thirty students were hit and three died. The press claimed students had fired, but a later investigation proved that no students had fired a shot.

The blame for what became known as the Orangeburg Massacre was laid on the slender, young shoulders of Cleveland Sellers, who had been on campus at the time of the shootings and had been shot. Sellers was arrested, found guilty of inciting a riot, and spent seven months in jail.

Sellers became a man haunted by history—the only person to be blamed for the tragedy at Orangeburg. The state of South Carolina never investigated why nine white police officers opened fire with shotguns, weapons not normally used for "riot" control, into a crowd of African Americans.

Even before he began serving his prison term, Sellers had earned a master's degree in education from Harvard University. Later in the seventies, he also earned a Ph.D. in education from the University of North Carolina at Greensboro, a move that he hoped would get him a job in a black college. He

Cleveland Sellers (photo courtesy of Cleveland Sellers).

never did get that job. Instead, he worked 11 years for the city of Greensboro as a planning supervisor and then another seven with the housing authority.

After his parents died within a few months of one another in 1990, Sellers returned to his hometown of Denmark, South Carolina, to manage his family's rental property. He has remained active in community affairs. Among other current activities, Sellers serves on the South Carolina State Board of Education and as program director of the Denmark Recreation Association.

In the meantime, he began to seek a pardon for his Orangeburg Massacre conviction. It finally came in July 1993, a few weeks before our interview. Sitting in Sellers's modest home in Denmark, it is hard to imagine that, more than 25 years ago, South Carolina authorities considered the soft-spoken and gentle-mannered Sellers one of the state's most dangerous criminals. It is also difficult to contemplate Sellers as the fiery young militant who once described himself as a "black revolutionary." But the articulate Sellers can vividly recall the events at Orangeburg, the history of the sixties civil rights movement, and his role as maker of history.

*   *   *

What were your feelings when the pardon you had been working so long and hard for finally came through?

We have been going backwards and forwards to clean as much of the record as possible and to get the Orangeburg Massacre put into its proper historical context. It's been extremely difficult because some of the major players were unwilling to give a different assessment and analysis than the one they gave originally, which we know is invalid and incorrect. A lot of the [South Carolina] state officials have been in a state of denial. So for me, the pardon represents the putting of the Orangeburg Massacre into its proper historical context. In terms of civil rights history, it should be placed alongside the killing of the four young girls in Birmingham and the murder of Chaney, Goodman, and Schwerner in Philadelphia [Mississippi].

In your view, is a thorough investigation still needed to set the record straight about what happened in Orangeburg?

I don't know if an investigation is needed. What is needed is a forum to discuss the incident in detail. The information is available, but a couple of things went bad. One of them was the media coverage. There was deliberate attempt to distort that incident and to distort history. The media wrote that the students at Orangeburg were shot as results of an exchange of gunfire. That was not true. There was no shooting from the campus. The press depicted me as falsely instigating and provoking what took place. The responsibility was shifted away from the officers who shot the students, to me.

Once lives are lost, it's extremely difficult to get people to turn around and admit that something wrong happened. The pardon lifts that burden, although it doesn't expunge the record. It's the first attempt to clear me of any complicity in the massacre.

What impact did the Orangeburg Massacre have on your personal and professional life?

As a result of the Orangeburg incident, I remained in jail for two and a half months under what I considered to be a very big bond and was restricted to staying five miles outside of Orangeburg. My home here in Denmark is actually five miles outside that limit. That was just the beginning.

When I was arrested in Orangeburg and taken to Columbia, a couple of things happened. The state actually opened the penitentiary for me in the middle of the night. They normally lock down about 5 P.M., and under no circumstances is the prison opened. That's a security precaution. But they did it for me. They locked me in the death row area. It was tough dealing with that kind of mind game.

Shortly after that, the federal government felt that Orangeburg was significant enough to try and then sentence me for refusing induction in the armed services. The judge denied me bond, using the Orangeburg incident as his reason. I was in jail from April 1968 to August-September 1968 before I was released on bond, which is normally a pretty standard thing. I had to go all the way to the Supreme Court to get justice. Justice [Hugo] Black signed a paper releasing me on bond.

During the period of my incarceration, I was transferred from the Atlanta city jail to the Atlanta county jail and then went to Noonan, Georgia, where I stayed four days before being transferred to Rome, Georgia. I stayed a week there before being transferred to Tallahassee Federal Correctional Institution. From there, I was moved back to Atlanta, to Knoxville, to Nashville, and then to Terre Haute, Indiana, where I did the bulk of my waiting for the appeal.

They set a hearing date, and I was released on bond, but the FBI and the Justice Department had officers there from the State of Louisiana. They created a charge—a gun possession charge—and I was arrested and put in jail until I could post another bond.

My attorneys chose not to fight the Louisiana gun charge because we were already dealing with the Orangeburg incident and the draft charges. We pleabargained, which I didn't want to do, but I had no choice. Because of Orangeburg, we were looking at five felony charges that could have put me in jail for 85 years. There was no fine on the Louisiana charge, but I did receive a one-year probationary sentence.

Many observers believe the authorities in South Carolina knew they screwed up at Orangeburg and needed a scapegoat to detract attention. Do you believe that?
That's a correct assessment. They had initially concluded that I had been killed with the other three students, which provided them with a scapegoat. I really didn't think the Orangeburg, South Carolina, police department in 1968 was sophisticated enough to develop such a plan. It had to involve both state law enforcement and the FBI.

And given what we know today about what COINTELPRO did to black civil rights activists and organizations in the sixties, that's a logical conclusion.
Absolutely! I was just lucky to get out of there alive!

One of the things that has always been curious to me is why the police used live ammunition. That was not standard ammunition used in riot control.
There is no rational explanation for anything they did. If the students were in downtown Orangeburg, I could understand their concern. But they were on campus. The officers actually walked on campus and shot the students. We can say it was poor judgment, but it was probably something

more sinister than that. People were killed and that fact should be addressed. We should find out what happened and why.

You said you were lucky to get out of the Orangeburg incident with your life. Did you worry that the authorities might want to "get rid of their problem," so to speak, and kill you?

I called the press the night before the Orangeburg Massacre happened, and said that, no matter what was going to happen at Orangeburg, it was going to be painted as my fault. There was no question in my mind about that. The shootings happened about five hundred feet from where I was living. They brought a tank and pointed it directly at my house. I knew it had live ammo, and I didn't want it to go off while I was sitting in a wooden house, so I moved out. On the night of the shooting, I was in a dormitory on the campus of South Carolina State College. I had no idea that the troops would come on campus and use deadly force.

But what happened at Orangeburg directly relates to my SNCC experience. We in the organization always talked about what it meant to live a long life. Many of us never really expected to live a long life, given the experiences we were going through.

I was in Mississippi in the summer of 1964 when there was a bombing every night. Many people were beaten, arrested, and murdered during the period the FBI was allegedly looking for Andrew Goodman, James Chaney, and Michael Schwerner. They discovered six additional bodies in various rivers. They were people who had at one point or another been active in the civil rights movement.

There was a lot of pressure. I was a teenager and there were some who were younger than I was. There was a tremendous amount of pressure! We would rig our cars to be faster than others and put them in areas where the hostilities were greater. We took the porch lights off and never stood in front of a window. You never knew when someone was going to plant a bomb or fire-bomb a house. The point I'm making is that we operated in a war zone, and we never knew if we would get out of there alive. Our parents were concerned, and they would write and implore us to come home. That was an additional pressure.

Did the experience at Orangeburg and all your other experiences in the civil rights movement shake your faith in the American system?

I still have concern about whether African Americans can receive justice from the judicial system. It took twenty-five years for me to get a pardon for what happened at Orangeburg. If it wasn't for the fact that I was shot, there would have been no way that I could have been tied in to the incident. I am a victim who was made to appear to be the perpetrator, so I don't think I got justice from the Orangeburg court system.

They surrounded the court house with trooper cars, and the first two rows of the courtroom were filled with troopers. I knew I got a bad deal on the Louisiana gun charge. I know the time I've spent in jail is not because of any kind of criminal activity I may have been involved with, but, rather, because of political expediency. Justice has been an elusive goal that I have sought to this day.

The same could be said about my draft evasion charge. I had sued the draft board both in South Carolina and Georgia because of the manner in which I was inducted and because of the fact that there were no African Americans involved in the process. We were just cannon fodder for the war! We did not make the decisions. They were probably thinking, "Send him off and let him be killed in Vietnam, and then we don't have to worry about another civil rights activist." I believe that was the backdrop to my being drafted in the armed forces.

Are you a better person for the experiences that you have gone through?

Initially, I had a tremendous amount of anger and frustration; but, if we want to be social change activists, one of the things we have to learn is that a lot of anger tends to do more harm than good and can have a negative impact on one's health, attitude, perspective . . . everything. You have to learn how to deal with the problem and how to release some of your frustration and anger or else you will become a reactionary kind of person. I chose not to be that kind of person. I chose to back off, regroup, and try to make a difference.

Is there anything you would do differently if you could relive the sequence of events that lead to the Orangeburg Massacre? Did you play it the way you should have played it?

I wasn't dealt a terrific hand to begin with, but I did do all that was possible for me to do. I don't look back with any regrets and say, "Well, if I did this, maybe this would have happened." I did everything I could do to provide for the security of the students, but, at the same time, we always knew that anytime you engage in protest activity, there is a possibility that something could happen. It could get completely out of control, and somebody could get hurt. I learned that from Mississippi and the other demonstrations I had been a party to. But no, I wouldn't do anything over again.

Orangeburg is a forgotten chapter of civil rights history and the history of the sixties. The incidents at Kent State and Jackson State are well known compared to Orangeburg. How do you explain that?

There are several reasons. One is that, during the period that Orangeburg occurred, the appeal to the moral conscience of America had reached its zenith. The sympathizers and empathizers were no longer concerned with individual civil rights events. You have to understand that Orangeburg comes after Watts and Detroit, when the mind of America is beginning to change and become more conservative and less responsive to civil rights issues.[2]

Another reason is that the FBI and the press were successful in distorting what came out of Orangeburg. A third and perhaps most important reason is that, as similar as Orangeburg is to Kent State, the students involved were not white and the lives lost were not white.

My contention is — and I will go to my grave believing this — if somebody had paid attention to what happened at Orangeburg, we might have been able to avoid Kent State.

What was in it for the press to distort the Orangeburg incident?
The news about the Orangeburg Massacre that got out to the world essentially came through local feeders, who made the incident a confrontation not a civil rights issue. People reading the newspaper said to themselves: "What's going on in Orangeburg? My goodness! Students are shooting the police, and they are getting killed! That's not civil rights. It's more like Detroit and Watts." So the readers moved on. That was the mindset the press created.

You came back to Denmark in 1990. Has your hometown changed much since you were growing up here in the fifties and early sixties?
I don't think there is a substantial change.

Is Denmark still segregated?
Yes, it is.

Is is as segregated as when you were growing up here?
Access to public facilities is OK. Blacks have that. But in terms of people working together, it's still segregated.

Is the Denmark of today a better place for your children to grow up than it was when you were a kid?
I would say it was better growing up in Denmark when I was a kid. There was more segregation, but we had a sense of community in which people supported each other. In its effort to become integrated, the African American community has lost a lot of that. We are not focusing internally as a community. Middle-class African Americans have kind of abandoned the rest of the community. So that's why I tend to believe my childhood was a better period. There was a lot of excitement! We had lots of heroes and heroines. We had a lot of people in leadership positions who had integrity and insight and could keep us focused on the issues. It was a much clearer period.

You didn't have crack in your childhood, and you didn't have a gun problem.
Crack and guns are serious problems, but the deeper, more insidious problem is the lack of hope and foresight. A lot of African American youngsters have given up hope. That's what concerns me. If you have hope, you will stay away from crack. If you have hope, you understand how destructive guns are. If you don't have self-respect and self-determination and you have a gun, you will shoot anybody. That's what we are beginning to see. The problem isn't going to be restricted to any one community. It's going to become all pervasive, and we are beginning to see that now.

How do young African Americans get hope? Does it come from the leadership? from jobs? from the family?

I think it comes from a number of things. It comes from organization, which we have a lot of today, but it's focused on material kinds of things rather than community. We have to reform those organizations and create new organizations, which can help refocus young African Americans by building a sense of community. During the period of 1968–1969, and even earlier, you will find that the statistics for black-on-black crime was at an all-time low. Those figures were even down in areas having the worst violent crime. That happened because people felt they were involved in something meaningful.

We have to get young people involved in determining their own destiny. That was the message of SNCC in the sixties. I'm still locked into the adage of the sixties: Don't trust anybody over thirty-five. I tell young people they have to step forward and be the catalyst for positive change. I can offer support, but after a period of time we lose the fire. We have to accept the fact that we must step off the stage or we slow the whole process down. That's not easy for [movement] people who have been on center stage. But they have to pass the torch. I can talk with young people about strategies, give them advice on what actions to take, and show them how to do certain things. I'm still good at that. But don't count on me to develop strategies.

That's interesting because in the sixties you looked upon yourself as a revolutionary, but now you are talking about having "lost the fire."

As we get older, we pick up a lot of baggage and tend not to do those things we did earlier. There was a time when, say, if I saw something was happening in Arkansas, I would jump in my car and go there to help out. Today, I would send a contribution, but I'm not going to go to Arkansas.

You talk with a lot of African American students and young people. Do they have the sense of commitment to make things better for the African American community that you and other young black activists had in the sixties?

We are moving in that direction. Civil rights history has been so distorted that it doesn't provide the basis African American students need to do the kind of analysis and the kind of preparation that is essential. If you see civil rights history on TV, you usually see a building burning and hear a voice explaining that that's the civil rights movement. They don't talk about the strategies and community organizing that went on in the civil rights movement. . . . It takes a lot of work to pull the pieces together.

We spent a lot of time in debate and discussions. We read Fanon. We read Malcolm [X]. We read [Jean-Paul] Sartre, Ché [Guevara] . . . a number of philosophers . . . Bertrand Russell.[3] That was expected of you. If you weren't willing to read, you couldn't participate in many of the discussions, which often went on day and night. You just didn't grow your hair long, step out, and were ready to go.

We considered ourselves good organizers, but we were trained by the likes of Saul Alinsky, who was a first-class organizer.[4] He could organize anything! He taught us skills that can be learned.

Today, however, we don't talk about strategies, how to mobilize people, how to establish goals. What are the goals of leadership? Is there a difference between mobilizing and organizing? What was the glue that held things together? Was it the principles and philosophies or was it the fact that people were just excited about being together?

What we get instead is the picture on TV of Martin Luther King as hero—a very sanitized Martin Luther King. I have problems with that. Most kids say, "I can't be a Martin Luther King because I can't walk on water." So we should teach young people about his commitment and his dedication—the human and political qualities that made him a social-change agent.

Young African Americans need to have their own experience. We have the African American students at the University of North Carolina [at Chapel Hill] who want their cultural center. They thought that by simply going to the administration and explaining what they felt was a legitimate issue the administration would say, "OK." [Laughs] They were really hurt when the university said, "No!" They thought there was no way possible that they could raise a legitimate issue and someone would turn them down. [Laughs] They didn't realize that their desire to have their own cultural center may be a moral issue for them, but it certainly wasn't for the administration. So the students at UNC learned a tremendous amount from that experience and are now different people.

You have talked a lot about how civil rights history has been distorted. Has that been true for the history of SNCC? Has SNCC been assessed fairly as far as the history of the sixties is concerned?

[Laughs] We have had to work to get SNCC to the center stage of civil rights history. Why? Because the folks who wrote the history of the civil rights movement made King the dominant figure. They sanitized him, and they didn't want to write about the people who were on the cutting edge. SNCC was always on the cutting edge. We did most of the things we wanted to do, but, if you look at the history of SNCC, you can see that it was impossible for the organization to continue any longer.

It ran its course?

Yeah, in the sense that it changed those things it wanted to change, but it had run into a formidable opposition.

What kind of reception did the SNCC volunteers receive from the black people when they came to Mississippi?

We use to tell organizers that if you couldn't survive in a community, you didn't belong there. Survival meant that if you went into a community and did the kind of work that was appreciated, then you were accepted. They did take care of us! They took us into their homes and fed us. That was the highest compliment that could be paid to us. We felt their generosity and respected it. They also warned us about different things and tried to protect us.

From left: **Reggie Rubins, Cleveland Sellers, Conny Curry and Julian Bond** (photo by the author).

They didn't flinch. There had to be pressure for them, but they never talked about it. They didn't say, "I'm worried because you are all here and someone may bomb my house."

I remember being in Marks, Mississippi, for three or four days. It is one of the poorest towns in the state. I went to live with a family—a husband, a wife, and three or four children. They lived in a two-room house with dirt floors—dirt floors! They had me sleeping in the front room, and they were all in the back. They fed me, and I'm certain the food they gave me was much better than what they ate.

They were so proud and so happy I was there; but I felt uncomfortable because I had taken their space and was eating their food which they probably had for special occasions. They would go to their neighbors and say, "We have a civil rights worker living with us." It must have been one of the few times they had excitement in their lives. I learned so much from those people about sharing and giving of oneself. It stays with you forever.

Did SNCC make a difference?

In terms of voter registration, in terms of the identification with the international struggles, in terms of public accommodations, we were able to make a difference. Dr. King's stand against the Vietnam War came a year after our statement of opposition, so SNCC helped push the civil rights movement toward an antiwar position.

SNCC was on the cutting edge and acted as a gadfly and catalyst. It forced

the civil rights movement to take notice and to move in a much more progressive direction more quickly than it would have if SNCC wasn't there.
SNCC took on the most recalcitrant areas. It picked Mississippi because it was
so hostile. SNCC didn't take on any powder puff issues. It took on issues that
had an impact.

That's the role we played, but you can't play it forever. Either you become
institutionalized or you go off the scene. SNCC just ran out of the energy and
life blood it needed to sustain itself.

*The concept of "black power" changed the direction of SNCC. Where did you
stand on that issue?*

After the 1964 challenge of the Democratic Party, there was a real question within SNCC about whether the Democratic Party was really behind the
push for the liberation of the African American people. Our conclusion was
no. So the organization began to move away from the Democratic Party.

We asked: "Who can do the best job determining the destiny of the
African American people?" We concluded that African Americans could do
the best job. We also concluded that we could not be strong enough to build
a coalition with whites until we were strong enough in our own communities.

The question of whites in the organization was one of the most difficult
issues we faced, but we made the best decision we could make. It had nothing
to do personally with the whites who were in SNCC. We were trying to be on
the cutting edge, and we felt that our decision [to expel whites from SNCC]
could make a difference.

Black power was no different than any other term used by the civil rights
movement. We had a new term just about every year: "Freedom '63"...
"Freedom Now".... All those slogans were just terms to galvanize and mobilize
the [African American] community.

*But no term upset or frightened many white Americans more than did the term
"black power."*

We were a little naive in not realizing how the press could take a term like
that and turn it around. But we got smart and backed away completely from
defining the term. That completely confused the press and they began to heap
their wrath on us. Then we said, "Okay. Anybody who wants to define the term
black power can do so. It has a lot of different meanings." Of course, the press
got upset again because it could mean A, B, C, or D. [Laughs]

When did disagreements start to surface within SNCC?

It started in 1964 over the bringing in of a large number of volunteers into
SNCC. That created anxiety and animosity. After that year, the terrain
changed. We had Watts in '65, and, from 1964 to 1965, Malcolm was still
around and there was a lot of discussion with him back and forth. A couple
of weeks before his death, Malcolm had actually gone to Selma at the height
of the Selma demonstrations.

Did you talk with Malcolm personally?

Yes, I talked with him. Malcolm was spellbinding. He could go and on and have you laughing half the time. He would call us "the students," and, for whatever reason, he didn't consider SNCC a civil rights organization. He would talk about SCLC, the Urban League, the NAACP as civil rights organizations, but not us.

Because you were young?

Because we were young ... because we were idealistic... We would challenge him and get on his case. [Laughs] That was the kind of challenge he enjoyed. Some of the students went up to see him in the summer of '64 to talk to him about life in Mississippi and nonviolence as a tactic and what it was meant to do. That dialogue kind of startled Malcolm.

Are you saying SNCC had an influence on Malcolm?

Yes, I think Malcolm had this view that people who believed in nonviolence didn't believe in self-defense. In his dialogue with SNCC students, I believe he was rudely awakened. The tactic of nonviolence made sense. In order to survive in Mississippi, we had little or no choice. If you were in a demonstration and started fighting, you would die! They had the law and everything else behind them. You had to take a little whopping in order to avoid a bigger whopping. If you were caught on the highway with a gun, they could just shoot you! You didn't want to be stupid. You had to know how to play it. Tactically, nonviolence was our salvation!

Did Malcolm have an impact on SNCC. Did he influence your strategy and tactics?

There were some groups that used to call SNCC "the children of Malcolm." Our ideology and principles were different, but we had a working relationship with the Nation of Islam on issues of mutual interest. We had a lot of discussion back and forth, especially on the issue of Black Power. He talked about black self-determination. We were talking about black self-determination. We talked about black political power. Malcolm talked about black political power. Malcolm did have a direct impact on the history of SNCC.

What about the packaging of Malcolm today—the X hats, the X shirts, the X movie? What is your view on that development?

I have a problem with commercialization. I think it's more important to understand Malcolm than to wear him. If it's a way to move African Americans forward, that's fine. But I'm not a big fan of people using Malcolm to commercialize themselves. They did that with King, too. We have to study Malcolm and his analysis of America. He talked about linking up African Americans and other blacks around the world, wherever they may be. Malcolm talked about a linkage based on common oppression. We can learn a lot of lessons from studying Malcolm.

So what's your opinion of Spike Lee's movie, Malcolm X?[5]

I thought the movie dealt with Malcolm as a Muslim, period, and it didn't deal with anything else. It didn't deal with Selma or the other extraneous stuff that was going on around Malcolm.[6] What was going on at the time of Montgomery bus boycott?[7] Did it have any impact on him? What about the sit-ins? What did he think of them? Of course, that's the choice of the director and that's fine.

Did Malcolm have any impact on you?

Absolutely! To me, Malcolm didn't symbolize all the negative things. I see Malcolm as a part of the civil rights movement.

That's interesting. [Laughs] I doubt if many whites would see Malcolm as an important part of the civil rights movement.

[Laughs] That's correct; and that's unfortunate because Malcolm impacted on the consciousness of the civil rights movement.

Did SNCC have a better understanding with Malcolm than it did with Dr. King?

It was about the same. I remember once when we were in Atlanta and Dr. King asked us to come over and talk about Black Power. He wanted to know if we had assessed all the reaction and the fallout and whether we had put any thought into the terminology. We spent six or seven hours talking back and forth; and, when we finished, we felt comfortable with each other.

We always had a great feeling towards Dr. King. He was a kind, gentle, genuine person who had a lot of integrity and was committed to what he was doing. Dr. King often disagreed with SNCC about tactics, and we would get upset over a particular tactic that SCLC would use, but we would get over it. We saw SCLC as a group that could mobilize a community, but didn't leave anything. We liked to think that SNCC organized communities and left a vehicle that could be used to change the course of history.

Getting back to what you said about SNCC running out of energy in the late sixties. You didn't mention COINTELPRO and its negative impact on SNCC and the civil rights movement.

COINTELPRO had a major impact on us. We had a number of people who were arrested on drug charges, and there was a conspiracy, I think, on the part of the Justice Department and the FBI to indict a lot of people from SNCC whom they knew were going to refuse to go into the armed services. There was an arrest of a SNCC member in Philadelphia [Mississippi] over some dynamite. Now why in the world would a SNCC person have dynamite in Philadelphia? That's absolutely amazing! We knew it didn't happen.

But the COINTELPRO influence was far more subtle than that. We had the FBI involved in personal relationships between people . . . between husbands and wives.

They were actually monitoring those types of relationships?

Not only would they eavesdrop, they would also make information available. For example, they would send a note to a wife and say, "Your husband is seeing such and such a person." The FBI created confusion and chaos, and their tactics became very problematic for the civil rights movement.

Then in '67 and '68, we have the Black Panthers emerge on the scene. They were very confrontational during a period [when] you weren't supposed to be confrontational. They made it a lot easier for the FBI to arrest, assault, and even kill people. It put the Panthers on SNCC. At one point—1968—there were a number of SNCC people who were on a Panther hit list to be killed.

That was because of misinformation?

Misinformation and disinformation. There was even a COINTELPRO memo sent out to people saying Stokely [Carmichael] was a CIA agent!

Is is accurate to say that the FBI was perhaps the most destructive force working against the civil rights movement in the sixties?

Absolutely! The FBI took a toll, believe me!

Did COINTELPRO set back the civil rights movement?

We had a lot of skilled and trained people, but COINTELPRO created so much chaos and confusion it made it impossible to exist.

Putting Orangeburg aside, do you ever get nostalgic for the old movement days and your movement buddies like Stokely Carmichael? Do you miss the rush you must have gotten from creating history?

I'm not so sure there was a "rush of history." At age nineteen, you know something is different and that you are on the stage of history, but what the hell does that mean? But the fellowship and camaraderie that people in the movement had for each other was so important. It was community, just like a family, and we shared so much. We still remain in contact and get together.

Have you had a reunion like SDS has had?

We had something similar to a reunion a few years back at Trinity College in Connecticut, where a lot of people came. It was interesting. We returned to the same groupings and the rhetoric was not far off. It's almost frightening. [Laughs] But we are still good friends.

The SNCC experience took so much energy that it has taken a long time for some of us to come to terms with it. It was an exciting time! There was lot of growth. You could almost see yourself growing.

Well, what about your future? The pardon has lifted a heavy burden from your life. What are your plans?

I've been thinking about getting into a research environment in higher education somewhere. The pardon will help make that possible. Universities were always linking my name with Orangeburg and saying, "Oh, he was at Orangeburg. He either shot it up or created the climate that led to it being shot up. [Laughs] We chose not to have him here." So the pardon is going to give me a little more leverage so I can get the door open and walk in.

3

Jane Adams

From Grassroots Organizer to University Professor

I had always felt like an outsider; and I guess that, being immersed in the black community in that kind of pressure cooker,
I very quickly came to see the world through black eyes. That
perspective permanently changed how I saw the world.

When I tried to understand myself as a woman later on, I drew
direct parallels between what I learned in Mississippi and my experiences as a woman.

SDS, because it was so open and freewheeling, was an organization to which people gravitated in order to come to grips with
the nature of the late twentieth century and the world we live
in without having to stick to old formulas. In the end, we failed,
but it was a number of years before that happened. I can say,
though, that the experience has stayed with me.

On February 1, 1960, four black students sat at a segregated Woolworth's
lunch counter in Greensboro, North Carolina, and waited to be served.
Although they were not the first sit-ins in the South, they sparked the biggest
student protest movement in American history and the beginning of the end
for de facto segregation in the South. Under the direction of the Student Nonviolent Coordinating Committee (SNCC), sit-ins hit the country like a bomb-
shell and spread like a prairie fire. In a year's time, more than 50,000 students
participated in sit-ins in over 140 places. The sit-ins inspired the freedom rides
in which idealistic students from the north plunged deep into the South to
work for SNCC and help desegregate public accommodations and register
voters.

In February 1964, SNCC appealed to black and to white students from
all over the country to come to work in Mississippi for the summer. More than
1,000 students answered the call and came to Mississippi for what became
known as Freedom Summer.

One of those students was Jane Adams, a 21-year-old anthropology student from Antioch College in Ohio. It was a dangerous time for a Northern
white — let alone a white woman — to go south. During Freedom Summer, six

people were killed and 80 beaten; 35 churches were burned and 30 other buildings bombed. But Adams braved the violence and hostility to go to Harmony Community in Mississippi, where she helped register blacks to vote and changed the American system.

Adams's Freedom Summer experience and her work as a SNCC volunteer changed her, and in 1965, after returning north from her second trip to Mississippi, she became an organizer and eventually Executive Secretary of Students for a Democratic Society (SDS).

SDS was organized in 1962 at the first national convention at Port Huron, Michigan. Fifty-nine participants representing 11 SDS chapters from 10 campuses, and an at-large delegation from New York City met and drafted the Port Huron statement, a document that became the manifesto for the emerging New Left as the sixties progressed. A loosely structured mass organization, SDS became increasingly more militant as the Vietnam War heated up and the draft calls mounted.

Adams was caught up in that militancy, and, during the second half of the sixties, she became an active participant in many of the major events that shaped the period, including the growing anti–Vietnam War movement and the beginnings of the budding feminist movement.

Adams cried when SDS disintegrated in 1969, and she disagreed with the violent campaign undertaken by the Weather Underground, an SDS offshoot. Like many other members of her generation, Adams became a burnt-out case, cast adrift as the counterculture wound down. During the early seventies, she and her boyfriend traveled the country, lived in communes, and worked at a variety of jobs.

In 1976, Adams reassessed her life and decided to return to university. After earning a B.A. in anthropology at Southern Illinois University at Carbondale in 1976, she went to work in California as a staff member for the Berkeley-based publication *Indigena: News from Indian America*. She researched and wrote articles, translated articles from Spanish to English, edited copy, and raised funds for the bilingual newspaper.

In 1978, she continued her education in anthropology, enrolling at the University of Illinois at Urbana and earning her M.A. in 1982 and Ph.D. in 1987. In 1987, Adams joined the faculty of the Department of Anthropology at Southern Illinois University as an assistant professor. At the time of our interview, Adams had learned the good news that the university had granted her tenure and promoted her to associate professor. But as our interview showed, neither the ivory tower, nor time, nor age had tempered Jane Adams's leftist views or faith in activism as a means to social change.

*   *   *

Could you describe the type of family background you came from?

It's unusual. My folks were urban Chicago intellectuals and socialists who

Jane Adams in Harmony Community, Mississippi, 1964 (photo courtesy of Jane Adams).

belonged to the Socialist Party. My mother was Jewish, and my father's family were New England Adamses who had moved to Downers Grove, a suburb of Chicago, when he [my father] was small. My dad got a job with Unemployment Compensation in southern Illinois when it started, but he always wanted to farm. In 1939, my parents bought a farm about five miles from Ava [Illinois].

I was born on May 12, 1943, and raised on that farm and attended a one-room school. After they consolidated that school in 1950, I went to grade school in Ava. Then my sophomore year in high school [1958], I transferred to the university school in Carbondale, twenty miles away.

Given your family background, I would imagine you were politically aware at an early age.

Oh, yes. There was a black man who worked in the office with dad, and he would come to our house. In those days, it was not the thing to do if you wanted to be popular.

Were you popular as a youngster, given your background?

People around here are good neighbors. My folks were good neighbors. My dad was on the school board and worked for school consolidation, while my mother was really involved with the PTA (Parent Teacher Association) and the library. But growing up, both my brother and I were really different. We had a house full of books and read a lot. We didn't believe in God, although I went to church for a number of years because it was a way of being in. It was not until the sixth grade that the divisions between us and our schoolmates came out. It became excruciatingly lonely. The university school kind of saved my life.

You found friends?

Yeah, a lot of my classmates were faculty brats with ideas. Some were beats, bohemians, and oddballs. I was really into existentialism and the beat poets.[1] I remember that, in my senior year, I was in a bathroom with a classmate and we declaimed Ginsberg's "Howl." [Laughs] It was an environment in which you could do that and it carried me right up until it was time for me to go to college at Antioch.

Why did you go to school there?

Actually, my mother wanted to go there, but it was the Depression and she couldn't afford to go to college. The banks busted and took her savings. That's where I probably got the idea. The Unitarian youth group had a regional conference at Antioch one summer in either my junior or senior year [of high school]. Yellow Springs was such a neat place. It had woods and a very bohemian type of atmosphere, and I just fell in love with it. There was no question I would go to school there.

Did it live up to expectations?

Yeah, in a lot of ways. I was a country kid, so, actually, it was a little New

Yorkish for me. But there was a lot of political activity. I had joined the Student Peace Union [SPU] the summer before and gotten into political stuff—mostly ban the bomb activities.

John F. Kennedy had an impact on a lot of young people of your generation. Did he have an impact on you?

He actually came to Carbondale when I was in high school, and I went to see him. Some of my girlfriends were practically having an orgasm when they saw him. I didn't understand it. I have never had worshipful attitude towards leaders or icons. Pete Seeger, maybe. Woody Guthrie, definitely. [Laughs] I never liked Kennedy much.

Why not?

While I was at Antioch [1962], I was in the workstudy program. My first work assignment was to go to Cleveland and work in a histology lab that was run by a Marcus Singer. My uncle, who did endocrinology research, arranged the job for me because he and Mr. Singer were friends.

Nuclear disarmament was an issue I was really involved with. I heard Kennedy make a speech about it. He had recently signed the Nuclear Test Ban Treaty.[2] In the first half of his speech, he talked to us—the people that wanted nuclear disarmament. In the second half of the speech, he talked to the military. It was the strongest part of his speech. He was playing the Cold War warrior. I was so upset that I used the occasion as an excuse to get some alcohol from the lab and get drunk for the first time. I got rip-roaring drunk. [Laughs] It might have been an excuse to see what it was like to get drunk, but I was disgusted by his speech.

[Laughs] Even though you didn't like Kennedy, did his assassination shock you?

Oh, yeah! I didn't like his policies, but to assassinate the President of the U.S. was a pretty horrible thing. One thing about Kennedy's assassination has stuck in my mind. There was lot of dyed-in-the-wool Stalinist kids at Antioch. One of them was a fellow I had a crush on.

The evening of Kennedy's assassination, we were gathered for dinner and he said something like "Good! I'm glad. Kennedy deserved it." I was really shocked and stunned by the attitude that fellow expressed. I may not have liked Kennedy's politics, but assassinating him really didn't seem appropriate.

Otherwise, how would you describe your experience at Antioch?

I guess I experienced culture shock. After two and a half years, I decided that I needed to get back to the real world, so I transferred to Southern Illinois University in 1964. That was the spring that Freedom Summer was organized. I heard what was going on down south, and I decided to go because I had been involved in civil rights activities in high school and Antioch.

Did you go yourself or did some of your friends go with you?

There was quite a group that went. Carbondale is an unusual town. It's a Southern town in a Northern state, but it had a movement there from very early. A fellow named John O'Neal, who was black and came from Carbondale, was one of the founders of the Free Southern Theater. He was sort of my hero. Two other local guys were founders of the Freedom Singers. But a bunch of us went south to Mississippi to experience Freedom Summer. There must have been eight of us.

How many of the group were white women?
    Maybe three or four of us. We were scattered all over Mississippi.

From what I've read, it was dangerous for anyone to go south, particularly for white women, given the racial stereotypes.
    Yeah. I guess it was scary, but, when you are twenty or twenty-one years of age, you think you are going to live forever. Youth is not fearful at that age.

But weren't you in Amite County in Mississippi in 1965 where someone was murdered?
    Oh, yes, during my second summer. That was Herbert Lee. I had gone down in '64. We were the second group to go in; and so, by the time we went down, we knew [James] Chaney, [Andrew] Goodman, and [Michael] Schwerner had been killed. That summer, I was in the county [Leake] next to Neshoba county where they were killed. That fall, I was in the Jackson Council of Federated Organizations (COFO), which was a coalition of civil rights groups that included SNCC and CORE (Congress of Racial Equality). It formed in 1962 to coordinate voter registration efforts in the South.
    I came back [to Carbondale] after Christmas to finish some courses, and then I went to Amite County, which is in the southwest corner of Mississippi. That was where Herbert Lee was killed and the song ["'Buked and Scorned"] was written about him.

What kind of reception did you receive from local whites? Were they overtly hostile?
    Well, we didn't see a lot of whites. I remember the first summer going to the launderette in Carthage, the county seat, the only town in the county, and a couple of white women were hostile to us. But there was a woman—I believe she was a librarian—who was really glad we were there. She had been very unhappy about Jim Crow and the virulent racism that existed, and she thought that by us being there we could break it open.
    That fall, when I was in Jackson [Mississippi], I remember talking with whites who were sort of urban upper-middle-class whites, and I don't remember anything hostile. Everybody was *very* nice to each other. [Laughs] Those people thought they were the elite and were very much into being aristocratic.

What about the local blacks? What kind of reception did they give you?
    They were enthusiastic about our coming. The community I went to the

first time, the Harmony Community, was an old Reconstruction community that was one of the few old plantations that had been broken up into forty-acre farms. The family I stayed with and a lot of other people were related to [Mississippi Governor] Ross Barnett, who did a lot of after-dark integration. The community has a lot of people who were very light. In fact, I passed for a member of the [black] family I stayed with. When Ross Barnett ran for governor, his campaign people said, "Vote for your cousin." The people I stayed with would laugh about that.

The black community had a Rosenwald school, but the local schools consolidated, and the blacks essentially lost it.[3] We tried to hold class in that school building, but the local whites said, "We own it now because we consolidated the schools." So they wouldn't let us use it.

Were you ever in danger?

Perhaps. One time, we went into town. A white girl from Detroit was driving the car. Some guys in a pickup truck pulled out in front of us and another group stayed behind us. They had guns and looked like they were looking for trouble.

Our driver was real quick thinking and pulled out in front of the car ahead and took off like a bat out of hell. We weren't far from the road that led into the Harmony Community, and she went down it. That was the most dangerous situation I was in. They wouldn't follow us in. If they did, they would have been in trouble.

There was just one road through the community, and most of the people were armed. They had walkie-talkie communication between houses at each end, so if someone came in making trouble, they would have found trouble before they got out.

Do you recall any other dangerous incidents?

A couple of times I saw some people with guns, watching us, but I don't think they were looking for trouble. They were just trying to show us that they were there. Earlier that year, some local white guys had been driving through, shooting into houses, and after some retaliatory shooting by people in the community, they got the message and stopped coming through. I also remember a cross being burned at the community center one night.

Did any of the local blacks have weapons to defend themselves?

Oh, yeah. The first night in Harmony, we were playing music, dancing and having a good time. Then we heard a car come down the road. The two brothers in the family picked up their guns, turned the lights out, opened the door, and looked at the car as it went by. After it went by, we turned the lights on and continued dancing. When I was in Amite County, there was always a gun in the car. Blacks didn't go anywhere without a gun.

What were some of the activities you were involved with while you were in the South?

I was put to work on the Federal Programs Project, but I can't recall doing much in that program area. We did do a lot of canvassing for the Mississippi Freedom Democratic Party [MFDP]. I would team up with a black, and we would beat the backroads and knock on doors of black people asking them to sign a petition for the MFDP.

One of the most memorable experiences was going to a house of a woman, whom I guess was a sharecropper living on a white man's land. She came to the door with her young kids and at first wouldn't talk with us. All she said was "yes'm" and "no'm." Then I don't know what we did, but she made a decision. She looked up at us and signed the petition. It was a remarkable transformation.

Why do you think she changed her mind?

I think she decided she was sick and tired of being used and was going to sign the petition, even though she might lose her home. That's when I realized the profundity of what we were trying to do in the South.

Do you feel your experience in the civil rights movement made a difference?

I don't know if, personally, I did anything, but I was a part of Freedom Summer, which broke the back of Jim Crow in Mississippi.

Do you think Freedom Summer was a turning point?

It was a real historic movement, and I was a part of it. And it turned my life around. Up until that point, I had been overwhelmed by white-bred America. I was caught up in a kind of existential angst. But my experience in the South gave me the feeling that the people can make history and transform the world. That was pretty heady for a while. [Laughs] We thought things were going to get overturned tomorrow. [Laughs] It was remarkable that powerless people without education and minimal leadership turned Mississippi upside down and really turned America around.

Did your Southern experience have any impact on you as a white woman?

I had always felt like an outsider, and I guess that being immersed in the black community in that kind of pressure cooker, I very quickly came to see the world through black eyes. That perspective permanently changed how I saw the world.

When I tried to understand myself as a woman later on [in 1966 and 1967], I drew direct parallels between what I had learned in Mississippi and my experiences as a woman ... the kind of stuff [Frantz] Fanon writes about and Ralph Ellison, the experience of the colonized and stigmatized, what we academics call "The Other."

Later, of course, SNCC kicked white people out of the organization.

I was in the North in the fall of 1965 when SNCC kicked out white people. I wasn't in SNCC, but I really believed the SNCC line that you organized at the base and that the organizer was somebody who made things happen and then went on. So organization was not important. But I began to wonder how effective I could be in the South. I was only twenty-one years old and white. I would try to organize blacks out in the rural areas, and these old ladies who had master's degrees would say "Yes, Miss Jane" and "No, Miss Jane." It drove me nuts. I realized I couldn't overcome that, so I returned to the North. Besides, the Vietnam War was beginning to happen.

It must have been a shock to a lot of white civil rights workers to have blacks all of a sudden want to control their own destiny?

I'm sure that was the case for some whites. For me, it was liberating and made perfect sense. I knew it had to happen. It was the same thing a little later when woman's consciousness began. I was really stunned that men didn't realize women had to have their own separate thing. Men, in fact, reacted with great hostility. But, of course, you have to have your own space. That's part of undoing oppression.

You made references to Vietnam. At the time of your involvement with Freedom Summer and SNCC's black power move, were you aware of the war going on in that Asian country?

Well, it wasn't at the center of my consciousness. I was very active in the Student Peace Union [SPU]; in fact, I was offered the national secretaryship of SPU in 1964. But it was actually a dying organization that was on its last legs. So my parents told me to go to Mississippi. They were right on that. The SPU was the first independent student organization to focus on Vietnam and what was happening there ... I guess as early as '62, or perhaps earlier. So I was aware of Vietnam. By October 1965, I left Mississippi to go back north and do Vietnam. That's what it was all about for white activists. I joined the SDS in the spring of '65.

Why did you join?

This fellow and I went to a SDS conference in Chicago, which is about one hundred miles north of Carbondale, where we heard talk about building an industrial society. I had been with the SPU while the YPSL [Young People's Socialist League] controlled it. So I had been around all these sectarian debates between left labor and the moderates. Then the YSA [Young Socialist Alliance, the youth wing of Socialist Workers Party, which were Trotskyites] tried to take over and I hated it. I hated all that left sectarianism. The SDS conference was a breath of fresh air. They were talking about the world we were living in in 1965, so I joined.

By 1966, you held the position of regional traveler for the SDS in the Midwest. Was that a full-time job?

Yeah, when I came back north, I wanted to be an organizer. I took the job and was based in Iowa City. I was given a TR-4 [a small Triumph car] and went tooling around Iowa, Kansas, Nebraska, and Missouri. [Laughs] I had this bumper sticker that said, "Make love, not war" and carried boxes of SDS literature, which I strapped on the trunk. The car was so small that when the boxes shifted, it felt like I was driving on a flat tire. [Laughs] I had to stop and adjust the boxes so I could drive.

One time, I needed tires, and some people in Lincoln, Nebraska, jumped over a fence and got me some. [Laughs] The whole operation was by the seat of its pants.

What kind of reaction did you receive from students when you tried to recruit them for SDS?

There were always students everywhere who didn't like the war, believed in civil rights, wanted to do activist things, and were glad to see someone come in from the outside and talk about the issues. I boned up about the [Vietnam] war, delivered literature, and organized a lot of conferences on the war. I thought it important that people talk to each other.

How successful were you in doing that?

We had conferences at every major university in my region.

Kirkpatrick Sale wrote in his history of the SDS[4] that the growth of the SDS was phenomenal. He said the SDS had one hundred thousand members by 1968. Do you think that number is accurate?

Membership was such a fuzzy thing. People would claim membership, although they never paid dues. A lot of people went to SDS-inspired demonstrations, but weren't members. You were in SDS if your soul was in the right place. SDS was a state of being.

Was the Vietnam War the galvanizing issue that increased membership?

Yes. Without a draft, there might have been just a small movement, not the large movement that eventually resulted. The fact was everybody's life was potentially on the line.

Those were heady days. A lot of activists actually thought a revolution was going to happen. Did you share that sentiment?

There were a lot of camps within the SDS and a lot of different views on how to carry out the revolution. In late '67, the Debray tendency had a lot of power in the national organization, but I never thought it was a good organizing model. Regis Debray had worked with Ché [Guevara] in Bolivia, and they had become extremely frustrated in Bolivia because they couldn't gain the support of the peasants.

So Debray wrote *Revolution in the Revolution* [Grove, 1967] and came up with the model of *cadres*, that is, dedicated bands of revolutionaries who moved surreptiously among the people. There were people in SDS who were very much into building cadres. But there was also Progressive Labor, which had its particular Maoist model. But I didn't like either model. I believed in building a mass movement, not cadres. In order to carry out a revolution, you had to have organizers.

How would you describe your political philosophy at this time?

I was a prairie populist who believed in marrying the cultural revolution with the social revolution and was for pushing the commitment forward. Around Christmas '66 — December 27 and 28, to be exact — at a National Council meeting in Berkeley, there was a big debate about the draft and whether we were ever going to get involved with actions against the war that would, in effect, make us illegal.

There was a feeling that we had to do something that would put us into radical opposition to the war and make us outlaws, while creating a mass opposition to the war. But later, I was really appalled by the Motherfuckers and the others who were talking about bombs. But about '67, people were starting to get really adventurous in their rhetoric. It was hot-headed rhetoric, but it really made it hard for us to organize.

How were women treated within the SDS?

Men virtually ran the organization. There was this fellow in the national office who told me point blank that he hated me, and I couldn't figure out why. What had I done? I don't think I had done anything except be this woman whom I was. I think I was this woman who didn't fit into categories, and that threw him for a loop. I started to get weird feedback from people because, clearly, I was doing things I wasn't supposed to.

Because you were a woman?

Yeah, that is how I interpreted it. It was a totally male environment. That's when I started to write stuff about women's liberation in the *New Left Notes* [an SDS publication].

So your consciousness was being raised. Were there a lot of women going through what you were going through?

A few at that point — the winter or spring of '67. It was lonely, but my mother was feminist, so I guess I got that consciousness from her.

How did you deal with men like that SDS worker who told you point blank he hated you?

I sort of went "Oh, I didn't hear that." [Laughs] I got deaf really quickly. [Laughs] Emotionally, I ran away from it. It took me years of therapy sessions in communes where we battered each other's egos before I learned how to deal with those kinds of non sequiturs.

Was sexual harassment prevalent within the movements?

When I was in high school, the cult of virginity was sacred, and we would sit around, talk, and agonize over our virginity. I really believed in a liberated sexuality, but it was not until '68 that I realized how exploitative men were of women who believed that. Men's construction of sexual liberation was a lot different than a woman's. After hearing a couple of men brag about their sexual conquests, I knew I had been naive.

Do you consider yourself a feminist?

I've been a feminist since the concept has been around.

Has there been a lot of progress since the sixties in dealing with discrimination against women?

The problems have shifted. The cult of virginity is no longer out there. The dark side of sexual relations today is both the diseases that came along with freer sexuality and the exploitation and coercion that women are subjected to by men.

In what way?

When I was in college, I could hide behind my virginity; if I didn't want to make it with a man, the man had to respect that. But that has gone, and a woman today has to say, "I don't want to make it with you." That's a much harder thing to say if you are a nice girl who doesn't want to hurt people. Today, it's much easier for a guy who is into sexual conquest to browbeat her into a sexual relationship she doesn't want. Today, it's much easier for a woman to be compromised into a guilt trip. I am glad that the cult of virginity has crumbled. It was oppressive and patriarchial. But male culture has not been transformed to conform to a more respectful kind of sexuality. Men are still raised to be conquerors.

So were you angry when you saw the Anita Hill–Clarence Thomas hearings on television?

[Laughs] I thought she [Anita Hill] was a tough lady and marveled at her cool. On the other hand, I was so disgusted when Thomas came out and did his legal lynching thing. But my feelings about the hearings are complicated.

When I was in the South in the early sixties, the cops hated white women more than just about anybody else. When we were arrested, the cops would beat the white women because they were there to protect white womanhood. That was a rationale for segregation.

Black men were made out to be bestial, lustful characters. That was how Clarence Thomas was characterized on the screen. He was extremely dark and looked like the stereotype. I believed Anita Hill, but I cringed when so much of what was said [at the hearings] reinforced white perceptions of black men. At the same time, I felt contempt for Thomas because I thought hc lost all dignity when he played the race card. From my point of view, it was hypocritical.

Do you think that incident has helped raise women's consciousness?

I believe it did a whole world of good for raising the issue of sexual harassment. It's on the table and out of the closet, really out of the closet. But I'm not sure it's being played out in the black community. It's so much more complicated there. But Anita Hill had so much dignity and poise! She was great!

You say you are a feminist. Does that mean you are still involved in women's issues like abortion and sexual harassment?

Jane Adams (photo courtesy of Southern Illinois University).

Well, my research has to do with farm women. I've taught courses about gender, and I'm involved with indigenous people. I was involved with Nicaragua as time would allow.

Fortunately, there is a network of progressive women in this area. My mother is very involved in pro–choice activities. In fact, she's just one of a core of women here who are in their seventies and eighties and involved in pro-choice. They organized the local women's center here in the early seventies. This is the only county [Jackson County] in Illinois that went for [George] McGovern in '72, thanks to the local network.[5]

You mentioned how you took LSD in '67 and how you were sexually liberated. Were you heavy into the counterculture scene?

I cut my eye teeth on folk music and Bob Dylan, whom I was really into. My relationship to acid rock was always derivative, dependent on what was playing around me; and while I developed a strong liking for some groups and songs, I didn't seek them out. Nor did I go to any big concerts, except Altamont, where the Stones sang and a man was killed and thrown up on the stage by the Hell's Angels, who were acting as "body guards," or such. I went to rock concerts as a part of a group, not on my own initiative.

But I really believed — and still believe — that psychedelics played a major part of the transformation that was going on at that time. They helped change white people's sensibilities in real important ways, deconstructing linear thinking and opening up possibilities.

That's interesting, considering how the drug scene deteriorated by the late sixties, when acid [LSD] and heroin was becoming much more prevalent.

Acid and heroin are two different things. I don't understand heroin, but there were people who used it as a way to cool out when everything has gotten too intense. As for the end of the sixties . . . change was happening so fast that everything is compressed. Today, it's hard to reconstruct how it was. Recently, I saw a documentary profile of [Richard] Nixon on TV, and I realized that Vietnam drove him crazy. Vietnam, in fact, drove all of us crazy! People were getting slaughtered, and any one who had a conscience had to be thinking of Nazi Germany.

The war wouldn't stop. It was like a juggernaut that kept going. We had masses of young people uprooted and traveling around, rootless and living hand-to-mouth. It was a pretty incredible time. What was happening, I believe, was that people had become unmoored, and drugs were one way to escape from existential anxiety. We did not know where we were going, and it looked like we didn't have a future.

The Vietnam War is long over, but one of its legacies is the distrust that a large part of the sixties generation has toward its government. Do you distrust your government?

I have no trust in government and society in some ways. I never had that innocence that people talk about and say we lost in Vietnam. I felt I had lost my innocence during World War II, even though I was born during the war. World War II fundamentally disrupted my notion of a benign universe.

In the fall of '67, you decided to go to Oklahoma and open a headshop. Why Oklahoma? Were you taking [Tim] Leary's advice to tune in, turn on, and drop out? [Laughs]

[Laughs] No. I met a fellow named Terry Roberts, and we hit it off. He was more of a druggie than me and introduced me to all that. He was from Brooklyn and had been to school in Oklahoma. I wanted to organize and try to bring the cultural and political revolutions together. We thought we would try to do it in Norman [Oklahoma].

So what was life like in Norman?

In that part of the West, you find a lot of libertarians,[6] and so Norman had a big libertarian streak. At that point, they liked SDS. There was a real community of the far right and the far left. The problem was that they [the libertarians] were too marginal and not able to break through. The dominant culture in Norman was into the football teams and the fraternities, so it turned out to be a real uncomfortable place to live.

So you left?

Yeah, we were there about a year and a half and went to Cleveland because we knew people there who had been in the ERAP project [Economic Research and Action Project, a community-organizing project of SDS inspired by SNCC's attempt to organize in poor white communities]. That was the branch of the SDS who, in the early sixties, had adopted the SNCC model and gone into community organizing. But it never got off the ground.

The women's movement, however, was beginning to develop while I was in Norman. We had a small consciousness raising group. We acted out a short play called *Sweet 16 to Soggy 36,* which depicted media images of femininity, from adolescence to middle age. We had a lot of fun doing it. It was a period when we said, "This is what they are doing to us."

Did you start to view your relationships with men different?

I argued with men a lot about how women were so badly treated. I was going through this period of self-affirmation and discovery. Terry was getting into an environment where he was supposed to be something he was anathema to; that is, the whole movement was getting very macho—John Wayne–like.[7]

By the end of the sixties, the scene had started to turn violent. The Weather Underground, for example, began to set off bombs. How did you view this turn of events?

By that time, we were really burnt out and didn't really know what to do. Terry and I had wanted to go to Seattle, but we went to Berkeley first to attend the United Front Against Fascism Conference, which the Black Panthers had organized. By that time, we had bald tires and had only enough money to buy tires or rent an apartment. We decided to stay and get jobs.

I got a job as a secretary in an insurance company, and Terry got one in an envelope factory. It looked like we were going to have a military coup. Things were getting pretty desperate in the '70 to '71 period. Of course, the logical extension was the townhouse explosion in Greenwich Village. I knew everyone of those people. I had lived with many of them.

So you weren't shocked by the townhouse explosion.

No, it was a logical extension—a trajectory that made sense. I was grieved by it, but I wasn't shocked.

What kind of relationship did you have with other women in the movement?

The emerging women's movement cut across factional lines. We were really trying to grapple with the women's issues. It was something new, so there couldn't be a party line that somebody could lay down. Even at the convention in Chicago when everything fell apart, there were many women like Diana Oughton who was very much a part of the Weather Underground, but who also participated very lovingly in the women's caucus. She later went underground and was killed in the townhouse explosion.

The SDS split into factions at the 1969 convention in Chicago. What were your feelings when you saw people whom you knew walk out, chanting?

I sat in the balcony and cried.

How did other people at the convention react?

I don't remember the reaction of other people, but I do remember going to meetings afterwards and trying to figure out where I fit. But I didn't fit anymore.

You must have thought a lot about the SDS legacy. You gave so much of your young life to the organization. What do you think the SDS accomplished?

Organizationally, its legacy is kind of dismal. In fact, as an organization it was kind of flaky. [Laughs] But it did give a kind of mythic focus for a lot of energy in the movement. SDS had a relatively small number of people involved at the organizational and policy levels, but we had a lot of influence in the movement. The literature we produced was important because we were a consciousness raising group right to the bitter end. But a mass movement did happen, and it would have happened whether or not SDS had existed and pumped out the literature.

But the SDS created a kind of arena for debating issues in a way that YSA and the Mobilization Committee did not. Those organizations had specific programs in place and had a correct line that one had to follow. But SDS, because it was so open and freewheeling, was an organization to which people gravitated in order to come to grips with the nature of the late twentieth century and the world we live in without having to stick to old formulas. In the end, we failed, but it was a number of years before that happened. I can say, though, that the experience has stayed with me.

Do you still stay in touch with some of your SDS comrades?

Yeah. We had two wonderful reunions. At the last reunion, I saw Bernardine [Dohrn] for first time since 1969. She lives in Chicago now, and I see her from time to time. That's been real wonderful. Some of the SDS folks are my lifelong friends, the kind of friends you make in your youth and don't make later in life.

I noticed that there is a blank spot in your résumé from 1970 to 1976. You mentioned you were burned out. How long did that continue?

Until I reassessed my life and went back to school in 1976. Dawn [her daughter] was born in '71, and that was the beginning of my rejoining humanity. I was living in communes in the early seventies. Terry and I built a house on the back of a Jeep truck, and we were going to use it to gypsy around.

Well, the truck was a disaster. [Laughs] It constantly broke down, and the roof leaked. I got pregnant, and we moved inside. There were eight of us in this little two-bedroom apartment. Then six of us moved into an abandoned house and squatted. But we got evicted while I was in the hospital having Dawn, so we went to Berkeley to live in a commune called The Circus, which Al Haber and some others started.

We lived there for a year until things started to get crazy. People in that commune were really into the psychologist R.D. Laing,[8] but he was a little too far out for me. They went around living out psychodramas and saying things like "I don't know if I get along with you if you don't like me using your toothbrush." [Laughs]

I'm not straight, but in some ways I was straighter than they were. So some of us jumped ship and took over a house that a commune had inhabited. I lived there a couple of years and then returned to Carbondale in '76 and went back to school.

How did you get involved with indigenous people?

I had majored in anthropology back in '61 at Antioch, but the social anthropology teacher was so dreadful, I shifted into other things. Under the influence of the counterculture, I had gotten interested in shamanism and had read a lot about it. Somewhere along the line, I had become aware of what was happening to indigenous people.

I had always been interested in Latin America. I had taken courses in Latin American studies and had been to Mexico through an Antioch program. While there, I studied land reform. From then on, Latin America and its indigenous groups were a part of my consciousness. I eventually worked for Indigena, a pro–indigenous organization, for quite a while. That was a good experience that got me into researching Latin American Indians.

Is doing research as exciting as being a radical in the sixties? [Laughs]

[Laughs] No, no, but the academic life is very demanding. I do a lot of public programming, which I consider research. I'm hoping to marry my academic life to my activism.

Teaching at a university, you have had a chance to observe students. How do students of today compare with those of your day?

I like to think there is a wave of activism coming. We are seeing kids in college today whose parents were a part of the sixties experience, and that will now be accelerating, I think the times are a-changing. I feel very hopeful about [President Bill] Clinton. In a lot of ways, he reminds me a lot of Kennedy, but I don't want to have the same jaundiced view of Clinton that I had of Kennedy. [Laughs]

You have mellowed. [Laughs]

Right. [Laughs] I hope Clinton is going to create some space. Reagan really pressed us [the Left and progressives], but he didn't destroy us the way McCarthy destroyed us in the fifties. But there is so much activism going on today in the communities, much more than when Kennedy was president. It's everywhere! People are just waiting to be released. My daughter is twenty-one, and I hope she will be able to join the new movement. [Laughs]

What will it take to create a new movement?

Hopefully, it won't be another war. I thought it might have been the [Persian] Gulf War, if Bush had fallen flat on his face. In the way it was able to control the press during the Gulf War, the U.S. government learned its lessons well from Vietnam.

What are your future goals?

I really want to reinsert myself into history, and hopefully, the time is going to come along when I can do that. We have been in a long period in which it has been very difficult to find a way to become more than another drop of water in the current. My other goals are to try and live in greater harmony with the natural world and to develop better human relationships.

If you could do it all over again, would you do anything differently?

In the interview or in my life?

[Laughs] It's too late to do the interview over, but what about your life? I am thinking specifically of the sixties.

I don't like organizations because I've found them to be very stressful. It takes a certain type of person to maneuver politically in an organization, and I don't think I have what it takes. Maybe I have to develop that in order to do what I want to do in life.

I wish we had had mentors in the sixties who could have given us leadership. That was one of the great things about the civil rights movement. While SNCC had a lot of hot-headed young idealists in its ranks, it also had a lot of much steadier older folks and grown-ups who were creating the context in which they could move effectively. That was the case, of course, until the mid-sixties when black power came to the fore.

If the movement comes along again, I hope those of the sixties generation can play that role to the younger folks. They can play the mentor role and help prevent the schisms and splits we had in the sixties.

4

Dave Dellinger
Radical for Peace

I've always tried to live in the present, as if the revolution had
already taken place. In other words, I live in accord with the way
I believe people will live in a decent society and not say, "Well,
after the revolution, I will start sharing my money, living simply,
and doing work whose purpose is to contribute to the well-being
of the community." Since the sixties, there has been a better
understanding that protesting and demonstrating is not enough.
We have to live the new way of life now. I'm encouraged by all
that.

It was one of the most dramatic trials in history. While the prosecution
tried to prove that the defendants had conspired to incite riots at the 1968
Democratic National Convention, the defendants — including such prominent
figures in the antiwar, counterculture, and black power movements as Dave
Dellinger, Abbie Hoffman, and Bobby Seale — disrupted proceedings by
shouting obscenities at the judge, wearing long robes, and even trying to hold
a birthday party in court.

The oldest of the "Chicago Seven," as the defendants became known, was
Dave Dellinger. Today, more than a quarter of a century later, Dellinger, at
the ripe age of 80, is still at the front lines of the American protest movement
and remains committed to nonviolence and radical social change. The Vietnam War may no longer be an issue, but Dellinger remains committed to a
host of left wing causes, including nuclear disarmament, Native American
rights, racial justice, and the problem of the environment, among others.

David Dellinger was a radical long before Vietnam erupted on the
American scene. Born on August 22, 1915, into a family of conservative Republicans and educated at Yale University, Dellinger rejected the comfortable
life laid out for him and followed his own path. It was at the Theological
Seminary in New York City, where Dellinger began studying in 1939, that he
started to reassess his life and begin to commit himself to pacifism.

In 1940, Dellinger joined with other divinity students in refusing to
register for the draft and was sentenced to a year and a day in the Danbury
Correctional Institute in Connecticut. Three years later, Dellinger refused to

report for a physical examination for induction in the armed forces and was sentenced to a two-year prison term at the federal penitentiary in Lewisburg, Pennsylvania. While incarcerated, the prisoner staged a six-day hunger strike to protest racial segregation.

Dellinger emerged from jail a committed radical for peaceful change. To support himself, he labored at a variety of jobs in factories and agriculture before opening a printing cooperative, the Liberation Press, in Glen Gardner, New Jersey, with several other pacifists. Throughout the fifties and early sixties, Dellinger became prominent within the movement, but it was Vietnam that made him internationally known.

Beginning in 1965, Dellinger helped to organize major antiwar demonstrations, and, in 1967, he became chairman of the National Mobilization Committee to End the War in Vietnam. Meanwhile, Dellinger became a major link between the American peace movement and the North Vietnamese government, especially after traveling to Hanoi to meet with Ho Chi Minh and other North Vietnamese officials.

All of the Chiago Seven were acquitted of the conspiracy charges, but Dellinger and four other defendants were found guilty of incitement-to-riot charges. In addition, Dellinger was found guilty of contempt for his conduct in the courtroom, which involved his shouting "bullshit" during the testimony of a prosecution witness. He was given the maximum term of five years in prison and a $5,000 fine on the incitement-to-riot charge and a concurrent sentence of two years, five months, and sixteen days in the contempt charge. Eventually, one contempt conviction was dropped, while another was upheld but never imposed.

When the U.S. involvement in the Vietnam quagmire ended in 1973, Dellinger continued his life as an activist—protesting, getting arrested, and writing articles as well as books, such as *Vietnam Revisited* [South End, 1986], *More Power Than We Know* [Doubleday, 1975], and *Revolutionary Nonviolence* [Bobbs, 1970], in which he outlined his views on pacifism, the role of the activist, and the injustices of the world. Today, Dellinger lives with his wife in Peacham, Vermont, which he uses as a base to lecture and teach, especially to a new generation of young activists.

Our interview took place soon after Dellinger, along with six other activists, completed a 42-day fast in October 1992 in Washington, D.C. Dellinger said the group was fasting "to reflect on what 500 years of the greed-oriented Columbus Enterprise has meant, and still means, to the people and ecology of the United States and the world. And like them, I fast to remember and draw strength from those who have resisted injustice and have tried to live in tune with Mother Earth and their fellow men."

                       *   *   *

I first contacted you last August [1992] when you were getting ready to participate in the People's Fast for Justice and Peace in the Americas. What was that all about?

The People's Fast called attention to the kind of society introduced in the Americas by Columbus and the Europeans who followed him and questioned celebrating Columbus's arrival in the New World and having a holiday in his honor.[1] We asked instead for Columbus Day to be called Indigenous People's Day or Native Americans' Day.

Did you petition Congress to do this?

No, although we have talked to some congressmen about it. The People's Fast also said that instead of glorifying the so-called end of the Cold War and talking about how the Soviet Union was falling apart, we should remember that we have had a doubling of the homeless population and a tripling of billionaires in the U.S. during the very period the Soviet Empire was collapsing.

When people came to talk with us at the fast, I would never start with Columbus. Instead, I began with something like the L.A. riots or the number of homeless and other poor and oppressed people. Then I would make connections with Columbus. Did you know that Columbus gave the indigenous population a quota for gold, and, if they didn't make it, he had their hands chopped off?

Then I would give the people I was talking with a quote from something Columbus said. I'll paraphrase it: "They [the indigenous population] have no concept of violence. When I handed them a sword, they cut their fingers on it. They would make excellent servants, and we could get them to do anything we wanted with about fifty of our men, whether we want to send them home or rule over them here."

What kind of response did you get from passers by?

Well, we certainly didn't get a response from the media, although I did have an article about the fast published in the *Los Angeles Times.* But people were very supportive and surprised about the facts. Sometimes, they had a general idea of what went on [with Columbus], but often they didn't know the specifics. They were very interested in what we had to say.

Why didn't you get a response from the media?

That's an interesting question. Why is the media controlled by huge corporations? [Laughs] Looking at it from a logistics point of view, our fast came just before the elections, and the media was concentrating on that to the exclusion of more profound questions and happenings.

Would you say your fast was successful?

Not as successful as we wanted it to be, so long as there are unemployed people, poor people, and people who "earn" a hundred [even a thousand] times what they pay their employees. But it was amazingly successful in terms of all the people we reached out to and the positive responses we received for our effort.

Dave Dellinger at Washington Goorsing Park, Pennsylvania, June 10, 1989 (photo credit: Bethel Agency, New York).

How long did you fast?

I fasted for forty-two days, but I'm seventy-eight years old and three different doctors told me that after twenty-one days I might do permanent harm to my body. So I had fruit juices the last three weeks. I lost close to thirty pounds.

But you're back to normal now?

Finally! I can't believe how long it took. I felt wonderful during the fast and afterwards, but it wasn't until four months later that I got back to my normal weight.

Is it difficult to be an activist at your age?

Not for me.

What keeps you going?

It's like the old line from [Charles] Dickens: "It's the worst of times, the best of times."[2] So I see how bad things are, and, at the same time, I believe the movement has lot of potential, mainly because of the many lessons we have learned. It's just a matter of a spark, like a Rosa Parks refusing to go to the back of the bus, to set off all kinds of activities, which will be on a sounder basis than in the sixties.

Are you involved with the same kinds of issues you were involved with in the sixties, or are there new ones?

Although I call myself a "nature mystic" who has always been interested in the environment, I wasn't involved very much with the issue politically until recently. Feminism is another issue I'm interested in today and have learned so much about in recent years.

I've always tried to live in the present, as if the revolution had already taken place. In other words, I live in accord with the way I believe people will live in a decent society and not say, "Well, after the revolution, I will start sharing my money, living simply, and doing work whose purpose is to contribute to the well-being of the community." Since the sixties, there has been a better understanding that protesting and demonstrating is not enough. We have to live the new way of life now. I'm encouraged by that.

Is the activism today as intense as it was in the sixties when there were very well defined issues like Vietnam and civil rights?

Well, I agree that in the sixties a couple of issues crowded out all the others, at least for many activists. But today, it's like Heinz catsup. There are fifty-seven different varieties of issues, and not everybody goes to the same event on the same weekend to shout the same slogans.

But a lot of the issues we have today—feminism, gay rights, and the environment—took root in the sixties. Is that the great legacy of the sixties?

It's an important part of the sixties legacy, but I think it has a lot to do with the seventies legacy, when people began to take stock and consider things that had gone wrong [in the sixties], especially the turning to violence at certain times.

In the seventies, a lot of people moved toward spiritualism and, in some cases, made the mistake of becoming slaves to a guru. Despite this aberration, there is within the movement a somewhat healthier spiritual background and understanding, including the most obvious example: liberation theology.

But it extends beyond that and includes people who are not a part of liberation theology because they have a more universalist position and do not want to be limited to one religion, even though they appreciate and work with those who are liberation theologists.

What type of activist organizations do you belong to today?

Belonging to a lot of organizations has never been a priority of mine, but I'm involved locally. After I talk to you, for example, I will go tonight to a meeting of the North County Coalition for Justice and Peace. I also belong to a similar committee in Burlington and to several other Vermont organizations for peace and justice.

I've been a member of CISPES [Committee in Solidarity with the People of El Salvador] and belong to the National Committee for Independent Political Action, which has been working towards a national but grass-roots-based independent political party. Also, I work with PVA [Progressive Vermont Alliance], which played a key role in electing Bernie Sanders as an independent member of Congress and is doing valuable local work in the field of education, the environment, and universal health insurance, etc.

I worked for several years with the Vermont and national Rainbow Coalitions, until Jesse Jackson[3] mistakenly decided it was more important for him to be president than for there to be a democratically functioning Rainbow Coalition that works for everyone and not just for his selfish ambitions. He has a lot of insight and strengths, so I hope he'll recover a broader outlook.

How do you support yourself?

I do a lot of things. First of all, I give lectures at colleges and other places and get some honoraria for that. Until recently, I taught part-time at different places — Yale for one year, Goddard College for a few years, Vermont College for several years. Usually I taught in an adult-degree independent studies program. But I stopped about three years ago to concentrate on the book I was having trouble finishing . . . my *From Yale to Jail* [Pantheon, 1993].

What type of trouble?

I had a lot of trouble in trying to get it done. I didn't have time!

Oh, I thought you might have had writer's block. [Laughs]

[Laughs] No, no. The trouble is that, since I'm old, I have so much to write about and my book went on and on. I've had to pare it down and decide what to use.

Let's talk about the peace movement. What impact has the Cold War had on the peace movement? Has it had to reassess itself?

Of course, but not as to the fundamental goals of peace and justice. But by now, most people realize that the U.S. is still acting like an arrogant superpower. The end of the Cold War has freed the U.S. to commit excesses in local places in what has been a terroristic and arrogantly militaristic fashion. But now I think that the peace movement is on the verge of coming alive today in a new way.

I suspect you don't accept the popular notion that the ending of the Cold War was a victory for the U.S. and capitalism.

I don't think that at all. As the Soviet Union failed, so did the U.S. They used each other as an excuse for a lot of their sins, particularly militarism and domination of other countries. Now they don't have an excuse anymore. The U.S. is desperately trying to find other excuses — cutting off the foreign flow of drugs by military means, for example, rather than doing away with the domestic need for drugs and with young inner-city kids running drugs, which is caused by poverty, unemployment, and helplessness.

I read where you were interested in finding a third way of development between the two super power blocks. What kind of society would you like to see?

It begins with what I said earlier. People should start living now the way they want society to become. That means sharing their worldly goods, not competing to rise above other people, but cooperating and sharing the rise together. In the U.S., it means a clear redistribution of the income and power. We are capable of having a society based on solidarity and cooperation rather than on individualistic and egotistical drives. I have advocated putting a maximum on incomes people earn.

We are capable of providing all the necessities of life free. That means food, clothing, shelter, and medical care. The American government believes the way to solve the economic problem is to go easy on corporations and to let the wealth trickle down to the poor, but it never does. Clinton, in an opportunistic attempt to gain votes, spoke about strengthening the middle class and letting the results trickle down to the poor. But it was an evasion of the need to deal directly and dramatically with the poverty of the poor and their lack of power over their lives.

Of course, when you talk about the redistribution of wealth, the average American thinks you are advocating Communism.

My theory is that the Communists proved it was impossible to have economic democracy unless you have political democracy and civil liberties. The United States has proved it is impossible to have political democracy and real freedom unless you have economic democracy.

You have written that "the military industrial complex and its do nothing political parties are sitting on a volcano of discontent that is bound to erupt." What makes you so sure that this will happen?

Because I travel around a lot, meaning I give a lot of talks and go to many meetings of different types that involve exploration of some of the many issues I have referred to. Over the years, I have gotten to know people from all over the U.S., and I've never known any other time when so many people were so deeply disillusioned and angry about the way things are.

Many people are becoming active in small ways, a sign which is often overlooked. For example, note all the cooperative activity that is taking place in such areas as child care, community safety, land trusts, loans, etc. People are living in the system as if they believe in it, but they don't subscribe to many of the things it represents. The press and the pundits say some ridiculous things like "The economy is in recovery," but I think it's in a permanent situation of human catastrophe. People aren't going to put up with that indefinitely.

How is the eruption going to occur, if it does happen?

I don't know. It's hard to predict. I think the movement is in a much stronger position today because of the lessons we learned from the sixties, as well as the seventies and eighties. I don't think it's going to be a single-issue response, although it might be a single issue that becomes the spark to give people more hope to deal dramatically and realistically with other pressing issues.

Are you still committed to nonviolence as you were in the sixties?

Yes, it's still my philosophy and practice. But I have supported and still support revolutionary groups like the ones in El Salvador and other imperialistically oppressed countries such as Cuba, Nicaragua, and Vietnam. By example and by being imaginative and creative, we have to promote nonviolence so that, if a revolutionary group of people in El Salvador, in the territories accepted by Israel, or elsewhere, wants to revolt, they will see it's possible to do so by nonviolent, not violent, action.

So is there no role for violence in achieving social change?

Violence is a two-edged sword that turns back on the people who use it. But I do give a kind of critical support to some violent groups. Unlike some peace bureaucrats, I don't wash my hands of them when oppressed peoples think it is the only way to liberate themselves. I don't call myself a pacifist because a lot of pacifist organizations are interested only in their own purity, or, at least, they overvalue their own purity by condemning everyone who, in despair, feels the only hope is to act violently. They don't value the importance of working nonviolently with other people, whether they are violent or not, in order to get justice.

You've been influenced by Gandhi,[4] I understand, but you don't follow him blindly.

I've never followed anybody blindly. I think the curse of America is that people are taught to follow other people. When I go out to speak, I quote Albert Camus,[5] who said "Beware of all veterans." I take that to mean civil rights and antiwar veterans, including myself. Listen to me and my ideas, but think for yourself.

People call you a radical. Are you comfortable with that label?

Yes, because I always explain that it comes from the Latin word *radex, radicis,* which means in English, "root." So I believe in going to the roots of our problems. I'm not a liberal and never wanted to be one. Most liberals accept our economic system, even though I appreciate the fact that they are at least questioning some aspects of the status quo. But unless they go deeper, the most they will accomplish is getting a few bandaids for people's wounds, not eliminating their wounds.

Can you recall your transformation into a radical?

Well, I guess it began in junior high. I lived in an upper-class part of town called The Park, and downtown across the railway tracks lived a lot of poor Irish and Italians. Junior high was the first time that all the kids from across town went to the same school. In junior high, I fell in love with a poor Irish girl, and a little later, my best friend was a poor Italian boy. He and I were the two best athletes in our class, as well as good students. I saw how prejudiced people could be against both of them. I saw class and ethnic prejudices in situations that were very painful to me.

So you developed a sense of social justice at a very early age?

Yes, at a very early age, although it doesn't mean I understood a lot of things. But in terms of my development, it was more important that I fell in love with Rena than that I read a lot of overtly political stuff. Still, I did read, particularly Shelley, Wordsworth, and various romantics, as well as the poet Thomas Hood,[6] who is not well-known today. After junior high, there was automatic ROTC for freshman students in my high school, and I don't think I thought much about it.

But we had this tough sergeant from the army, and he didn't know how to relate to the kids. When one of us did something he didn't like, he kept us overtime until someone told him who did it. One day we were marching down Main Street, and a car came by and somebody in it yelled something at us. Someone yelled back, "Fuck you!"

When we got back to the school, the sergeant said that he was going to keep us until we told him who had said it. I stepped out of line and told him he was being unfair. He grabbed me and shook me up, leaving claw marks on my arm. Various incidents like that turned me off to authoritarianism. Then we had Sacco and Vanzetti.[7] At first, I thought they were bad men, but step by step, I learned differently and became sympathetic to them. My father was a friend of Governor A.T. Fuller who could have pardoned them. So I tried to get my father to pardon them, and, when he wouldn't, I asked him if he would take me to see the governor. All these events seem isolated, but they were formative experiences.

And turned you into an activist.

At my fifteenth reunion, the only Yale reunion I ever went to, two of my former classmates asked me, "When did you become a radical? We don't remember you being so radical at Yale." But actually in my freshman year at Yale, I saw a notice in Dwight Hall about the campaign of the University Christian Association to help the nonacademic employees join a union. I joined the campaign and asked my black janitor and Irish maid about it. The janitor reported me to the Dean, who called me in. He said I had a great future ahead of me if I didn't mess it up by getting involved with such things. He said the Communists had organized the campaign.

Of course, I pointed out to him that I saw the announcement on a Christian bulletin board. [Laughs] So I was becoming aware, but, on the other hand, I was keeping busy with athletics and studies. I was asked to join the Radical Political Union by—guess who?—W.W. Rostow, who later became an adviser to Presidents [John F.] Kennedy and [Lyndon B.] Johnson and advocated policies that I can only call militaristically imperialist. I went to one meeting and decided it was only self-gratifying rhetoric—great bullshit talk—and didn't have time for that. But through the Christian association, I became aware of Gandhi and became an admirer of his.

Are you still religious?
    I'm spiritual. [Laughs]

[Laughs] Does that mean you don't belong to an organized religion?
    Actually, technically, I belong to the local Congregational church. But let me quote Joseph Campbell.[8] He said, "The fool has said in his heart that there is no God, but an even greater fool has said there is a God and he's ours." In other words, I don't believe literally in the Christian mythology or the exclusive merits of any one religion. But I do believe in loving one's enemies and doing good to those who hate you, which is a fundamental tenet of most religions, even though every one of them has some adherents who find excuses to act differently.

You don't have to be a Christian to believe that.
    Exactly. Today, I am as much in contact with Buddhists as I am with Christians and atheists.

Was there a defining event that changed you?
    One time, I left Yale with old clothes and without any money and went on the road in order to find out what was the real truth about all the people I had said were unfairly unemployed and whom my father and many others said were lazy and didn't want to work. I rode the rails and stayed in the Salvation Army and other missions. My life was different after that.
    I then went into a seminary but not necessarily with the intention of becoming a minister. I wanted to find out more about the Hebrew prophets and early Christianity and various dissident heretical sects that appealed to me. But while I was in the seminary, I became offended by the upperclass atmosphere and the isolation from nearby Harlem, which was just a few blocks away. When I and four other students said we were going to move into Harlem, the head of the seminary said he was going to expel us if we did. But we did, and apparently he didn't dare expel us.
    At the same time, in 1939, I got a part-time job in an inner city church in Newark [New Jersey] in a neighborhood that was gradually becoming increasingly black. Then in 1940, the draft law was passed, and I and seven others refused to register, even though we could have had a religious deferment.
    All we had to do was to sign our names to a piece of paper, and we were exempt. But our interest was getting rid of the war for everyone, not just ourselves. So we didn't do it. Then I went to prison. So you see there was no single defining event that turned me into an activist. It happened accumulatively, and I'm still learning from groups and individuals that have always been denied their full rights and are standing up for them.

And what impact did your time spent in prison have on you?
    Dostoyevsky[9] once said that if you want to know what a society is like, visit the prisons.

You have written that the fifties was a time for sowing seeds and the sixties was a time for harvesting them. Could you elaborate?

What I did in the fifties helped me play a role in the sixties movement. There was a woman named Sis Robinson, a black woman who was probably the best high jumper in the country, who refused to pay her war taxes. We went to Alderson, West Virginia, where she was imprisoned and held a hunger strike outside until she was finally released. For many of us, the sixties came out of those earlier types of experiences in which we stood up for what we knew was right.

When did you become aware of what was going on in Vietnam?

I heard a little bit about it at the Easter antinuclear march in New York City in 1963. I was one of the speakers. Some students—Trotskyites[10] and some others who were from the more democratic but socialistic Student Peace Union—raised signs that said something like "the U.S. out of Vietnam." Bayard Rustin,[11] the chairman of the event, ordered that they put their signs down.

Why?

Because it supposedly violated the focus of the meeting. Everything was supposed to focus on the nuclear issue. The same thing happened on June 12, 1982, when there were nearly a million people in New York and other places calling for a nuclear freeze. I was one of the M.C.'s, and we were told not to mention the current Israeli attack on Lebanon and the U.S. involvement in Nicaragua and Central America. The rally organizers thought it would divide the crowd.

Similarly, in 1966 and '67 a lot of the MOBE people, who were against the Vietnam War, were upset that we always had speakers at our rallies who talked about civil rights or Puerto Rican independence. In any case, back in '63, I told Bayard [Rustin] he shouldn't order the signs to be dropped. But actually the original order came to Bayard from the chairman of SANE,[12] and Bayard didn't dare offend him. I was the next speaker, and I spoke about Vietnam. I knew something about Vietnam, but I should have known more. But, in part at least, thanks to those students, from then on it became more of an issue.

How did you become one of the biggest organizers against the Vietnam War?

Beginning in 1964, we began to organize the opposition to the Vietnam War. The SDS called for the first national mobilization against it. After that, we organized something called The Assembly of the Unrepresented People. It was planned by a number of peace activists who had been active in civil rights and by a number of black civil rights activists in SNCC [Student Nonviolent Coordinating Committee] who were antiwar.

But we were not limited to the war and civil rights. We had meetings at the Assembly on practically every subject—American Indians, woman's rights, prisons... We marched on Washington in an attempt to get to the capitol.

We thought Congress had abdicated its responsibility by passing the Gulf of Tonkin Resolution. We were going to take the government's place and declare a people's peace with Vietnam. Our plan was to go up into the balcony of Congress and announce that. But, of course, we were stopped along the way and thrown into jail.

You did move to make contact with North Vietnam. You met with Ho Chi Minh, which was quite a bold move.
    Well, it wasn't a bold move.

It was bold in the sense that you did infuriate a lot of people, particularly the hawks.
    I had some trouble with the North Vietnamese leaders, too, because they didn't want me to travel into the danger zones. [Laughs] But I finally did, after announcing that I wouldn't attend any more meetings until after a trip into them.

The experience must have been fascinating.
    It sure was!

And revealing?
    Sure, in terms of the destruction. I put terrific pressure on the North Vietnamese leaders to invite in journalists. I told the North Vietnamese it would help the antiwar movement if the [U.S.] media could report what was happening in Vietnam. The North Vietnamese wanted me to select "the" journalist, but I didn't feel right about doing that. I didn't think it's an exaggeration to say that my influence led to Harrison Salisbury [of the *New York Times*] going to Vietnam. When he reported what he saw, it had a powerful effect on the public.

What did you think of Ho Chi Minh?
    I loved him! Before I met him, I had been suspicious. He had that wispy beard and gentle manner, and I thought his gentle appearance might really be hiding a sinister man. I had read a book by Bernard Fall[13] who claimed Ho Chi Minh had admitted to killing thousands of people during his agricultural reform of 1945. Before I saw Ho [Chi Minh], I met with several leaders of what were called mass organizations — about fifteen of them. I challenged them about the 1945 incident. They said it wasn't true. They said some of the angry peasants had come into the villages, killed people, and burned down their houses, but that Ho and his comrades had done everything possible to stop it. I believed it. I was impressed with Ho and Pham Van Dong, who was North Vietnam's prime minister. They were both simple, straightforward men. Of course, this all relates to what I said earlier. I'm a totally nonviolent activist, but I found out that I had more in common with Ho and Pham Van Dong than I did with some of the peace leaders in this country.

You did get a lot of heat from U.S. leaders about your association with North Vietnam. I believe Gerald Ford[14] [then a congressman from Michigan] said you were under the spell of Ho and that North Vietnam was leading you and other peace activists by the nose.

But unlike Jane Fonda,[15] I didn't agree to be photographed standing on an anti-aircraft weapon that was used to shoot down U.S. planes.

Was that stupid on her part?

She was very courageous in making the transition from a spoiled daughter of a Hollywood star to a person concerned with peace, justice, and real democracy. It was as if I had been in high school, newly concerned with justice, and went to Vietnam. I would have probably done something stupid in Vietnam, too, in an attempt to express something true and noble.

But she has apologized.

Did you actually see her apology?

No, I didn't.

Well, I did. I got advance notice of it and saw what she said on TV. Fonda didn't apologize for having opposed the war or for going to Vietnam. She said it was stupid to get on an anti-aircraft weapon and act like she was shooting down an American plane. Some of my antiwar friends said, "Oh, wasn't that terrible. Jane Fonda apologized for opposing the war." But she never did that.

A lot of people don't realize that by going to North Vietnam you helped save American lives. You helped get the North Vietnamese to release American POWs, didn't you?

After I had gone to Vietnam the first time, I was invited to go again to work out a release of some POWs. I decided that somebody else should go. I consulted with some other people, and we chose Howard Zinn and Dan Berrigan.[16] I didn't participate that directly in such a release until 1972. We brought the wife of one POW and the mother of another. They were extraordinarily grateful, and later one of the POWs took part in antiwar demonstrations. Cora Weiss, Barbara Webster, and I organized something called The Committee of Liaison with POWs, and we did arrange exchanges of mail between POWs and their families, which had not taken place until then. Also, the North Vietnamese began to allow the POWs to have some goods sent to them. Yes, some of the POWs and their families were grateful.

In the sixties, you were a lot older than the radicals around you. That's even more true today. Has that created any problems for you in relating to your fellow activists?

I don't think so. At our Chicago trial in 1969–70, Rennie Davis and I served as a bridge between the Yippies, Abbie [Hoffman], Jerry [Rubin], and Lee Weiner, on the one hand, and John Froines and Tom Hayden on the other.[17] The two groups were at swords' points all the time. Because I had their confidence, I was able to play a mediating role. In fact, I got into a lot of trouble with other peace leaders because I was so friendly with Abbie and Jerry.

They didn't like Jerry and Abbie.
Yes, they thought they were irresponsible.

Because of their thirst for publicity and attention and their use of guerrilla theater?
Exactly. I remember the big antiwar rally on November 15, 1969, which I had helped to organize. I proposed that Abbie, Jerry, and I speak at the rally. Jerry and Abbie were absolutely banned, so I invited them to stand on the other side of the podium while I spoke, as an act of solidarity with them and appreciation for their work.

So the movement wasn't monolithic. There was a lot of differences and disagreement and, I guess you could say, jealousies and competitions.
There was a certain amount of that, and a part of my role was to reduce it to a minimum. It was a job handling some of the meetings. [Laughs] I remember coming out of a meeting and someone saying to me, "What a zoo! They are all animals who want to fight each other. I don't know how you do it. Somehow you make them peaceful. [Laughs]"

So there was no generation gap when it came to communicating with Hoffman, Rubin, and the other movement leaders?
I believe I was able to communicate with them because I had a lot of sympathy for all of them, even though I didn't always agree with them. It's like what I said earlier—that even though I was dedicated to nonviolence, I have gotten along with people all over the world who haven't chosen the path of armed revolt. I respected what they were trying to do, although I didn't always agree with their methods.

And how do you relate to young activists today?
I get along well. I admire a lot of young people for their imagination and creativity, and I learn a lot from them. Today, I have marvelous meetings in high schools and colleges because I accept the fact that young people know a lot of things I don't. They also don't carry the baggage that I and a lot of other activists have to carry.

You became friends with Abbie and Jerry?
At the Chicago trial, I was closest to Rennie Davis, but I have always been on good terms with Abbie and Jerry. If we disagreed, we said so frankly. When Abbie went underground, I saw him many times. I was called in at one point to help him when he was in Canada and having a terrible time. He was going through all kinds of manic depressive stuff.
The way I saw it, Abbie was used to being the center of everything, but when he went underground, he had to avoid that, and, as a result, he couldn't follow his usual impulses and no longer knew who he was. He admitted that to me. He had to be cautious, and that was against his personality, which had always been dramatic and at the center of any gathering when he was present.

I know that, at one point, you thought the CIA had something to do with Abbie's death.

I still believe that's a possibility. We were unable to carry out the type of investigation that would have determined if it was. I know he wasn't depressed in the sense of being discouraged, as the media claimed. After August 1985, he would telephone me between eleven and twelve at night once every week or two. He also sent me a lot of letters. He was very enthusiastic about how things were shaping up. He said wherever he went, he got a huge crowd of young people, and they were eager to hear what he had to say.

How would you assess Abbie's place in the history of American radicalism?

He definitely has a role and legacy. He was an important figure for his sense of humor. He emphasized that one didn't have to be a rigid, boring ideologue to be a radical. At the Chicago Seven trial, Tom Hayden and Abbie were always at odds because Abbie thought Tom was too straight and mental and not enough the full personality. Of course, Abbie didn't always think through the consequences of his actions.

Hoffman was a real showman.

Yeah, but I remember reading his autobiography [*Soon to Be a Motion Picture*, reprint, Buccaneer Books, 1994]. I know some of things he said in that book that were, in a directly factual sense, lies. I was there. [Laughs] I know he was exaggerating.

Did he do so on purpose?

Abbie used to say to me that the spirit of what he reported was truer than the actual facts were. I wrote critical reviews of him for *Liberation* magazine shortly before we were indicted in Chicago. But I toned it down slightly because I didn't want what I wrote to be used against him at the trial.

Getting back to the trial, were you surprised at being indicted?

I don't remember whether I was surprised or not because I think I was too busy to care about it.

What significance did the trial have for the antiwar movement?

That's a tough question to answer. On the one hand, it could be said that the trial took too much money, time, and attention away from fighting the government. But we tried to compensate by turning the trial into something useful. We got a huge response when we traveled and spoke around the country weekends and evenings. We were drumming up opposition to the war.

But the press made us appear more important than we actually were. We were just seven men who were indicted and put on trial. There were a lot of just as important people in the movement. A lot of women played a significant role at Chicago and in the movement generally. There were also men in other places [the Seattle Eight, for example], who were mostly ignored by the media.

Did you expect to go to jail?

Whenever anybody criticizes Jerry Rubin today, I say I will not publicly criticize him or any of the others because we made a collective decision. We would all go to jail for ten years, if necessary, in order to get the most from the trial from a revolutionary point of view. We all wanted to turn the trial into something useful.

Are you disappointed that many of the Chicago defendants have changed so much from their revolutionary posture of those days? I think of Rubin, Hoffman, Davis. . . . Seale has come out with a book on barbecuing.

But even back then, Bobby was talking about publishing such a book. It doesn't conflict with what he stood for. I talked to Bobby Seale last night, and I don't believe that he has become a part of the system. While he was earning a degree at Temple, he had me and several other [Chicago] defendants come to the university and participate in a forum that had radical intentions. He has worked with underprivileged children and with the training of people for jobs. He is trying to help.

What about the sixties counterculture and the drugs, "free love," etc.? Did you relate to that scene well?

It depended. Basically, the counterculture was not into destructive things, although there were excesses. I remember an incident at the Chicago trial the night we got out of jail after the Appeals Court had ruled that we were eligible for bail. There was a big party. A couple of young people pressed me to sample some LSD. "Come on Dave. You should try it at least once," they said to me.

Abbie Hoffman said, "Shut up! Don't you see Dave doesn't need to take LSD. He already has had enough visions. He got them on hunger strikes in prison." I used to smoke [marijuana]. I never bought it or sought it out. When it was passed around, I would take a toke. I could go a month or twenty years without taking any. It didn't do a lot for me. I just did it for the company.

What about LSD?

I have never taken anything besides marijuana, and I never really had any problems with people who did. There is only exception to that statement. That was when Paul Krassner took LSD before he went on the witness stand in our trial [the Chicago Seven] and did a terrible job. Paul himself said afterwards that he did a terrible job because he had taken acid.

Is marijuana harmless?

Yes, and it might be even good for some people. When my son was dying of cancer, the doctors gave some marijuana to him and it helped.

And what is your attitude toward cocaine?

I remember going to a party in the seventies, and some people whom I loved and trusted said I should sniff some coke. I almost felt like doing it, but thought, "Well, no." [Laughs] My feeling is that people don't need drugs if they have enough self-esteem and mutual respect with others.

But should marijuana be legalized?

I spoke in favor of legalizing marijuana at a couple of rallies here in

Vermont. I advocate legalizing not just marijuana but all drugs. Then, if people do have problems with them, they could have medical care and not go to prison.

In the late sixties, a lot of radicals thought the country was moving toward civil war. Did you share that feeling?

If you mean military conflict, no, I never thought so. But there has been a kind civil war going on throughout American history. There have always been people in this country who try to change the system so that everybody will be treated like a human being, but ordinarily, suppress their more human instincts and live the way they think they have to in order to survive in an anti-human society. A lot of people in this country are going through the motions of working at useless jobs, holding a job, and staying afloat, but, in reality, are absolutely disgusted with the system.

The U.S. is still fighting the Vietnam War, isn't it? It was a big issue in the '92 election. Will we ever get over that trauma?

It has been a trauma for the government to fight a terrorist war and lose it. But I hope we never get over some of the positive aspects from that troubled war, such as the Vietnam Syndrome. The Vietnam Syndrome opposes selfish intervention in foreign countries in order to increase the profits and power of U.S.-based corporations and to entrench the U.S. as a superpower.

In their book Destructive Generation *[Summit, 1989], Horowitz and Collier wrote that "the decade [the sixties] ended with a big bang that made society into a collection of splinter groups, social interest groups, and newly minted minorities whose common belief was that America was guilty and untrustworthy." How do you respond to that critique?*

It's an oversimplified interpretation of the sixties legacy. First of all, people did learn a lot of lessons from the sixties that are a lot different than the conclusions that Collier and Horowitz came up with. The big lesson learned from the sixties experience was that violence doesn't work. Also, people learned to develop new issues other than the antiwar issue. So I disagree with Collier and Horowitz. It is the visible and invisible [U.S.] governments that are untrustworthy, not the attempt to replace those power groups with something more democratic, humane, and egalitarian.

What are your future plans?

As I said in my pleas to the jury in a couple of recent cases, I hope that, if I'm walking down the street and somebody's house is on fire, I will do what I can to help get them out of the house and to safety, even if it means breaking a window or door. I hope that for the rest of my life, I will respond to the social, political, and economic evils in society and learn better ways of dealing with them. At times, it may mean breaking down a locked door, participating in a sit-in, or going to jail.

But to be more humane and creative, I plan to take long walks in the countryside, climb some mountains, sit on a rock by the ocean, or read Dostoyevsky. . . . I will continue to be not just interested in problems of society, but also in the deeper meanings of life. Otherwise, our attempts to solve the problems tend to become shrill, self-righteous, and superficial.

I am thankful for a new understanding that the personal is political and the political is personal. The way I use the word *spiritual* today, I also think that the spiritual is political and that the political is spiritual.

5

Bill Ayers
Radical Educator

We had a grand idea that we thought was important, and we were willing to spend a very important part of our lives reaching for it. We didn't reach our goal, but I think it made me a better person. The final chapter has yet to be written.

In 1968, Bill Ayers was a teacher in the radical Children's Community School when his strong opposition to the Vietnam War moved him to quit and go to work for the Students for a Democratic Society (SDS) full-time. Two years later, Ayers, frustrated by the continued escalation of war, became a leader in the SDS splinter group, the Weather Underground, and a fugitive from the law. For the next 11 years, Ayers and his comrades, who included his future wife Bernardine Dohrn, were on the run, issuing communiqués, exploding bombs, and trying to foment a revolution they hoped would transform American society and the world.

Life's direction had certainly taken an unexpected turn for a young man who had grown up in the white, affluent, but segregated suburbs of Chicago, the son of a prominent father, who served as chairman of the Commonwealth Edison Company. The young Ayers may have led a sheltered and privileged life, but, from an early age, he had a social conscience. After attending prep school in the early sixties, he enrolled at the University of Michigan, a hotbed of student activism, where he met and was influenced by SDS leaders such as Tom Hayden and Al Haber.

Ayers began to take an activist interest in politics in 1965, the year the United States began to escalate the war in earnest. In October of that year, he was arrested with 26 other University of Michigan students during a sit-in at the Ann Arbor draft board.

In the same year, Ayers became interested in progressive education and began teaching at the Children's Community School. Established in 1964, the school was integrated and based on the radical teaching principals of A.S. Neill of Summerhill in England.[1]

During the late sixties, Ayers became increasingly active in SDS, and, at the organization's national convention in June 1969, he was one of 10 members who authored a paper titled, "You don't need a Weatherman to know which way the wind blows," the name taken from a line in Bob Dylan's song, "Subterranean Homesick Blues." The paper, Ayers later explained, argued that "the responsibility of white Americans, who enjoy the benefits of living in the most powerful imperialist power that's ever been known in world history, was to join forces with the Third World and struggle for the end of the system of imperialism."[2]

At that national convention, a faction led by Bernardine Dohrn, which included Bill Ayers, expelled Progressive Labor from the SDS and took over the organization. But the move destroyed the organization, and it quickly withered away. Meanwhile, Ayers and Dohrn were helping to build an underground organization called the Weathermen (later renamed the Weather Underground because group members decided the original name was too sexist).

On March 6, 1970, three members of the Weather Underground, including Ayers' girlfriend Diana Oughton, were killed in an explosion at a townhouse on West 11th Street in Greenwich Village, New York, after one of the three incorrectly crossed the wires while teaching each other how to build a bomb. Feeling they would be arrested because of their close association with three dead comrades, Ayers and Dohrn decided not to show up for their next court appearance. The FBI listed them as fugitives.

Durig the next 11 years, Ayers stayed one step ahead of the law, constantly changing names, identities, phone numbers, and addresses. In a 1990 interview, the radical estimated that he had had at least a dozen different aliases and had lived in about 15 different states, although he never left the United States.

When the Weather Underground dissolved in 1976, Ayers, unlike many other group members, decided to stay on the run. During the next five years, he held a variety of jobs, which included working in a bakery and a day care center. He also took up with Dohrn with whom, in 1977, he had his first son, Zayd Shakur (for fallen Liberation Army "soldier" Zayd Shakur).

The two radicals surfaced in 1980 and turned themselves in to the authorities in Chicago. Bombing conspiracy charges against Ayers had been dropped in the mid-1970s because of illegal government surveillance. Prosecution for the bombings themselves were never pursued, which meant Ayers was charged with nothing.

Ayers returned to the university, earning his M.A. in early childhood education from the Bank Street College of Education in 1984. He worked as an instructor in the curriculum and teaching department at Columbia University Teacher's College from 1985 to 1987, when he earned his M.Ed. and Ed.D. in curriculum and teaching from the Teacher's College. In 1987, he accepted a teaching position with the education department at the University of Illinois at Chicago.

Bill Ayers and Bernardine Dohrn (see chapter 15; photo by the author).

Today, Ayers remains a committed activist who believes the country's educational system needs radical overhaul. This interview took place at Ayers and Dohrn's home in Chicago.

*   *   *

How does a former member of the Weather Underground end up on the faculty of a university, teaching elementary education?

I had been a teacher of young people in the sixties, and, then again, when our kids were born, I got back into early childhood education. I taught in a day care center in New York for about seven years. When I finished my doctorate in elementary education at Columbia Teacher's College, we began talking about finding a teaching job that would allow me to be a professor. I got a nice job at the University of Illinois at Chicago. We moved here in the fall of 1987.

As fate would have it, we arrived at the time of the devastating teacher's strike that hit the Chicago school system. Being who I am, I found myself on the picket line about a week after arriving. I then got swept up in a very democratic and far-reaching school reform movement.

How are you accepted by your colleagues?

I have gotten along well with them. Some of my colleagues consider me weird, not necessarily for anything I did in my past, but because I don't do research that involves getting data and analyzing it. Rather, my research proselytizes for school reform. This may, on occasion, bring me into conflict with my colleagues, but I wouldn't say our differences lead to animosity. In fact, I have lots of friends on the faculty.

What's the school reform movement about?

The explanation is long and involved but let me summarize it: The Chicago school system is a big failing system. It's failing in a massive way. There have been nine school strikes in the last eighteen years. In 1987, the year I arrived in Chicago, the focus of the conflict had changed from a board-union struggle to a parent-community struggle against the system.

All of the grievances that had built up over the years just crystalized around the strike, which dragged on for thirty days. In time, a real coalition formed among the parents and community organizations. I became involved with that. The best friends I have in Chicago today are the result of that development. I got involved in drafting law and then lobbying for its passage. Then I spent a year as Assistant Deputy Mayor for Education under [Richard] Daley, Jr.,[3] of all ironies. [Laughs] My work has mainly involved setting up the parent councils that now run the schools and helping to educate parents about the educational issues.

Because the educational system is struggling, there are natural antagonisms between parents and teachers. The teachers are inclined to blame the parents for the failure of the system. The teachers are inclined to blame the parents for the problems they encounter in the classroom. It's not a very productive kind of tension. It's my view that you can structure a kind of partnership between parents and teachers, and that's what I've spent a lot of my energy trying to do.

Is Chicago a microcosm of the problems the country is having with education?

In some ways, it's a microcosm; in another, it's an example of urban failure. When you talk about school failure, it's like anything else in America: it's selective failure. It's not a failure across the board. The kids at Exeter aren't failing. There are problems at Exeter, sure. And there are things that I would improve, but that's another issue.

The fact is we have a two-tier school system: those schools that succeed and those that fail. Chicago is a part of that tier that fails. Its failure is predictable and based on race, class, and poverty, and the kids are being cheated. It's predictable that black and poor kids will fail.

Is the question of how resources are allocated a big reason for the failure?

It's partly that, but the problem goes beyond that and has to do with human resources like teachers, access to buildings, transportation, libraries, and other support services. There are other dimensions to the failure as well. For example, the bureaucratization that can exist in a school system of a half million kids. It's a bureaucracy that is top heavy and wasteful; but, more than that, though, it breeds conformity and obedience.

If you allocated resources but didn't address this problem, the educational system would still be in deep trouble because it translates into having a school system where teachers dutifully march through the given curriculum without much thought, much feeling, or much interaction with students.

It sounds like the analysis that was made of the educational system in the sixties. [Laughs] Has anything changed?

[Laughs] If anything, the situation has intensified. Maybe there have been some changes during the past twenty-five years, and perhaps some of those changes have been for the good; but the changes are not too quantifiable because they are mainly in the hearts and minds of many of us.

How do you mean?

We are living our lives — I'm certainly living mine — quite differently from the scripted life that was laid out for us. That's because I had the good fortune of coming of age at a time of turmoil and upheaval. The changes that occurred in the sixties impacted on lots and lots of people, not just people in the movement. But in terms of things that are quantifiable — racial segregation, the oppression of the masses of black kids, the intensification of the pain of poverty for young people — the situation has gotten worse in the past twenty-five years.

Is the critique of American society that you had in the sixties essentially the same one you have today?

Oh, absolutely! My analysis hasn't changed noticeably, although I would deflate some of the rhetoric today. But in terms of my analysis of race and society and what they have done to distort class contradictions . . . of the international policy of the U.S. government . . . I would say my analysis of those things remains the same, though, I'm a bit more agnostic in terms of trying to change things.

By agnostic, I mean I don't bring to the discussion the certainty I had twenty-five years ago because things didn't work out the way I predicted. As an educator involved with local restructuring, I'm highly agnostic. I have a lot of ideas on how to reform the educational system, but I'm not certain they will lead to success.

Critics like Allan Bloom[4] bashed the sixties and said the social turmoil and so called permissiveness of the period are responsible for a lot of the social problems we have today, especially with the educational system. It was very fashionable for conservatives, especially in the Reagan-Bush era, to adhere to this analysis. How do you respond?

I use Allan Bloom's book in my teaching. About a year after Bloom's book hit the bestsellers list, it became available on "Books on Tape." I thought that was wonderful. [Laughs] Bloom had written his big critique of how none of us can read and now his book was on "Books on Tape."

But I don't think we should accept the conservative framework for analyzing society. My big problem with the whole "family values" thing that the Reagan people pushed so hard was the liberal response. The liberals accepted the conservative framework. Why didn't they define *the family* in broader terms?

We need a larger collectivity than "the family." We should be encouraging people to take responsibility for other people's children, for other people's lives. It's not enough for me to say, "I'm doing good for my family and the rest of the world can go to hell." That's a deadly kind of morality. That kind of selfishness is what defines our society and makes us crazy. It walls us off from one another. It makes cooperation across categories, classes, and issues almost impossible.

That's an interesting analysis. What you are espousing is the quintessential philosophy of the sixties, namely, that community is the focus for changing your life and changing the world.

That's exactly right.

We seem to be getting more and more away from that focus on community. How do you explain that?

I think we live in a culture and educational system and society that is characterized by capitalist social relations, which define how we interact with each other. These relations are competitive and selfish and teach people to use other people for their selfish ends. That, in fact, is so common we don't even see it. We don't have the right to walk down the street and rape someone or beat someone up. That's bad. Yet that attitude characterizes the way we relate to each other.

The teacher of my kids, who are in the fifth grade, recently did a clever thing. He gave each kid in the class an imaginary $1,000 and told them that they could invest it in the stock market. I am very proud of my son because he wouldn't invest in Coca-Cola stock. [Laughs]

The teacher used a clever teaching exercise, but what if he had said to the class: "I've got $1,000, and we are going to figure out collectively what we can do to better the world." Everyone would have thought that was propaganda. The point I'm making is that we swim in a sea of capitalist relations and don't even see it. It's like the fish trying to see the water. We breath it in every day and act in it every day.

It's rare when our society and culture encourages you to be your most generous self. And that's what the sixties were all about. Take the civil rights movement. There is a different feeling when you are part of a mass movement that is led by a moral idea. It's such a different feeling! I've never had that feeling since. To be a citizen today means to be cynical and to have a low level of participation. That's disgusting! That's a very sad and tragic thing we are living through.

With the demise of Communism, capitalism is now the model for what a society wants to be. That's especially true for Russia and Eastern Europe. Is there really an alternative model to capitalism which a society can use to build economic and social relations?

There is a wonderful article in *The New Yorker*, written by Robert Heilbroner, the economist, and titled something like "After Communism."[5] He argues against the notion pushed by Reagan and Bush that "we won and they lost." Heilbroner says it's a crisis for everyone, and the notion that "they are bad and went down, and we are good and we are on the up," glosses over the common problems that face both the western countries and former communist societies — bureaucracy, voicelessness in mass society, ecological destruction, economic chaos, lunacy, and overpopulation — all of which American society is experiencing. We haven't experienced it the way they have there [the former Soviet Union and Eastern Europe], but we haven't resolved our contradictions nationally or internationally. The L.A. riots[6] are the real tip of the iceberg, and they remind us that the crisis is not going away.

Can we really resolve the crisis? [He points.] You walk two blocks that way and two blocks that way [from Ayers' house], and you are in the heart of the largest black ghetto in the United States! You get the feeling you are in the Third World. It's unbelievable that that kind of community could exist in this country, especially when it's right next to this prosperous middle-class enclave we are sitting in right now.

We see some progressive things developing in Eastern Europe, but we also see some reactionary things. It hasn't yet played itself out. We shouldn't be so smug and so sure. Fifteen years ago, we thought the Shah [of Iran] would be on the throne forever.[7] Look at Yugoslavia. My God! What century are we living in? If you look at the world, you can see chaos, not solidity, is the rule.

You still sound like the sixties activist who believes that radical reform is the way to go when we look at solutions to the problems facing society.

Absolutely! The problems are doable; but how we can do it, I don't know. It's inconceivable that a place like Chicago or Manhattan can go on forever when they are in a situation where the most fabulous wealth sits cheek to jowl with the most desperate poverty. It's just not conceivable! It's not fair and it's not right!

Can this contradiction be resolved?

Yes, but it will take some restructuring that we haven't seen yet. It will also demand an international approach, or we will all go down together.

What are your feelings about the change in U.S. government from the Reagan-Bush era to Bill Clinton?

I see differences between Reagan-Bush and Bill Clinton, and they are important. I voted. I've voted in every election since I was eighteen. I always held my nose and voted for the lesser of the two evils. I'm not at all deluded.

So who did you vote for in the 1992 election?

I voted for Jerry Brown's[8] delegates and my twelve-year-old son Malik for president, who was the best candidate. [Laughs] I vote because I believe it's a democratic right we should insist upon and struggle to reform. But I don't believe for one minute that the system, the way it's drawn up now, is democratic. I don't believe that it's representative of democratic action.

I have another practical reason for voting in the '92 election. It's very important what happens with the federal judiciary. It matters in the measurable concrete lives of people that we do not get another Clarence Thomas or William Rehnquist.[9] It's important for the environment . . . abortion . . .

But Clinton didn't part company with Bush on more substantive issues that are important. Clinton doesn't part with Bush on the issue of whether to socialize medical care because he represents the capitalist class as a whole.

Well, do you think Clinton is going to be good for education?

I had written an open letter to Bill Clinton in *Rethinking Schools,* a journal that is based in Milwaukee. Then the Clinton transition team asked for my résumé, so I sent the letter along with my résumé to Washington. I never heard from them. [Laughs]

I said in my open letter to Clinton that he has a great opportunity to make a difference in education, especially in his appointment of a secretary of education. Theo Bell and William Bennett[10] taught us that the position could be used as a bully pulpit in a very forceful way.

The fear I have of Dick Riley[11] is that he is enamored of national testing and national standards, which is very much like the conservative agenda. In my view, it will be very destructive to push that. But what did we get when we got rid of Bush? We got the notion that every national discussion on education has to focus on the issue of privatization. When the reactionaries were in power, every question concerning education had to turn the corner around the question of vouchers. We got that pushed off to the side. That's good.

I know Chris Whittle[12] wants to turn the classroom into a marketplace, and he does seem to have some influence. Does that disturb you?

I think it is a very real and serious threat. Twenty years ago, what Whittle proposes would have been a marginal, nut-case scenario. Three things have changed my mind about it, though. One is the fact that Reagan and Bush were in power for twelve years, and the guys in key positions in their administrations whom we thought were nuts in the sixties, such as David Stockman,[13] were in positions of power.

Stockman was at Michigan State University, and I knew about him. Nobody took him seriously, but then he was not running the [country's] budget. Secondly, individuals that tend to be ideological like them, tend to stick to their principles. They have an agenda, so you can't dismiss that. Thirdly, the problem in the schools is difficult. I'm not saying it's intractable, but it's complex and ongoing. But do I think the Chicago schools will be dead in five years? Yes, I do.

You mean finished?
  Yes, as a system.

What will happen then?
  I don't know. Right now in the [Illinois] legislature, which is run by Republicans, bills are circulating to create twenty-five different districts and do away with the Chicago district.

Which is good or bad?
  It's a reactionary push, but it wouldn't be all bad because there would be major lawsuits. My point is that the system is in such a crisis, such mismanagement, such chaos, a lot of things are possible. So I can't predict what will happen. I'm pretty sure that the north Chicago schools will not open this September [1993]. I'm pretty sure the $300 million shortfall isn't addressable by any human means. I'm pretty sure that the Republican legislature will not come up with the money.

Is this type of situation developing in other parts of the country?
  Oh, absolutely! It's happening. [William] Bennett said Chicago had the worst educational system in America, but they are also symptomatic of big urban systems. They are impoverished, overbureaucratized, and underfunded. We've got a fifty percent dropout rate in high school.

I'm no expert on American education, but here is how I look at it. The country puts $100 billion into the War on Drugs, which is like throwing water into the ocean. If you have fifty percent of the kids dropping out, what are they going to do? Can society really expect them to settle for working at McDonald's?
  Yes, it's like South Africa. What we are witnessing is a boycott of the schools by half the kids. They are saying the schools aren't working for me. They won't pay off for me. You and I submitted to a lot of bullshit in high school, but we did so because we believed, our parents believed, our community believed, that education would pay off. Fifty percent of the kids in Chicago are seeing no payoff and are leaving. As you suggest, they end up in prison, costing a lot more. The system is completely fucked up!

It sounds like you are saying that the country is at a crossroads and is not facing up to it.
  Yes, we are on the road to crisis. But I think the American people sense it.

So how does a sixties radical end up in elementary education?
  I was in early childhood education at the same time I was a radical in the sixties. I went to a conservative prep school called Lake Forest Academy, where, interestingly, of the academy's thirty-nine students, four ended up in the SDS. [Laughs]

I was blown away with the image and courage of the black students from the South and the white students from the North standing up and getting the shit kicked out of them. It consumed me! During my senior year, the school recruited the first black kid for Lake Forest. He was extraordinary—the son of a federal judge. I was designated to be his mentor and big brother.

I enrolled at the University of Michigan, mainly because my parents went there; and one of the first things I did at the university was to join a picket line of people protesting a pizzeria that wouldn't hire blacks. I took a liberal arts degree and got peripherally involved in the movement in 1965 when the war in Vietnam was escalating and I decided to participate in a sit-in at the draft board. I was arrested along with some of the other people. That was an altering experience because I spent ten days in jail.

One of the people I spent time in jail with was the husband of a woman who has just been hired to teach in an alternate school. He told me about it, and the school sounded fascinating. When I got out of school, I went to see the place. The [Children's Community] school was located in a church basement, and I got swept away! I never thought I would work with kids and be a teacher, but I had such a great time that I went back the next day and the next day. . . . In a year and a half, I was director of the school.

It was an interracial school?

Yes, very consciously a counterculture institution. It was a conscious attempt by parents to create a school that would reflect the culture and was consistent with their own values and against the culture of capitalism that we live in. They wanted a school that was not capitalistic and not racist.

So I was drawn to early childhood education. It was what I did well and what I liked doing. It was only after the school failed that I became a traveler for SDS.

Why did the school fail?

For a variety of reasons, including my own incompetence.

You are being kind of harsh on yourself.

Well, I didn't know how to run a school. It was always in trouble financially. The school was a hard thing to sustain over a number of years. When we lost the lease on the building, we had trouble finding licensable space. So we went out of business.

When you are a radical, you ask yourself what kind of work can I do that can make a contribution? I met Bernardine in 1966 at a "Radical in the Professions" conference in Ann Arbor, Michigan, which brought together social workers, lawyers, teachers, architects . . . all kinds of professionals. The idea was what were you to do if you were a movement person? At the time—this was before we thought the apocalypse was upon us—that was an important question for us.

Did you learn anything at that school that is helping you as an educator today?

Absolutely! It was a great school! We were trying to build an integrated cooperative. The school had a dozen good people and some wonderful families that had a sense of what a school should be and then tried to create it.

You sound as if you are proud to be radical.

I'm a radical, Leftist, small "c" communist... [Laughs] Maybe I'm the last communist who is willing to admit it. [Laughs] We have always been small "c" communists in the sense that we were never in the [Communist] party and never Stalinists. The ethics of Communism still appeal to me. I don't like Lenin as much as the early Marx.[14]

I also like Henry David Thoreau, Mother Jones, and Jane Addams...[15] Those are people who articulated a vision of a fair and just world. But frankly, I don't see how we are going to survive unless we are willing to talk about justice and fairness. In a period like this, in which there is no large movement to carry us along, the way to try and make sense of things is to undertake small projects and become involved in small movements that try to create the conditions where people raise issues.

This was what I was doing this morning. I was having breakfast with thirty-five teachers, and we talked about how they could control their training and the content of their work. It was a helpful, bold, and frank discussion, and, in a period like this, I frankly can't see anything else we could do.

As the sixties progressed, you became increasingly more militant. Is that because of the way the Vietnam War was going, the way it was escalating?

A part of it was frustration; but what we did in the summer of 1967 constitutes one of the most heroic chapters in American history. It's a chapter most Americans don't know too much about. We went in droves into working class communities and knocked on doors and talked to people. We opened coffee houses to meet with GIs, and we became a mass movement — not in the way the civil rights movement was — but in the sense that it touched and reached millions of people. We helped create a growing feeling that the war was wrong, immoral, and couldn't be won.

We convinced people that the war was carried out by an aggressive superpower against a peasant people who had the right to self-determination. We created a sense of solidarity with the Vietnamese people. They weren't different from you or me. They had kids, too, and hopes and dreams, and went to work every day. The idea that the Vietnamese represented a faceless enemy was bullshit! Vietnam was invaded by us. That was wrong!

But by '68 and '69, frustration was beginning to set in. We began to feel that no matter what we did, they could escalate the war, and we couldn't stop that escalation. So we began to think the best tactic was to inflict on them the kind of pain that would make them draw back. I remember the serious discussions we had about ways to disrupt their capacity to carry on the war.

I was a longshoreman for a period of time, and I remember many serious discussions radicals in the longshoreman's union had about how we could stop them. That was when you began to see the blockage of troop trains and sit-ins in research laboratories. It was not a Communist union but a Revisionist Communist union, which was willing to pass resolutions against the war but wasn't willing to have a political strike and refuse to load any boat going to Vietnam. We could have done that, but we didn't.

Certain things defined the New Left as the New Left. One was a radical belief in democracy—Let the people decide. Now we had the people on our side. They had decided, and we couldn't stop the war. The other thing about the New Left was that you had to act on what you believe. You couldn't just believe it.

For me, at least, the late sixties became a period of deep questioning and anquish. I believed these guys should be stopped, but how do you do it? We tried a lot of things—for example, disabling B-52s in California by blowing out their tires. My brother was in the service, and he put sugar in the gas tanks of airplanes on a regular basis before he was court-martialed. We tried a lot of things, but the war, we found out, was very hard to stop.

So was the idea to go underground and become a real revolutionary?

What real militants do is put their lives on the line and take risks for their values. It's not the throwing of a brick through a window but the risking of something that makes you a militant. When Bobby Sands starved himself to death, he did the only militant thing he could do while he was locked up in prison.[16] His action was militant because he took a personal risk to make a point. I don't think he intended to die, but I think he knew that death was a possibility.

So again—how do you align your actions with your values? I felt the Vietnamese had reached a critical point in their struggle, and I had to do something. I felt supportive of their struggle to resist the U.S. invasion. But how do I help them resist the invasion? That became a real quandary for me.

We didn't plan to go underground the way we did it, but the government has always been good at one thing. They can disrupt you by tying you up in legalisms and making you pay a price every time you build a defense committee. I felt that we shouldn't submit ourselves to that kind of harrassment.

Also, we began to escalate our actions because we, in the movement, were being beaten and arrested and even tortured in the precincts in Chicago. It was becoming routine. They would break into our houses, hang some guy out the window, terrorize us, and then leave. They broke into our national office every other day. We were going crazy. Nuts by then! Then the bomb explosion in the townhouse went off, and we went underground.

How did the disintegration of the SDS contribute to events?

It created a more barricaded mentality, which is always dangerous. You become more shrill, less reasoned and thoughtful, and more dogmatic and more insistent.

What impact did the townhouse explosion have on you?

It was devastating! I lost my best friend and my girlfriend. I was twenty-four years old. Diana [Oughton] was twenty-seven. I was numb for a long time . . . disoriented . . . and I had a lot of grief. I felt a sense of responsibility for their deaths. It was our own craziness that led to that. It wasn't an act of God.

Did it temper your subsequent actions when you went underground?

Oh, absolutely! We—the leaders of the Weather Underground—spent the next year going around the country making contact with people in the former SDS and others on the periphery, trying to get them to disarm and to convince them that the way to go was not in a blaze of glory. Rather, the way to go was to be more sensible, more thoughtful, more strategic, and more careful. We thought we had learned from our mistakes.

Was that prudent attitude the reason why you were able to stay underground for eleven years without being caught? That was an embarrassment for the authorities.

Well, one of the things keeping us underground was that we wanted to be an embarrassment to the government. One of our political messages was: You Americans think the system can't change, but we are here to tell you that they aren't as strong as they look.

We did have mass support. That seems crazy because we were a group of nut cases on the fringes.

What kind of help did you get?

Often, we would run into people who would recognize us and didn't turn us in. That happened all time! We always had people help us when we needed money or an ID or a place that could be used as a drop-off point for our mail. Some knew who we were; others didn't and could care less. There was a large network of young people who knew the illegal world that revolved around being underground.

I remember after we bombed the capitol.[17] We were sitting in our apartment in New York like this [mimics being in a straitjacket]. The landlord came into our apartment to do repairs and saw the news about the capitol bombing on television and said: "God! I think it's great that they did it." He was a guy—a hard working immigrant from Europe—who had no reason to be a radical. We got a lot of signals like that. We weren't as isolated underground as one would think.

But the ending of the Vietnam War in 1975 led to the end of your underground organization, right?

It completely set us adrift. We thought we had a larger agenda, but our organization was held together by the war. When the war ended, our differences surfaced. We ended up in typical left-wing fashion: We ate each other . . . cannibalism. [Laughs] It was sad but typical, and in some ways predictable. You unite around a very large purpose and sacrifice immensely for that purpose. Then that large purpose goes away and what do you do?

The sensible thing would be to shake hands and say, "Let's agree to break up for a while, and we can still be friends." But the more typical thing that happens is we end up saying, "You bastard! You don't agree with me!" It was a painful time, but we survived and today are friends with most of the people who went underground. We still agree that the world needs to change dramatically.

Looking back, do you give yourself, the SDS, and the Weather Underground much credit for stopping the war?

The contribution of the American antiwar movement was to limit the ability of the American government to escalate the Vietnam War beyond what was humanly tolerable. They [the U.S.] didn't bomb the dykes in the north, even though they talked about it. They didn't use nuclear weapons. I think we played a big role in subverting the U.S. Army, which became a decisive factor in the sense that they couldn't count on the reliability of the fighting force. That was terribly important but very sad for the people involved. Read the *Fourth of July*.[18] The cost was high, but the cost of going the other way could have been higher.

We were never anti–GI in the sense that we felt they should be hurt. We spent a lot of time working with GI troops, whom we felt should be brought home and saved.

Within the antiwar movement, I think the SDS made a serious contribution to ending the war, as did the Weather Underground, which helped to wear down the war makers. It became obvious that political bombings and our opposition to the war would be a part of the political landscape until the war ended. If you look at the newspapers after the capitol bombing, you saw the Senate leadership making statement after statement . . . freaking out! This happened in my house! The fact that we were indistinguishable from their children freaked them out. We were their enemy, but we were the kids of parents who were successful in the American sense of the term.

[Peter] Collier and [David] Horowitz would disagree with you. Have you read their book?[19]

Parts of it.

Their chapter on you and your wife [Bernardine Dohrn] is savage.

You know why? David and Peter were the editors of *Ramparts*. Peter has a background basically like mine, but David grew up in a Communist household. His parents were Stalinists; so when he broke with the Left, he broke with a vengeance. I spoke to him a couple of times when he was going through the period of self-doubt before he emerged as the most severe critic of the Left. It is the same thing as David Greenglass, who ratted on the Rosenbergs,[20] or some of the people who went before HUAC [House Unamerican Activities Committee]. When you have a conversion experience, everything in the old days is wrong.

I remember talking to David and him saying, "But the Panthers are like the Stalinists. They lie! They lie!" Of course the Panthers lied. They weren't saints. Whoever thought they were! Whoever thought Stalin was God! I'm sure it was a big disappointment to many people when he turned out to be a real prick. But I didn't think Stalin was God, and I didn't think Huey Newton was God. I didn't have a problem like David, who was relating to his own experiences and his parents' experiences.

You are saying he reacted like a fundamentalist.

Yes. That's the danger of being dogmatic and sectarian. You shrilly insist upon certainty in an uncertain world. When our organization fell apart, a lot of the anger was directed at Bernardine [Dohrn]—and, to some extent, me— because she was the leader who was supposed to be perfect. The best thing a person can do is to always question the so-called verities and truths.

In 1980, you negotiated your way back from the underground. You must have assessed those eleven years of your life.

We had a grand idea that we thought was important, and we were willing to spend a very important part of our lives reaching for it. We didn't reach our goal, but I think it made me a better person. The final chapter has yet to be written.

Recently, a friend and I visited a very nice Montessori school.[21] The entire time we were there, the school director kept saying, "See that child playing over there. Maria Montessori would say such and such. And she would say such and such about those children over there." I got irritated and said, "Carl Jung once said: 'I'm glad I'm Jung and not a Jungian because I can still change my mind.'"[22] [Laughs] The teacher said, "Maria Montesorri said the same thing." [Laughs]

My point is that when you are into dogma, you can't grow or change. But I'm changing, growing. . . .

Do you ever get nostalgic for the sixties experience?

I'm too busy to get nostalgic, although the sixties were the touchstone for my experience today. Something goes off in mind when I see an event like the Gulf War, the invasion of Panama or Grenada unfolding.[23] I don't need to know too much about it to know it's wrong. I know it instinctively. I learned so much coming of age during the civil rights movement.

There's nothing like participating in a mass movement! I'm not nostalgic for that feeling exactly, but I long for that feeling of being part of a beloved community that is working toward a greater goal outside ourselves.

6

Warren Hinckle

Unreconstructed Radical

> It wasn't so much that *Ramparts* made a revolution in radical or
> left-wing journalism. All we did was apply the techniques of the
> marketplace to produce a slick non-leftist-looking publication
> that looked appealing on the newsstand. Then we promoted the
> hell out of it. Nothing like that had ever been done to a left-wing
> publication before.

In 1964, *Ramparts* magazine was a two-year-old liberal Catholic publication with a circulation of 4,000. Four years later, it had become a big-time,
slick, muckraking magazine with a circulation of 250,000 subscribers. In its
heyday, from 1964 to 1968, *Ramparts* played a significant role in making the
public aware of the stories about U.S. government skullduggery that were circulating in smaller left-liberal publications.

Many of *Ramparts'* stories pried the covers off CIA operations. Nobody
paid much attention, for example, to a *Viet Report* investigation revealing that
Michigan State University had been serving as a cover for CIA operations in
South Vietnam; but when *Ramparts* reported the story, it became a national
exposé. The same was true of other revelations, including the stories about the
National Student Association working as a CIA front and the CIA using phony
foundations to channel funds to various groups it wanted to support. The
public began to take notice when *Ramparts* reported on the stories.

In *Ramparts'* heyday, Warren Hinckle was the editor that made the
magazine work. A fourth-generation San Franciscan and grandson of a Bar-
bary Coast dance hall girl, Hinckle became associated with *Ramparts* in 1962,
the year Edwin M. Keating, a San Francisco lawyer, founded the magazine.
Not knowing much about publishing, Keating hired the 22-year-old Hinckle to
do a promotion plan for *Ramparts*. Hinckle suggested that Keating rent a hotel
ballroom where *Ramparts* would throw a party for priests, leading Catholic
laymen, journalists, and important people in publishing, with a few models
and movie stars thrown in to help grab attention. Keating didn't think too
much of Hinckle's plan and fired him.

Hinckle started his own publicity company, which quickly folded, and

Warren Hinckle (photo by the author).

then went to work for the *San Francisco Chronicle* before approaching Keating and asking if he could help with the promotion, advertising, and editorial design of *Ramparts*. In 1964, Hinckle became executive editor and associate publisher of *Ramparts*. In effect, he ran the magazine.

Hinckle stayed with *Ramparts* until 1969, when the magazine went bankrupt. He then started another muckraking magazine called *Scanlon's Monthly*, but it folded as well. In the mid-seventies, Hinckle edited filmmaker Francis Ford Coppola's[1] experimental *City of San Francisco* magazine and went to work for the *San Francisco Examiner*, where he was an associate editor from 1985 to 1991.

He has also written and co-written more than a dozen books, including his autobiography, *If You Have a Lemon, Make Lemonade* (Putnam, 1974), as well as *The Fish Is Red* (Times Books, 1980), which chronicles the United States government's covert obsession with destroying Fidel Castro and the disastrous consequences for the domestic scene as the secret war turned inward. In 1992, *Fish* was updated and republished as *Deadly Secrets: The CIA-Mafia War Against Castro and the Assassination of JFK*.[2] Hinckle and co-author William Turner describe the history of the U.S.'s Cuba project, which began in the early sixties soon after Castro came to power, as "the CIA's most ambitious domestic undertaking and its most expensive failure" and conclude that "the secret war corrupted American institutions in ways that set up the destruction of two presidents."

In 1992, Hinckle launched his latest publishing venture: a new quarterly magazine *The Argonaut*, which harks back to a muckraking journal of the same name, published from 1877 to the 1950s and edited for a time by the famous writer Ambrose Bierce.[3]

Our interview took place in San Francisco at the Dover Club, a hole-in-the-wall Irish pub that is one of Hinckle's favorite hangouts. I knew about Hinckle's pro–Irish Republican Army (IRA)[4] sympathies and mentioned that I had been in Ireland several times and interviewed IRA leaders Gerry Adams and Danny Morrison. "Tell that to the boys in the bar, and you'll get along great," Hinckle advised enthusiastically.

Waiting for Hinckle to arrive at the Dover Club, I had a couple of pints of Harp, chatted with the patrons at the bar, and learned that Hinckle is considered a local legend, albeit an eccentric one. Hinckle arrived an hour late for the interview, sporting the customary black patch over his left eye and dressed in a blue sweater, blue jeans, and a tweed sport jacket, which he slung over his right shoulder. Hinckle's dress, along with his long hair and youthful manner, made him look a decade younger than his 54 years.

We talked belly up to the bar, with Hinckle imbibing a few bottles of non-alcoholic O'Doul's, while I sipped a few more pints of Harp. Hinckle's description of himself in one of his op-ed pieces that appeared in the *New York Times* as an unreconstructed radical was verified time and again during the course of our conversation.

*   *   *

I found Deadly Secrets *very interesting reading. I got a review copy from your publisher, Thunder's Mouth Press. It's a story you have been chasing since the sixties, right?*

[Laughs] It's a never-ending story that originally came out in 1980 as *The Fish Is Red,* but we tore the book up and added a lot of material to it because of the stuff that has come out. The new edition is a lot bigger.

It seems that nothing has changed since the sixties. The CIA seems to be getting away with the same shit it's always been getting away with.

[Laughs] The French were right. The world never changes. And nothing is going to change with this administration [Clinton administration]. There is always stuff that is going to come out. There is a guy who is floating a book around New York publishing circles. He claims that Clinton was involved in all the Contra trading stuff. Clinton knew about it, he claims, and covered it up.

How does his theory work?

There is a town in Arkansas that is a kind of a hot-rod town for money laundering and pilots involved in smuggling operations. A lot of stuff went through there in the 1980s during the secret arming of the Contras. A federal grand jury investigated what was happening, but nothing ever came of it. People figure Clinton must have been involved. After all, he was governor. One of his biggest financial contributors was up to his ass in the thing . . . up to his ass in profits from drug smuggling. I don't know if a book will come out of that, but it's the same old shit, the kind of CIA stuff *Ramparts* exposed in the sixties.

If his theory is correct, I can guess that you are not enamored of Bill Clinton?
    They certainly did miss a lot.

So is Argonaut *going to be the* Ramparts *of the nineties?*
    That's what a lot of people are saying, but we'll see. The kind of journalism *Ramparts* practiced comes easy and is openly successful when the rest of the press is so bad. So it doesn't matter if *Argonaut* is the most brilliant piece of shit that ever happened. [Laughs] It depends on how bad the rest of them are. It's a pretty low period for journalism.

It's said that the stories Ramparts *dug up were stories that the mainstream press knew were around but were afraid to publish.*
    It's not that they were afraid to report them. They didn't pay any attention to them. *The Nation* ran the Bay of Pigs story before it happened, but nobody paid any attention to it. The fact that *The Nation* had the story meant nothing. All Kennedy had to do was call the *New York Times* and say, "Look, don't print it." *The Nation* didn't have enough power to force the story out by itself.
    It wasn't so much that *Ramparts* made a revolution in radical or left-wing journalism. All we did was apply the techniques of the marketplace to produce a slick, non-leftist-looking publication that looked appealing on the newsstand. Then we promoted the hell out it. Nothing like that had ever been done to a left-wing publication before.
    We took a lot of whacks at Clinton in the first issue of *Argonaut*. He's going to serve the corporations the way [Franklin Delano] Roosevelt served capitalism. He's going to make it safe for the corporations, and he's going to do it by soaking the taxpayers. It's a pretty good trick, and everybody is going along with it. It's amazing!

Will it work?
    It [the system] will putter along. What's the alternative? Cuba had the only efficient socialist system that came close to working, but it's been fucked over the most. No socialist system has ever worked. Basically, a socialist system eventually becomes institutionalized capitalism. It comes to have the same government perks and eventually ends up fucking over everybody. [Laughs] It's human nature to rat fuck whether it's a capitalist system or a socialist system. There is no such thing as democracy.

Are you going to try to stake out the same kind of role for Argonaut *that* Ramparts *played in publishing in the sixties?*
    There was only one magazine like *Ramparts*.

What I'm saying is that, in the sixties, Ramparts *exposed so much of what the mainstream press had missed. You said it was a pretty low period for journalism.*

*Everybody thinks that investigative journalism has come a long way since Wood-
ward and Bernstein exposed Watergate.*

But did we really learn anything about Watergate? It's always been my
position — and it's not singular with me — that the entire Watergate thing was
a CIA operation to overthrow the government because Nixon was wacko and
out of control. He was fucking with the CIA and the FBI and was going to
create his own operation within the White House. That was too much for the
CIA. Besides, Nixon was an outsider; so the CIA overthrew him and used the
Washington Post to do it. So Watergate involved one branch of government
overthrowing another branch of government and using the government to do
it. [Laughs]

How did you come to work for Ramparts?

Well, basically, I didn't feel like working for a mainstream publication.
The *Ramparts* publisher had gone broke, and we restarted the publication as
a monthly. I ended up with the goddamn thing. I didn't know anything about
raising money for a publication. We essentially had to invent it as we went
along. We decided that if we are going to do it, let's go for broke. Let's be like
Time magazine. What do we care if we go broke? We shouldn't be here
anyway. We are broke! [Laughs]

*So it kind of helped that you were young and inexperienced. You didn't know any
better. [Laughs]*

Yeah, we didn't know any better. We didn't care about the establishment
or saving our ass.

*You say in your autobiography that you hated magazines, even though you
worked for* Ramparts. *So you applied a newspaper approach to the magazine,
didn't you?*

Oh, yeah, especially in the way we dealt with breaking stories.

And rewriting the stories that Ramparts' *correspondents sent in to you was your
specialty.*

We would do a lot of team journalism, where we would put several re-
searchers and a couple of writers on a story. They would write a draft and I'd
say, "Give me the goddamn thing." And I would rewrite it.

Where did your love of newspapers come from?

I put out a paper in grammar school . . . high school . . . college. I don't
know where the hell it came from! There must have been a journalist in the
woodpile.

[Laughs] The milkman must have been a journalist.

[Laughs] Nobody knows.

What kind of background did you have?

It was a typical Catholic middle-class family background. It was not an intellectual type of background. I had sixteen years of Catholic schooling, so where would I get it? We barely had *Reader's Digest* in the home.

But you are obviously well read. Where did that desire to learn and question come from?

I guess it came from experiencing the authority of the [Catholic] Church and not liking it. I ended up going to school at the University of San Francisco. I couldn't major in journalism because the school didn't have a journalism major. I did all that fucking work in the school newspaper and didn't get a unit's credit! The pricks! I majored in philosophy because they wouldn't let us read the important books unless we did. I discovered I couldn't study [Immanuel] Kant[5] unless I majored in philosophy. I said, "Fuck this! I'll major in philosophy! Don't tell me I can't read books. What is this stuff!"

But Jesuit education is good. You learn how to fight. You come to the conclusion that no fucking institution was any fucking good. It's a short step to go from the Catholic Church to the government of the United States. If you come to the conclusion that the Catholic Church is full of shit, you know that United States government has to be full of shit.

So ex–Catholics make the best radicals. [Laughs]

I think so. I think that was certainly true in the sixties. What I'm saying is that, if you grew up in a traditional liberal upbringing and were raised in an environment in which you were familiar with the liberal issues and causes and you knew what socialism is, you are more or less apt not to pull the temple walls down and you are more willing to operate within the established liberal traditional system. But who were the guys that ended up supporting the [Vietnam] war? They were the goddamn liberals!

Are you still pissed off at the Church?

I still subscribe to the *National Catholic Reporter*. [Laughs] I have a kid who's three years old, and I just had him baptized in the Church. But I'm certainly not going to drag the kid to church! Ultimately, you kind of stay within that framework, even though you know it's full of shit. But you just don't want your kid to get conned into it. I keep up with the Church and its issues and beefs. I use to write about the Church in my *Chronicle* column.

Getting back to Ramparts, *did it have any impact on journalism?*

I think *Ramparts* had an impact on the style of intellectual publications, helping them get away from the old grey look they had. After *Ramparts*, magazines like *Harper's* and *The Atlantic* started to retool and use color illustrations. Since *Ramparts*, there have been attempts to start another left-wing magazine similar to it, but they have been underfinanced and much too cautious.

Yeah, but Ramparts *never seemed to have enough money.*

We weren't underfinanced. We just knew how to use debt. [Laughs]

That's what capitalists use, don't they? Some of the more serious leftists were always griping at me, saying "Oh, you can't do that." I'd say, "What the fuck's the matter with you? You are supposed to be leftists. Besides, that's what General Motors does."

[Laughs] But it finally caught up with you.

Oh, sure. I was always ready to shut it down. What the fuck! As long as you can do what you want to do, fine. If you can't, stop. Eventually, *Ramparts* went under. That's no great distinction.

Ramparts' *demise must have been a letdown for you. The magazine had received such fame, and you were so young. What do you do for an encore?*

You don't care, if you live in San Francisco. It's a magical city. If you live in a little village, you can go back to the bar. [Laughs] We did *Scanlon's* [magazine] for a while. . . . Another magazine followed.

Did Ramparts *have any impact in terms of Vietnam?*

Ramparts was the largest magazine to be against the war, and it certainly helped to change the press's opinion of the war, which initially was in support of it. I think we made the press a little more willing to question and criticize the government. Many of the stories we broke ended up on the front page of the *New York Times.*

Did Ramparts *have any impact on the public's perception of the war?*

Oh, yeah, sure it did; but *Ramparts* was just one of many particular forces trying to expose what was going on in Vietnam.

Isn't it ironic that many people ended up blaming the press for the U.S. losing the Vietnam war?

Television couldn't help itself. In terms of the coverage of the war, pictures of villages burning were never shown before. But it wasn't the intention of television to undermine the war. Compared to television, *Ramparts* was a small fish that had barely enough circulation to get the *New York Times'* attention.

Looking at your place in the sixties, you were always a gadfly, weren't you? You never really fit in in terms of the so-called movement. You weren't really a part of the New Left, even though you probably shared a lot of their beliefs.

Yes, I was at odds with a lot of them. I didn't like them. I did get to know Abbie [Hoffman] pretty well in later years, and I kind of liked him. Rubin and some of the others were jerkoffs as far as I was concerned.

You thought they were phonies?

Just jerkoffs . . . their Yippie thing against the war. Come on now!

But weren't they working toward the same goals as you were? They were challenging the system and trying to get the country out of Vietnam?

Well, I certainly didn't go around exposing Abbie Hoffman and Jerry

Rubin, which would have been easy to do. But they are certainly not the type of guys I would go out drinking with.

That was one of your points in your autobiography. Many of the activists didn't drink, which made it hard for you to get along with them.
Fuck them! They were like fundamentalists.

So even though you grew up San Francisco, you were never a part of the hippie scene?
I didn't care for it.

Why not?
It was completely hedonistic and nonpolitical, and the message was to drop acid at any time while the country was in a real political crisis with the war in Vietnam. So to package acid, beads, the perfumes, and preach: "Hey! Let's not get involved. Let's drop out and tune out." . . . That was totally irresponsible and a rip-off. Those kids were totally fucked over. *Ramparts* became the first critic of the Haight-Ashbury and the love generation scene. Bill Graham,[6] the rock promoter, would never speak to me. When I was a columnist for the *Chronicle*, the newspaper sent me to cover a Rolling Stones concert tour. I told them, "Please don't send me on a Rolling Stones tour." [Laughs]

[Laughs] You went on a Rolling Stones tour? What happened?
Graham kicked me off the tour.

Because of what you wrote about him or the tour?
No. He just hated me from the sixties and because I didn't show a great appreciation for rock music in my writing. I was more interested in writing about the politics behind the scene. Graham went bananas. He said, "You get off my tour!" I said, "Fuck you!"
But, given the luxurious hindsight of history, *Ramparts* was right about all that. It [counterculture] crashed into a complete debacle and was ripped off by merchandisers. It turned into a crass commercial thing, and kids were left at the mercy of murderers, drug dealers, and filth. . . . It was a disaster.

But I understand from something I read somewhere that you respected the Diggers.
Yeah, the Diggers were the legitimate thing.

Did you know some of their leaders—Emmett Grogan, Peter Berg, Peter Coyote?[7]
Yeah, but not really well. All of those guys, I respect. Peter Berg is an extremely interesting thinker. There is a lot of difference between an Emmett Grogan or a Jerry Rubin.[8] Emmett Grogan was out there seriously, in his crazy way, trying to take care of people, feeding people, and fighting off the marauders who were fucking over those very innocent young kids. He was

protecting them and doing a good thing. Jerry Rubin was basically a show-boat and a fuckoff who was out to promote himself. When you watched those two guys it wasn't difficult to reach a decision about who was real and who wasn't.

In the context of the Vietnam War, I never did do a cover story exposing Jerry Rubin. Why bother to do that!

Did you ever get any heat from people in the movement or the counterculture. Did anyone ever come to your office at Ramparts *and say, "Wait a minute, Hinckle! What are you doing! It's not helping the cause."*

They knew better than to tell me that shit. I would have told them to fuck off. But yeah, sure, there was some of that shit. But I told them: "Fuck you! What you are doing is not helping the cause." I have no use for ideologues and moralists. They couldn't have a good time. They couldn't see the absurdities and contradictions.

Speaking of ideologues, [David] Horowitz and [Peter] Collier worked for Ramparts. *They wrote a book called* Destructive Generation: Second Thoughts on the Sixties,[9] *which really savaged the legacy of the sixties. Did you read it?*

No, I haven't read it, but I guess I'm going to have to since the *Argonaut* is coming out with an issue devoted to the sixties.

You should because the book is almost vicious in its critique of the sixties. Essentially, they argue that the problems American society has today can be traced to what happened in the sixties.

That's ridiculous!

You must have known Horowitz and Collier well?

Oh, yeah. Peter was always nonpolitical.

What was he doing at Ramparts, *which was such a political magazine?*

He was our literary editor and did a lot of literary essays. Very, very bright. Very good writer, Peter. Nice guy, Peter. Horowitz was the ideologue and the most left of the two. I remember when *Ramparts* reached the point where we had used every tax dodge possible, and no one would give us any money because of our politics. We had trouble with the Jews on Israel, even though we were pro–Israel. But we weren't pro–Israel enough. We couldn't get ads because we were too radical.

When the end came, I devised this crazy plan. I had run into an under-writer who said he'd put money up but wanted a new thing. He didn't want all that debt. I said, "Yeah, that makes sense. I'll start a new magazine." *Ramparts* was ruined anyway. It was about '68.

I went back to the staff at *Ramparts* and said, "Here's the deal. We are go-ing to fold this thing and walk across the street. I'll probably get fucking sued, but we'll start a new magazine. We'll call it *Barricades*. Someone shouted, "Oh, no! We can't do that. It's too risky. We should have been smaller in the first place. . . ." He went on and on. Finally, he said, "Besides, it's immoral. What about all the people that had invested money?"

I said, "What money? [Laughs] It's gone! This is reality we are talking about." Horowitz was the only guy who understood that. He said, "Yeah, it's just a corporation. What we are doing is killing the old corporation and starting a new one."

Then later, Horowitz did a complete flip-flop and went completely in the opposite direction ideologically and took Collier with him, even though he wasn't particularly political in the first place. But I saved Horowitz's ass.

Oh, yeah? What happened?

I was in the bar, and a group of gays were having a meeting next door. Horowitz ran an article in *New West* magazine, or its successor, attacking promiscuity among gays as a cause of AIDS, or something like that. I really forgot his point, but it may have been a valid one, such as the bathhouses should be shut. Anyway, the gays were outraged by what Horowitz wrote. Horowitz came to the meeting like the big fat dumb jerk he is, wanting to answer questions. But those gays were ready to lynch him.

I couldn't care less about it, but I was in this bar, and they all came over from that meeting. I don't know how the hell I ran into him [Horowitz]. I could see those guys [the gays] were really mad and about to kick the shit out of him. I told them, "Horowitz is right-wing. What can you do about the guy? Take it easy." I got those guys off his back when they were literally going to kick the shit out of him.

[Laughs] Maybe that's what they should have done.

Yeah, there's some people who believe I shouldn't have saved his ass. But I remember Eldridge [Cleaver]. I still like him. I remember when Cleaver was in the can—the fucking hypocrisy of the Left—because he changed his political views!

He actually became a born-again Christian.

Yeah, but I remember when he came back to the U.S. from exile overseas and had to serve time in jail because of what he did in the sixties when he was active in the [Black] Panthers. Those were the charges, and those fucking hypocrites in the New Left made the moral judgment that, because the guy changed his politics, he's not on our side anymore. Therefore, he belongs in jail because we don't like his ideas. I say, "Wait a minute! [Laughs] Where's the principle here? A guy shouldn't be in jail because of his ideas whether we agree with him or not. Nobody should belong in jail for his ideas! And furthermore, this guy is in jail for something he did in the sixties, and you bastards won't lift a finger to help him!" The phony moral hypocrisy of the Left—I've never had any use for it!

[Laughs] So do you get nostalgic for the sixties?

Not really, although *Ramparts* was a lot of fun. But I always have fun.

[Laughs] There's always something going on in San Francisco ... a great town. [Laughs] I wrote a column for the *Chronicle* in the seventies and eighties that just burned this town down! We had so many great controversies... Things just never get dull in San Francisco. The city really hasn't changed that much [from the sixties].

That's interesting, because at Ramparts *you were at the center of the national scene, but at the* Chronicle *you had a local audience.*
    But I never left here. [Laughs]

[Laughs] And you never look back?
    No! [Laughs] Bad guys will always be around.

7

Peter Berg

From Digger to Environmental Activist

> I think everything I'm doing today comes from the Diggers...
> The ideas of the Planet Drum Foundation — bioregionalism,
> rehabilitation, finding ways to restore the natural systems,
> finding ways to fulfill human needs — are the ideas of the Dig-
> gers. The Planet Drum Foundation and all it stands for is the im-
> plicit ecology of the Diggers made explicit. You can't have a
> social system anymore that doesn't have ecological conscious-
> ness at its center. It just has to be that way.

In 1966, Peter Berg helped found the San Francisco–based Diggers, an informal group dedicated to nonviolent anarchy. Described as "the conscience
of the Haight," the Diggers took their ideological roots from a seventeenth-
century anarchist communal farming group in Cromwellian England, also
known as the Diggers. They lived on wastelands scattered across the countryside and promoted the idea that the land should be free for all those who
needed to use it.

The modern day Diggers wanted everything to be free and worked to
establish an entire economic network based on bargaining and sharing rather
than profit. Many of the Diggers came out of the San Francisco Mime Troupe
and effectively used their theatrical experience as a means for organizing the
hippie community.

The Diggers railed against the merchants who called themselves hippies
but profited at the expense at the counterculture. They began daily free food
handouts for the young hippies who poured into San Francisco's Haight-
Ashbury District and operated a "Free Store," inviting passersby to help themselves to household items. They showed their antipathy for money by publicly
burning it and staging a "Death of Money" parade. The Diggers spread to New
York and influenced some of the political leaders of the counterculture, including Abbie Hoffman, who, by the summer of 1967, began to identify himself as a Digger.

By 1968, however, the San Francisco hippy movement had begun to
disintegrate into gross commercialism. In the words of Berg, "The high point

of vision and optimism had peaked and started to pass." So the Diggers held a ritual ceremony in which they buried the "hippy" and declared themselves "free men."

Like many who had become disillusioned with the counterculture, Berg drifted until 1972 when he attended a UN-sponsored conference on the environment in Stockholm, Sweden, where he mixed and talked with some of the 10,000 people in the streets who were not part of the official conference and did not attend the meetings. Like many of the other "unofficial delegates," Berg concluded that the world needed a deeper level of understanding about the condition of the planet and the social, economic, and political factors affecting it.

In 1974 Berg helped found the Planet Drum Foundation in an effort to create a culture, a life-style, and a political philosophy that would help mankind live in harmony with the Earth. Since then, Berg, in collaboration with a diverse range of people, from poets and ecologists to Native Americans and community activists, has helped develop and refine a concept known as *bioregionalism*.

A *bioregion*, according to Berg and other adherents of the cultural concept, is "the natural conditions of the planet, which are distinct areas with coherent and interconnected plant and animal communities often defined by a watershed."[1] Bioregionalism stresses sustainability, community self-determination and regional self-reliance, and ways to begin sustaining and maintaining the natural systems in which people live. The movement is growing in North America and worldwide. There are 2,000 bioregional groups and publications in North America alone and the fifth North American Bioregional Congress was scheduled to be held in Texas in 1994.

As Peter Berg explains, "[We] ecology-related social reformers recognize that the earth is essentially self-governing and that humans have a task of rediscovering what a realistic relationship to the rest of planetary life entails."[2]

Our interview took place at the Planet Drum Foundation in San Francisco, a city that bioregionalists say is in a naturally defined area known as the Shasta Region. Dressed in blue jeans and a plain white T-shirt, his graying hair tied in a ponytail, Berg talked enthusiastically about bioregionalism as a cultural concept whose time has come. Members of a younger generation of activists, the spiritual heirs of the Digger movement, moved about the office. As our interview progressed, it became evident that Berg still possessed the idealism that fired the Diggers during the sixties counterculture.

* * *

As part of your postal address, you include the term Shasta Region. *Does the U.S. Postal Service recognize that term? Do your letters get delivered without any problem?*

Not only does the Planet Drum Foundation use the term, but other people in the San Francisco area do as well. We get correspondence all the time that has something like *Delaware Valley Watershed* in the address, or whatever, and there is no problem. I believe that, in the future, the Postal Service will use the term *Shasta Region* to designate Northern California.

How long will it take before that comes about?
It has taken the state of California fifteen years to adopt the term *bioregion* to mean "habitat for endangered species," which they currently do. The state of California published something last year titled a "Memorandum of Understanding: Agreement on Biodiversity." They established ten different bioregions for the purposes of identifying endangered species habitats. And they advise local residents to form bioregional councils in those areas. It's an unprecedented move.

You use a lot of new terms like Shasta Bioregion, *but you need to introduce a new language, don't you? Ecologically, you are trying to push the world in an entirely new direction in the way it treats the planet.*
Actually, what we are trying to do is very old. There is not much difference between what we are doing and what the people did in the Pleistocene period about fifteen thousand to forty thousand years ago. The only difference, really, is that, today, we recognize humankind is on a finite planet. The big news for the human species is that the biosphere is limited.

When you say the biosphere is limited, are you talking about things like fossil fuels?
Fossil fuels are just one aspect. You can also say that water supplies are also limited. The ozone layer is limited. The number of species on the planet is limited. The industrial era is ending because of the limited biosphere we share. That's the news. That will eventually affect humankind in the same way the notion of personal freedom affected us at the beginning of the industrial revolution.

When did the environmental movement, bioregionalism, begin?
When it became obvious that our society was inadequate to solve its own problems. The publication of *Silent Spring* in 1962 could be considered the beginning.[3]

Were you influenced by Rachel Carson's book?
Not at the time. I was absorbed by my own personal experiences.

In San Francisco?
I was involved with the Diggers. Someone at the time said we were actually practicing a different kind of human ecology. We were trying to establish a different approach to how human beings could live together by providing free food, free housing, and free cultural events for a quarter of a million people in San Francisco. That is why some people viewed the Diggers as performing radical revolutionary and ecological acts. Paul Krassner[4] told me the first

time he saw the word *ecology* was in something I had written in a Digger essay.

Did you come up with the term bioregion?

No. the first time I saw the term *bioregion* it was used to describe an area of natural resources conservation, but I thought it could be used to denote a place where people live as well. So a bioregion just doesn't include plants and animals. A city and its urban environment are in a bioregion. Human beings are in a bioregion. The characteristics of a bioregion include unique plants and animals, watersheds, soils, land forms, climate, and other natural characteristics, as well as the adaptive ways people have lived in those places. The term *bioregion* can be used for human beings as well as a way of seeing what's around them.

I understand from my reading about bioregionalism that it's not a back-to-nature movement.

We are in nature. We are nature.

But you accept the fact that cities and urbanization are here.

Cities are currently opposed to nature.

So do you want to get rid of cities?

No.

Limit their growth?

There are a lot of ecologically valuable aspects to cities, for example, people in the country use a lot more gasoline. Say you live in the country and have a truck that gets twelve miles to the gallon, and you have to travel thirty miles a day to the store and back. That's a lot of fuel.

I feel confident, though, that bioregional precepts are eventually going to guide most people who live in rural regions because the demographics are changing. There are a lot of new settlers who are very ecologically aware. I feel confident that the rural areas will go bioregional. Suburbanites have every good reason to do the same as well because they are more directly attached to the resources they use than city people.

Could you give an example?

Take water use in the West. When urbanites in that part of the country consume water supplies, they often do a good job of conservation. But on the other hand, urbanites can be difficult. When I give a talk, I say, "I know you're not ordinary suburbanites. You are smarter than New Yorkers. But if you were a New Yorker and I was to ask you these questions, what would your answers be? Where does the water come from? Answer: 'The faucet.' Where does it go? 'The drain.' Where does the garbage go? 'Out.' Where does the food come from? 'The store.' What happens when you flush the toilet? 'It goes away.' Or as somebody said, 'Who cares?'" [Laughs] Okay, a lot of times that's the urban response to really critical ecological issues. And it is suicide or ecocide.

We just had fun laughing at it, but if that is the point of view of urbanites, forget the planet! Forget *Homo sapiens*. We aren't going to make it. You have to know where the water comes from. You have to know where it goes. You have to know where the food comes from. You have to be involved with those processes. No city in the U.S. has thorough gray-water recycling. No city has dual water systems. Every ship in the navy does, by the way, but very few homes do.

We are resources bound in the biosphere. It's a limited situation with X people and X resources. There is no new water. In fact, there is less water — clean water — all the time. So urbanites have got to be biospherically aware and have to start carrying out appropriate activities. This will make for much different-looking cities.

If this was done, how would, say, San Francisco look?

This city would be a series of villages, the way cities once were. And there would be rooftop gardens everywhere, gray-water systems, no single-passenger automobiles, and half the streets torn up. Forty percent of the land area of the average American city is covered with pavement for automobiles — that is, for streets, parking garages, and gas stations. Two-thirds of the land in downtown L.A. is used for automobiles. So cities would look different, and city people would be different. Their life-styles would be less nine-to-five in orientation and more like a couple of hours of this and couple of hours of that. There would be more neighborhood interaction, for example, in which people help to plant gardens or get involved with things like retrofitting buildings to save energy.

I would imagine one of the big challenges to the bioregional movement, especially here in the U.S., is to change a capitalist system that is based on consumerism and waste.

Both communism and capitalism are failed ideologies. The problem is the industrial growth economy. We have to change our thinking if humans are to live within the limits of the biosphere. We have to start practicing interdependence instead of independence and sustainability instead of growth. Bioregionalism is the key to the question "how do you think locally and act globally?"

The bioregional movement is actually a conservative movement, isn't it? What you are really trying to do is to return decision-making power to the people.

Liberal and *conservative* are very relative terms. Thomas Berry, an ecological who has been influenced by bioregionalism, is a real conservative, that is, he is a conservative because he wants to conserve resources. The radicals, he says, are the ones who want to clear cut the forests.

But one of your prime goals is to turn decision making away from the big corporate interests that run this country and back to the local community?

Right. The big urban planner in the U.S. isn't a city planning department.

It's Donald Trump.[5] He is the guy who says, "I want to do such and such." But the planning department says, "Wait! You can't do all that. You can only do two-thirds of that." So the planning department can modify what Trump or his fellow developers want to do, but the planning department doesn't carry different possibilities through. And citizens are almost never part of the planning process. We have charades where the power structure holds meetings and says, "Now we will have citizen input." But it doesn't mean a damn thing. Financiers, construction companies, labor unions . . . those are the ones that make the decisions.

How strong is the bioregional movement? In addition to San Francisco and northern California, where are some of the other major bioregional centers of operation?
   The Pacific Northwest—Seattle and Portland—are big centers. Even New York State and Chicago have bioregional groups. . . . There are centers in other parts of the world, too, particularly in Italy, Spain, England, South America, and Australia.

How does the Planet Drum Foundation fit into the bioregional movement?
   We are the mother networking group for the bioregional movement. We publish directories and other publications, teach workshops, and give lectures and presentations. And you've seen all the people who have come through here since we sat down to talk. One of them is from Vancouver Island, British Columbia. He's a forest activist and is also involved in restoration ecology. People call us all the time, too, to find out about information resources and to be put on mailing lists. Our biggest role is to present positions about the bioregional concept to show how it applies to various activities and to state its long-term goals.

You say "establish a position on bioregionalism." How does that come about?
   When the state of California adopted the term *bioregionalism*, I went to Sacramento and told them that it was a cultural concept. It's not a new natural resources designation for only managers and agencies to play around with. The Shasta Bioregion is different from what they were calling bioregions. They had six bioregions in what we call Shasta. I said, "Bioregionalism is an ongoing cultural phenomena. It's our life; therefore, it's a cultural concept."

When did the idea of bioregionalism originate?
   Planet Drum was founded in 1973, but it took until 1978 to get a good definition of *bioregionalism*. It's in an article titled "Reinhabiting California," which I coauthored with Raymond F. Dasmann. Ray is a world class ecologist. We wanted to publish an earlier essay of mine in *The Ecologist*. They read the essay but didn't understand it because it was advanced beyond their point of view. Ray said he and I could rewrite a couple of things and the magazine would accept it. I was honored because I'm an activist, and he is a recognized scientist.

*The [Bill] Clinton–[Albert] Gore ticket just got elected to office. People assume
they will be more pro-environment. Will the change in presidential administration help the bioregional movement?*

I'm not an uncritical fan of the [Clinton] administration. I think it's
primarily a management-oriented group. They are process people, facilitators.
They are probably not going to divide all the government departments with
all their jurisdictions into watersheds. It could be done, by the way. In fact,
FDR [President Franklin Delano Roosevelt] almost did it. He was going to set
up all the major watersheds in the country into units for dealing with water,
energy, and agriculture.

Let's talk about yourself. Where were you born and educated?

I was born in New York and entered the University of Florida at
Gainesville in 1954.

What subject did you major in?

Psychology, but I didn't go to classes faithfully. I read novels instead and
eventually dropped out of school.

That was during the height of the McCarthy period?

During the height of the McCarthy period when we were suspended for
putting up signs that said "Integrate in 1958."

You were suspended for doing that?

Somebody was, but I wasn't. I did put up signs, though. The editor of the
school newspaper was a McCarthyite and he tried to get professors to take him
home and have drinks and make homosexual advances so they could be kicked
out of school. At one blow, we lost about eighty percent of the best professors
we ever had at the University of Florida.[6] [Laughs] Wap!

*So McCarthyism had a chilling effect on the University of Florida like it did at
other schools?*

Yes, for a certain group of students, it had a very chilling effect. It was like
apartheid as far as the social relationship between blacks and whites was concerned. You have to recall that a lot of people went through a tremendous
Calvinistic period during the Second World War. Many went without sexual
partners for four years. Women went to work in factories. My mother was saving grease at home for war drives.

For the people that did that, the fifties were a chance to get a car, a house,
a washing machine, a grey flannel suit, and an office job. They were straight,
really straight, and if you weren't in that groove, it was almost as if you were
a traitor who was betraying your country. We grew up in that atmosphere, but
it started to crack up.

How did that happen?

I think Elvis Presley was a symbol of how this happened. Elvis is black
music with a white face. During the fifties in the South, there were only two

types of music to listen to: country and western and "race" music. It was called "race" music — apartheid of the airwaves. But the most interesting musicians were on the Race station. You know, all that heavy duty Mama Mae Thornton rock and roll. "You ain't nothing but a hound dog...." Then Elvis sang it. Elvis the Pelvis — a male figure.

I remember the first time I was ever around an Elvis Presley concert. I didn't actually go in to it, but I remember the girls — screaming, hysterical, fourteen-year-old girls. I dropped a girl off at one of Elvis's concerts and picked her up later. She had literally peed in her pants at the concert. It was sexual apotheosis. It was camouflaged integration, even though he sounded like a Southerner, acted like a Southerner. He could have been a bigot for all I know. But he was liberating for teenagers.

After an Elvis concert, they came home and said, "Why are we wearing these stupid looking clothes?" I want to wear a leather jacket and look like Marlon Brando in *The Wild One*.[7] I don't want to do this anymore." Young people became curious. Reefer? What's reefer? Reefer[8] gets us high. What's high? [Laughs] Sex, drugs, and rock and roll: each one of these categories had major cultural breakthroughs.

So you dropped out of the University of Florida. What did you do? Did you go to work?

I hitchhiked around the country. I went to Chicago, San Francisco, and L.A. A small underground culture called North Beach was rooted in San Francisco, and the police were resenting it. [Laughs] Musicians played on the sidewalk. Poets actually read in the coffeehouses. Shops had signs like "Co-existence Bagel Shop." Co-existence Bagel Shop. [Laughs] In Florida, the sheets — the KKK — would have come out. Communists! [Laughs] It was like heaven.

What did you do to support yourself in San Francisco?

I had a hard time getting a job because I was still in my teens. I lived with friends and had no money. At the time, there was a draft, even though there wasn't a war, and opposing it was very difficult, given the climate of the country. I wasn't equipped to do it, so I went into the army to get rid of that obligation. When I got out of the army, I went to live in New York. But while in the army — this was the early sixties — I became involved with the civil rights movement.

What were some of the things you were doing as part of the movement?

I was in the second sit-in at Thalheimer's department store in Richmond, Virginia, even though I was in the army at the time. I went to Thalheimer's in civilian clothes, and I was the only white person there. At that sit-in, they used German shepherd dogs to rip dresses off young girls. You should have seen that, man! South Africa doesn't look any different than that!

What was the reaction of your superiors to your civil rights activities?

You know, I falsified my background when I went into the army and gave myself credit for a huge number of college credit hours in statistics, a subject that doesn't actually interest me. I think I claimed twelve hours of statistics. [Laughs] The military did a search of its records to find people with certain qualifications, and I ended up doing some sort of nutty morale study involving statistics and personnel in and around the Pentagon.

That morale test was invented by some of my superiors who had doctorates in psychology and, like me, were getting rid of their military obligation. You know who scored highest on the morale test? Paratroopers in the stockade. Jailed paratroopers had the highest score of anybody. [Laughs] It turns out they were the red, white, and blue guys, even though they had gotten into fights. Who has the best morale? The trained animals do. [Laughs]

Anyway, I felt guilty about being in the army while the sit-ins were going on. I'm absolutely sure where I stand on race and human rights. So I became a part of the underground movement that challenged that.

So you left the army, went back to New York and got involved with the civil rights activities.

Civil rights, black activists, and black culture.

How did it come about that you returned to San Francisco?

I had a strange experience. I hallucinated a message to myself that said, "If you don't know who you are, someone else will tell you." So I decided to drop out of the straight life completely. I hitchhiked out to Detroit with a friend of mine who was an artist and a woman friend whom I had met in New York. We eventually ended up going our separate ways. I made it to Whidbey Island in Puget Sound. Then I jumped a lumber freight train in Portland. When the train would slow down, I would get out and suck ice for water.

The train ended up in the Albany freight yard, which is next door to Berkeley. The year was 1964, the pre–Free Speech period. I ran into some people and stayed with them for a while. I went to Mexico where I went a little crazy from culture shock. I came back, lived in Haight Ashbury, and got a job. I got involved with the scene that was emerging. I took LSD there.

Can you recall the experience?

I was with a woman. We fell in love taking LSD together. So I remember the experience very nicely.

Was LSD the first psychedelic drug you took?

I had taken some very powerful psychedelic drugs before. The first was peyote.

In David Zane Mairowitz's book The Radical Soap Opera,[9] *which you suggested I read in preparation for this interview, Mairowitz said that LSD had a profound influence on the Digger movement. Was that true?*

[Pause] Mairowitz knew that the Diggers were theater.

Yes, a lot of Diggers were actors. Were you one?

I was mostly a director and playwright. I invented the term *guerrilla theater*. Ronnie Davis, the director of the San Francisco Mime Troupe, gave me credit for the phrase in an essay he wrote. We [Diggers] developed a kind of play where we would arrive at a location and start performing without telling people they were going to be watching a performance.

I wrote one titled *Center Man*, which had an American Army MP bossing a bunch of prisoners around. I remember doing that play in the middle of Sproul Plaza, Berkeley. We arrived in a VW van, got out, and the MP marched the prisoners over to a certain area where he made them pick up cigarette butts and brutalized them. Then this play breaks out, which has dialogue between the performers, and the people watching didn't know whether it was theater or not.

There was an ROTC officer in the audience who actually congratulated the MP for the way he was handling his men. [Laughs] He thought it was real. The students watching the play, of course, were appalled. They were students on their way to study the Greeks and Chaucer.[10] Suddenly, they see this supposedly brutal scene.

After the play was over, some of the people just left without applauding. Others said: "Stay! stay! We're going for a cop." [Laughs] I couldn't believe it. [Laughs] We did that kind of theater in different situations. Later, people thought of guerrilla theater as cartooning propaganda stuff. But I thought guerrilla theater could be a weapon, not a tool, that could blow people's minds.

Jerry Rubin was there at Berkeley while this was going on. He was involved with the Free Speech movement. Later he went to Washington to testify dressed up as a revolutionary soldier.[11] Did you influence him?

I didn't know him, but the one I had influence over was Abbie Hoffman.[12]

In what way?

Right from the beginning, Hoffman caught on to what we were doing. He was at an SDS convention in Denton, Michigan, which we [the Diggers] took over for a couple of hours. He watched our guerrilla theater, and you could see him being transformed on the spot.

While the other people were saying, "Get them out of here. They are disruptive." Hoffman said, "You don't know what they're doing. You don't know what's going on here. You just don't get it." I'm not a fan of Abbie Hoffman, but I believe he knew what we were doing because he had a little background working with black people. He had gone South and worked with SNCC. So in spite of being as straight as the other people at the meeting, he had enough background to say to himself, "Hey, wait a minute. There's white hipness going on here. That's what this is. These guys are doing what the black activists have done to the old black establishment." I could see his wheels turning. He said, "Wow! I can't believe it. It's finally happening." So he was converted.

Do you use guerrilla theater today in the bioregional movement?

Well, Judy Goldhaft is a veteran of all that, and she does performances that use very skillful mime and narrative to get things across that are associated with bioregionalism.

So you are still using your sixties experience to help you as an activist today?

Sure. I'm no longer a performer, but I use what I learned as a performer to make my talks better. I can work audiences.

Could you talk about how the Diggers got started and evolved?

The seminal event was when Emmett Grogan and Billy Murcutt watched the Fillmore riots in San Francisco. That's when black people rioted.[13] They asked each other: "What is the white equivalent of that? If we were those black people in white society, what would we be?"

They were both in the Mime Troupe and a guerrilla play of mine. One of the two had read a book on anarchism and came across the Diggers, who were the Winstanley group during the 1600s enclosure movement in England. They were peasants who were shoved off their land, went into the cities and towns, and dug up the commons to plant vegetables and so were called Diggers. Billy and Emmett thought that "Digger" was such a great name. It meant like "I dig it."

The Diggers believed in sharing and in communal ownership of property. The idea was: What's the appropriate Digger model that could be used for a quarter of a million people who have come to Haight-Ashbury and have tuned in, turned on, and dropped out? Emmett and Billy nailed a piece of paper to the door of the building where the Mime troupe performed. It was like the ninety-nine theses.[14] It said things like "fuck money, fuck property, fuck the Mime Troupe, fuck the president, fuck the protesters"—just a list of negatives.

I thought the Digger ideal could be applied to guerrilla theater. We could perform guerrilla theater free in the parks. The thing was to act out a situation that described how we thought the world should be—a utopia. I called this "life acting." There would be two precepts—one was "Everything is free," and the other, "Do your own thing."

I didn't invent those things. I just put the formulation together. The Mime Troupe had about seventy-five members at the time and had grown enormously. We took about twenty of them with us. Peter Coyote,[15] Emmett Grogan, and a lot of women—Jane Lapiner, Judy Goldhaft, and Ann Linden—split to start the Diggers. A lot of the recruits were seventeen- and eighteen-year-old college dropouts, who had recently arrived in San Francisco and were completely into serving the vision. We started doing a lot of different activities.

Today, some former female activists from that period say the movement was sexist, and its male leaders were unaware of women's rights and women's needs. You said that you weren't like that . . .

No, I didn't say that. I said I was aware that there was a feminist imperative.

But was there a lot of sexism in the movement?

You should really ask the women that question. But I would suspect yes. When men call women "chicks" and talk about "scoring" as we did, you have sexism. The Beatles were sexist. Listen to their music.

And so were the Rolling Stones.

Even more so. And a lot of black music was sexist and homophobic. But let me tell you about one of the interesting things about the Haight-Ashbury scene. A lot of gays who weren't out of the closet were able to use the hippy scene to their advantage. They saw it was possible to wear something like a dress without getting their heads bashed in. [Laughs]

You said the Diggers began to undertake a lot of activities. What were some of them?

Talk about human ecology! We were serving people food in the park, delivering food to the communes, creating communes, liberating buildings... We had a free store. We held events for up to ten thousand people in the park every weekend. We were hitting on all the basic human needs—food, shelter, water, culture...

Mairowitz says you were not interested in overthrowing the system per se, but rather burrowing radical enclaves within it. Is that true?

Oh, yes, definitely. I had been in the civil rights movement and was against the war and very much for human and civil rights. I was an early supporter of gay rights and feminism. But I thought society per se wasn't going to change, only parts of it, aspects of it. I felt that part of the counterculture revolution should certainly be a group of people who were willing to act out the furtherest vision of what society might be.

And according to Mairowitz, protest in itself wasn't that important to the Diggers.

Well, we did protest some, but I have always been interested in being proactive. In my view, the conflict between the New Left and the Diggers and [between] the SDS and the Diggers has been exaggerated. I think a lot of people in the New Left were simply squares. They weren't into sex, drugs, and rock and roll.

You mean members of groups like Progressive Labor?

They were strict Calvinists—Puritans, in fact. They just didn't understand what we were about. I'm a feeling person. I love art and esthetic values. Those people weren't even into art. You couldn't talk to them about what [John] Steinbeck wrote.[16] They were fundamentalist dumb reds. [Laughs] A great expression. [Laughs]

[Laughs] You did get a lot of criticism from activists who weren't dumb reds. They thought the Diggers' brand of activism dangerous to the movement.

Consider the source. They said that about everything. But here we have activists who were unesthetically inclined — squares — fighting for the rights of people who have outrageous music, do dirty dancing as a norm, smoke pot — if they can get their hands on it — and dress flamboyantly. To me it was like Protestantism!

Or Southern fundamentalism.

Which is worse. It was like, "What church are you going to today?" Not, "Are you going to church?" [Laughs]

A lot of hucksters came into the movement, and you had a lot of fun with them, didn't you?

If you are in a Digger frame of mind, hip merchants and political protesters are on the same level. Political protesters are going to go about Calvinistically trying to change things that aren't going to change that much. The hip merchants are looking for the "experience" and trying to make a commodity from it. From a Digger point of view, there is little difference between the two.

This is coming from a guy who is into politics. "Berg is going to tell you about civil rights, the [Vietnam] war. He's a pain in the ass." But when the Black Panthers started up, we related to them immediately. No problem. They got their "free breakfast for school kids" idea from us. We told them that they ought to be doing it. "You guys got panache. You can do it. Show how fucked up the system is!" They did.

So the Diggers had a good relationship with the Black Panthers?

I remember when we made a trip over to Oakland and met with Bobby Seale. Bobby was in a pin-striped blue suit, really dressed. He looked at us closely. We were a ragtag bunch, looking like bums or winos, because we were in our hippy outfits — torn jeans, vests, long hair.

We brought him a case of sole. We said to him, "We want to talk to you about forming an alliance. We believe in what you are doing, but we also want to give you this case of fish." He looked at the fish and said, "What kind of awful looking fish is that." We said, "It's sole." He said, "Hey, man. That's not sole. [Laughs] Sole is filleted." But we said, "Yes, it is. It comes from that." He said, "No kidding? It actually comes from that ugly looking thing with both eyes on one side of its body." Talk about nonecological. [Laughs] He didn't even know what the fish looked like. Very urban was Bobby. [Laughs]

[Laughs] There was a cultural difference, but you Diggers got along with the Black Panthers.

Years later, Huey Newton came to Emmett's [Grogan] wake. And I always liked Bobby Seale. I always thought he was an interesting person. He had a lot of style.

He sure did. He came out with a book titled Barbecuing with Bobby. *[Laughs]*
[Laughs] This is a guy who came out with a book on barbecuing and had
never seen a live sole in his life.

How long did the Digger movement last?
Until the summer solstice of '69. We occupied the city hall steps from the
spring equinox to the summer solstice.[17]

Why did the Diggers end? Was it a conscious decision or did it just fizzle out?
Two things happened: The bloom came off the rose. It was very hard to
live out a thing like the Diggers for two years without any break. And we did
it for three years actually. Secondly, the whole psychedelic movement started
to collapse. The high point of vision, optimism, had peaked and started to pass.

*People started to get burned out. It wasn't just the Diggers, was it? It was the
whole movement.*
Yes, very true. That's a good point. A little known fact is that the police
heavily oppressed the Haight-Ashbury neighborhood. They made Haight
Street one way, which is guaranteed to have cars moving at forty-five miles an
hour. They put in mercury vapor lights that burned all night with an eery
orange glow. And they started to send police cars into the neighborhood to
pick up kids, to ask them their age, show their IDs, and so forth. So people
were hassled.

We moved the Diggers onto the city hall steps and occupied them for
three months, giving out food to city employees, washing our hair in the foun-
tain, reading poetry on the steps. We made a film about that titled *Nowsreal*.
We made a decision that the Diggers would end when the event ended on the
summer solstice. On the last day, we put "San Francisco is Entering into Eter-
nity" on a theater marquee. We held events in five different parts of the city,
watched the sun go down, and asked each other: "What are we going to do
now?"

What did you do?
After that, I ended up on a commune in northern California for a year.
Then Judy Goldhaft and I went across the country with our two children and
a group of former Diggers. We split off from that group when we got to Pennsylvania and went to Maine, where I talked to the poet Allen Van Newkirk.

He had discovered this term *bioregion*. But he meant it as a natural
resources area. I wanted to use it as a social idea. He told me he was through
with social ideas. He had been supportive of the Newark riots and was wanted
by the police. He went into exile in Canada, very burnt out on politics.

Then I heard there was going to be an UN conference on the environment in '72. I went there and told the conference organizers and delegates that
I was a representative of the land-based North American communes group.
Then I came back to San Francisco in 1973 and started the Planet Drum Foundation as a way to communicate with all the people that I had been involved

with and to stimulate discussion about what was an appropriate social form for living on the planet together. It didn't seem to be the nation state.

Slowly, biregionalism came to be defined as including people. Ecologists got involved. Gary Snyder[18] got involved. He uses a lot of our language today. *Rehabilitation* is my word, and he used it as the title of an essay. But we have been so busy doing things — salmon restoration, Green City program — that we weren't thinking about influencing the wider public. Now, of course, these ideas are much more accessible to the general public.

Is it because more people today are environmentally conscious and so are more receptive to your ideas?

Yeah, but, Ron, you shouldn't ask me why people do things. I'm just saying we were ahead of our time for at least ten years, and during the last three years, there has been a lot of catching up to our positions. I'm just glad.

Do you ever get nostalgic for the Digger part of your life?

The hardest thing about all that is that I've not remained as tight with everybody from that time as I was with them then, although, of course, there are some who I do still share things with. When they are in San Francisco, they will stay here. They don't have to call. And I can do the same thing if I'm in their neighborhood. If it wasn't for the Digger group being an extended family, we wouldn't have been able to do Planet Drum Foundation.

What I miss most is the tremendous camaraderie we had. We were outlaws, outside of society. We were completely self-reliant and tremendously interdependent in a way that was beautiful. We covered for each other when we got busted. We got each other out of jail. I must have bailed out at least a dozen people. Our family eventually grew and grew to include more than two hundred people. We had good relationships, and for that not to be the case today is a loss. I have nostalgia, not for the period, but for the camaraderie.

What is the legacy of the Diggers? How would you assess the group's place in American history?

I think everything I'm doing today comes from the Diggers. I'm not involved with money. I'm director of an educational foundation that has less than $100,000-a-year budget. The ideas of the Planet Drum Foundation — bioregionalism, rehabitation, finding ways to restore natural systems, finding ways to fulfill human needs — are the ideas of the Diggers. The Planet Drum Foundation and all it stands for is the implicit ecology of the Diggers made explicit. You can't have a social movement anymore that doesn't have ecological consciousness at its center. It just has to be that way now.

8

Noam Chomsky
Radical Intellectual

> It was a very different culture in those days. If the American peo-
> ple read today about the U.S. bombing a country like it did Viet-
> nam in the sixties, they would get very upset about it. But in
> those days, people didn't bat an eyelash. You couldn't get two
> people to sit in a room and talk about Vietnam. There has been
> a big cultural change since the sixties, and it's a great improve-
> ment.

Until the early 1960s, Noam Chomsky had the academic life of a scholar-
intellectual laid out for him. Then his life changed radically when he joined
the protest movement and became prominent as an outspoken critic of the
Vietnam War. His work as a member of the steering committee of RESIST (a
national movement that counseled young men against the draft), his participation in such important demonstrations as the October 1967 protest march
against the draft, and his involvement in the trial of Dr. Benjamin Spock as
an unindicted coconspirator made Chomsky one of the most prominent
figures in the New Left during the sixties.

Time has not tempered Chomsky's radicalism. Today, he is one of the
world's most interesting intellectuals. As a scholar, he has transformed traditional thinking in his chosen professional field, linguistics, by challenging traditional ideas about language development. As an activist and writer, he has
provided one of the most penetrating and eloquent analyses of global politics
and U.S. foreign policy.

Norman Mailer, who shared a jail cell with Chomsky after a demonstration at the Pentagon, described him as a "slim, sharp-featured man with an
ascetic expression and an air of gentle and absolute moral integrity." Many
who admire Chomsky would agree that this is an apt description of the radical
intellectual.

Chomsky was born into a scholarly Jewish environment on December 7,
1928. His father had emigrated to the United States from a small village in the
Ukraine to avoid the draft in Russia. Chomsky was a precocious youngster
who, at age 10, could read and understand the proofs of his father's edition of

133

the thirteenth-century *Hebrew Grammar.* After earning his Ph.D. from the University of Pennsylvania in 1955, the young scholar began teaching at the Massachusetts Institute of Technology (MIT) as an Institute Professor in the Department of Linguistics and Philosophy.

It was not until a decade later, when the Vietnam War began to escalate, that Chomsky's interest in radical politics began in earnest. His classic essay "The Responsibility of the Intellectual," which was first published in *Mosaic* in June 1966 and then expanded into an article in the February 23, 1967, issue of the *New York Review of Books* and reprinted in his book of essays *American Power and the New Mandarins,* helped define the sixties peace movement. Chomsky characterized the New Mandarins as the liberal intellectuals who helped construct the intellectual justification for their role in serving the giant corporations and federal government; he charged that they shared a major responsibility for the Vietnam War.

For Chomsky, the Vietnam War was no grotesque aberration in American history but, rather, was in the imperialist tradition of a nation that pursues its self-interest as ruthlessly and violently as any great power in history. His anti-establishment critique has meant that Chomsky has been effectively shut out from participation in any discussion, debate, or critique of U.S. foreign policy. The mainstream media rarely reviews his books. He is unwelcome on the op-ed pages of such influential newspapers as the *New York Times* and the *Washington Post,* and he never appears as an expert commentator on any of the establishment radio or television shows. No wonder then that the average American doesn't know too much about Professor Noam Chomsky.

But, as this interview found out, this blacklisting hasn't blunted Chomsky's determination to continue dissecting U.S. foreign policy and challenging the conventional political and economic orthodoxies of our time.

＊　　＊　　＊

Did you vote in the '92 presidential elections?
　　Yeah, I voted.

You don't seem too enthusiastic?
　　I voted more against [George] Bush than for anybody.

Does anybody mean the other mainstream candidate, Bill Clinton?
　　I voted for Clinton, not necessarily because I approve of his position, but because I think Bush would be worse.

How would you judge Clinton's performance so far?
　　Some of his rhetoric is in the right direction, although the policies are continuing more or less the same. He has recognized that the problems of the American economy are structural, and he can't fix them with bandaids. He understands that. The impact of the Reagan years has put an extreme burden

Noam Chomsky (photo credit: Donna Coveney/MIT News Office).

on the poor and on future generations, which is not going to be easy to over-come. He recognizes that state interventions in the economy are not going to be confined by the forms preferred by radical Reaganite statist conservatives. You can't hide things behind the Pentagon anymore.

Can anything be done to alleviate the serious social, political, and economic problems facing this country?

There are some marginal differences between Bush and Clinton, but they are not enormous. They roughly have the same commitments. They differ on how best to provide for the needs of the corporate sector, although there might be some openings in the Clinton administration for some of the other sectors.

One thing that is significant in my mind is that another four years of court packing by ultrastatist reactionaries would be extremely harmful to civil liberties in this country. The Reagan and Bush administrations say they are conservatives trying to give a right-wing thrust to the courts. But they are actually statist reactionaries who believe that the courts should control you. That's exactly what's happening in the courts.

And that is quite ironic because conservatives are always preaching about how they are against big government and the intrusion of the state into the lives of citizens.

Yes, but the Reaganites are not conservatives. I'm much more conservative than they are. Any old time conservative would turn over in his grave if he could see how the term *conservative* was used in the 1980s.

It seems that with each presidential election, sound bites, and not the presentation of substantive issues, are becoming more and more important. I know you've written extensively about the impact of the media on society. Could you elaborate on what effect that development is having on the American system?

In one sense, it's serving a useful effect. It's revealing that the system is essentially vacuous. We are becoming like what we derisively call "a banana republic."

Take the election in Honduras, an election that George Bush described as "an inspiring example of democracy in action." Well, they had two candidates, both representative of landowners and right-wing businessmen. There were no issues because they agreed on everything, so they spent their time throwing mud at each other. It was like a circus.

We are getting more like that. The people who own and run this country want to distort and marginalize the public. They are deeply antidemocratic. The idea that the public should have some role in anything that is happening is an idea foreign to both American liberals and conservative right-wing reactionaries. Yes, the circus type atmosphere in which sound bites and mudslinging predominates has been the style in American politics.

But do you really think the average American buys your analysis? He would probably say, "That's not true. The U.S. is the freest country on earth."

No, he wouldn't. The polls show that the level of alienation, the feeling that the "institutions do not work for me," is at the highest level it's ever been. The Harris polling organization has done a study of this every year for years. The Harris Poll shows that the sense of alienation reached its highest level last year [1991].

About two-thirds of the public feels alienated from every institution. About eighty-three percent respond that the economic system is inherently unfair. You wouldn't find figures like that in Stalinist Russia. I think that was the reason for the growth of the Perot phenomenon. He came out of nowhere and was the leading candidate, even though he had no positions on any topic. A candidate could come from Mars and the American public would vote for him. They [the American electorate] realize the American system is totally bankrupt.

You are one of the most severe and outspoken critics of U.S. foreign policy, and what you have said so far shows that. But you have been shut out of the mainstream press. In fact, I think the only time I have heard you in an interview in the mainstream [broadcast] media was on National Public Radio. Does that frustrate you?

National Public Radio . . . [Laughs] I was on for five minutes in the sixties and maybe an equivalent amount of time in the eighties. But no, I don't. I do have constant access to the media in Canada, Europe, Australia, and other countries. But if I did have access to the mainstream media, I might begin to wonder if I'm doing something wrong. Am I being so supportive of power that they are willing to let me have access to the media? I would begin to question what I'm doing.

I guess the reason you haven't been invited to present your views in the mainstream media is because you are considered a "radical." Are you comfortable with that label?

A radical is someone who tries to get at the root of things. That's what I try to do.

How would you describe the role of the radical in the American political context?

In the tradition of Thomas Paine and the better part of Thomas Jefferson.[1] In modern times, Eugene Debs[2] . . . and other people who have done something decent for this country.

Were your views on politics always outside the mainstream?

Yes, ever since I've been ten years old.

How did your family background shape your political views?

I grew up in the Depression. My family on both sides were immigrants. My parents were teachers and very much a part of the Jewish community. They were [Franklin Delano] Roosevelt Democrats, which is what you would expect. One wing of my family, my father's side, was extremely conservative Jewish. In fact, they lived in the seventeenth century. The other side, which I gravitated toward, was Jewish working class and mostly unemployed. They had little formal education in the sense of going to school, but were very educated people. In fact, that part of my family life was the most lively intellectual atmosphere I've experienced in my life. That includes my years at Harvard. They read and went to concerts and represented every kind and brand of radical politics. That had an influence on me.

Were you a part of the Jewish cultural tradition?

Oh, yes. I was a part of an immigrant community that hung on to that tradition.

But you have been described as a self-hating Jew because of your outspoken criticism of Israel and your support of the Palestinian cause. Has that criticism bothered you?

It bothered me when my parents were alive because they lived in the Jewish community and were hurt by all the slime and mud that was thrown at me. They felt hurt by it even though they agreed with my position. In fact, in Israel, my position is not particularly controversial.

The Jewish community in the U.S. is like other ethnic communities in the U.S. For reasons I don't entirely understand, ethnic communities in this country regress toward chauvinistic and fanatical aspects of the original culture. That's apparently true in the Jewish community. In the techniques it uses, the Jewish community these days acts like old-fashioned Stalinists. They are constantly dividing the world up into three categories. You got to follow the straight right-wing party line in Israel. If you do that, you are okay and fit the first category. But if you don't, you are either one of two categories: Jewish or non–Jewish. By definition, if you are non–Jewish, you are antisemite. If you are a Jew, you are a self-hating Jew. Okay, that takes care of the world.

Once upon a time in this country, the Jewish Anti-Defamation League[3] used to be a civil rights organization. Now it's more like a Jewish Stalinist organization. It heaps piles of slime and fabrications on people who are "not loyal to Israel." They circulate all kinds of lies and fabrications just like the old Communist party.

So you have been cut off from the Jewish community.

Well, that's their decision. If they want to cut me off, that's fine. I can't lead my life for them. I don't belong to any organizations.

Why not?

I don't know of any to belong to. At one time I did. I was one of the founders of RESIST during the 1960s and the anti–Vietnam War movement.

Counseling young people?

It began as a support organization for the antiwar resistance and then it expanded to become a support group for all sorts of activism.

Could you recall how you got involved in the antiwar movement?

I got involved in 1964 as an individual who was very much opposed to Kennedy's war, which used to be Eisenhower's war. I reached the point where I decided I couldn't keep quiet any longer, and I started to give talks wherever

I could—churchs, peace groups... It was extremely hard because nobody cared. You just couldn't find an audience.

That was before the teach-ins, right?

Yeah, when sometimes four people would show up—the organizers and a couple of drunks off the street.

What kept you going and wanting to speak up?

It got so horrible over there [Vietnam] that I couldn't look at myself in the mirror anymore. I thought there was absolutely no hope of any political opposition to the war developing. What was going on over there was no secret. One could read the front page of the *New York Times* and find out that the U.S. was bombing South Vietnam. It was a very different culture in those days.

If the American people read today about the U.S. bombing a country like it did Vietnam in the sixties, they would get very upset about it. But in those days, people didn't bat an eyelash. You couldn't get two people to sit in a room and talk about Vietnam. There has been a big cultural change since the sixties, and it's a great improvement.

By 1965, I was involved with trying to organize tax resistance and had refused to pay taxes. By 1966 and '67, I was involved practically in every kind of activism. There was plenty to do.

Did the U.S. government put pressure on you because of your refusal to pay taxes?

Not on the tax issue, which kind of surprised me because I was one of the organizers of the tax resistance campaign. I expected it, but nothing happened. I knew the FBI kept a file on me, and I was on Nixon's enemies list. I was an unindicted coconspirator in the Spock trial.[4] In fact, on the first day of his trial, they said I was next in line to be prosecuted. The only reason I wasn't was because the FBI was so incompetent it picked all the wrong people to prosecute.

How did it come about that you became an undindited coconspirator in the Spock trial?

It was a classic example of the total incompetence of the U.S. government. The national organization was very public. We did little in secret in our efforts to support people in the armed forces. Our people would get in the town hall and say, "We are going to do this." So it was an open and shut case. The question was: Who is organizing the resistance? They could never figure that out, although it was public.

The authorities zeroed in on two incidents. The first occurred in New York, where an organization called "Call to Resist Illegitimate Authority" held a news conference. The other incident was at the Justice Department where a demonstration occurred.

Anybody involved in those two things was considered a coconspirator, except they got people mixed up. In fact, during the whole trial, the FBI couldn't get the Jewish names right. All during the trial, I was confused with Herschel

Kaminsky. The guy they were after was Art Rasko, but the guy they picked up was Marcus Raskin. They didn't look at all like each other. The whole thing was like a comic opera.

Ben Spock and Bill Coffin were asked to come everytime we had a public event because they were visible and brought the press. They were quite happy to show up. The only reason I wasn't picked up was because, while everybody was walking into the Justice Department with their draft cards, I was haranguing the crowd outside and couldn't go in with them. In fact, I was the guy who brought down the draft cards from Boston where they had been collected. But the FBI investigating was totally incompetent and couldn't figure any of this stuff out.

What was the outcome of the trial?

They were convicted, but it was overthrown on appeal. The judge was out of his mind and made all kinds of errors. In the midst of all this, the Tet Offensive happened. It changed everything. After Tet, the corporate sector decided the war had to end because it was becoming too costly, and they basically fired Lyndon Johnson and told the government that it had to start pulling out of Vietnam.

Now that had a big effect and made for an enormous change. Up until December 1967, everybody was a hawk. Starting in February 1968, everybody who was not a dove was saying they had been a dove all along. One of the effects of this was that the government gave up. A classic example was [U.S. Attorney General] Ramsey Clark, who prosecuted the case against the draft resisters, but now he turned against the war.

So, in your opinion, the Tet Offensive was the watershed?

Absolutely! No question about it. It changed the country's elite totally. If you look at the Kennedy intellectuals like [Arthur] Schlesinger[5] and that crowd, they have two versions of what happened [with Vietnam]. There are the memoirs they wrote before the Tet Offensive, and the books they wrote after it; they are radically different. In the books before Tet, there is no hint that anybody wanted to withdraw from Vietnam. The books after Tet are full of explanations about how Kennedy had plans to withdraw from Vietnam. The game was over by that date, of course, and they wanted to cover their asses.

As the war got out of control for the U.S. war machine, U.S. officials constantly lied about their actions in Vietnam...

I don't think the military lied much, to tell you the truth. That's where I disagree with a lot of people.

But isn't that why a lot of Americans got disillusioned with the war?

I don't think the military or even the government lied that much. The idea that the government lied and military lied is really press impression. Take the secret war in Cambodia or the secret war in Laos that Nixon was attacked for. Were the bombings secret? I knew all about them.

But the average American didn't know about the secret bombings?

Yeah, that's because the press wasn't reporting what it knew. Until this day, we don't know a lot about the secret bombing of Cambodia, for a very simple reason — journalists like Sidney Schanberg, who is supposed to be "the conscience of the press," was sitting in Phonm Penh, refusing to interview the million and half refugees who were literally across the street.[6] That's why we don't know about the secret war. It's not because of government lying.

That's an interesting analysis because the people who said we should have won the war blame the press for what happened in Vietnam.

The press was totally servile. I wrote a couple of hundred pages about this in a book called *Manufacturing Consent*,[7] which deals with the media's coverage of the Vietnam War. To this day, the American press supports state power. Take a recent news story, for example: A few days ago in the *New York Times*, there was an article about the Emperor of Japan going to China and how he hadn't been forthcoming enough in admitting Japan was guilty for its actions against China in World War II. To the left of that story was another one about Vietnam and how George Bush had said he was going to insist on retribution against Vietnam for all the so-called crimes committed and how we want them to come clean finally.

Speak of war guilt! If the Emperor of Japan had gone to China and said, "We forgive you guys for allowing us to invade you, but we insist on retribution," that would be regarded as a reversion to Naziism. That's the front page of the *New York Times*, and nobody batted an eyelash. Americans accept that kind of thinking.

The elites [in this country] accept that we are Nazis, that we want to attack a country, wipe it out, and destroy a couple of million people. The U.S. even insists on retribution! Find someone who questions that. That's a good example of the servility of the press. I don't think there is any totalitarian state in history that ever achieved this.

You have written that the U.S. has never ended its efforts to win the war in Vietnam and that this is an extension of what the U.S. has been trying to do since 1945 — establish a world imperial economy dominated by U.S. capital.

That's not even arguable. It's stated in the open record . . . in the public documents.

What have been the consequences?

It's a long story that began about 1945. The U.S. elite knew at the time that they were in a position of unimaginable power that had no historical precedent. They wanted to organize the world in the interests of the forces they represented, which is the U.S. corporate sector.

The first step was to reconstruct the industrial societies of Japan and Germany, which were under U.S. control. The industrial societies, including the minor ones like France and England, had to be returned to conservative business rule. That meant anti–Fascist collaborators, including outright war criminals, had to be put in power. The anti–Fascist resistance had to be destroyed, which was done all over the world.

The labor movement had to undermined . . . things of that kind. That was done everywhere, including throughout the Third World. The next step was to organize that restructured world. The U.S. was the only productive economy at that point, and we had a huge surplus of goods and nobody to buy them. The U.S. elite worried about the dollar gap. How could we overcome that, they thought? One way was to implement the Marshall Plan. Another way was to reconstruct the old traditional colonial relationships so there could be triangular trading patterns. The U.S. would use dollars to purchase the raw material from the colonies. So, if we bought, say, rubber from Malaysia, Britain would get the dollars because they would sell that country something or other, and then Britain would use the dollars to buy manufacturing exports.

That was the rough idea. The Third World had to be returned to the state it was before World War II. It's in the documentary record. Africa had to be exploited for the reconstruction of Europe after '45. Latin America was to belong to the United States. Southeast Asia had to fulfill its main function as a source of raw material. That meant any kind of radical nationalism in the Third World was intolerable and had to be stopped.

That was the basis for intervention, which is what happened in Vietnam. If a nationalistic movement looked like it was going to be successful, it had to be extinguished or other nationalist movements might get the same idea. That was history of the post–World War II period to 1970.

So the Vietnam War was not an aberration in American history?

It was not an aberration, but it got out of hand. They expected it to be a small war.

Looking back to the period of the late sixties and early seventies, it looked to many activists that America was on the brink of civil war. Did you share that sentiment?

The Pentagon certainly shared that belief. In fact, one part of the Pentagon Papers, which surprisingly has not received a lot of attention, has to do with the post–Tet period. In early 1968, the Pentagon Papers showed that the Joint Chiefs of Staff were very concerned about sending another couple of hundred thousand troops [to Vietnam] because they thought they would have to use them here in the U.S. to quell civil disorder. No one really wants to comment on that because it reveals how effective the movement was. The people aren't supposed to know they can be effective.

So the movement was effective?

Oh, yes. If there hadn't been a movement, the U.S. would have ended up probably using tactical nuclear weapons, or at least escalating the war.

How would you explain the eclipse of the peace movement? It seemed to have disintegrated by the end of the Vietnam War.

That's just propaganda! It was big in the sixties and seventies and was much bigger in the eighties than the seventies. The movement began to include much broader sectors of the American public and became more deeply rooted in American life. For example, when Ronald Reagan took office, he tried to emulate Kennedy as far as Central America was concerned. He published a White Paper that was just like Kennedy's 1961 White Paper. Reagan's paper was a precursor to a possible invasion of Nicaragua and the sending of troops to El Salvador.

But the public reaction was enormous and negative, so he had to back down. He went the clandestine route and developed a secret international network since the public wouldn't tolerate anything overt. That's because the antiwar movement was so vast it covered most of the country. So any talk about the demise of the movement is just nonsense. It's still strong.

But it doesn't seem to have the cohesion the Vietnam antiwar movement did. The movement today seems fragmented.

Yeah, but suppose the Anita Hill episode had happened thirty years ago. Nobody would have given a damn. But things have changed. Or suppose the Columbus centennial had happened in 1962.[8] It would have been another celebration of the liberation of the hemisphere. But it wasn't, and that's because of the enormous changes in public attitude on every issue.

But if the movement was so strong, why was there so little protest against the Gulf War?

That's a fabrication of the real situation. There was more protest against the Gulf War than against any U.S. action in history. There was a huge protest against the Gulf War before it started. In the case of Vietnam, there were 200,000 troops in Vietnam, and we had been bombing the country for five years before there was any protest.

But I live in South Carolina, and all I saw on television was a few isolated protests, mainly in San Francisco. Polls showed the U.S. public overwhelmingly backed its government in the Gulf War.

In January [1991], there were two protests in Washington involving a couple of hundred thousand people, one before the war started and one after. There has never been anything like that in the history of any imperial power. Can you remember another instance where the American people protested a war before it began?

Your essay, "The Responsibility of the Intellectual," defined the sixties peace movement as much as any document of that period. Does that essay still have relevance today?

There is nothing particularly profound about that essay. It points out something that goes back to the origins of history and illustrates the fact that any system of power, whatever it is, is going to have a priesthood—a group—that is going to guard the official doctrine and try to indoctrinate the people. You go back far enough in history and you find it was a religious priesthood.

Today, it's a kind of secular priesthood. People that obtain wealth and privilege within a system are those who are overwhelmingly system suppor-tive; that is, they sell out to the power. They are the so-called respected in-tellectuals. Then there are people of integrity who take justice and honesty seriously and try to break free of the power.

The mass media is a classic example of what you are talking about, isn't it? You have a select group of journalists in Washington who represent and are a part of the power elite in Washington . . .

But it's also true of the universities and many other areas of American society. The mass media is a more visible example because it is easier to study. It's much more difficult to make a systemic study of the universities.

Looking back to the sixties, apart from your anti–Vietnam War activities, were you ever a part of the sixties counterculture life-style . . . the drugs and sex, etc.?

Not really. I'm kind of old-fashioned. Some people might describe my life-style as being in the mold of "Leave It to Beaver."[9] [Laughs] I like rock music but the old-fashioned kind.

[Laughs] Today, it's fashionable to denigrate the sixties. I ran across a statement from Daniel Bell, the noted sociologist, who said, "The decade [the sixties] repre-sented the last gasp of American romanticism gone sour by rancour and impa-tience."[10] Is there any merit to Bell's critique of the sixties legacy?

It's nonsense. In 1959, Daniel Bell wrote a book called *The End of Ideology* [Free Press, 1965] in which he predicted there was never again going to be any more protest; in effect, it was going to be the end of history.[11] Then the coun-try blew up. That shows the value of his analysis.

The sixties created a big mass movement involving a lot of young people, so naturally it had a lot of freaky things about it. But it had an enormous impact on this society and other countries. Daniel Bell probably didn't like what happened.

But today, there is much more concern now over oppression and the questions of peace and justice. There is more respect for other cultures. Of course, the elites in this country hate it, but they are the commissars and con-trol the writing of history.

Are you opposed to Western capitalism?

I'm not opposed to Western capitalism. Look around the world and you find various systems that differ in many respects. Some have better features than others and that includes the U.S. The U.S., for example, has more provi-sions for freedom of speech than probably any other country, but there has never been a country that allows any kind of democratic involvement on the issues. There never has been a society like that.

Could you sketch a society that you would like to see?

I would like to see a society in which the public plays a meaningful role on matters of public policy. That includes everything from how to run the local schools to where resources should be invested. That requires a lot of functioning organizations. People can't do it alone. They have to be organized. I would like a society in which workers have control of factories and the community controls what's in the community—pretty much what the old-fashioned anarchists described.

You are a world renowned linguist, as well as a full-time activist. How do you manage to balance the two careers?

It's pretty wearing. [Laughs]

[Laughs] It was tough scheduling an interview with you. Your schedule is like one the president of the U.S. keeps. You have it laid out by the hour.

I'm already working on my 1995 schedule.

Wow! [Laughs] Why have you been at MIT so long?

I like it. I have plenty of opportunities there. I like the atmosphere . . . the intellectual atmosphere.

One might ask why do you work at MIT when it's a part of the military industrial complex running the "imperial" power you criticize?

Isn't everything in this country [a part of the military industrial complex]? I have been at universities around the world and this [MIT] is the freest and the most honest and has the best relations between faculty and students than at any other university I have seen. That may be because MIT is a science-based university. Scientists are different. They tend to work together, and there is much less hierarchy [in the field].

Has MIT put any pressure on you to curb your radical views?

None whatsoever. In fact, by general standards, they have quite a good record on civil liberties. That was shown to be particularly true during the sixties when I got into a lot of trouble. I'm sure they were getting a lot of alumni and community pressure because of my activities.

Is that pressure still there?

No, not really. It's interesting. The MIT faculty would be regarded as very conservative, but we all get along better here than faculty do at a lot of other universities.

In looking back at your long activist career, can you really say you made a difference?

Probably, but it's hard to say. Anyway, people keep wanting me to come back and give more talks. [Laughs] And I have a huge correspondence. I must spend twenty hours a week just answering letters.

Where do the letters come from?

From all over the place. A lot of people in this country feel isolated. They may have heard something I said on the radio or read something from one of my books and it struck a chord.

And what about your future?

I don't think I will be doing anything different. I don't see any major changes in the way things are in the world. Over the last few years, there have some wins but mostly losses for the kinds of issues I think are important.

Could you give an example?

Well, there has been a chipping away of labor rights to the extent that we are now back to where we were sixty or seventy years ago in terms of labor rights. The fact that Caterpillar Tractor was able to hire scabs when its workers went on strike puts us back one hundred years. That that could happen in an industrialized society today is amazing. So I see a lot of things to fight for in the coming years ... which is what I plan to do.

9

Tim Leary

From High Priest of LSD
to Guru of High Tech

> I think the experiences I've had have strengthened me. I've had
> an incredible life! I've been at West Point for two years. I've been
> a respectable professor at Harvard. I've been in prison. . . . I've
> drunk from the bowls, and I know where Man is coming from.
> I don't have to take shit from anyone!

I first interviewed Tim Leary at Yale University in 1988. The poster on
the front door to the building known to Yale students as SSS read: Dr. Tim
Leary, Former Drug Guru and Harvard Psychologist: A Discourse on Millen-
nia Madness." Inside, a half hour later, the Yale Political Union president introduced Leary to a jam-packed audience, most of whom were not even born
when the former guru served as the high priest of LSD and the prime mover
in the counterculture that flourished in the late 1960s.

Leary, then 67 years old, looked trim and fit as he jauntily approached the
stage and gave a big wave and a warm smile to the audience. He leaned on the
podium draped with the Yale Political Union flag. In the background, a large
American flag hung from a chalkboard.

"He's into computers now. That's neat," squeaked one fuzzy-cheeked student who had his hair tied tightly into a bun à la sixties style. His friend
hummed the words "Turn on, tune in, drop out" to a familiar punk rock
melody. They both looked stoned.

Leary introduced himself as a "performing professional philosopher, the
Pete Rose[1] of philosophy," who had been a "hustler" for 38 years. For the next
hour, Leary, exuded energy that belied his age and gave a rambling talk in
which he reminisced about the sixties, commented about "The Roaring Twentieth Century," explained why it was so important for everyone to think for
themselves, and offered predictions about the future. He talked enthusiastically about how interactive technology would transform our lives.

When I interviewed Leary again five years later, he had not changed
much, nor had his message. Whatever subject arose in the interview, Leary

Tim Leary (photo courtesy of Tim Leary).

drew heavily on his experiences as a major participant in the events of the sixties. There is a lot to draw upon, for Leary's life reads like a highly improbable novel, the stuff that legends are made of.

Born in 1920 in Springfield, Massachusetts, the son of a pious Roman Catholic mother and a hard-drinking father, Leary grew up a rebel. He was expelled from high school, from the U.S. Military Academy at West Point, and from the University of Alabama before finally earning a Ph.D. in psychology from University of California at Berkeley. Leary began a promising academic career that led to an appointment to the Harvard University faculty in 1960.

Then he discovered psychedelic drugs on a trip to Cuernavaca, Mexico, and his life changed forever. "In four hours by the swimming pool in Cuernavaca," Leary wrote in his autobiography *Flashbacks,* "I learned more about the mind, the brain, and its structures than I did in the preceding fifteen as a diligent psychologist."[2] He experimented with LSD for three years at Harvard before being fired in 1963. With the emerging counterculture providing Leary a big audience for his message, he put together a traveling light-and-sound show and toured the country expounding on the virtues of psychedelic drugs.

Leary became famous as "the high priest of LSD," but in 1970 he was jailed for possession of a small amount of marijuana. President Richard Nixon called Leary "the most dangerous man alive."

With the help of the radical Weather Underground, he managed to escape from prison and make his way to Algeria where Black Panther Eldridge Cleaver also thought Leary was pretty dangerous and saw that he was put under house arrest. U.S. authorities eventually nabbed him in Kabul, Afghanistan. In all, Leary spent 42 months in U.S. jails.

Today, Leary is a leader of the futurist movement and president of Futique Inc., a company that designs highly interactive software programs for personal computers. *L.A. Weekly* called his first program, "Mind Adventure," the best computer game ever.

Tim Leary is not the easiest of interviews. In fact, at times, with his puzzled expressions and long pauses, the one-time guru looks as if he has taken one acid trip too many. Leary is also a challenging interview, for he is always questioning the prevailing wisdom and often puts a new twist on subjects brought up in conversation, whether they are about the sixties or his enthusiasm for high tech.

*   *   *

Is lecturing to students the main way you make a living today?

Yes. I give about forty lectures a year, but I don't just give lectures to college kids. I also go around the country giving talks at lecture halls, theaters, comedy and night clubs. I perform philosophy.

What does that mean? Are you a kind of standup philosopher?

Sometimes I sit down. I would do it more often but sometimes there is no chair.

[Laughs] What are some of the things you talk about?

I talk about the stages of evolution and the evolution of the human race — from the hunter-gather period to the information age we are in now. Sometimes I talk about the Roaring Twentieth Century and the great changes that have taken place. What I'm actually trying to do is encourage people to think for themselves. I use humor and satire, which I believe are the keys to evolutionary change. I believe making fun of or ridiculing an establishment or institution or the powers that be is the best way to loosen its clutches over our minds.

Well, humor helped you, right? The powers that be were after you for a long time. You escaped from prisons. You were in hiding. If it wasn't for your sense of humor, do you think you could have survived those traumas?

[Long pause] [Laughs] It helped.

In an earlier interview, you talked with a lot of students at Yale University. What was your impression of them?

I was apprehensive of the type of students I would find there. The Yale Political Union members, who took care of me, dressed and talked like bankers. So it was with heavy heart that I went through that lecture. But as for the general student body, I have found them to be the best looking, smartest, wildest I've lectured in years.

What was your impression of Yale University campus?

We had this interview in a building (the student cafeteria) that is pop Gothic or some sort of feudal monstrosity. [Laughs] You have to enter the building through gates that resemble those you would use to enter Folsom Prison. The corridors and staircases comprise a dark, twisting, tortuous maze of brick dungeon. The construction of the building reveals a mind that has an insane, bizarre, psychotic worship of the past. So it [Yale] truly represents the mentality of the East Coast Republican Party and the puritanical culture that has controlled America since Abraham Lincoln. It's no accident that George Bush, Robert Bork, and Pat Robertson come from Yale.[3]

[Laughs] I gather you didn't like Yale's physical facilities?

I have been in forty jails and prisons in my life, and I immediately began looking for ways of escape.

Speaking of jail, I guess you would include being incarcerated by Eldridge Cleaver in the mid-seventies when you were on the run and ended up in Algeria. Could you recall how that came about?

I arrived in Algeria when Eldridge Cleaver was involved in a bitter, violent struggle with Hughie Newton for the leadership of the Black Panthers. Cleaver represented the most militant and violent of the factions. He thought my views on political reform were hopelessly out-of-date; therefore, he considered me dangerous to the cause. Cleaver openly boasted to the press that he arrested me for my "dangerous views and lack of discipline."

Did you ever feel that Cleaver might kill you?

The Panthers had claimed to have killed some others, but they couldn't do anything because I was so visible. Worldwide publicity was focused on my being in Algeria. But before we come down too hard on the Black Panthers' motives, we have to remember the times.

Cleaver and Newton were filled with black pride, anger, and frustration. There were about twenty Black Panthers in Algeria, and they knew they were not going to overthrow the most violent empire in history. Cleaver kept my wife and me enslaved for just four days, while the white man in America had kept the black man enslaved for over four hundred years.

You have spent several years in prison. How does a free spirit like you manage to adapt?

Since I left Harvard in 1963, I've always had a hard time paying the rent. But for five years while I was in prison, I didn't have to worry about that. [Laughs] I was also in solitary confinement for two years, which simplified my life. [Laughs]

Why were you in solitary confinement?

Because the authorities thought I was an escape risk and because I was considered a danger to incite a riot and stir up disrespect for authority. They weren't too far wrong. When I was in Folsom Prison, I was part of a group of prisoners who were continually filing suits trying to reform the prison system.

Let's talk about the new Tim Leary. Recently, I read a profile about you that described how you have gone from being the high priest of LSD to social butterfly who is tight with Los Angeles high society. A lot of people who remember your anti-establishment ways in the sixties might find that disappointing.

I believe an interview tells more about an interviewer than it does about the interviewee.

Does that include this interview?

Yes, your interview will tell more about you than it does about me.

But back to the question. Have you become a social butterfly?

The author of that article made me sound like someone who is totally obsessed with how my car was parked, name dropping, and the frivolities of life—a person who has no interest with philosophical, psychological, or political issues. Of course, it's not true.

In the '92 elections, the Democrats defeated the Republican Party in the presidential race for the first time in twelve years. Does it make a difference which political party leads the country?

We shouldn't allow people to volunteer to run for president. That means the most combative, noisiest, best-debating candidate usually wins the fight. Instead, the American people should draft or hire the team that is best able to pilot them. I have facetiously suggested—although there is some truth to it—that we should make a trade with the former Soviet Union for Mikhail Gorbachev[4]—the MVP political leader of the world—to acquire his services as team star and manager.

I think the Republican Party plays the same role in our country that the Communist Party played in the former Soviet Union. It controls the military, police, education, industry, and press. On the other hand, there is no such thing as a Democratic Party. That is an oxymoron. The Democratic Party has a loose, confused, chaotic association of minorities, the poor, and the avant garde groups. They all have one thing in common: They have been fucked over by the central party—the Republican party. So I would never vote for a Republican for president.

You are very critical of the system. So what about your views? Have they changed much since you were involved with the drug culture? Take the phrase, "Tune in, turn on, drop out." Does it still have relevance for today's people?

I don't know what you mean by today's people. There are more than four billion people living on the face of the Earth and two hundred and fifty million living in America. For several million of them, anything would have relevance.

Okay. Are you still gung ho in your belief that psychedelic drugs like LSD can liberate the mind?

I believe that to use drugs in the collective sense like you are using them is very confusing. People talk about drugs, drugs, drugs! Are we talking about caffeine, aspirin, sugar, or heroin? I'm obsessed with language these days. Like a lot of other philosophers, I believe it is language that closes the mind and keeps us oppressed and that, if we use the language of the past, we will never be able to create the language of the future.

Also, if we continue to use the language created by the establishment and media, we will never be able to think for ourselves. So the word *drugs* is totally ambiguous and dangerous. It's like the two words *communist* and *leftist*. Anyone who disagrees with Ollie North[5] is considered a Communist. Anything that the power structure does not approve of is dangerous and should be suppressed. But it doesn't consider booze and nicotine to be drugs. Since 1960, I have used psychedelic drugs like LSD that can expand consciousness and accelerate thoughts in one's mind, but my name has never been linked to heroin and cocaine.

That raises an interesting point. You mentioned nicotine and heroin. They are mood-enhancing drugs that are the drugs of choice for many people today. But LSD seems to be making a comeback among the young. What does that mean?

[Long pause] [Laughs] I really don't know. But let me say this: It's obvious that people will take drugs that are available. It's impossible to find good acid [LSD] today. In the early seventies, the U.S. government estimated that seven million people were taking LSD. Ironically, since the late sixties, there hasn't been any pure LSD around. So those seven million people, as well as others since then, were using and have been using a chemical that was and is, at best, homemade and, at worse, a concoction of speed and God knows what else thrown together and sold as LSD.

But no thinking person could have avoided the challenge of psychedelic drugs in the sixties. Allan Ginsberg, Cary Grant, Henry Luce . . . I can go on and on and list thousands more, including William F. Buckley.[6]

Buckley! That's interesting.

To this day, Buckley is a crusader for the legalization of psychedelic drugs. There are many kooky right-wing libertarians who, because they want to use psychedelic drugs, are willing to make them legal.

Are you in favoring of legalizing all drugs?

Yeah, but whether I'm in favor of legalizing drugs or not, they are still going to exist. Why not legalize all drugs? We would then have accurate critical evaluations of them, as well as quality control, good labeling on packages, licensing, and information on how to use drugs intelligently. We would teach people how to use drugs just as we teach people to ride a bicycle and drive a car. An intelligent society will do this. I'm like everybody else. I don't want a bunch of acidheads wandering about my neighborhood shouting "Wow" and other expressions like that.

Do you still use LSD?

I guess I do.

How about other drugs? Are you still experimenting?

Drugs are no longer the central interest in my life, but I do keep abreast of what's going on. Every few months, a new drug will come out, and I will get it from a reputable chemist.

Influential Americans have said that casual drug users are just as responsible for drug abuse as any drug dealer. What do you say?

I think that's vicious nonsense. Of course, minors or juveniles should be prevented from having access to drugs. But the age should be determined individually by the family. Society is in no position to say that a person under eighteen or twenty-one should not take drugs. There are a lot of immature people over twenty-one who can't handle drugs or alcohol, money or cars, for that matter.

Ten percent of the population may have addictive personalities that lead them to abuse drugs. They are dangerous to themselves and to others and should be discouraged from using drugs. But that doesn't mean the other ninety percent should be denied access to drugs. That is totally irrational! That's like saying because there are two million diabetics in the country who can't use white sugar, none of the rest of us should use it. It's an all or nothing monolithic, puritanical caste of thinking symptomatic of the fundamentalist Christian or Islamic mind that wants to control the activities of everybody else, probably because they have no discipline or self-control themselves.

Do you think we will ever get back to period like the sixties where there was lot of interest in mind exploration?

When you talk about "we," who are talking about? I have never left.

[Laughs] Okay, pardon my language. I mean the general public—the young people, for example.

[Long pause] Yes, certainly. By the year 2000, a wide variety of neurotransmitters will be available, which are more precise, effective, and safer than the primitive drugs we were using in the late sixties and seventies. They will be used very much like we use vitamins today. The drugs of the twenty-first century will be seen not so much as medications but as tools for activating or booting up various circuits of the brain.

The main preoccupation and business of the human species in the twenty-first century will be to learn how to operate the human biocomputer—that is, the hundred billion neurons in our brain, each of which, we are told, has enormous thought process capabilities. So in the next century—which will truly be the information, cybernetic civilization—it will be taken for granted that everyone's responsibility will be to program and reprogram his or her own brain.

You are optimistic about the future. But what about America? There has been a rash of books and articles analyzing America's decline.

The feudal idea that America is locked in mortal combat with an evil Communist empire is finished. America will be a source and inspiration of the cybernetic age because creativity, innovation, independence, and disrespect for authority is still much in evidence in America, much more than any other country.

America has the characteristics that will bring the next civilization about. I think countries like Russia and Japan realize that. That is why there has been a tremendous influx of Asian scholars and scientists coming to study in America. They don't want to be like us, but they want to share and emulate our creativity. So I'm far from being pessimistic about America. I'm prouder than ever to be an American.

You're very much involved with how technology is changing society. How do you keep up with what's new in society?

By hanging around young people. They show me what's going on. The kids who are growing up in the eighties and nineties are an entirely different generation. They're the first generation to use interactive technology and to experience digital communication. They are the high tech kids. People over thirty have a hard time understanding this Nintendo generation who think digitally.

I recall the first time I saw my grandchildren in a video arcade moving electrons around on a screen. It was about 1980. I knew they were using a new language, a new mode of communication, and a new way to operate their brains. So since 1980, I've been working very hard trying to learn how to package thoughts. I don't see how anybody involved in psychology would not get involved with electronic reality.

It has certainly changed the way I interact with audiences. I don't give a lecture anymore. I perform with an audiovisual tape to reanimate my lecture through very powerful audiovisual images. The idea of a lecturer just standing there at the podium and moving his vocal cords is thirty thousand years old. In the future, teachers in the classroom will be communicating with their children by creating images on a screen.

It sounds like what you call digital communication has a psychedelic quality to it. What implications do these developments have for mind expansion?

The average American watches television for seven hours a day. Study the situation and you will see that the people who do commercials are trying to put viewers in what I call a "trans state." Watch a commercial, and you don't know what is going to happen to you. Then bang! Marlboro! What I'm saying is that already brain programming is happening all the time. That's what got Bush elected. That's what got the people to support the Gulf War. The way to do that is to shock, shake, and create constantly changing images so a viewer doesn't know what's going on.

The Gulf War was history's greatest commercial. We were hypnotized by the fireworks, the noise, the electronics. Then they said, "We are winning! [Laughs] If you use the electronic multimedia on someone without their knowledge, that is brain washing. But we are taking that power and developing software and making it available to individuals. Kids can't do an ABC or an NBC show, but they can create their own reality in class and then, through electronics, get it to other people. In the future, everybody will be doing what ABC and NBC do right now.

But won't the authorities want to monopolize this new technology, given its potential for mind control?

Big Brother[7] has already hooked the individual to sit down in front of the TV for an average of seven hours a day. The way to fight that is to develop software and get people to learn how to communicate.

We are developing technologies that can reprogram the brain from its right-brain state. We know the brain is made up of hundreds of millions of neurons. It's like a computer. The problem is that the brain is programmed at an early age, for example, to speak the language of your culture, and it's very hard to change your reality as you get older. But with new interactive programs, you can escape a right-brain state and reprogram your brain.

I understand you own your own computer company. What are some of the things you are doing with it?

That again is the vocabulary of the capitalist age. I belong to a network of people — a cooperative of writers, artists, designers, musicians, and others — who are interested in pooling their efforts and talents to develop computer programs. The cooperative is called Futique [the opposite of antique], and one of our major projects is to take books and translate them into a software program that is interactive.

It sounds interesting, but what does it mean?

It means you perform a book, rather than passively read it. The process is very similar to the way that a group of technicians, artists, and writers will take a novel and make a movie out of it. We put the book into a performance mode so that the book can be performed.

Are you making the software available to the public?

Yes, but we are running into the problems that many movie producers have. We are literally having to develop the programs in our backyard on a very low budget. We distribute some of our books through normal distribution channels, but we also distribute some via mail order.

What kind of response have you received?

My first software, called "Mind Mirror," sold about forty thousand copies in the first year. You have to figure that three or four times that amount has been pirated. So perhaps between one hundred twenty thousand and one hundred sixty thousand copies of that program are out there. It wasn't a bestseller, but it was a respectable start. It's a brand new field, and we are learning. We expect future programs to do better.

Do you target specific audiences?

In my mind, the target audience is the fourteen-year-old kid in the ghetto who has no opportunity in her life. We can make software available to her for less money than it costs to buy the books she is using in her school.

How are you trying to reach the fourteen-year-old kid?

We are targeting teachers. One of our projects is developing a performing software program version of *Huckleberry Finn*, the most subversive book ever written.[8] The program, which will have good graphics, will allow the child to perform it as easily and as naturally as he would shoot basketballs or play baseball. The game awards the player for performance. That's something the kid can understand. Once those programs get into the schools, we think the reception will be so explosive that in a few years the kids will have access to information as easily as they have access to water, air, and basic medical care.

Given the potential for digital communication, I would assume you are not nostalgic for the sixties?

I still like to listen to the Rolling Stones and Jimi Hendrix. The fact that you are evolving means you can enjoy them more. It also means you don't have to give anything up. I still like to read books, even though I consider books to be very old-fashioned. As I said, we are now developing methods to communicate without books.

Do you think books will disappear?

Electronic communication is certainly going to replace books. We are going to package ideas at light speed.

Given the mind-boggling changes you describe, do the sixties look like the Dark Ages to you now?

No, because the sixties generation was the first electronic generation. It was a very exciting time.

So were those of the sixties generation pioneers?

Oh, yeah. The average person of my generation was very shocked when the sixties generation came along. Actually, each of the last three generations — those who are past fifty, those between thirty and fifty, and those younger than thirty — are different but heroic breeds. Together we have come farther than Captain Kirk and Captain Spock.[9] So we have to be kind and compassionate to each other.

The irony is that, before 1920, the idea of a generation did not exist. People sang the same songs, listened to the same music, and wore the same clothes as your grandparents. People of my generation didn't like television, just like a lot of hippies today don't like computers. The two older generations are outdated, so it's up to the youngsters to teach older people new techniques.

One last question: How would you like to be remembered? What would you like on your epitaph?

I was sitting next to a distinguished-looking elderly black woman on a plane. We talked a bit. She asked my name. She then took my hand and shook it fervently. She said, "Yes, I know who you are. You have given Man fits for a very long time." [Laughs] "He gave them fits" would be a very nice epitaph.

[Long pause] I think the experiences I've had have strengthened me. I've had an incredible life! I've been to West Point for two years. I've been a respectable professor at Harvard. I've been in prison. . . . I've drunk from the bowls, and I know where Man is coming from. I don't have to take shit from anyone!

Philip Berrigan
Radical for Christ

I am trying to get to the roots of the problem, and that is the true nature of a radical. I try to show Christian people that Christ was an outlaw, and, to have any sort of inner freedom, they have no choice but to put themselves up against the system. A person who believes in that philosophy must be willing to pay for the consequences of his actions. He must be willing to go to jail if necessary.

In the early years of the anti–Vietnam War movement, resistance to the draft was largely confined to a number of individuals who chose to burn their draft cards publicly. In late 1967, this form of civil disobedience culminated in a mass burning of draft cards at the Pentagon by hundreds of young men.

Draft resistance took a new turn in October 1967 when Philip Berrigan and three associates conducted a raid on an inner-city draft board at the Customs House in Baltimore. They poured containers of blood over the Selective Service records and then waited for the authorities to come and arrest them. As one observer noted, the action of the activists, who became known as the Baltimore Four, marked "a quantum leap in the antiwar movement, for it expanded draft resistance, permitting those ineligible for the draft to take effective action against the Selective Service mechanism and the corporations profiting from war manufacturers."[1]

Berrigan's action made him a high profile activist against the Vietnam War and eventually led to his imprisonment for challenging public authority. In effect, he became the first Roman Catholic priest to be sentenced to jail in the United States for political crimes.

Philip Berrigan was born in Two Harbors, Minnesota, on October 5, 1923, and raised in Syracuse, New York, where he attended Catholic parochial schools. During World War II, Berrigan saw action in some of the fiercest battles of the Allied offensive in Europe. After the war, he graduated with a B.A. degree in English from Holy Cross College in Worcester, Massachusetts, and then entered the Society of St. Joseph (more commonly known as the Josephite Fathers) in 1950. After earning a B.S. degree in secondary education from Loyola University of the South in 1957 and an M.S. degree from Xavier University three years later, Berrigan began teaching English and religion and counseling students at the Josephites' St. Augustine High School in a New Orleans black ghetto.

During his six years at the school, Berrigan took up the cause of the black civil rights struggle, taking freedom rides, working with black organizations like SNCC and CORE, and trying to get scholarships for black students. Berrigan's leftist views and activism put him in conflict with the Catholic hierarchy in the South, and he was transferred to the faculty of the Josephite seminar in Newburgh, New York. Undaunted by the conservative blue collar milieu of Newburgh, Berrigan worked on behalf of the poor and became increasingly more outspoken in his opposition to the escalating Vietnam War. Once again, his Catholic superiors felt compelled to transfer him, this time to the black inner-city parish in Baltimore, Maryland.

Berrigan continued to work for peace, but his increasing frustrations over the ineffectiveness of the "respectable" means of peace protest led to his actions at the Baltimore Customs House. Another raid on draft records in the Baltimore suburb of Catonsville followed in 1968. After being convicted for the two raids, Berrigan and his brother Dan, whom Philip had recruited for the raid, jumped bail and eluded police for weeks before his capture in 1970.

Eventually, Berrigan and six other activists, who became known as the Harrisburg Seven, were charged with an elaborate but bizarre plot to kidnap Henry Kissinger and blow up heating tunnels in Washington's federal buildings. The jury failed to reach a verdict, but Berrigan and his wife Elizabeth, a former nun whom he had married in 1969, were found guilty of smuggling letters in and out of prison. The conviction was later appealed and reversed.

After the signing of the Paris Peace Accords in 1973,[2] the Berrigans broadened their antiwar resistance to include challenging the arms race and U.S. militarism. More than 20 years later, age has not diminished Berrigan's commitment to turning swords into ploughshares. For the peace activist and devout Christian, war is still "an expression of the American addiction to violence," which is "destroying us, driving us mad."[3]

Our first of two interviews took place at the federal prison at Lorton, Virginia, where Berrigan was serving a six-month term for the destruction of government property (A five-year contempt of court sentence was pending). Berrigan was angry at the judge for not allowing the defendants to testify about arms research at Johns Hopkins Applied Physics Laboratory in Columbia, Maryland, which they had trespassed in 1991. Released in December 1992, Berrigan talked with me a second time from Jonah House, a small religious commune in Baltimore, where Berrigan and his wife live with their three children when not getting arrested for antiwar activities.

* * *

You just got out of the prison at Lorton, Virginia. For how long were you in?

I was in for four and a half months on a six-month sentence. The charge was destruction of government property because of what we did at the White House. A five-year contempt citation was pending, but it was dropped.

Why were you cited for contempt?

My wife and seven other people were on trial, and the judge was suppressing everything. I got up and started challenging the way he was handling the trial. I did it twice. He warned me once, but I got up a second time and said the trial was a disgrace and was being held in a neo–Nazi courtroom. The judge locked me up for the day, and, when I wouldn't apologize at the end of the day, he gave me a five-year sentence.

How many times have you been in jail?

Oh, I don't know. Maybe thirty to forty times. I've been married since 1969, and I guess I've been in jail nine or ten years of that time.

Has being in jail so much been hard on your marriage and family life?

I've been married twenty-three years, and my wife Elizabeth is not only a great wife but also a committed activist.[4] Our kids have been brought up in the atmosphere of the resistance. Our son Jerry, who is seventeen years old and presently in Germany for a year of study, was arrested at the Pentagon on August 6 [1992], the anniversary of the bombing of Hiroshima.[5] Our two other kids are eighteen and sixteen, and they have been arrested six or seven times. But we've never forced the resistance on our children. They have come to us and asked if they could do civil disobedience.

You have received some of the toughest sentences ever handed down by U.S. judges for protesting war and civil disobedience. Do you think that the American judicial system has tried to make you an example?

All I know is that it's impossible to get a fair trial in an American court. I cannot use international law as a defense or appeal to a higher law. I cannot say, "I view human life sacred, and that's why I did it." The American judicial system is a travesty because the courts are identified with the military and the government.

When I talked to you on the phone after you had called me from prison, you said to me that "there aren't many of us left." You seemed kind of down. Was that true? In terms of activism and changing the system, does it seem like an uphill struggle today?

It's always uphill, but I really don't have any reason to be down. There are always a lot of hopeful signs around. It's better to be doing what I'm doing than to do nothing.

You say signs? What kind of signs do you see that there is a viable movement to change the system?

I meet rather frequently with people along the eastern seaboard who haven't quit. They don't stop. They have a pretty solid analysis of what's going down, of the new [Bill Clinton presidential] administration, of what's happening in Somalia[6] . . . on and on and on. They know there is no option but to continue, so they continue. They plan, they resist, they go to jail.

You have never quit. You are sixty-nine years old. What keeps you going as an activist?

Two things—one is the scripture. The Bible is our manifesto. The other is Jonah House, which is an excellent community, one of the best in the country.

Could you describe what Jonah House is like?

We have been going since 1973. We're a nonviolent religious community that is really open to anybody. Membership fluctuates. Right now, we have about seven members. We hold everything in common because we know God is the only owner of material things and we are just holding it in stewardship. We have only one bank account and no health insurance, so we have to be very careful about our health, especially when we do contract work like printing, carpentry work, and so on, which are our main means of support. We are involved in resistance work with movement people from Maine to North Carolina.

Jonah House sounds like an old-fashioned sixties commune.

Except that we are gathered for a purpose: to resist war and to resist imperial government.

When you look back at your life of political activism, can you say your involvement has been a catalyst for change? Or is it important to see tangible results?

It's only important to see results in a secondary sense. The important thing is to do the most truthful and most honest thing one can do and then rely on God to cause the result. Often, we don't see the result, so the thing to do is to keep going and do the best we can.

Are you still involved in organized religion?

Only in the most superficial way. Whenever I get the opportunity, I will speak to church groups. Often, I go to church-related colleges and universities and high schools to speak.

I guess rocky and volatile would be the words to describe your relationship with the Catholic Church, right?

Right. I first got in trouble with the Church in the civil rights era when it chastized me for my involvement with black rights. Then I got in trouble again when I got involved in the antiwar movement. Yes, it's been on the rocky side.

What is your current standing with the Church?

Under the new Code of Canon Law, I'm no longer excommunicated. I can receive the sacraments, but, of course, I can't officially perform them.

Is it difficult to endure prison life at your age?

It was easier twenty years ago. [Laughs] But I do keep myself in shape. I try to run every day, and I don't have trouble with the prison food. I did have a bout of pneumonia and a [problem] in my right leg the last time I was incarcerated. They shackled me to a bed.

Why did they do that?

For security purposes. They also had an armed guard at my door twenty-four hours a day.

You are real dangerous. [Laughs]

Real dangerous. [Laughs]

You have been a unique kind of prisoner. When you go to prison, you are not in for car theft or murder. You are in because you want to be in. You are in for your political beliefs. How do prisoners relate to you?

The prisoners' reaction is very cavalier to begin with because they don't know anything about the struggle against the war in Vietnam or the Cold War. The prisoners, both black and white, are not politically oriented, so only in time do they become familiar with what we are doing and why we are in jail. That takes an awful lot of conversation and a lot of work in the Bible study classes we conduct. But when they get a handle on what we are doing and why; they even begin to think about joining us.

Do you actively proselytize the inmates?

Oh, yeah, we do the best we can. Another peace activist and myself worked for over four months with a select group of prisoners. One of them — a homeless guy from Jamaica — is now living at the Catholic worker house in Washington, D.C., and doing well.

Being in prison so many times, you must have some definite ideas about prison reform.

It's kind of hard to reform a system that is totally counterproductive and wasteful. The prison population is expanding at an enormous rate — an almost geometric rate.

I believe the U.S. has the highest incarceration rate in the world.

Yes, we do, hands down! So we can't do anything intelligent to reform a rotten system. If one was to point out that there is no damn point at all incarcerating nonviolent criminals, it would be totally lost on the system. You wouldn't get any reaction at all. The recidivism rate is staggering! The same people keep coming back to prison. We saw that at Lorton. When a new shipment of prisoners come in, we can see the relationships renewed between guards and prisoners. Everybody knows everybody because the prisoners have been in there so many times. [Laughs] There is nothing for them to do. Society has written them off and made them expendable.

It's a revolving door. But what is the point of you going to prison?

We are involved in a hearts-and-mind thing. It's matter of conscience. We are trying to get people to think about not just what is going down, but about what needs to be done. By sacrificing our liberty, we are making an appeal to people of conscience and their sense of responsibility. It's the only way it can really be done.

You are talking about changing people, but there are such enormous problems in this country — drug addiction, high unemployment, high homicide rate . . . The U.S. is a tremendously violent country. Why haven't the American people been radicalized? Why hasn't there been a larger radical movement in the U.S.?

The U.S. government gets constant study reports on the nature of the population, so it knows what may make the people erupt and insist on change. Then the government gears their propaganda to prevent that from happening. The other factor relates to the nature of the economic system. By locking themselves into materialism, the people create their own prisons.

Are you saying the American people are willing to be bought off? If they have a good standard of living, they are willing to put a blind eye to a lot of bad things that are going on?

Precisely! But there is a lot of despair in this country. As politics becomes increasingly corrupt, as the number of homeless increases and drug use rises, and as the economy deteriorates, people, more and more, are preoccupied in trying to survive and are struggling to remain human.

Are you comfortable with the radical *label?*

Yes, I am. I am trying to get to the *roots* of the problems, and that is the true nature of a radical. I try to show Christian people that Christ was an outlaw, and, to have any sort of inner freedom, they have no choice but to put themselves up against the system. A person who believes in that philosophy must be willing to pay for the consequences of his actions. He must be willing to go to jail, if necessary.

Is there a role for violence in achieving social change?

I would say violence is circular in nature. When [violence is] employed, violence just breeds more violence. We saw that happening in Somalia when the U.S. Marines went in for supposedly "humanitarian" reasons. The U.S. hopes that something positive and humanitarian would come out of its presence in Somalia, but it's just not going to happen. My brother Dan and I draw our pacifism from the Gospel. We have a Biblical view of land, a condemnation of human law by God's word. So we are immensely critical of the entire court system, the justice system, and the penal system.

You have criticized what you call the "American empire." Is there any indication that it's declining?

It's very definitely in decline. We are the largest debtor nation in the world, and our trade imbalances are way off. The national debt is staggering. It's over four trillion dollars now and increasing all the time. So the very idea that that Clinton administration or any other American presidential administration will bail us out is an unlikely prospect.

If the U.S. is in decline, isn't there the strong possibility that it will increasingly become more violent?

Yes, I think that's a threat. Do you remember the concerns about the USSR when it was still a formidable opponent and in terrible economic trouble? We worried that the USSR might embark on the path to nuclear war and take the world with it. But war has always been an expression of America's addiction to violence. On the international level, we seem to think that violence is the only option that works. Take Somalia. We couldn't see any option but to send American troops into that country. It's an almost automatic response. By generating an awful lot of violence during the Cold War, the U.S. government has corrupted its own people with violence.

So I assume you are not impressed with the so-called "New World Order."

What new world order? It's the old world order.

The Cold War has ostensibly ended. Where is the U.S. nuclear disarmament movement now?

Anyone thoughtful would say that the threat of nuclear holocaust has not abated at all because the world is still under a definite threat from nuclear war. The nuclear club is expanding all the time. For example, it's pretty factual that Pakistan has had the bomb and has even threatened India with it once or twice. So the danger of nuclear war has not abated at all.

What type of nuclear disarmament activities are you involved with today?

We are going to protest what is going on at Johns Hopkins University's Applied Physics Lab, which is probably the most prominent weapons lab in the eastern part of the country. Its military contract is largely with the navy. Only a minuscule part of its budget is for civilian and peaceful purposes. The lab is involved with Star Wars, the Trident II program, with guidance systems for a whole new family of cruise missiles, and various other things. Johns Hopkins would boast about it if you asked the university.

In looking back to your youth, can you recall what radicalized you?

I've cultivated a strong sense of justice because of my upbringing, my family, and the good range of friends I've had through the years. My first experience with injustice occurred during World War II, when, as a GI, I was sent to the European theater of operations. I saw how blacks were mistreated in the armed forces, how they were strictly segregated in those days. I promised to do something about it after the war, and so I joined a religious order that ministered to black Americans. I became a Josephite priest.

Was there a turning point in your life?

I think the Cuban missile crisis was it. Seeing what happened in the European theater during World War II and being in the service for three and a half years, I was just appalled by the crisis. The politicians were back to doing the same old crap and now were threatening the world with an even more destructive war that involved nuclear devastation. I was so infuriated I vowed to do something about it.

The Cuban Missile Crisis pushed me to do my homework and investigate what was happening in Indochina. I discovered there were three nuclear powers involved in Indochina [the Chinese, the Russians, and ourselves] and that the dangers were really profound. I concluded the real danger was that the regional war could develop into a nuclear exchange. I knew that at one point we had sixty-five nuclear warheads in South Vietnam and that they were of the tactical variety and ready to be fired.

What led to your actions in 1967 when you broke into the Customs House in Baltimore and destroyed those draft records?

I went to a number of antiwar conferences where people talked about raiding draft boards and stopping buses that brought conscripts to local draft centers. I listened very intently, talked to some of those people, and became convinced that acting against the Selective Service was the key to the whole thing. Contrary to the Fourteenth Amendment, we were sending conscripts to kill and be killed in Indochina. We started by pouring blood on the A-1 draft files, and later we destroyed them with homemade napalm.

Other activists criticized your actions. How did you answer your critics?

Merely by explaining over and over again that this property [the draft files] was dehumanizing and destructive of life and that God's law and international law had precedence over U.S. law. The draft files were like a weapon and had no right to exist. You patiently make your point time and again and those of good will listen to you and those who aren't, won't.

There's an addiction to property in this country, so there's always an outcry whenever property is destroyed, no matter how threatening the act may or may not be to human life. So at Catonsville, we were trying to say something about property and what it was doing to human beings, especially for young draftees in Indochina. Such actions don't go over very well because people are so enslaved by their damn property!

You were convicted of those draft board raids at Baltimore and Catonsville, but instead of going to jail, you decided to jump bail and go underground. Why?

It was very offensive to Dan, myself, and others to show up, hat in hand, simply because we were told that our appeal had been rejected by the Supreme Court and we had this surrender date. We had not done anything wrong. We had actually performed a public service, so why should we suggest that they were right by showing up for a long jail sentence, six years in my case? We didn't do it. Instead, we went underground, even though we didn't know anything about how to conduct ourselves underground.

But there was a support network that helped you, right?
    Oh, sure. If I hadn't tried to surface for a very large and important rally in New York City, I could have stayed underground indefinitely.

A lot of activists were going underground at this time. Were you in contact with them?
    My brother was. He talked to the Panthers, Weather Underground, and various other segments of the Left resistance to the war.

You were part of the Harrisburg Seven. That was a very bizarre episode. The resistance was talking about blowing up tunnels and kidnapping [Henry] Kissinger. Were those options seriously considered?
    I was actually at Lewisburg Penitentiary at the time, and Elizabeth and I had secretly married. She had attended a meeting at Greenwich, Connecticut, where there was talk about making a citizen's arrest of people like Kissinger, and she wrote me to ask what I thought about it. I didn't think much of the idea at all. In fact, I thought it was kind of ridiculous and wrote her back saying so. But an informant seized and xeroxed those letters and turned them over to the FBI. That was the basis of the Harrisburg indictment.

But you survived the indictment.
    Yes, we hung the jury, and I got a short concurrent sentence out of it . . . two years or something like that.

That was an exciting period in American history. Activists had a real commitment to the issues. Do you ever miss that part of your life?
    It was a very intriguing and intense period, and I do get nostalgic from time to time. I think those years were among the finest in what is the People's History of the United States . . . the stuff that Howard Zinn writes about[7] The tragedy of that period is twofold: First, the U.S. may have been kicked out of Indochina, but it came out of that war with a new family of first-strike weaponry and a counterinsurgency doctrine. Secondly, the movement had quit and was miniscule in strength.

Do you think the official end of the Vietnam War, when the U.S. pulled out, was the reason why, in your words, the movement "quit."
    It's a part of the country's national character. The American people don't stay with complex, perplexing social issues for very long.

The American people have a short memory span, so to speak.
    Yeah, and amnesia and a lack of historical perception. That was certainly one factor. Another is the illusionary, willful thinking we in the movement indulged ourselves in. We told ourselves that we got kicked out of Vietnam, and things are going to be better now.

Do you think a movement of the scale we saw during the Vietnam War will develop again, given the problems the U.S. faces today?

I hope so, Ron.

Does such a thing happening involve more hope than reality?

You just have to keep working for something like that. We plan to have a session in Washington soon. We will have thirty to forty people, that's all. Yet we worked hard on this for a period of the months and did a lot of a mailings and solicitations. But one has to be content with that kind of response these days.

Of course, the movement in opposition to the Vietnam War began small and it grew to millions.

There is always the possibility, but now if the Russian threat continues to recede and if the economic picture gets better, those are factors that will make it more difficult.

How do young people in the movement today compare with those in the movement in the sixties?

I don't think there is a considerable difference. Whenever a challenge is put to young people in the movement today, they respond, provided the challenge is realistic and truthful and is presented by somebody who knows about commitment themselves.

Where you into the so-called scene of the sixties — the music, drugs, and sex — the counterculture?

No, not at all. [Laughs] Only in a marginal fashion. I never got into drugs. I don't think I smoked marijuana, and I never was part of the loose sexual traffic that was going on in those days.

Did the "loose sexual traffic" lead to an atmosphere of male chauvinism in the movement?

Males in the movement often didn't consider the opinion of women because they didn't have much sense. We automatically assumed that women should have a secondary role, that they weren't leaders and shouldn't take risks. We assumed all that and acted on it.

What changed your attitudes towards women in the movement?

People helped me to change, especially some of the women in the movement.

You mean like Elizabeth, your wife?

Very definitely. She has always been a strong supporter and has had a lot of influence on me and my thinking, as have some of the other women in our community.

Looking back to the sixties, how would you summarize the period's legacy?

I see the sixties legacy in a very positive light. It was a tragic period in

American history that involved degradation and genocide and four million dead in Indochina. But America's eyes were opened. Thanks largely to the movement, the American people didn't buy a war the U.S. government tried to sell them. Because committed people offered a thoughtful critique of our government and national life, it was one of the noblest periods in American history. For the first time, we woke up as a people. The sixties made those who continue the struggle more sophisticated in how we analyze what this country has done and become.

Ironically, Vietnam is still with us, isn't it? It still haunts and influences our thinking as a country.
     That's true. We never got into a national analysis of what we did there. We didn't want to live up to that responsibility. The Germans and the Russians have come to some accommodation with the crime of their history, but this country never has.

I ran across an article in the American Scholar, *written by James Hitchcock. He wrote that the Berrigans' activism represents "a reaffirmation of the central importance of religious values in American life, a denial that religion and activism cannot be separated in any real sense." Would you agree with that assessment?*
     Yes, most definitely. We have faith in commitment and a belief in universal justice and the idea that we have to remake the world in order for man to survive. The Bible has been a handbook for us, as we seek to change society. In order to be Christians, we must love our enemies and believe in universal justice for all. That's perhaps the most breathtaking aspect of the whole thing.

Do you miss the priesthood and ministering to people?
     I like to think I minister in a different way.

So what about your future? Is there any chance that you will retire from the activist life?
     I can't see any change in what I'm doing or plan to do, so long as health and community hold up. I will continue to meet and work with a whole range of community people from Maine to North Carolina. That's continuing. I will continue, so long as I can walk, talk, and shoot my mouth off. [Laughs]

11

Anita Hoffman

Reluctant Radical

> In terms of psychedelics, sexual liberation, women's liberation, gay liberation . . . we had a tremendous impact. And I think the idealism we had in the sixties—the desire to make the world a better place—still exists. I see ourselves as part of a huge transformation that is now going on and that will go on for the next twenty years as we move into the next millennium.

In his biography of Abbie Hoffman, Marty Jezer wrote, "Despite his need for personal independence, Abbie did not find his life complete without a woman, so his optimism about his life's direction was confirmed when . . . he met Anita Kushner, a volunteer at Liberty House."[1] Abbie and Anita quickly found they had a lot in common. They both had studied psychology in university, and, in their desire to become actively involved in making the world a better place, they both shared the idealism of sixties youth.

"If I had been a woman. I would have been Anita," Abbie later wrote. "Sometimes couples take forty years of living together to get to look and act alike: we began right off."[2]

Born in 1942 in Baltimore, Maryland, Anita grew up in a middle-class Jewish family in Queens, New York. A bright student, she graduated with honors from Goucher College and was awarded a Danforth Fellowship to study English literature at Columbia University. But she found the academic life stifling and dropped out to work in publishing. She then returned to school and earned her M.A. in psychology at Yeshiva University.

After meeting at Liberty House in 1964, Anita and Abbie moved into together, eventually married, and went on to participate in many of the significant events and activities of the sixties experience. In 1967, they were together with 10,000 other New Yorkers at the East Coast's first Be-In and later at the Spring Mobilization against the Vietnam War, which was also held in New York City. The following year, they and thousands of other protesters marched on the Pentagon. Together, they shared the music, the life-style, and the drug experience of the counterculture.

Anita remained a radical activist for nearly ten years until she became

169

Anita Hoffman (photo courtesy of Anita Hoffman).

disillusioned with the movement after making a trip to Algeria. At Abbie's request, she had joined a Yippie-Weathermen delegation to celebrate the birthday of LSD guru Tim Leary, who had escaped from jail and fled to Algeria to
join Eldridge Cleaver and a number of other Black Panthers who were living
in exile. Cleaver, who had jumped bail and escaped to Algeria after a gun battle
with police, was the Black Panthers' leader.

Anita was turned off by Cleaver's "power trip"; his treatment of his wife,
Kathleen; and the timidity of the other white radicals who had come with her
to Algeria in the face of Cleaver's strong-arm tactics. Anita fled Algeria and
made her way to Paris to join Abbie. But other radicals criticized Anita for her
defiance in Algeria and ostracized the Hoffmans.

In 1974, after being busted on a charge of selling cocaine, Abbie jumped
bail and went underground. Anita decided not to join him. Instead, she went
through many changes and started to stake out a new life for herself and son
America, whom she and Abbie had conceived in Paris. She got interested in
the emerging women's movement and found a self-help center for mothers on
welfare. Later, she moved to Los Angeles and found jobs working in publishing
and in Hollywood. Today, Anita Hoffman seems to have found her niche in
the electronics revolution as a producer of multimedia.

*   *   *

Do you recall when you became politically aware?

When I was in high school, I began to read newspapers like the *New York Times*. The whole family use to lounge around on Sundays and read the *Times*. That started it.

I can also remember doing a report in high school on *Profiles in Courage* and reading a book by Chester Bowles in which he wrote about going to India and seeing the poverty there.[3] That book was real important to me. The poverty he described was so overwhelming, but he also wrote about starting programs to feed the people and working to improve their living conditions. After reading that book, there was no question about what I was going to do with my life. I was going to try to help make conditions better for people.

Then at age sixteen, my parents enrolled me in a small woman's college in Baltimore named Goucher College, mainly because, I think, they wanted me to marry well. I was a very bright kid, but they were not ambitious for me. They knew about Goucher College and looked up to it. In their mind, Goucher represented what was the finest but it turned out to be a huge disappointment.

Why was that?

It turned out to be very cloistered. It was a women's college with seven hundred mostly southern debutantes, along with some Jewish girls from New Jersey. I happened to be a Jewish girl from Queens [New York]. It was not very intellectually stimulating, but it did have small classes and some good professors. I was bored, so I just kept on reading. I majored in English literature.

I recall that in my second year [at Goucher], there were civil rights demonstrations in Baltimore. I participated in the first integrated sit-in at Woolworth's. The feeling at the sit-in was so completely different than what I experienced in college. There was no hierarchy and none of the superficial things that I had grown up with or that separated people at school. It didn't matter who had this title or that title, or who was in charge, or what you were wearing. For the first time, I saw black college students — black male college students — in leadership roles. It was a terrific experience! I went on to participate in two more sit-ins.

Did you get arrested?

No. In fact, I don't think anybody was arrested. The sit-ins in Baltimore that I experienced were pretty pallid compared to what was happening in the South. But I did graduate from Goucher with honors in 1962 and then went on to Columbia University graduate school to study English literature. I was interested in eighteenth century English literature, but my adviser was Jeffrey Hart, who later attained fame at Dartmouth as founder of the *Dartmouth Review*, a very conservative publication. [Laughs] But I dropped out of the program because it was too academic and totally removed from real life.

I left school and took a job in the publishing industry, only to discover that women like me, who have no connections, have a tough time getting a good

job. I was put in the Rights and Permissions Department, which involved totally boring work that had nothing to do with being an English major. It was
just a glorified secretarial position. I knew I wouldn't get an editorial position —

Because you were a woman?

Yes, because I was a woman. That was the time before women's liberation. So I quit and went to graduate school in psychology at Yeshiva University. I didn't have a background in psychology, so I studied on my own and then
took the Graduate Record Examination and passed.[4] The year was 1964.

Why did you decide to go into psychology?

Because of my idealism. I saw it as a way of helping. I once visited a mental
hospital, where a friend of mine was undertaking a residency in psychiatry. I
saw how poor women, most of whom were black, were treated. I thought
maybe psychology was a way of helping people like them. I also thought that
graduate school was a way for a female to get ahead because she would be
respected for her brain.

I saw a notice on a Columbia University bulletin board, advertising for
students to work as Pinkerton cops at the World's Fair in Flushing Meadows.
I applied and got hired. A lot of the guys were either former cops or rejects
from the police department. The women were the wives of other police
officers and New York City detectives. They were mostly white, lower middle
class, and racist. They didn't read. I remember remarking with shock, "They
don't even read movie magazines!" They were not even embarrassed by their
racism. I felt estranged from them.

Then the SNCC [Student Nonviolent Coordinating Committee] sit-ins
happened at the Florida Pavilion. The Pinkerton cops were vicious in the way
they arrested the protesters and took them away. They beat them up! I was
shocked and disgusted! As a way of protesting what happened, I made a contribution of one-week's pay to SNCC.

Given your budding activism, why didn't you join SNCC?

It was like another world. It was a step that, at the time, didn't occur to
me. Besides, it would have meant quitting a job I needed.

*Nineteen sixty-four was the year of Freedom Summer. Did you consider going
south?*

No. I was not that ballsy. I was just a conventional young, liberal woman.
I hadn't reached the point where I thought of myself as a movement person.
So I completed graduate school and got a Master's degree.

But I once again became disillusioned. A single mother, who was a fellow
graduate student, cracked up. She actually had a breakdown. One of the
woman professors started analyzing what had happened to her in a presump-
tuous way that turned me off. I was repelled by psychology's pomposity and
its smug assumption that it understood everything; so rather than continue in
graduate school, I dropped out.

By this time, the Vietnam War was starting to go strong. There were stories about the napalming of civilians. I had seen this powerful film about the Holocaust, and I felt this strong urge to do something.

To me, it seemed the best thing to do would be to work for the New York American Civil Liberties Union. I liked the fact they were so principaled. It wasn't like joining a faction of the Left, which at the time, was very confusing and threatening to me. I always thought of the Left as consisting of people always telling you what to do.

I went to work as an assistant for the head of the public relations at the New York ACLU. I did a lot of low-level stuff like copying documents on the mimeograph machine. I eventually quit the job because of sexism. When my supervisor quit, I thought I deserved a shot at her position, but I wasn't given it. So I quit.

I vowed that I had had it with the white collar world. I wasn't making any progress. I thought I would drop out and be a waitress. I collected unemployment benefits, lived in the Village [Greenwich Village], and was kind of confused.

But then I thought that, being unemployed, it might be a good idea to do some volunteer work one day a week. A fellow graduate student told me about the work being done at Liberty House. I had read something about it in the [Village] Voice.

I went to Liberty House on a rainy day, and Abbie was there alone in the store. That's how we met. [Laughs] The scene is still vivid in my mind. He was wearing these brown cordoroy jeans and a cowboy shirt, and he looked incredibly sexy to me. I thought, "My god, this guy must have founded the store." I was intimidated.

But we spent the whole day talking. I found out that he had a graduate degree in psychology and that we had a lot in common. I realized he was just another graduate student like me. I was less intimidated. Sometime during the day, he put a tab of acid in my hand. I had never seen one before. [Laughs] He wasn't really offering it to me, just showing off.

Beatles music played on the radio all day — songs like "Strawberry Fields." We made a date for that night. I was thrilled! I had never met anybody like him before. He wore tight clothes and seemed like a dancer . . . so light and comfortable in his body. I think he was the first guy in my life whom I really thought was sexy. I didn't care about anything else in my life. All I knew was that I would be with him that evening.

I didn't even care if he lived with another woman. I actually thought he could even be gay, or bisexual. He shrieked sex to me and that sex could be any kind. I was not very experienced, but it didn't seem to matter.

How did your relationship with Abbie develop?

Very quickly. He came to my house that night carrying a lunch bag, which I later learned was typical of movement people. They didn't want to impose or give you the impression that you had to feed them. So he showed up on our first date with this little brown bag. [Laughs]

We put on the Beatles "Revolver" album. At the time, you were supposed to regard Red China with horror, but he told me Mao wrote poetry and that he had eliminated poverty in his country. Of course, I was pretty impressed. He was giving me a message and challenging me: Reality isn't exactly the way you think it is.

We smoked grass and started dancing to the Beatles. Then we made love. We were together every night after that, and two weeks later, we moved in together and started living together.

So Abbie introduced you to the movement.

I had noticed young people — hippies — walking around in the Village, but I didn't understand what they were about. Eventually, we took acid together, went to Be-Ins, etc. I thought of myself as his mate.

I think Abbie was the most fearless person I had ever met. We went to a lot of demonstrations together. I remember going to one in New York City called "Support Our Boys in Vietnam," where we were pelted with eggs and tomatoes. The situation was really scary because it looked like some of the people would attack us. With Abbie, my courage was tested because I was put into situations I wouldn't have chosen for myself.

Did Abbie encourage you to grow as a person?

At the time, he would tell me that he considered me a female version of himself, which I thought was very flattering. But I told myself I knew it wasn't true. [Laughs]

Did he talk with you?

Oh yeah! We had a wonderful dialogue. I think he liked me because I am smart and gave him back appropriate feedback. That is the thing I miss most about those years. In good matings, there is tremendous feedback and give and take, as well as ongoing dialogue. We had all that!

Did you have an influence on him?

I'm sure I did. I was more of an ethically concerned person than I was a Lefty. Thay is how I see myself today. Abbie was a part of the Left, but he wasn't ideological. Only if it suited him. He was concerned about solving problems and issues. He was a grassroots organizer. Both of us had this love-hate relationship with the Left.

How did other people in the movement perceive you? Did they take you seriously and view you as an activist or as simply "Abbie's woman"?

I was never a person who aspired to power. I sort of accepted Abbie as leader, although I did have some original ideas myself. The idea of calling the Free Store "heaven" was mine, although there is some dispute about who coined the name "Yippies." Paul Krassner says he did. But it's not really worth arguing about.

I did feel a part of the movement . . . a respected member of the group. But then after the trial [of the Chicago Seven], there was this Yippie visit to see Eldridge Cleaver, who was a fugitive in Algeria. The idea was to celebrate Tim Leary's birthday after he [Leary] had escaped from jail. The idea was to bring all the groups in the movement together and have a media event.

Abbie couldn't go because federal restrictions on traveling overseas had been placed on him. Abbie wanted me to go in his place, but the truth is I didn't want to. I had no interest in going because I was going through changes.

Women's Lib had already started. I really respected what Robin Morgan and those other women were doing and saying. But I also knew Robin Morgan would take every opportunity to attack Abbie. I wouldn't go to [women's] consciousness raising sessions because everybody would be waiting for the opportunity, as every word came out of my mouth, to attack Abbie: [In a sarcastic tone] "So he doesn't really want to do housework."

I became very isolated and went through a lot of changes. I had a lot of discussions with Abbie, too, about our life together. It was one thing for him to come out publicly with very progressive ideas about women's liberation, but it's another thing when I was the only one cleaning the house.

But I ended up going to Algeria as a substitute for Abbie with a group of radicals. It was a rigid atmosphere and a very complex situation. Eldridge Cleaver turned out to be this authoritarian person who ran a militaristic operation. He was probably worried that the Yippies might embarrass him because he was a guest of the Algerian government, so he kept us locked up in this apartment.

Tim Leary and [his wife] Rosemary were terrified; but they lived in this seaside hotel, so, at least, they didn't have to live with Eldridge. Eldridge was also controlling Kathleen [Eldridge Cleaver's wife], and it came out later, I think in the *Village Voice*, that she had had an affair with one of the other Black Panther fugitives who had come over with him, and Eldridge allegedly had had him killed. Meanwhile, he was having an affair with a half–Belgian, half–Arab mistress, and we were kept imprisoned in the mistress's apartment. Very ugly stuff.

I only had one chance to meet Kathleen, but I liked her. It was at a dinner where all the men got the food first, and the women later had to go off to another room, where they sat on the floor. It was like the Panthers were influenced by the Algerian treatment of women.

Were you afraid?

I was more angry than afraid. When I rebelled, no one took my side, which really shocked me because I thought they would. My mistake was not lining up any allies before I made my stand. Not being a political person, I didn't understand this.

It wouldn't have changed anything any way, would it?

No. It wouldn't have changed anything. Eventually, I climbed out of a window and escaped. I had to talk my way out of Algeria because I was leaving without Eldridge's permission. I went to Paris where Abbie and Jerry [Rubin] were staying.

While all this was going on, Tim Leary was on a good will tour of the Arab countries. He heard about what happened when he came back to Algeria. Tim and I have somewhat of a close friendship now because, through the years, he has really respected me for doing what I did in Algeria.

In Paris there was this big Yippie split. Nobody believed my version of events in Algeria except Abbie and a few friends. Jerry Rubin didn't take my side. I knew that when I got back to the U.S. and the story got out, nobody was going to believe the word of a white woman against the Black Panthers. I became so disillusioned with the movement that I wanted to drop out to have a baby . . . finally. So we conceived our child, America, in Paris.

Given the "Yippie split," what is your relationship with Jerry Rubin today?

We have had our ins and outs. I just spent Thanksgiving at Jerry's, where he had a little gathering. He's incredibly wealthy and not very political anymore. But back in those days, Jerry didn't have an endearing personality like Abbie's. In fact, there were times I resented him.

Why was that?

It seemed to me he was rigidly leftist. You know that idea leftists have — that the world has got to get worse before it gets better. That if people suffer enough, they will eventually rise up. I loathe that idea! I think it's evil!

Given what Jerry Rubin is today, do you think he was a genuine leftist in the sixties who was serious about what he espoused?

I think he was. The weird thing, though, is that I like him better now. I guess that's because I know him better today and accept him as he is. It may also be because I was always comparing him to Abbie, and, if we didn't agree on every point, I would get angry. But I thought they were a great combination and good for each other. They had complementary talents and abilities.

What is your opinion of the controversy surrounding Jerry's desire to do a biography of Abbie? [Paul] Krassner wrote an article in the Utne Reader *about Rubin signing a contract for $400,000 to write a biography of Abbie.*[5]

Abbie's got a lunatic brother, Jack, who went to the publisher and prevented Jerry from getting the contract. I said to Jerry, "Why don't you do a book about Abbie in which you write about the years you knew him? That makes more sense than writing a straight-forward biography." I think what Jack did was horrible because I do believe in free speech. It put me more on Jerry's side than I was before the whole thing started.

I don't understand why the publisher would knuckle under to Abbie's brother.

Jack warned the publisher that nobody would talk to Jerry if it went ahead with the book. The irony is that Jack was never close to Abbie, but he now goes around saying he talked with Abbie each day and how close he was with him. Jack wasn't even a politico! After Abbie died, Jack was the first one to appear on TV and to hustle to get an agent for a book. It got quite ugly after he [Abbie] died.

What impact did having a baby have on your relationship with Abbie?
I remember the headline in the newspaper: "ABBIE HAS BABY." [Laughs]

[Laughs] Like you didn't have anything to do with it.
Right. [Laughs] But it was a very stressful time when I had the baby. Abbie and others in the Chicago Conspiracy Trial were being assessed for huge taxes on money they had actually raised giving speeches to help them pay for their defense. As expenses mounted, Abbie had to go out and keep making speeches, which meant I was left at home with the baby a lot.

Yeah, it was really hard on me. Abbie loved the baby, but I was basically the one stuck at home taking care of him. It was a stressful situation, because we never had any money—

That's ironic, because you and Abbie were often criticized for getting "rich off the movement."
Rolling Stone [magazine] wrote that we lived in a penthouse, but we actually lived in a little apartment on the roof of the building on Thirteenth Street. While I was pregnant in 1971, we attended this demonstration against the U.S. invasion of Cambodia, and Abbie was arrested and put in a stadium. Abbie somehow managed to escape, but the FBI arrested him in the hallway of our apartment building one night while we were waiting for the elevator. When I spoke to the press, I mentioned that the incident had happened in "the lobby" of our apartment building. *Rolling Stone* and other publications jumped on that and wrote it up to imply that it happened in the lobby of a fancy building.

But we didn't believe in establishing some gray socialist or party-line Communist life-style. The idea was not to reduce everyone to a subsistence level to make it fair. The idea was to work to establish a system in which everyone had the middle-class life-style that we prosperous American have. We wanted to bring everybody up, not push everybody down.

We lived modestly. In fact, we gave $25,000 to the Black Panther Defense Committee. But we enjoyed ourselves. We enjoyed going to the movies and traveling. Abbie lived a lot of stuff that [Abraham] Maslow[6] preached and which presaged the New Age. The Left has always had a puritanical streak that we resented.

According to Jezer's biography of Abbie, he got a lot of heat from women's groups.
He did. Robin Morgan attributed a quote to Abbie that actually came from John Sinclair. It was something like "Yippies were about wine, women and song." Abbie would not make such a stupid statement! He did not knowingly make such sexist statements. He believed in women's liberation.

But at times it was difficult for me because Abbie met all kinds of women in the movement, including the famous ones, such as Germaine Greer.[7] Abbie would joke that he wanted to seduce her. I remember when Germaine Greer came to our house for dinner. She flirted with Abbie and ignored me. At the time, it was hurtful because I was then pregnant with America.

Looking back now, though, I see that period from a different perspective. A lot of what I thought I saw was the result of my shyness and lack of experience in the world. Women were always flirting with Abbie. He did have a strong sex drive and a big ego. I think the disease — the manic depression — has a sexual component.

Given the criticism Abbie experienced and the way the movement was going, was he getting disillusioned?

Women were attacking him. . . . He had a dispute over *Steal This Book* [Amereon Books, 1976].[8] It was his idea. He had done all the writing for it. Those things bothered him. Abbie wasn't interested in power. He was just a charismatic leader and speaker who was totally committed to his cause. He slept very little and was completely immersed in his work. But I do believe his disease made him increasingly irritable over the years. There were times when he was difficult to live with. He was getting frustrated because he knew he was right and what was wrong and what needed to be done, but he had to be polite and let newer younger people play more of a role.

Looking back now, those times seemed so chaotic . . . we were so young. . . . In the late eighties, Abbie talked about the "arrogance of youth." [Laughs] We did have the arrogance of youth. We believed we were right. But being young, we did some stupid things. That's understandable.

Were you aware of Abbie's manic depression in the sixties?

That was my major mistake, although I probably couldn't have changed anything. I had a degree in psychology, but I didn't know he was manic at certain times. The disease did increase his energy to do what he was doing. At times he was like Superman! I don't think it was a bad thing at that time. Only when he went underground did he start to get depressed because it was hard for him to be alone.

Why did you decide not to go underground?

We had a baby, and I didn't know what going underground would be like. We feared he would be caught if we traveled together. I always knew that Abbie, even with all his macho posturing, was more vulnerable than he appeared. But it was only later that I understood why he was vulnerable. It was, of course, because of his illness — his manic depression.

When Abbie was underground, there was a time when I thought he was actually cracking up. I went to see a famous psychiatrist to see if there was any way he could help him. He couldn't because there was no way the psychiatrist could see Abbie. It was too dangerous.

Abbie was accused of selling cocaine. Did he?

No. I don't think he ever bought or sold cocaine in his life. We could never afford it. But he did know a lot of rich people—movement hangers-on, artists, movie people—who gave it to him. Like a lot of people at the time, Abbie didn't realize cocaine was bad. It was like: Here's this new thing! Freud used it. I really think it helped set off his illness.

Do you ever regret not going underground with him?

If I had gone underground, I would probably have put Abbie in danger of being caught. He would have had a wife and kid to worry about and maybe we would have had fights. Abbie was a strong personality, and I don't know if I could have controlled him if he became manic while underground.

In a way, then, maybe my ignorance of not knowing about his manic depression was for the best. On the other hand, maybe I could have sought treatment for Abbie if I had known. But in those days, of course, we were antipsychiatry because psychiatry was antigay, antiwomen, and antimovement.

Looking back, it was a difficult situation, and I feel bad about it! I really miss him! He was the love of my life. I've never had that type of relationship with anyone since. I never had those types of feelings since. I just miss him terribly.

While Abbie went underground, your life was kind of hell, wasn't it? I understand the FBI had you under surveillance.

Yes, but the first two years after Abbie went underground were probably the two most important years of my life. The women's liberation stuff had been eating away at me, and I now had a chance to be on my own. Everything I did, I got credit for, even if it was just myself who knew about it.

Of course, Abbie had inspired me. I had learned so much by osmosis, and now I had a chance to use it. I founded a self-help center for women on welfare. To get it started, I arranged training in welfare advocacy from the ACLU and raised money from foundations and Wall Street firms. The Downtown Welfare Advocacy Center lasted a long time; but eventually I got burned out, and other women took it over.

I did the letter book [*To America with Love: Letters from the Underground* (Stonehill Publishing, 1976)] and started to move into spiritual things and indulge in new interests. I left New York and went to Santa Fe where Abbie, Johanna,[9] another couple, and I tried to establish an underground commune. But it didn't last too long. Nobody really helped me take care of the kid, and I was resentful. We split up, but I stayed on in Santa Fe for eighteen months.

I then went to Los Angeles and worked for the *L.A. Weekly* as a reporter. After that, I worked for actor Jon Voight[10] as a story writer for three years. Abbie and I had met Jon at the Chicago Conspiracy Trial. That was my first real job after becoming a single parent. There should always be the option for mothers to stay home and raise children, but I remember being on the L.A. freeway with all the other commuters and feeling great. I felt I had joined mainstream society. I really love being a part of the world, as opposed to being a single mother stuck at home.

Being a single parent, do you have thoughts on how society can help women in your situation?

I think for the electronic revolution to happen — HDTV [High Definition Television], fiber optics, access to the Library of Congress from home computers, and all those sorts of thing — huge numbers of people are going to have to be trained in the new technology. I would like to see a job-training program put in place for everyone who has been left out of the system. Train the disadvantaged so they can enter this new world.

Some aspects of the new technology are boring. Sometimes it involves nothing more than people just entering data into a computer. But there are creative aspects as well, and the real possibility of true participatory democracy through interactive TV, voting electronically, networking, and the town hall concept. These things will happen within the next ten years.

Looking back to your sixties experience, was that part of your life one quick psychedelic experience or did you and other radicals accomplish anything?

Well, it's debatable.

You know conservatives have disparaged the sixties and have criticized what they see as the era's "narcissism."

I think we were the last gasp of romanticism, and we did have a strong cultural influence on what followed. Abbie was right in his belief that a dedicated minority can bring about change. In terms of psychedelics, sexual liberation, women's liberation, gay liberation, we had a tremendous impact. And I think the idealism we had in the sixties — the desire to make the world a better place — still exists among baby boomers. I see ourselves as part of a huge transformation that is now going on and that will go on for the next twenty years as we move into the next millenium.

What's going to happen?

I believe the electronic revolution is creating a new nervous system for the planet. We are becoming one planet, one world. I know we have a lot of problems and that there have been setbacks, but it is a part of the process. It's important that the Cold War is over. That was so insane! It was an insanity that my generation had to live with, but, to our credit, we reacted against it.

Do you still see yourself as feminist?

Of course, but I'm surprised that feminism is still somehow considered controversial and that some young people get turned off by the term. I work with some young women who consider themselves Leftist but are contemptuous of feminists. Many of the feminist issues of the sixties are still around today. It's something to get angry about.

Did you, like a lot of other feminists, get angry when you saw the Anita Hill–Clarence Thomas hearings?

Of course! I feel her side made a big mistake by letting the other side hog the media. I learned from the sixties experience that you have to flood the airwaves with your information. Otherwise, people will just believe the other side.

Do you think the hearings helped raise women's consciousness?

Oh, a tremendous amount! So many women have been victimized by sexual harassment at work. A lot of women who didn't believe her [Anita Hill] immediately after the hearings have now come forward and say they believe her. I think a lot of black people believed her but were angry with her because she did it publicly. They felt she had embarrassed the [black] community.

Issues like sexual harassment have to be dealt with openly. That's why steps are now being taken in so many workplaces to deal with the problem. The issue has entered mainstream.

You seem optimistic about the way society is going. How about your life?

My life has been one long learning experience—a quest to make a better life for me and my kid. I haven't always succeeded. Now for the first time, I'm doing work that I want to do, that is, producing multimedia. I'm excited about the new technology and the wonderful ways it can communicate information. Communication is what brought down the Iron Curtain.[11]

The challenge for young people from the First World [the developed nations] is not to become too decadent. The danger is that young people will get wrapped up in the trivial aspects of the new technology and get cut off from the rest of the world. That's the danger and the challenge the electronic revolution presents.

12

Jerry Rubin
A Man for All Seasons

> The true flowering of the sixties will come in the nineties when the children of the sixties come into power in politics, government, and business. Bill Clinton being the first baby boomer to be elected President is an indication of that. It's going to be exciting because the sixties are going to come back in the nineties without the shrillness and with the generation working within the system.

Jerry Rubin was the sixties rabble rouser who gave us such choice and blunt admonitions as "Do it!" and "Don't trust anyone over thirty." He even advised his generation to make its day by killing their parents. Rubin stood at the center of the turbulent period as a kind of court jester who egged on the establishment and fomented discontent. Rubin and Abbie Hoffman became the "Abbott and Costello"[1] of guerrilla theater in the sixties. Among other antics, the two threw money on the floor of the Wall Street Stock Exchange, campaigned to elect a pig as president, and stood trial as a member of the now mythic Chicago Seven on charges of inciting a riot during the 1968 Democratic National Convention in Chicago.

Rubin appeared before the House Un-American Activities Committee (HUAC) dressed first as an American Revolutionary War soldier, then as a bare-chested urban guerrilla, and finally as Santa Claus. He wrote the book *Do It!* (1970), which became a manifesto for the counterculture. He even spent time in jail, not, however, from a conviction at the Chicago Seven trial, although he was one of five defendants convicted of crossing state lines to incite a riot. The convictions were later overturned.

After the sixties became history and America crawled through the seventies, Rubin gradually withdrew from the public scene. Then in 1980, Rubin went to work on Wall Street, moving in a new direction as an unabashed yuppie and aspiring entrepreneur. In the mid-eighties, he began to generate almost as much publicity as he did in the sixties by operating a networking business in which working professionals paid Rubin large fees to go to parties he arranged, where they hoped they would meet people who could advance their careers. Thousands flocked to such famous Big Apple hot spots as the Palladium and Studio 54 to meet, exchange business cards, transact business, and mingle with the opposite sex.

My first interview with Jerry Rubin took place in 1988 at my hotel room in Manhattan, New York, a few blocks from Rubin's office, where, explained Rubin, the interview would not be subjected to the distractions of his busy schedule. About 5 feet 6 inches in height and delicate looking, Rubin was nattily dressed in tie, shirt, dress slacks, and tennis shoes in quintessential eighties yuppy style. Rubin had just turned 50, but could have passed for a man 15 years younger. He looked relaxed and in good shape for a man any age.

Before the interview began, I asked him if he would like something to drink. He ordered—what else?—Perrier water. Speaking in a clipped tone, Rubin was relaxed, cordial, and articulate and talked enthusiastically about his transformation from sixties radical to business entrepreneur, his future with his wife and child, and his career as an entrepreneur.

Our second interview took place four years later in Los Angeles in Rubin's luxurious $4,000-a-month apartment in the city's Westwood suburb, a few miles from the UCLA campus. The 54-year-old Rubin was no longer married or running a networking business. This time, he was dressed in blue jeans and t-shirt and constantly on the phone establishing his latest entrepreneurial venture: multilevel marketing. No relaxed posture for Rubin this time. He may have been dressed casually, but his demeanor revealed a man—a business man—under pressure.

As I waited patiently for the interview to begin, Rubin talked with associates about the sale of bottled water and health products distributed by Omnitrition International, the company with which he is associated. They include a line of so-called smart foods that are promoted as nutrients for the brain and that go by the names of WOW, Focus, and Go for It.

Once again, Rubin was at the center of controversy. In late 1992, he and Omnitrition were hit with a class action suit, which charged the company was associated with a pyramid scheme that stacked the odds against its investors. The plaintiffs claimed the distributors earned their bonuses and concessions based on how many new distributors they recruited, not on the products sold.

In a letter to *USA Today*, Rubin defended multilevel marketing, saying, "In the 1960s, I scorned money; in the 1990s, I am now helping to make money in a real and honest way," and added, "Through network marketing, we will create an economic transformation in the 1990s as profound as the social changes that took place in America in the 1960s."

Did Rubin really believe this, or was he, as his critics contend, on another self-promotion trip? I began to find out, once he put down the phone and began answering my questions.

*   *   *

Jerry Rubin (photo by the author).

Good to see you again. I don't remember that serious expression the last time I interviewed you.

Okay, now I'm smiling. I've got all your questions laid out, too. Why aren't you smiling, Jerry? Do you have ulcers yet? Why don't you have two phones? Why don't you relax? . . . Stop being my father. You're not president of the Help Jerry Rubin Club.

[Laughs] Anyway, the last time I interviewed you, you were in New York City, and now you are living on the other side of the country. What happened?

The police ordered me out of the city.

[Laughs] No, those days are gone, Jerry.

[Laughs] Well, it was a volunteer move.

A business move?

Business, yes. Personal, yes. Change, yes. California is a visionary state. New York wasn't giving me much space to think. I can think with less limitations here. In New York, the world crowds in on you, and you have to create your own reality. I'll probably move back to New York some day. If you look at my life, you will see that I've shuttled back and forth between New York and L.A.

Are you still into running?

I do less of it.

But I see the bottle of Perrier water on the table in front of us.
   Yes, it's good for you.

Running less, Perrier more.
   Yes, but getting back to your question of why I came to L.A. I'm into the beginning of decades, and I feel more comfortable in L.A. because it is a kind of barometer of what is happening in the rest of the country. A lot of what happens in the country happens first in California.
   Also, I have a five-year-old and a three-year-old, and I felt it would be nice to be around them the early part of their lives. They live with their mother. We are divorced, but the kids live with me half the time.
   I'm also involved with a national sales organization that sells nutritional drinks, bottled water, and packaged food. That's how I make my money and support myself. It's better to do that kind of entrepreneurship on the West Coast than the East Coast.

You had a networking organization in New York the last time I saw you. You brought business people together in a social situation so they could interact.
   That's what I did then, but I stopped in the late eighties when the business fell apart. I got involved in what I believe is the boom industry of the nineties: multilevel marketing. In multilevel marketing, you make a commission on people by teaching them to build their business organization. It's entrepreneurs teaching entrepreneurs to be entrepreneurs.

It's a controversial activity.
   Yes, it's got a lot of problems, a lot of challenges, and a lot of possibilities, but it's very democratic. It's almost socialistic capitalism in a strange sort of way. It's people working together . . . supporting each other.

Why did your [New York] networking enterprise fall apart?
   The social trends changed. People began to stay at home more and weren't going out as much. The yuppies as a force crashed.

Part of the controversy of multilevel marketing is that critics contend it is nothing more than a pyramid scheme. In fact, that is what a lawsuit against you charges.
   It's a frivolous sort of lawsuit because it's not a pyramid scheme. The guy who sued me has nothing to do with me. Suing me was the only way that the law firm, which blackmails genuine multilevel marketing companies, can get publicity. Sue a person like me, and you get a headline in *USA Today*. Sure, there are pyramid schemes in multilevel marketing. That's the case when there isn't a genuine product. People should be warned against those pyramid schemes. I can name twenty right now, but what I'm involved with is not a pyramid scheme.

Well, how would you describe it?
   It's an alternative way of moving products right from the manufacturer to the individual—

But it still sounds like a pyramid scheme to me.

Yeah, in the sense that everybody is at the top of his organization. If you look at society, every big organization is a pyramid. The Democratic Party is a pyramid—the President is on top. GM [General Motors] is a pyramid. Apple Computer is a pyramid. But those enterprises are undemocratic, while ours is democratic, which means that anybody at the bottom of a pyramid can start his own pyramid.

But the point is how can everybody make money in a system like that?

Yes, they can, but they have to work hard. It's not a lottery ticket. You can make money from Amway. It's a great idea! Why can't you buy products from yourself and make money by recommending products to other people. That's a fabulous idea! That's the great capitalistic secret big corporations don't want you to know. They want you to go to their stores and buy from them. Amway is a revolutionary idea!

But here is the defining question: Is there a retailable product that people outside the money-making structure want? If there is, it's not a pyramid. If there isn't, it's a pyramid. In our situation, we see incredible nutritional supplements and bottled water that comes from one of the few springs in America. The products we sell have a retail market.

But your critics say that what you sell is "horsefeathers." That's the exact word one of your critics used.

Well, no one ever built a statue to a critic. We sell high-powered vitamin supplements, and there are people who are against the vitamin industry. Vitamins are essential to take. People who don't take vitamins will be looked upon in the next ten years the way people who smoke cigarettes are looked upon today. You are nuts if you don't take care of yourself! I believe in health self-reliance. It's one of my bedrock beliefs. My parents were dead by the time they were in their late forties, but I am as healthy a person as you will find in the world.

So are you happy?

Deliriously happy ... deliriously happy... So—

Are you serious or being sarcastic? I can't tell by the tone of your voice.

Of course, I'm serious ... but I don't want the critic's comment to go by unchallenged. The media can always trot out some expert who says certain products don't work. We sell a product called "Wow," which I believe is the product of the nineties. It's a caffeinated, amino acid drink.

We sell another product that contains Arginine—an isolated amino acid. If you don't know what that is, I suggest you go to the library and find out. The critics can say what they want, but our products are based on scientific credibility. They work! They are in demand; they are high quality. We are selling the idea of people looking good, keeping their weight down, and being as sharp physically and mentally as one can be. That's important when you consider the health care costs in this country. If doctors were paid to keep people healthy and not sick, they would recommend our products.

I read an article in which you called the nineties "the freedom decade" and that people-to-people marketing is going to be the vehicle to personal freedom. That sounds kind of grandiose. What do you mean by that?

I think people have to save the economy. The government isn't going to do it. People can save the economy by being self-reliant businessmen. I've already talked about being self-reliant in health. I'm very much into self-reliance. Self-reliance is the most revolutionary, radical idea in the world today.

What I mean by business self-reliance is that a person has to be responsible for his own financial security. A job doesn't mean security anymore, and the government can't give you financial security.

On the subject of security, will that lawsuit hurt your business?

No, it's not going to hurt business. That happened months ago. Sales keep going up.

What's your exact relationship to Omnitrition International?

I'm a distributor.

How many are there.

About thirty thousand. As I said, I'm my own boss. Everybody in multi-level marketing is their own boss.

Your detractors call you trendy, but, in looking at your life story, it seems to me that you have had a strong streak of self-reliance. Judging by what I've read about you and from what I learned talking to you, you seem to me to be a person who depends upon himself to make tough decisions.

I'm kind of an inner-directed person, but I'm sensitive to the external environment as well. I'm not an elitist, really. My background is pretty typical. I grew up in Cincinnati, the son of a truck driver.

When did you become political?

Growing up in Cincinnati, I could see that there was a big gap between blacks and whites. I felt uncomfortable with that and thought it was wrong. I remember when they started to build bomb shelters in Cincinnati. I kind of protested the arms race. I remember putting on a suit and handing out fliers.

One of the interesting things about your young life was that you actually met Ché Guevara.

I went to Cuba in 1964. We had a group interview with him. I had been editor of the high school newspaper and wanted to be a journalist at the time. I got hired by a newspaper every summer and did interviews with baseball players. I also interviewed [President] Jack Kennedy when he came to my college. I've always liked to be around action people. They make things happen.

Does your early background in journalism explain where your tremendous sense of how to use the media came from?

I'm a journalist, so I know where a story is, what makes news, and how to get people interested in a story. That's what makes a good political activist. That's what makes a good marketeer.

Why did you go to graduate school at the University of California at Berkeley?

I came to Berkeley because, at that time, in my mind, I was a political activist and wanted to go to the hotbed of activism. I came a year before the Free Speech Movement. I didn't like the economic inequality throughout the country. From that issue evolved the Free Speech Movement and then Vietnam. It was an exciting period when anything went politically. We had a sense of power in that we believed we had the answer and could make a difference.

What was the impact of the Free Speech Movement on the subsequent history of the country?

It showed what mass action could accomplish. It showed what a crowd could do if it was motivated by morality. It showed the power of an idea. It showed that you could stand up for an idea . . . and more.

Is that where you realized the power of theater in a movement?

Yes, I think the Free Speech Movement was theater. I remember the impact on the crowd when Mario Savio was dragged off a stage when he tried to make a speech. That was theater. Yes, that was one of the things that gave me the idea of theater. But anything that happened after that was theater. I helped to create the antiwar movement. We stopped troop trains. We burned draft cards. We had teach-ins. We marched on the Oakland Army Terminal and tried to close it down. We fought with the Hell's Angels.[2]

When did you fight with the Hell's Angels?

I can't recall exactly. There was some big demonstration, and the Hell's Angels attacked us. A big brawl broke out.

You had to defend yourself?

I was involved, but it didn't prevent us from marching again. Then it seemed like the whole country was marching. The House Armed Services Committee called me to Washington. I dressed in a Revolutionary War Soldier uniform . . .

Why?

To show that protest was American.

But a lot of your colleagues in the movement thought you were making a bad move.

Yeah, most people were against it at first but liked what I did after it happened.

God, that was almost thirty years ago! Which reminds me: In the sixties, you were one of the guys that helped popularize the slogan, "Don't trust anyone over thirty."

Gee, that's '68 and the time of the Democratic National Convention and the height of the protest movement. Yeah, I know I said, "Don't trust anyone over thirty," but I didn't mean it literally.

[Laughs] Are you serious, or has time clouded your memory?

We said a lot of things then, didn't we? [Laughs] No, I think turning fifty was much more traumatic.

It seems like you hate the idea of growing old.

Yes, because I love living so much.

Does it really matter what a person looks like? Isn't it a superficial way of relating to people? The conventional wisdom is that one should consider a person's inner beauty — his character and personality — more.

It's not superficial because how you look and take care of yourself indicates your attitude toward yourself. I'm not talking about surface beauty. I'm talking about reverence for life. And that begins with how you treat yourself. How can a revolutionary who wants to change the world eat junk food?

That contradiction escapes me completely. You're against corporations because they are poisoning the environment. You're against corporations because they dominate Latin America. Then you go into a restaurant and eat corporate food and think nothing of it. That's the contradiction of so many activists. To me, a revolutionary has to have a positive attitude toward others and to himself. I think the first responsibility of a revolutionary is to live a long life and to be healthy while you live a long life.

Do you still consider youself a revolutionary?

No, not at all.

Then do you consider yourself a part of the establishment . . . the established corporate world of America?

No, not really. When I think of the establishment, I think of the major corporations. I'm not an official in General Motors. I'm an entrepreneur who has created his own business and a new kind of industry. It works, it's profitable, but it's truly a self-creation. I'm not filling a corporate slot.

Also, I don't have an establishment approach to things, and I no longer believe in the credo "Are you a part of the establishment or part of the revolution?" If that were the case, then everybody is part of the establishment because there are so few revolutionaries. In fact, I don't know of any.

But do you now share the ethos of American business and the conservative values it holds? For example, do you believe in the familiar slogan "What is good for business is good for America"?

Well. I think that's too general and too much a cliché. What's the alternative to that? The state owns everything. To me, bureaucracy is as big a problem as business. Get rid of business? But we don't think what the alternative is.

Look at the Soviet Union. Business is good for the Soviet Union. I rejoice at the idea of business getting a foothold in that country. I would love for the Soviet Union to become a consumer society. If there is anything I would like to see right now, it's the growth of the middle class, the building of supermarkets, and the encouragement of entrepreneurship in the Soviet Union.

Look at the Soviet Union. It was antibusiness. It tried to organize itself around a rigid ideology where everyone would be equal. It failed! People suffered. But in this country, we have to encourage more entrepreneurship and less corporatism.

America is a corporate society dominated by major corporations. We don't know who is making the decisions. The object of corporate America is to make everything as cheap as possible so as to maximize profits. That's what's wrong with America. There has to be a better climate that allows entrepreneurs to flourish. That would be exciting. So in answer to your question, I don't subscribe to a corporate business philosophy. I wouldn't survive in a corporation.

Getting back to the sixties, what is your most vivid impression of the period?

It's sad that the sixties went up in a puff of smoke. No great novels came out of the sixties. No great sociology came out of the sixties. No great ideas came out of the sixties. The sixties generation really hasn't recorded itself or interpreted itself well. Too many of us got trapped in our own myths. We got stuck trying to relive our lives each year like we lived them in the sixties.

Didn't any good come out of the sixties?

Oh, an enormous amount! I think the sixties transformed America, making it a more pacific society. What the Right calls "the Vietnam Syndrome" has permanently changed America. Beginning around 1964, the people stood up and said that the American government was wrong about Vietnam and we the people were going to change it. By 1970, that resulted in having hundreds of thousands of people against the war. The country realized it was in a war that couldn't be won.

To me, that permanently changed the soul of the country. We didn't have the stomach to be an occupying force again. That's all because the sixties generation didn't say "Business as usual." They said "Morality first." That's a total transformation.

But the true flowering of the sixties will come in the nineties when the children of the sixties move into power in politics, government, and business. An indication of that is the fact that President Clinton is the first baby boomer to be elected President of the U.S. It's going to be exciting because I think the sixties will come back in the nineties without the shrillness and with the generation working within the system.

Are there any other positive things to come out of the sixties?

Sure, of course. The sixties, for example, increased the diversity of American life. Blacks became proud to be blacks, women proud to be women, and, to some extent, gays to be gays.

You had a lot of fun in the sixties, didn't you?

I certainly did! I do get nostalgic for it. It was an irresponsible time. We said things like, "Don't get married and don't have kids." Not growing up was a big part of the sixties. "Stay young forever," we said. Demonstrations were fun; riots were fun. Going home at night and seeing yourself on TV was fun.

But the greatest fun of all was being part of a moral movement that you thought was changing history. We believed we had a purpose . . . that our lives made a difference. What we did was important. Also, the sixties did a lot of things for the first time and that was fun. For example, collectively, it was the first time a generation smoked dope. It was the first generation to do acid. In the sixties, America lost its innocence.

Is today as exciting a time to live in as the sixties?

Oh, yes. America is such a colorful society today. There is so much excitement. But our expectation level for excitement has gotten too high. That's why we get bored so easy. In the sixties, we could get excited over a rally. [Laughs] We got an orgasm over that.

How would you compare the youth of today with that of the sixties? Is there much of a difference?

The youth of today are totally different. They are young adults. They try to act like mature adult men and women, although they lack the maturity. They are the product of the society they are living in now. They are exactly as they should be.

When you think back to the sixties, do you recall being embarrassed by anything you did?

No, but I regret not investing in real estate.

[Laughs] You should have invested in real estate!

I shouldn't have been so dogmatic. I should have had a few things going on the side.

Yeah, but you weren't into money in those days. You were into trying to transform the system.

But money can be a tool for positive things. I didn't realize that at the time.

So you regret not being more materialistic in the sixties?

No, not materialistic. I could have invested in real estate, let my investment sit, and now reap the dividends.

You're not serious! [Laughs]

I am serious. If I had known what I know now and I had a chance to relive the sixties, I'd probably buy real estate. I should have done that at least in the seventies, for God's sake! I was still against money in the seventies . . . and the early eighties.

But your experiences as a political activist in the sixties did help you make the transition to businessman and entrepreneur in the eighties.

Yes, do it! It's exactly what my book said when it came out in 1970. Don't talk about doing something. Don't come up with reasons why something can't happen. Be positive; go out and do it. That's the key to being an entrepreneur.

But on the other hand, the key thing to being an entrepreneur is handling money. Nothing in my sixties experience, unfortunately, prepared me for that. It was not a money-oriented generation. I had so many negative feelings toward money in the sixties.

Would you say you activists in the sixties were entrepreneurs—political entrepreneurs?

Yes, and the antiwar movement was our business. We created it and directed it. We didn't want to work for the government or for corporate America, but we did want to create our own society.

Whether a political activist or entrepreneur, you have been ambitious, haven't you? Didn't you tell one of your family members that you were going to be famous when you grew up?

Yes, but the drive goes out of you as you get older. I was telling somebody the other day that I want to lead a very normal life.

What's a normal life for Jerry Rubin?

Well, I want to have my children grow up to be healthy. I want to grow, to be rich. I enjoy being healthy. I'm not interested in experiencing ups and downs anymore. I want a moderate level of experience. Those aren't the statements of an ambitious person.

Yes, and what you seem to be saying is that you want a middle-class life-style like most Americans.

That statement would have horrified me in the sixties, but I have to be honest about myself.

But as we know, history goes in cycles. Say in fifteen or twenty years from how, your daughter comes to you and says: "I want to smoke pot, Dad. I know you did it in the sixties." What would you say to her?

Good question. I know the best way to drive her to pot would be to say no. I got a lot of pleasure out of pot . . . tremendous amounts of pleasure.

So were you heavily involved in the sixties drug scene?

I chain-smoked marijuana. Nothing much more than that.

How about acid?

Occasionally. Once every six months . . . a year . . . special occasions . . . I loved it. It opened up my mind.

Do you still smoke marijuana?

Occasionally, about once every three years. I stopped smoking about four years ago. But about three weeks ago, I had a few puffs of a joint at a friend's house.

What did it taste like after all that time?

It was strange. Your arms get loose and your body parts get kind of watery. I liked it for about an hour, but then I got to dislike it because it sapped my energy.

Well, what would you tell your daughter?

I'd say, "Try it." Nothing wrong with seeing what it's like. But if she got dependent on it, I'd know there was a big hole in her life. Marijuana can make you feel really secure. It can make you think you are really close to people. Marijuana is an anxiety reducer. I think that if I had more self-esteem in the sixties, I would have smoked less marijuana.

Did marijuana do any good for you?

I think it broke down the linear categories in my mind. I think marijuana merges the categories of a person's mind together so that he is more creative. You think of different ways of doing things. You can make a breakthrough in your mind, which is usually a prison.

So why aren't you smoking it anymore?

The main reason is that it interferes with my health purposes. I just don't know what it does to the body, but I'm convinced it's cancer producing. It's got to be negative healthwise. It may be positive for breaking down the categories of your mind, but the effect on the liver, lungs, gall bladder, stomach, arteries—any part of your body—has to be negative.

So is there any argument for the legalization of pot?

I would be in favor of legalizing all drugs, if by legalizing them, we could get rid of them. In other words, I would be in favor of an enormous government campaign of education against drugs as it is doing against smoking cigarettes. The main argument for legalization is that people are going to do drugs anyway and it's creating a criminal class of dealers who are responsible for so much violence in our society. So I believe we can eliminate the criminals but put very tight controls on drugs.

Tax the legalized drugs, and the money can be used for education against drugs. America is being destroyed by drugs. I know so many people whose lives have been destroyed by drugs. But I don't know how to keep drugs out of this country. The problem lies with the consumer. The production of drugs can't be stopped if people want them. So long as money can be made, someone will find a way to get drugs to the consumer. Why can't we use the genius of our advertising to point out the dangers of cocaine and hard drugs and the overuse of marijuana?

Do you think perhaps the fact that Americans are willing to use drugs says something is wrong with our society?

Yes, America has no collective purpose. Many people lead empty lives and take drugs, which they believe helps fill the vacuum. I'm for drug testing.

You're for drug testing! [Laughs] That would make Abbie Hoffman have a fit!

Well, Abbie and I disagreed about a lot of things. I'm not for the abuse of drug testing. I'm for our society using every means possible to combat the drug epidemic. It's the greatest threat to our society. In the sixties, I would have said, "Great! Problems for the establishment. How thrilling." I would have said, "How wonderful! America is falling apart." I don't feel like that anymore. I want to see our country work and our people happy.

But what about the civil libertarian argument that drug testing is unconstitutional because it involves illegal search and seizure.

That's a legitimate argument, but you can weigh one argument against another. We can have all our civil liberties and then have criminals running through the streets, our young people falling apart, and adults being miserable.

You are talking like a real conservative.

Maybe I am a conservative these days. I am outraged by how victims of crime are brutalized and perpetrators of crime get away with it. I don't think civil liberties are absolutes.

But you know about Big Brother.[3] You take one civil liberty away and then the authorities will go after another. That's the nature of power. It has happened time and again in history. And why can't it happen in America?

It doesn't necessarily follow. I think the people and not the government should support drug testing. On the grassroots level, the people should say, "We don't want drugs in our neighborhoods, in our athletics, in our factories, in our society. Drug testing? Give me an alternative." If the ACLU [American Civil Liberties Union] is upset, let it come up with another, more effective suggestion.

Okay. A lot of the drug abuse occurs in the inner city where there is poverty and little hope. Instead of the government concentrating its efforts on drug testing, why doesn't it work harder to develop programs to combat poverty, create jobs, and you give people hope?

Yeah, but you get rid of poverty by getting people off drugs. Drugs perpetuate poverty. People are getting involved with drugs instead of finding jobs. I believe in what Jesse Jackson has said: "Hope, not dope!"

Some observers have argued that the permissive attitude towards drugs in the sixties has lead to the drug problem we have today. Is that an argument?

I can see that argument, but I don't necessarily agree with it. What's the alternative? Do we really want a repressive antipermissive society? In a way, the whole drug thing is a money-making operation. Maybe society should find better ways for some of its people to make money.

From what you've said so far, I gather that you are an unabashed yuppie[4] and make no apologies for it.

But I would define *yuppie* my way. I would define *yuppie* as someone who is first a professional. I guess I'm that. Also, he [a yuppie] is personal-growth oriented. I don't see a yuppie as being a creature of materialism. Personally, I'm not all that materialistic. To me, a yuppie is a person who jogs, cares about what he eats, takes care of himself, and tries to enjoy life.

But critics say that's bad. We have a generation of yuppies—a "me generation" into itself—with no social conscience.

It's a very unfair criticism. I don't know what that means, really. The seventies were characterized as a very selfish decade, but to me, it was one of much personal growth. First, to be into yourself, you have to get out of yourself. I believe yuppies are changing America. In Russia, they are developing a yuppie class. I think the U.S.-Russian yuppie alliance is going to dismantle the world's war machine. That's my prediction for the nineties and the twenty-first century. We will see if that happens.

Do you have a lot of people come up to you and say, "Jerry Rubin, I can't believe this! What are you doing in a suit and tie chasing the conventional American dream? Boy, did you sell out!"

It used to happen much more than it does now. It annoys me and sure it bothers me. But I'm not here to live up to other people's expectations. Look, the change is totally legitimate. Almost everybody from the sixties generation has made this change. Perhaps I'm a symbol of this change because I was so well-known in the sixties and then moved to Wall Street. That may appear traumatic to some people. But America has accepted that most of the sixties activists have gone into business today.

I've interviewed several activists from the sixties, including William Kunstler and the late Abbie Hoffman. Neither seemed to have changed much since the sixties. Have they failed to move with the times?

Yes, but I'm glad they are around. The world needs a Bill Kunstler. He's the Clarence Darrow[5] of our time, while Abbie was the veteran activist who reminded us of the injustices in society and that our underpants are showing. That's great! We need that.

Abbie never changed much over the years, but you did. Did the fact that you became an unabashed capitalist and no longer a revolutionary have any affect on your relationship?

There was some conflict, but I believe our friendship was stronger than our conflicts, although at times our conflicts tested our friendship.

Were you surprised by his suicide?

Yes, although I knew he was manic depressive. He was pretty down near the end of his life.

That's interesting. I interviewed Anita Hoffman for this book, and she told me that she didn't really know he was a manic depressive until he was underground.

In the sixties, it was easy to hide your manic depression because it was kind of a manic decade. Abbie would do things like write a book in three days. That seemed like normal behavior in the sixties, but looking at it now, you realize it's manic behavior.

After his death, there was speculation that the CIA may have had something to do with his death.

I don't question the conclusion that Abbie took his own life. I think the evidence is overwhelming.

Were you really going to write a biography of Abbie?

At the time of his death, I had that thought. I knew Abbie as well as anybody did. I was aware of his brilliance, as well as his humaneness and contradictions, which made him so interesting. The book idea, though, was kind of blackballed by his brother and other people. So I had to make a decision — did I really want to spend my time rummaging back through the sixties when I am such a forward-looking person?

How would you assess Abbie's place in history?

I think he's one of the great rebels of American history. He's one of the freest spirits who has ever lived in this country. He has to be seen as the Groucho Marx[6] of American politics. He's going to become more significant as time goes by.

How would you assess your own place in history?

No, I don't think one does that to oneself.

If Hoffman were alive today, could he serve as a model for today's youth?

No, I don't think so. Today's youth have to figure out how to lead a normal life while still being politically active, whereas Abbie's life statement was: To be a political activist, you have to devote your whole life to activism.

Was Hoffman your mentor in the sixties? He introduced you to the political uses of guerrilla theater, didn't he?

I taught him some things, too; namely that he should take his street theater out of the village and into the international arena. Concentrate on Vietnam instead of the local cop. And Abbie taught me that politics can be street theater and not just a lecture in a room. So I think we taught each other.

I read an article in which the author said you were booed at Hoffman's funeral.

No, I wasn't.

That's what the author claimed.

I don't care what he said! He wasn't there. That's totally false. Who booed me?

[Laughs] The writer didn't list names. But now it's on the record. I asked you, and you gave me an answer.

Not that I care.

We've talked about keeping healthy and succeeding in business. What about religion? Does it play in any role in your life?

No, not really. That's one of the conflicts I had with my wife. She is a Unitarian and is more ritualistic than me. I guess I'm an agnostic. Maybe I'm too young to worry about God. Maybe I should start worrying when I'm eighty.

[Laughs] Maybe it will be too late. That reminds me of one of my philosophy professors in college. He used to chide the class with: "You don't want to wake up at fifty and start thinking about the great questions of life."

Why not? I don't think there are any answers to the great questions. I really like to think there's a man up there in the sky with a grey beard looking down on us right now. I really pray there is! I would hope there is some kind of afterlife. I hope that this isn't all there is. I would love to be reincarnated.

Would you want to come back as Jerry Rubin?

Yes, maybe that's the ultimate heaven and hell. Everybody has to come back and relive their life. But I would be happy to do that. I've enjoyed my life.

Maybe God has a sense of humor, and he'll bring you back as Abbie Hoffman.

[Long laugh] That's real funny!

[Laughs] Or maybe God has a twisted sense of humor, and he'll send you back as Lyndon Johnson.

[Laughs] Maybe I'll be back as Ronald Reagan. Now that would be something!

13

Ericka Huggins

From Black Panther to AIDS Activist

> If people in the movement had a spiritual container to hold all
> the feelings and emotions and hard times we all experienced, it
> would have been a different movement. Love did have a role to
> play in the movement, but it was played down. I'm not just talk-
> ing about the love that led us to call each other comrades. We
> did have love for humanity, but that love needed to be more in-
> ternalized.

The Black Panther Party for Self Defense was founded in 1966 in Oakland, California, when two college students, Huey P. Newton and Bobby
Seale, got together to find a way to protect the black community against police
oppression and brutality. Taking their inspiration from radical freedom fighter
Frantz Fanon, the party formulated a ten-point program, a combination of
beliefs and demands that expressed a desire for black people to determine the
destiny of their community.

The Panthers demanded that blacks be exempted from military service
and receive reparations for centuries of exploitation. They worked for neighborhood control of institutions such as education and law enforcement. Initially, they patrolled the ghetto areas with guns and lawbooks to protect blacks
against police harassment, but this quickly led to several well-publicized armed
crashes with the police in which Panthers were arrested or killed. In 1967,
Huey Newton was found guilty of killing an Oakland policeman. Chicago
police killed Panther leader Fred Hampton in his bed in 1969 under suspicious
circumstances. In all, police and the FBI killed more than 20 Panthers.

The Panthers and their allies accused the authorities of carrying out a
campaign to intimidate, disrupt, and ultimately destroy the party. An FBI
memo made public in 1971 at hearings of the Senate Select Committee on Intelligence revealed that the purpose of the FBI campaign against the Black
Panthers was to "prevent the rise of a black messiah who would unify and electrify the militant black movement."[1] Hoover believed the Panthers were "the
greatest threat to the internal security of the country" and implemented a
counterintelligence program against the Panthers called COINTELPRO.

But the Party grew quickly, as it implemented innovative programs such as liberation schools, medical clinics, and children's breakfast programs. By 1972, membership had jumped to over 5,000 with 45 chapters nationwide. The *Black Panther,* the party newspaper, reached a circulation of 30,000 in Chicago, and 35,000 in New York.

The party allied itself with other revolutionary groups, such as the Weather Underground, and identified itself with Third World liberation movements in Asia, Africa, and Latin America. The Panthers were adherents of Marxism and maintained that white people are not the enemy; the capitalist system is.

By the early seventies, however, differences within the party began to surface. Eldridge Cleaver favored violent revolution and split with Newton and Seale, who favored more peaceful methods. The differences eventually sapped the Party, and by the late seventies, it had declined in membership and influence.

Ericka Huggins joined the Black Panthers in 1967, a year after its founding, and eventually rose through the party hierarchy to become the deputy minister of education. Huggins' involvement with the Panthers came at a heavy price: Her husband John was killed in 1969, the result of a Panther disagreement with another black organization called US; and shortly after moving to New Haven to bury her husband, she was arrested for murder, along with Bobby Seale, and jailed for nearly two years. The charges were later dropped.

Today, Huggins lives in San Francisco and directs a program called Crossings, which operates under the auspices of the Shanti Project and provides services to HIV-positive people. She has practiced Siddha meditation since her incarceration in New Haven and, today, teaches it to Bay Area prisoners.

The interview began at Huggins's small office at the Shanti Project headquarters in downtown San Francisco; but she had an unexpected dental problem, which led us to continue the interview in a cab and later at her dentist's office. Huggins is tall and rail thin, and her short-cropped hair is flecked with gray. Most of the time during our interview, Huggins spoke in a quiet, measured monotone, but her voice fired with passion when she recalled the injustices of the sixties or society's attitudes toward people with AIDS in the nineties.

*   *   *

Tell me what the Shanti Project is about?

The Shanti Project started in 1974 to help people with life-threatening illnesses. About 1982, the project became involved with men who had Kaposi's sarcoma, a cancer specific to people with AIDS. In 1984, the Project moved its focus from working with people who had life-threatening illnesses to working solely with people with AIDS. The project plan was to continue this targeted service until the epidemic ended. Of course, that hasn't happened.

Ericka Huggins (photo by the author).

After I was hired in 1990, I saw that the Shanti Project was doing wonderful work, but its specific target was white middle-class males. There were no services for addicts, women, children, adolescents, and poor men and women of color. I worked to change the project's focus.

People think of AIDS as a gay white disease. What impact has AIDS had on the black community?
I'll give you an example. In a certain section of the Bronx in New York City, one in five women has tested positive for the HIV virus. They are African American and Puerto Rican women. Children, many of whom are black, are now the highest at-risk group. This is due to a number of factors: the high level of intravenous drug use, men who are bisexual don't disclose this information to their partners, and the concept that the disease cannot touch them. HIV does not discriminate.

That's quite a revelation that doesn't show up in media accounts of the AIDS epidemic.
The media has one slant on things as you know. [Laughs] When I started with the Shanti Project, a colleague and I wrote a proposal for a program that would help the underserved, the same people who are underserved in every other aspect of their lives. We couldn't think of what to call the program, but my friend was inspired and said, "Let's call it 'Crossings.'" It fit everything we wanted to do.
Volunteers from Crossings give emotional support and practical assis-

tance to people and families with AIDS. They go to their homes, apartments, or places of residence. Those services the people need, we provide. It could be having a volunteer come by and chat, do laundry, or run errands....

We are federally funded, and, by the terms of our contract with the federal government, our clients have to be indigent. We target people living in certain districts—the Mission, the Tenderloin, and South of Market. Our clients are poor, white and heterosexual, newly poor gay white men, bisexual men of all colors, teenagers of all colors and sexual orientation, children of all colors, and women who are primarily heterosexual. This focus is on a different population from the one that Shanti Project has served historically.

You are federally funded? What do you think of the federal government's response to the AIDS epidemic?

I think that limited and biased thinking exacerbates the problem. We can't blame the government entirely. We are all part of the government. If people want to stop the rising AIDS statistics, they can do something about it. The general public still attaches such a stigma to AIDS. In the first five or six years of the epidemic, the average American didn't even think about AIDS as a disease that could touch their lives.

It's human nature. When drug addiction started to rise in poor communities, did anyone pay attention? No! Then the white middle-class kids started getting addicted, overdosing, or jumping out of windows. That's when Americans started to pay attention.

I can't say that the government is to blame without including all of us. In addition to the need for more funding for services, people with AIDS also need love and care. That's what everybody can give. Have we done that? People have died at home alone, totally ostracized and isolated because of the backward attitude toward certain life-styles. People are still dying at home alone; however, the situation is far better than it was.

What is it like working with children with AIDS?

The children are so amazing, knowing what they are living with and that they can die at any moment. Kids with AIDS have so much courage. They are so ready to speak out about life, about death, about love and its healing quality.

There is one eleven-year-old boy, a fifth grader. He just made a public statement, announcing to his elementary school classmates that he has AIDS. The principal supports him; the parents' group supports him. This is phenomenal because he made the decision to let people know he has AIDS. He's making it easier for all the children with AIDS who will come after him at that school.

It sounds like you are doing extremely rewarding work.

Yes, I am; but federal funding is being cut everywhere, and Shanti Project is no exception. So I don't assume the program will last forever. I certainly hope that AIDS won't last forever; however, I know it's going to stay with us.

You have talked about the prejudice AIDS patients experience. Do black AIDS patients experience an extra stigma because they are black?

Yes, especially gay black men. They receive a lot of flack, not only from the society in general but also the black community. Oppressed people don't like additional oppression meted upon themselves. So there is a lot of denial about AIDS in the black community. Attitudes, however, are slowly changing. The churches, for example, are beginning to pay more attention to the problem.

Let's backtrack and talk about your background. Were you born in San Francisco?

No. I was born in Washington, D.C. I have lived in California since 1971. I came from a working-class background. My mother worked as a secretary in the State Department, and my father worked as a clerk in the Pentagon. I'm the oldest of three children. We lived in southeast Washington, which is poor to lower middle class. I never had to want for food, but I do know that my parents did a lot to put us through school and to send me to college.

Where did you go to college?

I went to two [colleges]: first to Cheney State Teachers College in Oxford, Pennsylvania, and then Lincoln University in Nebraska. I was at Lincoln when Professor Charles Hamilton, coauthor with Stokely Carmichael of the book *Black Power,*[2] was there. It was an exciting place to be. I was a part of the Black Student Congress. During the year 1967, I had read a *Ramparts* article about Huey Newton. He had been shot by Oakland police. I decided that day I was going to go to California and join the Black Panther Party. It was October.

One month later, I left school and went to California with a friend, John Huggins, whom I later married. We attended a "Free Huey" rally in early '68 and joined the party directly after. I was eighteen and a half [years old]. John Huggins was killed on January 17, 1969.

You were so young. Going to California was a daring move.

That's the way I am. I have a very stable way of living day to day, but when I decide something needs to change, I just do it. Going to California was very disconcerting to my mother, who was using her hard-earned money to send me to school. My desire to go wasn't whimsical. I felt sure it was the right thing to do. I knew I had to do it.

What happened when you arrived in Los Angeles?

Well, we stayed at the home of John's cousin for a while, and then we found an apartment. We started working in an auto parts factory and sought out the Black Panther Party. We talked to people who were selling party newspapers, found out where the office was, and got involved.

A couple of months after that, we quit our jobs and started working for the party full-time. We did this until John's death. After he was killed, I returned to the East Coast to bury his body in New Haven, Connecticut. Students from Yale and the local black community asked me to stay and start a party chapter, and I did. Two months later, I was arrested and charged with conspiracy to commit murder.

Why did the Black Panther Party grow so quickly?
It's obvious, right?

There was a need?
There was a need. People were tired of living the way they were, under the foot of everything. They saw that the [Black Panther] party was willing to stand up to what was unjust. The party constantly received bad press, which led to defensive stances it wouldn't have ordinarily taken. Some people loved the NAACP, but turning the other cheek didn't work when you were being shot down by the police. The period of the late sixties was the height of racism in the U.S. It was wild!

You said the party got a lot of bad press. Were there a lot of misconceptions about the Panthers? For example, people generally thought that Panthers stood for nothing but Black Power, but I understand from my reading that the Black Panthers did a lot of good things for poor people of all colors.
We never used the term "Black Power." We always said "All Power to the People." The oppressed were, and are, people of all colors. We happened to be black, but we had alliances with a wide range of groups representing people of all colors. We aligned ourselves with student organizations, women's organizations, antiwar organizations... We didn't have a nationalist perspective.

Eventually, Latinos and white people joined the Black Panther Party. Few people know that. We were open-minded and had a broad world view. In fact, from the mid-seventies, Huey Newton recognized the legitimacy of gay liberation, something no other black organization would publicly acknowledge. Yes, we were totally misrepresented.

Is that because of the fear that white America had of the Black Panthers?
White America had a fear of black people! If we had only talked about "black power," they would have said, "Oh, those fools!" But we were talking about changing the distribution of wealth, so that poor people who had nothing could have something. Why should children have to starve in such a rich country? It's because the country was founded on a self-centered economic system!

Those were the things we talked about. But we frightened the power structure, and the government created a means to destroy us from within and without. This led to the Black Panthers arming themselves to the teeth.

One of the most memorable impressions I got from reading Elaine Brown's autobiography[3] was that she had serious doubts she would live through the police crackdown.
I woke up everyday and thanked God I had lived to see another day! I

didn't have any concept of living to be forty-five years old. Everybody around me was being killed or thrown in jail. After John's death [he was twenty-three], I said to myself, "I will be going soon."

The Panthers had violent differences with another black organization called US.

The FBI had violent differences with the Black Panther Party. The US organization was a pawn in their big game. There was phenomenal infiltration of organizations all over the country by COINTELPRO. It was phenomenal! There were people who infiltrated the US organization and the Panthers and orchestrated many jailings and deaths.

Ten years after John's death, the FBI made a statement in the *L.A. Times* about the murders on the UCLA campus on January 17, 1969. In effect, the bureau admitted that, although it didn't pull the trigger, it did orchestrate what happened. It's easy to say "The Panthers versus US," but then people will say, "Oh, yeah, black folks fighting black folks." It was set up to look that way.

Given what you lost and what you experienced, I would think it would be very hard not to be bitter toward the U.S. government. How do you feel toward the American system?

I'm not bitter. I believe everybody's destiny unfolds as it is meant to, so people with understanding don't harbor hatred and bitterness. Actually, if I harbored bitterness, would the government be hurt? No. I would. I want to live my life in a meaningful way, and I want to continue to be of assistance to people. I couldn't do that if I harbored bitterness.

Even though COINTELPRO was, in fact, responsible, I don't hold bitterness to those people. My spiritual beliefs tell me I shouldn't be bitter. I believe good actions return good actions and ugly actions return ugly actions. That's been my experience in life.

Have you learned from your bad experiences?

Yes. I learned a lot from both the positive and negative ones. I do miss John, Bunchy Carter,[4] . . . all my friends who were killed physically or mentally. I have a lot of friends who didn't want to go on anymore. I have friends from that period who are bitter and depressed. Sure, I grieved when I had to grieve, but I had to move on. That's the way to stay healthy.

I'm surprised that there hasn't been more public indignation about the abuses carried out by the FBI and the U.S. government. I think the argument can be made that the U.S. government wanted to wipe out the Black Panthers.

I think people care about what happened. Elaine Brown's book and David Hilliard's book[5] are really going to wake people up. The Department of Justice really did want to wipe out the Black Panther Party.

You mentioned Hilliard's book. He writes about the Oakland Community Learning Center, which you had a lot to do with. He says it was one of the Party's most successful programs. What was it about?

The school started in 1971, and we moved into the building we called the Oakland Community Learning Center in 1973. I was the school's director until 1981. It was a school for two-and-a-half- to twelve-year-old children. After we started it, we realized that we couldn't work with children without working with their entire families. So we did that.

Is the center still in existence?
No. It closed in 1982.

Are any of the programs the Panthers started in the sixties still in existence today?
In spirit or in another form. I often run into children who say to me, "I remember you from the school. Didn't you serve me breakfast in the free breakfast program?" The irony is that the federal government saw how successful our food programs were, and so they started free breakfast and lunch programs. The government was so embarrassed by what the party was doing.

When I say another form, I meant there are other programs in existence today that derive from what the Black Panther Party did. There are alternative schools all over the country that are modeled after the Oakland Community Learning Center. They came to us, and we showed them what we were doing. The free clinic came from the party. There were thirteen original free clinics, and at least seven or eight of them are in existence today.

How is the Black Panther Party viewed in the black community today?
I can't speak for the black community, and I won't even try. All I can say is that people remember the Party in different ways. Some people remember it as a horrible thing. Some people remember it as something they wish they could have taken part in, but couldn't. I have a number of friends who say to me, "I wish I had the courage to join the Party, but I didn't." Other people look back at it and dislike it because they wanted to look good in the eyes of white people.

My mother went through every possible feeling about the Party. She didn't change her view until the state of Connecticut put her daughter on trial. She realized that what I was saying was true and came to understand what that government was all about. She saw how the FBI lied!

My mother is this typical black lady from Washington, D.C. They followed her when she got on the plane to visit me on trial or in jail. What was she going to do? My mother was so changed by what she experienced that her friends couldn't talk to her anymore because they thought she was exaggerating.

I think more people from the party have to write about their experiences. When my newer friends read Elaine Brown's book, they say, "Oh, is that what you mean? Is this how you lived?"

In a New York Times *article about Elaine Brown's autobiography, you are quoted as saying that the sixties lacked a "spiritual dimension."[6] That's an interesting comment. Could you elaborate?*

I was not just talking about religion. If people in the movement had a spiritual container to hold all the feelings, emotions, and hard times we all experienced, it would have been a different movement. Love did have a role in the movement, but it was played down. I'm not talking about the love that led us to call each other comrades. We did have love for humanity, but that love needed to be more internalized.

That's why people drank, did drugs, and were brutal with each other. They didn't do that because they were horrible. The movement attracted sensitive, wonderful people. Then people became addicted, or began harming people close to them, or whatever happened to them because that shit takes a toll. If you have a spiritual base, you have something else to hold on to, something that connects you to a power greater than your mind or body.

Your spiritual base is Siddha meditation. How did you get involved with that?

I had always been interested in yoga and meditation. I taught myself to meditate when I was in prison. I needed to do something to keep sane because I was in isolation for fourteen months. I spent the last six months in the general prison population.

I'm so glad I did meditate and practice self-inquiry in prison. A lot of former members [of the Black Panthers], who have remained my friends, have taken on a spiritual path.

I hate reading articles that say, "Well, they were this way in the sixties, and now they meditate." We aren't any different than we were in those days. I know all my friends who have some spiritual backdrop to their lives today feel the same way about the state of the world. But we are still the walking wounded. Many of us live like war veterans with post-traumatic shock syndrome.

You were in a war.

We absolutely were! There wasn't a day that went by during that time when I didn't leave my house and ask myself: "What's out there? Will I have to duck bullets?" In fact, I was pregnant with my daughter under those circumstances. The really awful thing was that I became used to it.

At one time, I was living in L.A. and visited Oakland. When I left the house, I wasn't thinking about ducking bullets. I could walk from my house to the corner store without worrying about who was following me. I thought to myself, "Ericka, there's something wrong in L.A. [Laughs] That isn't how people are supposed to live." Oakland was bad, too! Don't get me wrong! But L.A. was much worse! The L.A. police force was one of the most racist in the country.

So, yeah, a part of me still suffers because we were at war, but I'm not suffering as badly as I would have if I didn't have a spiritual base. The movement would have stayed together if it had spirituality built into it. Students who talk about starting a new movement ask me, "What didn't work [in the sixties]?" They really want to know. I tell them that poverty of the spirit was at the core of the movement's destruction.

The idea of separatism is gaining strength among young blacks. You see it at the universities in the black-student demands for separate black unions. What's your opinion of that development?

There was a movement in the sixties for black separatism. There was a movement in the fifties, too. There will always be a movement for black separatism. It's nothing new. It will always be that way so long as there is racism in this country.

Do you think the country has made much progress in terms of race relations since the sixties?

No. Racism is very deeply embedded in the minds of European-Americans and all Americans. I don't think it's something that's going to change easily. This may be the reason why African-Americans gravitate towards separatism.

African-American families don't raise their children the same way European-Americans do. We don't raise a young child to think, "Oh, there's a white person. Hate him! Aren't they ugly! They don't look like us. Don't play with them, children!"

It wouldn't have dawned on my mother to teach us that way. But she did tell me that white people really don't like black people. She did that because she didn't want me to go out into the world thinking like Pollyanna. But right down the road in Maryland, the young children who were white were being taught by their parents to spit on us! They were being taught to hate us. They were being taught to call us "Nigger."

Didn't the Black Panther Party believe that racism was imbedded in the capitalist system?

Yes, racism aids and abets capitalism.

Do you still hold to that Black Panther critique?

That's a funny way of putting it. What I believe in is what I believe in. I don't call it a critique or a philosophy. It's real simple. Anybody with eyeballs can see it. I believe that when people want to make money, they will create any excuse to justify their exploitation of others to get it. It's that simple!

If you want to make money, go find some people you can force to work for free or who will work cheaply. Then take them from wherever they are, drag them across the oceans, and imprison them to do that. Tell them repeatedly that they are no good and that they don't deserve anything better than they have. Say it over and over again, and those people will believe it and pass this belief on to their children.

The reason for slavery is simple. People need to have power over other people. It can be called the "Black Panther critique" so that it seems outside our perspective, but we know the truth of what happened.

It doesn't sound like you have much hope for the future of race relations in this country.

I always have hope. I live with hope. I believe people at the core of their beings don't want to live nasty, small-minded lives. They do so because they don't know a different way. In working with so many children over the years, I have found that children will play with each other in a sweet way until they are told to play in a different way. Look at the Korean and African American communities and see how much friction there is between them.

It has to do with a belief system that the Koreans were exposed to before leaving home. They are told that, when they come to America, they will find that black people are lazy, they steal, they are looked down upon by other Americans. So when the Koreans leave their homeland to come to America, they are only interested in selling goods to African Americans and won't have anything else to do with them.

African Americans pick up on that, and the battle begins. But it's not just Koreans and African Americans. Humans interact in this way. We all struggle with what I learned to call the "inner enemies." One of them is greed; another is envy.

If human beings accept responsibility for their behavior, they can change. We are going to have to change. That's what the music of young people today is telling us. They don't say it politely like the love songs of the sixties. They say change or die!

Is that why a lot of white people are afraid of rap music?

Yeah, but aren't white people afraid of everything? Tell me something that mainstream white people aren't afraid of? That's why many white people want power over everybody and everything. They feel powerless. But remember that a lot of young white people like rap, and some of them are writing and performing. Also, a lot of young black rappers love Bob Dylan. The rap music stations don't play him, the rap musicians don't allude to him. But they do listen to him ... and Jim Hendrix, Janis Joplin ... all those folks ... because the message is there. Listen to rap and you'll hear poetry and philosophy!

So you are in tune with young people?

I like hanging out with young people, so I have the finger on the pulse of what's going on. I learn a lot from young people. My daughter, who is twenty-four, worked at ABC-TV during the Gulf War. She was appalled! She saw the news come in one way and go out another. She couldn't believe it! During the war, she was sad all the time. Not just because of the war but because of how the public was denied the benefit of the truth.

Yeah, the power structure learned its lessons from Vietnam and was able to control and manipulate the media better.

That's right. I'm glad my daughter got to see it with her own eyes.

Were you aware of the feminist movement that began to spring up in the late sixties?

Women in the Black Panther Party were aware of that movement, but we thought those white women were out of their minds. We were so busy trying to live one more day that we couldn't understand why white women wanted equal pay with white men. We just wanted black women to get a job, period!

Feminism, as it was called, didn't ring true for black women and other women of color because its foundation was white and middle class, so full of envy of men. The kind of things white feminists in that period were fighting for didn't have any connection to the lives of women in the black community.

Did some of the feminists try to recruit you to the cause? Did they say, "Look, we are women. We have to stick together"?

No, they didn't try, but they invited us to speak to them, and we did that often. We talked a lot about how our situation was different, and they listened to a certain degree.

But let me tell you something. Remember earlier [in our interview]? I spoke earlier about the need for white people to work on their racism? Well, it's not enough to be a feminist. White women have to rid themselves of their racism as well. You can be a feminist and still be a racist. We found that out constantly.

In what context?

Think about it for a moment. Let's say you have somehow realized that poor people aren't so bad after all. Is that going to change your attitude about race? About culture? Not necessarily, unless a person looks racism and classism straight in the eye. There were white women in the movement who wanted to work with us and with white men, but not with black men.

Why not?

They were afraid of black men because their mothers said black men would rape them.

Are you interested in women's issues today like, for example, abortion or sexual harassment?

I am interested in every issue affecting human beings. I don't think women in this society have been treated with compassion and humaneness. Women have not been treated well in societies all over the world. So it's a good thing women are standing up for their rights. I feel the same way about children. They need to be treated in a loving way; however, we live in a society where nurturance and mothers of the heart are secondary to money, so women and children are going to be looked down upon, used, and abused.

Elaine Brown in that New York Times Magazine *article said Anita Hill was crucified. Those were harsh words. Do you feel the same way?*

Yes, I do. She was up against the "good old boy" network. She is not just a black woman. She is a woman. This event left a message in people's minds that it's okay to do anything you want to with women in the workplace. She was great! She handled herself with poise and dignity.

Let's talk a little more about your involvement with the Black Panthers. What was it like working with the whites in the movement? I know the Black Panther Party was allied with the Weather Underground in the early seventies.

I thought some of the things they [the Weather Underground] did were crazy.

So why did the Black Panthers align themselves with the Weather Underground?

I don't know everything that went on in the Party, so I can't answer that. The Weather Underground was a revolutionary organization. We tended to align ourselves with revolutionary organizations all around the world. When I say the Weather Underground was crazy, I meant it did some spontaneous things that weren't in the best interests of the Party and the people we attempted to serve. Of course, there are people who say that the Black Panther Party was crazy. And it was to a certain degree.

It got that way in 1972, didn't it, when the Party divided into factions?

COINTELPRO was behind that rift. For that matter, perhaps COINTELPRO was behind a lot of the things the Weather Underground did. Will we ever be given the truth?

What are your feelings today about that period of your life?

I don't get nostalgic for those times, but I do get nostalgic for the people who are no longer here. I do remember that part of my life with love because I miss a lot of people I grew up with in those times. We went through a lot together.

Do you see another organization like the Black Panthers forming again?

There have been many organizations that have tried to replicate the Party philosophy and actions, but they haven't done it. It's possible a similar organization will arise, but there will never be another Black Panther Party. It has its own place in time and history.

14

Jim Fouratt

Gay Rights Activist

> Today, there is not a more vital movement in this country than
> the gay liberation movement. It has diversity, and it's exciting,
> although there is a lot of disagreement. There is no question that
> gay liberation has transformed what it means to be gay today. It
> will never be like it was before. Never! No matter what happens.
> And it all goes back to that tacky bar and historic moment in time
> in 1969.

The seminal event in the birth of the gay liberation movement began on
a Friday night, June 27, 1969, when New York police raided a Greenwich
Village gay bar called Stonewall. In the past, police would routinely raid the
city's gay bars and intimidate their patrons, who would submissively endure
the police harassment. This time, however, the gay patrons of Stonewall confronted the police, first jeering them and then attacking them with a battery
of coins, paving stones, and parking meters.

The Stonewall rebellion, which lasted for five days, became a defining moment in history for gays, marking a new era in gay politics and changing the
face of gay and lesbian life. Within two years after the Stonewall rebellion, gay
liberation groups emerged in every major city and university in the United
States, Canada, Australia, and Western Europe.

As Martin Duberman wrote, "*Stonewall* has become synonymous over
the years with gay resistance and oppression. Today, the word resonates with
images of insurgency and self-realization and occupies a central place in the
iconography of lesbian and gay awareness."[1]

Jim Fouratt, a gay and a political activist, was at Stonewall. Since the early
sixties, long before the beginning of gay liberation, Fouratt had been involved
in the ferment of the decade. He was a prominent Vietnam War organizer and
protester, an ardent member of the counterculture, and a friend and associate
of many of the movement leaders, including Abbie Hoffman, Allen Ginsberg,
and Jerry Rubin.

Born into a Catholic working-class family from Rhode Island, Fouratt was
still a teenager when he moved to New York in the early sixties to study acting.

While a student in the Actor's Studio, he was introduced to radical politics when he attended Ban-the-Bomb demonstrations with artist friends.[2] Soon after, he joined the emerging New Left and helped organize a radical support network in New York City for young hippies that included the founding of the Free Store, which, in typical Digger fashion, recycled used clothes and other household goods by giving them away free at the store. He also singlehandedly published and distributed a newspaper, which he called *The Communication Company*.

After Stonewall raised the consciousness of the gay community, Fouratt became a founding member of the Gay Liberation Front and, since then, has remained a radical and gay rights activist. Fouratt was a cofounder of Act Up and founding board member of the Lesbian and Gay Community Service Center, the Gay Community Service Center in New York, and Wipe Out AIDS (now known as H.E.A.L.). Today, he works as the director of national publicity for Rhino Records, while serving as a contributing writer for *Spin* magazine and authoring a cultural column titled "Ear Candy," which is syndicated in the gay press. Fouratt divides his time between New York City and Los Angeles, where this interview took place.

*   *   *

Let's start at the beginning and get some background. Where did you grow up?
I was born in New Jersey but lived most of my youth in Rhode Island. I grew up the only son of a working-class Irish family. My stepfather, who brought me up, was the son of an Irish cop and a telephone operator. My mom was fifteen when I was born. Most of the families in the Irish-Portuguese neighborhood where I grew up had lots of kids, but I grew up an only child. As a kid, I went to parochial schools.

It sounds like you grew up in a tough, macho, working-class neighborhood.
No, although there were the odd Saturday night fights. My grandfather and stepfather used to go out to the [American] Legion with the boys and drink a lot. There was a lot of alcohol in the family . . . mostly beer and cheap stuff.

You have an interesting background, but it doesn't seem the kind that would produce an educated radical.
Well, I was this little, smart, queer kid who was sickly as a child and spent a lot of time by himself, reading, watching television, learning to do a lot of things by himself, and having a very active fantasy life. My parents may have been working class, but they sent me to the best schools.

Do you recall when you became political?
I can remember my first political act. I must have been six or seven, watching television, when I saw this ad for the Committee of One Million Loyal Americans. I remember calling up the number mentioned in the ad and

Jim Fouratt (photo by the author).

getting this package sent to me. I was supposed to go out into the neighborhood and get people to sign this petition, but no one would.

My mom got very upset when she saw what I was asking people to sign. She said, "You can't do this!" It was a petition for Joe McCarthy. [Laughs] It's interesting that the neighborhood was conservative working class, but my neighbors wouldn't sign the petition.

But in terms of really becoming political, that happened when I was seventeen and went to New York to study acting under Lee Strasberg.[3] There was a woman in the class who was rumored to be a Communist.

Remember this was the early sixties, a time when Communism was not something one talked about. I was an actor, and I knew that, because of Joe McCarthy, an actor didn't talk about politics. In 1962, I went with her to a demonstration that took place in Times Square. There were about fifty demonstrators and about twice that many plainclothes police and Secret Service agents.

I was arrested, along with the other demonstrators, and charged with using profanity, which I didn't use, and with generally being wild in the streets, which I wasn't. I thought, "This is America, so all I have to do is tell the truth and that would be it."

Before I went to trial, my lawyers found out that NBC television had footage of the demonstration, but the government had confiscated it. That was my first experience with freedom of the press. I was found guilty because, as the judge said, "the police do not lie."

You said you were withdrawn as a kid, but you became an actor. How did that come about?

I was poor and from a working-class family, but I grew up determined to become something that I was not tracked to be. Being an only kid meant my father wasn't in the financial situation of other fathers who had several children. I had more advantages. I would have one pair of pants or one pair of shoes, but they would be from the best store or have the best label. It gave me a superior attitude.

When it was time to go to school, I got accepted to Harvard, but there was no scholarship money, so I couldn't go. I was tracked to go to a school like the University of Rhode Island or some other God-awful place, but I thought I was much better than that. That's when I decided to leave for New York and become an actor.

You also said you were a "queer kid." When did you learn that you were gay?

I use the word *queer* in the very contemporary sense of the word, not in the way all of us grew up understanding the word to mean. [Long pause] I was different, but I didn't understand why that was. I was very popular with girls I dated and did all that kind of stuff. In the Catholic environment I was raised, it was easy not to sleep with girls. It was expected that you didn't.

It wasn't until I arrived in New York City that I realized I was a homosexual. In the artistic community I became a part of, differences were respected. It was okay to be a part of the community if you were gay. So I evolved into someone who didn't pretend he was straight. Remember: This was the early sixties, before gay liberation, and you didn't come out for fear it would ruin your life.

When you came to New York in the early sixties, were you aware of the need to fight for gay rights and to stand up for yourself as a gay person? I know it was the time of the Mattachine Society and the budding gay rights movement?[4]

I knew about those things and identified with them, but I was trying to figure out how I could be an actor and do it. While at the Actor's Studio, I spent time coming to terms with myself and learning who I was. At that time, there were no role models, but I accepted my homosexuality and decided I was going to be a beatnik. This was like 1962 or '63. I got in on the end of the beatnik era. By the mid-sixties, I had become involved with the avant garde in New York City.

At this point, the New Left was gaining strength. Were you a part of this development?

I was aware of what was going on in the South, the SDS, and the Vietnam War. I had two parallel life-styles going: the Andy Warhol,[5] downtown, avant-garde, art-scene lifestyle, which was apolitical, and another, which I had been drawn into as a result of being arrested, tried, and found guilty. The two life-styles did not cross over very much.

It was an exciting time, but I had to constantly live with the fact that I was depersonalized in the New Left. The moment someone found out I was gay, I didn't become a fully dimensional person with a point of view. I became a person who did something different in bed. I had no power over that then, and I still don't. What can a person do if someone calls you faggot? I may be an asshole, and it's okay to call me that in an encounter, but it's not right to call me a faggot. What does that have to do with what I have to say?

So what's your view on "outing"?[6]

I'm very opposed to it because deciding to come out is very personal. One should not come out unless he wants to. Yet today, you see homosexuals being forced out before they are ready. My experience from the sixties taught me that what you gain in personal terms from coming out can't be measured, but what you give up though is measurable. I think that's still true today.

But isn't it important for gays to come out? Prejudice breeds from the unfamiliar. People are afraid of the unknown.

Yes, that's true. I grew up in a poor neighborhood that was mostly Catholic. I grew up thinking that all Jews were rich and that the biggest neighborhood in Rhode Island was where all the Jewish people lived. On Saturdays, our family would get into our car, drive through the neighborhood, and look at the houses.

When I got to New York and Lee Strasberg's class, I met Bobby Walton, who went on to play in the TV show *Lou Grant*. Bobby was Jewish and wanted to introduce me to his grandmother. We went to the bowels of the Lower East Side to this old, old building, where we walked up five flights of stairs to reach this tiny grungy apartment. That was where Bobby's grandmother lived. I remember saying to Bobby on the way home, "Bobby why does your grandmother live like that? All Jews are rich." [Laughs] But that was all I knew.

So, yes, it's important for gays to come out. I have a great friend here in L.A. who is a psychiatrist. He's thirty-five years old, unmarried, and his mother doesn't know he is gay. I've been very systematically but gently telling him that none of his other work matters unless he goes home and tells his mother he is gay. She probably knows that her unmarried, strange-bird, psychiatrist son is queer, but he has got to do it for himself. That's what coming out is all about.

How did you become a part of the hippy movement?

I contracted hepatitis in 1965 and had to go to the hospital, where I almost died. When I got out, my hair was grown long, and the hippy movement was just beginning. I remember reading about a Be-In in California and deciding that we should have a Be-In in New York [City]. So I got some people together, and we organized one in Central Park. That really tied Abbie [Hoffman] to me.

How did you first meet Abbie?

I met Abbie before the Be-In when he was in transition from being a part

of SNCC [Student Nonviolent Coordinating Committee] to trying to figure
out what to do next. I had become very visible. I was the hippy who the *New
York Times* wrote about. I could explain things well. I think Abbie was impressed with the acceptance and visibility I had within the movement. He
came to me to find out how I had started a small underground newspaper and
some other things.

*Nineteen sixty-five was also the year of the West Coast Homophile organization
and its big protest in Washington.*[7]
    Those were the kinds of people I didn't like.

Why not?
    In retrospect, I'm much kinder to them and realize the heroic actions they
took, but at the time I said, "Who the hell wants to be like them!" They wanted
to be accepted, and I didn't care about acceptability. They said they were like
everybody else, and I didn't care to be like everybody else. In fact, there was
tremendous conflict between the gay liberation sensibility and old homophile
movement. That happened in '67 or '68 . . . before Stonewall.

You were highly visible and a spokesperson. People knew you were gay?
    It wasn't talked about.

Why? Because it wasn't important?
    Well, it wasn't something I talked about. It wasn't like I was pretending.
I had a lover whom I lived with and went around with. I tried to live my life
honestly. Still, someone was always trying to fix me up with some girl.

Were they trying to make you straight?
    No, it was because they wouldn't accept that I was gay. It was very much
a sixties mentality.

*Given what you say is a "sixties mentality," there must have been incidents where
people took things out on you because you were gay.*
    I was an actor, but I had to find other work to supplement my income. I
would work long enough to become eligible for unemployment, which allowed
me to do my own thing. I went to work for Eastern Airlines and got fired
because I was a homosexual.
    It bothered me, but gradually the hippy sensibility came in, as well as the
use of drugs and psychedelics, which relaxed people and made them more
fluid. People began to respect diversity more. I felt a part of the counterculture
from the beginning. But today, it pisses me off that you don't find me in most
of the histories of the sixties. That is homophobic! People don't like to write
about the "queers" who were running around during that period.

Did that make you more militant?
    I wanted to change the world! I saw the hippy movement as a political
movement, although many other hippies didn't see it that way. They were

middle class, bourgeois, and privileged. I didn't have a trust fund, but I discovered that practically everybody I knew had money and trustfunds. The sixties were different from today. You could live on practically nothing then. The FBI would ask me where did I get my money from? [Laughs]

When did the FBI ask you that?
From the first time I was arrested at the demonstration in 1962.

Have you had a chance to look at your FBI file?
As much as I could get. Most of it is blacked out.

They thought you were a subversive?
Yeah, a homosexual subversive.

The fact that you are homosexual was in your file?
Oh, yeah.

That's quite ironic, given what we know about Hoover now.
I'm not surprised at the hatred Hoover had for homosexuals. Homosexuality is often internalized.

He was obsessed with homosexuality, wasn't he?
And black men.

Yeah, remember the tapes that Hoover made of Dr. King's conversations.
He [Hoover] used blackmail and the threat of blackmail to keep people in their place.

Getting back to your involvement with the counterculture, were you heavily into drugs?
No, not really. I just pretended that I was. I was different from the other hippies. I'm not a dionysian. I'm a good Catholic boy at heart. Deep down, I'm very moral. I think that's the reason why I'm alive today. I could easily have gone off the deep end with drugs, sex, or despair. Look at all the people in the New Left who eventually got involved with heroin.

Were there other homosexual leaders in the movement like you?
Closeted—

They weren't out in the open like you?
In fact, they thought I was a threat.

Were you a part of the sixties gay scene?
Sure I was, but I've never lived my life in a homosexual ghetto. I've always had straight friends, but I don't particularly identify with the homosexual who hangs around gay bars or who lives in the ghetto.

What relationship did you have with black militants who were fighting for racial justice?
I think every gay person identifies with the desires of the underdog,

whether they are conscious of it or not. They know that deep down in their soul things are so hard to change. Historically, for example, you can see that there have been a lot of lesbians in social work.

The Panthers were very important to me, but I remember that, in the early days of gay liberation, I had to justify Eldrige Cleaver's use of the word *faggot*. I explained he was using a different language—prison talk. I didn't realize it at the time, but I was wrong.

Cleaver meant it?

Oh, yeah, he meant it. It was vicious! It made it difficult to put our two movements together. I had to get up and publicly apologize for Cleaver.

What about the women's movement? What kind of relationship did gay activists like you have with it during the sixties?

You couldn't have had gay liberation without the women's movement. The women's movement opened the door by teaching us that the personal is political. That is the key. That is the gift of the women's movement to all of us, including heterosexual men. What goes on with you is political. How you feel is political. So I was gung ho in supporting the women's movement.

Was that support reciprocated?

Not always. No. You see, the women's movement was led by women who turned out to be lesbians. Many were women who wanted to fight alongside me but were in roles where they had to serve coffee.

In the late sixties, people in the movement began believing that a real revolution was actually going to take place. Did you share that conviction?

Yes, absolutely, but things were getting crazy. I was taking a lot of speed at the time. Everything was very intense.

You became a part of the Yippies and then dropped out.

Well, I didn't exactly drop out. We had a serious disagreement about Chicago.[8]

About strategy?

We knew there was going to be a blowout.

So you were against violence. You didn't want to see a violent confrontation?

I am the type who will stand up and be counted, but I believe you shouldn't manipulate young people. Today, I still feel that way. You have to let people make their own choices. I believe that, if given enough information, people make the right choices.

That belief is very American. [Laughs]

Yes, and idealistic. [Laughs]

That's interesting. Did you get turned off as the sixties progressed? More and more people, especially those in the Weather Underground, thought violence was the answer.

I very much supported the Weather Underground because their violence was against property and not against people.

Isn't that a fine distinction you are making?

Not in my mind. But as I said, I don't support violence. Random acts of violence terrorize people, but they don't accomplish anything. What is the message?

Could you relate your experience at Stonewall?

You know the story about Stonewall, don't you?

No. Tell me about it?

I was coming home from CBS, where I was working at the time, and happened to be in the vicinity of Stonewall when the riot broke out. I immediately called up all my New Left friends and told them, "There is a riot taking place over here. Get on down!" Nobody came. NOBODY SHOWED!

Did you call Abbie?

Yes, everyone!

They sympathized with you but weren't going to stick their necks out for you. Was that the idea?

It wasn't even a question of sympathy. They just didn't care. It wasn't important to them. We were just fags! Oh, of course, some of them later said that they showed up, but they didn't. That taught me an important lesson. That's when I became a leader in gay liberation.

When the riot happened at Stonewall, did you realize its historical significance?

Yes, I did. I saw ordinary people who normally wouldn't do that sort of thing. I knew it was a moment in history where everything changes.

The gay community was never the same after Stonewall?

I remember going to consciousness raising meetings after Stonewall where Mattachine and Homophile people tried to put a clamp on everything. A number of people in the New Left whom I knew were gay came out.

I became one of the five founders of the Gay Liberation Front. We attracted a large number of people, including women. We were different than other gay organizations that followed, which were either all male or all female in membership.

I confess I didn't know the significance of Stonewall until I started researching this interview. I now know it's one of the seminal events of the sixties. But you don't read about Stonewall in mainstream history books. Does this bother you?

Yes, absolutely! A film was made about the Free Speech Movement at Berkeley. I attended the press conference when the film premiered. I asked the filmmakers why weren't there any homosexuals in the movie? The producer had the temerity to say to me, "There weren't any." I caught my breath and said, "They were in Berkeley. They were in San Francisco..." I began to name organizations that homosexuals were members of. We weren't represented in that film, and it happens again and again. A long time ago, I made a decision to forget all of that because I could become consumed with bitterness, frustration, and resentment.

How important is the gays-in-the-military issue to you?

It's not an issue I would have chosen. I have contradictory feelings about it. It took me a long time to get behind the issue. It took a dyke from the National Gay [and Lesbian] Task Force to tell me, "If you believe in equality, you got to buy the whole package. There has to be equality in everything." So I finally got it. Everybody in this country has got to have equal protection under the law, although being a movement person, I find it difficult to support the military.

But who's talking about the issue? I turn on the TV, and I see Ted Koppel with some heterosexuals — men, usually white. We gays don't really have a say in the thing. There is something discriminatory to me about heterosexual men talking for us all the time, even though they may be nice people.

I sense you think there are more important issues facing gays today than the one about gays in the military.

I think domestic partnership is a more important issue. That issue is as important for nonmarried heterosexuals living together as it is for same-sex people living together.

Doesn't it disturb you that at this point in time there is a trend to restrict gay rights? I know states like Colorado are moving to do that.

It's the most exciting time in my life! It's exciting for many gays because we think we won. We ain't going back! Recently, I went to the annual meeting of Gay and Lesbian Journalists in Mainstream Media. I was one of the oldest people there. I looked at a generation of gay journalists that are visible and working for the *New York Times* and the *Washington Post* — the mainstream media. They were discussing such things as ethics. They weren't talking about gay issues, such as coming out on the job. To me that was exciting.

But there is no guarantee that there will be continued progress for gays. It could backslide . . .

There is no guarantee. A lot could depend on the economy. We are the new "niggers." The [anti-]abortionists realize they have lost, so who is going to be their next target? It could be gays and lesbians.

I know some conservatives are saying that the big issue for them in the nineties is not going to be abortion, but gay rights.

Well, for the last ten years, they have used the gay issue to fund-raise. But it's a lot better today for radicals than it was in the early seventies when everything fell apart. The Vietnam War was over. Our lives were fucked up. We had two choices: either we recanted and joined the system or stayed outsiders.

So what happened to you?

In the early seventies, I was in the gay collectives in New York City. In 1972, I joined a collective in Washington, D.C., that organized an alternative radio network and covered the 1972 convention. We then went to San Francisco and set up the Unicorn New Service. We produced feeds for one hundred and sixty radio stations and were the only media allowed into Wounded Knee.[9] We had access to the Weather Underground and other radicals. In San Francisco, I had hepatitis and nearly died.

Then I went back to New York [City], and from there to Hollywood to resume my acting career. I became active in trade unions in Hollywood and got blacklisted. Trade newspapers would report what I said about producers at closed-door meetings. So I went back to New York and got involved with running nightclubs.

Where you still political?

Yeah, but in the seventies the gay movement began to fall apart. That was the situation until the eighties when AIDS changed things. I was involved with the AIDS issue right from the beginning. I became active in two AIDS organizations. If anything good came out of the AIDS issue, it was that it revitalized the gay liberation movement.

How did it do that?

It brought gays and lesbians together to work together.

Because of what AIDS was doing to the gay community?

Yes, because the government didn't care about gays dying from AIDS. That set the stage for radical activity. The same thing happened that happened in 1969: Gays began organizing around the issue of empowerment.

How would you describe the response of the government to the AIDS crisis?

The government has certainly responded, but Bill Clinton has taken public positions on AIDS only because of the vitality of the AIDS movement. My views on AIDS are very left of the AIDS movement. I think AZT is a toxic drug foisted upon the gay community because it's highly profitable. I think the HIV theory doesn't hold up. AIDS is a much more complicated disease. It has a lot more to do with poverty and life-style than gays and nongays are willing to admit.

My view is that the government allowed bathhouses and bathroom bars to exist to contain the gay community. A lot of energy that could have been used to transform society was dissipated by encouraging people to fuck themselves to death!

You say it an exciting time to be gay and a radical. Do you ever get nostalgic for the sixties?

Honey, the nineties are going to be everything that the sixties were not. If the eighties were the fifties, then the nineties are going to be the sixties without the mistakes that our generation made. The good thing is that there are still enough of us around who have hope that is tempered with realism. I have as much hope as anybody you are going to interview for this book.

Yet it's sad. I've seen ten years of death wipe out almost every gay leader that I saw emerge in the seventies. Any person who had any cultural impact is dead. Some died of AIDS; some died of drug addiction; some died of natural causes. I might be the fag who will have the last word, so to speak.

Today, there is not a more vital movement in this country than the gay liberation movement. It has diversity and it's exciting, although there is a lot of disagreement. There is no question that gay liberation has transformed what it means to be gay today. It will never be like it was before. Never! No matter what happens. And it all goes back to that tacky bar and historic moment in time in 1969.

What about your future?

I worry about it. I have no money, and, as I said, most of the people I know from the sixties are dead. Occasionally, I see Paul [Krassner], Anita [Hoffman], and Jerry [Rubin].[10] I don't trust Jerry, but I don't wish him ill will. At one point, I did.

I don't want to be like those old Commies from the thirties who had fucking resentments for something like forty years. Bitter! Fighting with each other. It was horrible! I don't want to be like that.

At the same time, I want the Todd Gitlins[11] to acknowledge that they have written a skewed history of the sixties that needs correcting. Gays and lesbians have been a more vital part of the New Left than anyone has yet acknowledged.

15

Bernardine Dohrn

From Revolutionary to Children's Rights Advocate

> The charge that most sixties people joined the establishment
> and became sellouts is preposterous. Most people have stayed
> the course. Most people are trying to do work that is meaningful.
> Most people are trying to live lives that are whole. Most people
> are trying to live in harmony with their values. Most reject the
> dominant measure of success: money, power, and fame. Today,
> our work doesn't amount to a movement, because most of us are
> involved in single issues — law reform, the environment, health
> care, education, political organizing. . . . But this local work is
> part of the sixties legacy.

On March 6, 1970, at a townhouse on Washington Square in Greenwich
Village, New York City, several members of the radical Weather Underground
were building a bomb when it accidently exploded, completely destroying the
building and killing three of the group's members. Three days later, Bernardine Dohrn, a leader in the Weather Underground, one of the group's leaders,
missed her court date in Chicago, where she was to face several riot-related
charges for the so-called Days of Rage, during which the Weather Underground went on a violent spree in Chicago, breaking windows, building
bonfires of park benches, and attacking police with rocks, lead pipes, and
baseball bats. Dohrn issued a communiqué, which began: "Hello, this is Bernardine Dohrn. I'm going to read you a Declaration of War. . . ."

It was another stage in the radical development of a woman who became
a legend in the antiwar movement. A decade earlier, Bernardine Dohrn was
growing up in the small conservative suburb of Whitefish Bay, Wisconsin, just
north of Milwaukee. Nobody could imagine then that the beautiful, popular
young girl would grow up to be a radical, bent on violently attacking the American system. A high school classmate of Dohrn's told *Esquire* in 1970 that
"about the most remarkable thing about Bernardine was how absolutely ordinary she was. The whole family was very, very normal."[1]

Dohrn spent her freshman and sophomore years at Miami University in
Oxford, Ohio, before transferring to the University of Chicago, where she

223

earned a B.A. degree with honors in political science and education. By the mid-sixties, she was one of several hundred young idealistic volunteers involved in the antiwar movement, civil rights, and the poverty program. Among other activities, she worked for Dr. Martin Luther King's Southern Christian Leadership Conference in 1966 in its efforts to integrate Chicago's white working-class suburbs.

But, as the Vietnam War escalated, Dohrn became increasingly radicalized. She graduated from law school in 1967 and went to New York to work for the ultra-liberal National Lawyer's Guild, where she began to become known in leftist circles. She helped organize law school students and others to resist the draft and to stage Draft Week, one of the first big antiwar demonstrations. Returning to Chicago in the summer of 1968, she joined the Students for a Democratic Society (SDS) and was eventually elected national intra-organizational secretary, one of the group's three top co-equal offices.

By early 1969, however, SDS began to fragment into two main factions: the Progressive Labor Party—the austere Maoist wing that eschewed the counterculture and wanted to organize the working class—and the more hip Revolutionary Youth Movement (RYM)—which embraced the counterculture and wanted to unite white students with more militant blacks. The conflict came to a head at the national SDS convention in June 1969, when Dohrn, on behalf of RYM, read a statement expelling Progressive Labor from SDS.

She then proceeded to lead the faction in the takeover of the organization's headquarters and the seizure of its assets. Soon after, Dohrn and a cadre of SDS members splintered off into the Weathermen (from Bob Dylan's lyric: "You don't need a weatherman to know which way the wind is blowing"), the name eventually being changed to Weather Underground because group members thought the original name too sexist.

From 1970 to 1974, the Weather Underground took credit for 12 bombings, as Dohrn and her compatriots managed to elude the authorities with the help of an elaborate underground network. But when the Vietnam War ended in 1975, the Weather Underground no longer had a political rationale for existing, and so it dissolved in 1976. Many members turned themselves in, but Dohrn and her husband, Bill Ayers, also a leader in the Weather Underground, decided to remain in hiding, even though the bombing conspiracy charges against Dohrn had been dropped in the early seventies because of illegal law enforcement surveillance.

In 1977, Dohrn and Ayers had their first son, Zayd Shakur (named for Black Liberation Army member Zayd Shakur). Later, another son (Malik for Malcolm X) was born. When the two finally turned themselves in after a decade on the run, Dohrn plea-bargained the remaining charges against her to three years' probation and a $1,000 fine.

Today, Dohrn is still a committed activist, working as a children's rights advocate and directing the Children and Family Justice Center at Northwestern University School of Law. Founded in 1992 with a multiyear grant support from several philanthropical organizations, the center is trying to transform the Juvenile Court of Cook County, Illinois, into "an effective center for the legal representation of children and families and a model of juvenile justice in the nation."[2]

The Juvenile Court of Cook County, the world's first juvenile court, was founded by the women of Hull House to protect children held in poor houses and adult jails and to help troubled children get a new start in life.[3] Since then the Cook County Juvenile Court has become "a backwater, inundated by enormous caseloads, exuding hopelessness and despair, isolated from Chicago's communities and professions."[4]

The plight of children in Chicago and Illinois is not unlike the crisis facing children throughout the United States and other parts of the world. Today, 21 other industrial nations have a lower infant mortality rate than the United States. In fact, each year 40,000 infants in the United States die before their first birthday. By the year 2000, it is predicted that one in four American children will be poor. Internationally, an estimated 35,000 children worldwide die each day from malnutrition and disease.

Our interview took place at Dohrn's home in Chicago. At age 51, Dohrn no longer wears the thigh-high boots and miniskirts that were her trademark in the sixties, but she still exudes the charisma that helped make her one of the era's most prominent radicals. Dressed in blue jeans, a tweed sports jacket, and a blue golf shirt, Dohrn's hair was sun streaked and she had a deep tan, the product, she revealed, of a recent vacation her family had taken to Maui.

Dohrn rarely gives lengthy interviews, but she consented after I assured her we would talk as much about today as the sixties. She was eager to talk candidly about her new life as children's rights advocate, and, later as the interview progressed, she opened up about her experiences as a sixties radical.

*   *   *

In your work at the [Children and Family] Center, you must have a formidable task ahead of you. I understand from my background reading that the Cook County Juvenile Court System is one of the worst in the nation. How did it get that way?

The Juvenile Court System has been officially neglected and is held in very low esteem. The legal profession tends to look down upon children and family law because money is not involved. Children and family law has always been looked upon as "kiddy law," and it's only recently that it has been taught in law school. Another factor is that the family court is usually isolated professionally and geographically in most cities and is hard to get to. Judges, lawyers, and professionals tend not to know where it is unless they work there full-time.

But children and family law involves some of the most intellectually challenging issues of our time and certainly the most human issues, that is, children and the family and the obligations, duties, rights, and the relationships that go with it. During the last fifteen years, we, as a society, have exacted a heavy toll on children, especially those in poor families. There has been a tremendous amount of neglect. The poor make up a powerless constituency, so the situation has gotten worse and worse in a kind of slow and invisible way. You don't see the true dimension of the crisis unless you work in the family courts or have to go there.

Is the crisis one of the legacies of the Reagan-Bush era?
    Yes, I'd say that's true.

Isn't that kind of ironic, because Reagan and Bush were always talking about family values.
    It's perfectly ironic, really. [Laughs] What they really meant was "some families."

White upper middle class families.
    Yes, and I think the middle class took it on the chin, too. The real irony of the era, though, is that children have been left behind, and the consequences will reverberate for decades. Almost eighty percent of the children who appear in juvenile court in Cook County are African American and Hispanic. The juvenile court is supposed to represent Cook County as whole, but, in fact, the white middle class have different solutions for their problems. If their children get arrested, they don't have charges pressed against them. Instead, they tend to get treated in private mental hospitals or private drug treatment programs.

Conservatives argue that the so-called permissiveness of the sixties is the big reason the family has broken down and why we have problems with children today. What do you say?
    The concept of the family is constantly being redefined, decade after decade. The notion that there was this wonderful nuclear family before the sixties and that there was no need for government support for families is ludicrous. Research shows there has been government subsidization of the middle class and the upper middle class families throughout American history. And, of course, the subsidization of the suburbs, the highway systems, and the funding of public education isn't considered permissiveness or dependency or a pathology or any of the other words that are thrown at the poor now. It's considered what we've earned or deserved.
    The fact is the [American] government has always nurtured and supported some families. Look, for example, at the roads, infrastructure, and subsidization of the suburbs. It's not something that started in the sixties. It's a legacy of the fifties, the forties, the thirties. . . . It's a historical phenomena. The sixties didn't create the impoverishment of children. On the contrary, it raised the question of the values underlining American society and why certain sectors were excluded.

So should the government play a bigger role in alleviating some of the problems affecting the American family?

Well, I think everybody should. [Laughs] Adults should; the private sector should... And, of course, the government should support families through promoting child care, maternal and child health care, and jobs. But it should do so in a more systematic and conscientious way. We don't want a system that is a welfare bureaucracy, but kids should grow up believing they have a role in the future.

You can call it government support or government obligation, but all societies have taken some obligation for the helpless or for poor people in crisis. Children are a big part of that.

Realistically, the family has changed, so we need a definition that is more reflective of the reality. For example, it could be a male, female, and a small child, or it could be grandmother, an aunt, and mother with three kids, or it could be a lot of different combinations in which people rake responsibility for the future of children and the family.

So what about the family Reagan always talked about? [Laughs]

As we all know, it wasn't his family. [Laughs]

And as you've pointed out, it's just one type of family.

You're right. Children do need families, but we have to be realistic about how we define families.

Do you have any thoughts on—I hate to say the word solutions *because of the magnitude of the problem—perhaps I should ask if you have any thoughts on new ways to deal with the crisis children are experiencing?*

I believe solutions are possible. People seem overwhelmed by the crisis and don't believe anything can be done, but a lot of things can be done. When you look at other countries, like Norway, which are very child centered, you can actually see that it's not complicated. And there are some juvenile courts— I wouldn't call them models—where people feel that their point of view is being heard and that some sense of justice is happening there. Yes, it's doable.

But can we solve the world's problems around a simple strategy? No, but we can do things that make the families feel human and feel like their problems are being heard, that their voice is being presented in the proceedings, that children have some options, and that, if they do something wrong, it won't ruin their lives, but they will have options, encouragement, and support.

The problems are complicated, but first they involve an attitudinal change. In the sixties, there was an attitude change when people said, "You know, we can solve the problems. Maybe we have an idealistic notion about how you can solve them, but we can make a dent." We can turn the world upside down in a very short time. What looks immutable to us today can be transformed very quickly.

We need an attitudinal change, but we also need a reallocation of resources. We are spending millions of dollars on foster care, but foster care has been a disaster for children. If you use that money to help support families at the front end, eighty percent of them would be able to raise their kids. Maybe ninety-five percent, maybe eighty-five, maybe seventy-eight. . . We can argue about the percentage of families, but not the outcome. So reallocate the resources and then devise a strategy to make a permanent and stable home for kids. But that's not the way we are doing it now. We are creating a Kafkaesque situation that's really incredible.

Do children need an international movement similar to the one that developed for the environment if any progress is to be made on the issue of children's rights?

I think that's a great idea, but I don't know how possible it is. The interesting thing is that it took ten years to write the UN Convention on Rights for Children, but the U.S. is still one of the few countries that hasn't signed it, although I think the Clinton administration probably will. There will be a fight over the extent and nature of the reservations to the convention the U.S. will want to get.

The realization that children are human beings entitled to human rights is a recent breakthrough, and we haven't seen the implications of it yet. You've got to remember that it was just twenty-eight years ago that children in the U.S. got constitutional rights.

You mentioned the environment. When I went to Norway last year [1992], I learned that country was interested in two issues — the environment and the plight of children — and they believe both are tied together.

In what way?

Well, it makes sense. Both issues concern the future; they show that people shouldn't just live for the present and for their immediate enjoyment, but they should have an obligation and duty to the future. Norway sent a huge delegation to the U.N. Rio de Janeiro Conference on the environment.[5]

You've written that the U.S. bears a lot of the blame for the worldwide plight of children. What's your reasoning on that?

The U.S. has just six percent of the world's population, but consumes some sixty percent of the world's wealth. The only way the U.S. controls so much of the world's wealth with so little of the world's population is through plunder and exploitation. So I believe the one-hundred-year experience of the U.S. being an imperialist power is something that has to be transformed. If we looked at ourselves as one nation among many, instead of assuming the trappings of super-power status, we wouldn't have to worry so much about other people wanting our "stuff," and we wouldn't have to worry about penetrating the Southern Hemisphere.

So does the critique you had of the U.S. in the sixties still hold true for the U.S. today?

The world has changed, of course, but the U.S. continues to exploit the rest of the world. This has created a distorted economy and culture here at home. You can see in the Clinton administration's attempts to modestly reduce the military budget how hard it is for this country to shift away from a war economy. Can we retool and retrain something that is destructive into something productive? That's one of the major questions this country faces.

One of the primary issues of the sixties was accountability. What is the government doing in our name? We have a situation now where people don't feel like they can hold a system accountable. Reagan and Bush ran on a platform of fiscal accountability. What the heck! [Laughs] They've tripled the deficit. In Illinois, they've created this huge statewide government agency [The Department of Children and Family Services] that was supposed to protect children. Can we hold it accountable? Don't children and families have the right and the responsibility to hold it accountable?

Do you still see yourself as a radical?

Yes. I still see the world in radical terms. I fit the world's stereotype of a radical. [Laughs] Abbie Hoffman said a lot of great things. One of them was, "If I were in the Soviet Union, you'd call me a dissident; but here [in the U.S.] you consider me a kook." [Laughs] We have different words [for radical] depending upon where we live. [Laughs]

A lot of people were enthusiastic about Clinton's election. They believed they would see changes. The enthusiasm was reminiscent of the enthusiasm many felt when Kennedy got elected in 1960. Does Clinton's election make you optimistic?

I think the change will be limited, although it's a relief to have the Reagan-Bush period over with. That's for sure! [Laughs] It remains to be seen, though, how much one single person can do while in power or how willing he's really going to be to go up against the interests that make a lot of money from the way things are ... the military interests, the health care interests, the insurance interests...

But I'm hopeful the same thing will happen as happened when Kennedy came to power. Kennedy created a lot of expectations for improvement, which gave rise to powerful social movements and pushed him beyond wherever he intended to go. The same thing could be said for LBJ. Without powerful social movements, Clinton will move as far to the right as the powers want him to go.

Are you talking about the civil rights movement, the peace movement, the youth movement?

And the beginnings of the ecology and feminist movements.

Are there any signs that a movement is taking shape today?

It's difficult to say. Of course, it's going to be different from the sixties. I think the level of anger and discontent among black kids in the inner city is very high, and where it will lead is anybody's guess. Can all the white people who have been thrown out of work identify with black teenagers in the inner city, and can women who are angry identify with gays? Can these various groups join their interests? That's always been the question in American history. I don't know where it will go exactly. But I think the conditions are ripe. A lot of people have found life a lot less good than they have grown up to expect it to be.

Making it difficult to have any kind of coalescence among movements is the fact that there is no real broad compelling issue like there was in the sixties with Vietnam. Some people thought the Gulf War would be that issue, if Bush fell flat on his face. But he handled the media well, didn't he?

The interesting thing about the Gulf War was that tremendous popular opposition to the war developed before it began. That was really surprising. Remember that on January 15, about forty-nine percent of the Congress voted against sending troops to the Gulf. It was interesting to see how much unrest about the war there was among young people, even though the draft wasn't in place. It was very reminiscent of the sixties in the sense that the arguments for the war are so easy to defeat. I did a lot of traveling in the five months [surrounding the Gulf War] and was surprised at the dissent that was growing. It took a tremendous amount of arm twisting and media campaigning on the part of Bush and the Republicans to get support for [U.S.] involvement.

The power structure had certainly learned its lessons from the sixties. The opposition ended up dying and watching the war on TV. It's now clear to everybody that the Gulf War was a fraud.

So far, we've spent a lot of time talking about the plight and rights of children. I understand from my research that you had a good childhood, which gave you the confidence to go out into the world and do things.

My parents were lower middle class, and they had a great belief and trust in the system. They didn't have any radical ideas, but they were loving and devoted—

And understanding?

Remarkably understanding, given their backgrounds. My mother was an orphan at a young age and was passed around from family to family. She went to work at eighteen. As a parent myself now, I respect what they did. Because there weren't any boys in the family, my sister and I were given opportunities we might not otherwise have had. One or two summers ago, I went back to my high school reunion...

Oh, yeah. What was that like?

It was wonderful! It was really wonderful because I hadn't been back there since college.

Were you nervous?

Extremely nervous. [Laughs] Everyone was. Reunions make you that way. [Laughs] I had been part of a group of girls who had been best friends from the fourth grade through high school. I had only seen two of them over the years. At the reunion, we stayed together and had a sleepover and stayed up all night, talking about our lives. One of the funny things was hearing other people's memories of you. People remembered me as more outspoken, radical, and political in high school than I remember. There was no way to know if they were reading backward or if it was really true.

Of course, that was before there was a feminist movement and before women, in many instances, realized that they were being discriminated against.

Indeed. Last year, some twenty-five of us met as a group of women who were turning fifty. We continued to meet for a year and talked a lot about growing up in the fifties. At one point, someone asked, "How many of us got a teaching degree in college?" I think twenty-two of us raised our hand. [Laughs] We were all expected not to go to work, but to be married a month or two out of college. But I remember my mother saying to me, "You should get a teaching degree in case something happens to your husband." That was the image of women at the time — not as working human beings but as people who might in a crisis have to support kids. That is how recent that attitude was.

Was going to law school an unusual thing for a woman to do in the sixties?

Completely. There were only six of us in my law school class.

Did you face discrimination because you were a woman?

Oh, yes, I did!

Did that experience help to radicalize you?

I think I was pretty well down the road by the time I went to law school. I was already involved with the civil rights movement, but I wasn't conscious yet of the gender issue. I remember how astounded my advisers in undergraduate school had been when I told them I planned to go to graduate school in Chinese studies. They told me that it would take six years to learn Chinese, but by that time, I would be married. In 1963, it was bluntly assumed that was the way things were.

Do you recall when you became political?

I think it's always a gradual process. My friends [at my high school reunion] reminded me that I had written a paper about the Algerian Revolution[6] in my senior year in high school. I was only an observer at the University of Chicago when students occupied the administration building. I wished I were daring and courageous enough to be demonstrating, but I didn't know those students and I couldn't imagine breaking into their world. I raised money for the civil rights movement, but that was a big step away from getting directly involved.

When I graduated from college, I went to work as a case worker for the Illinois Department of Public Aid, which was a tremendous learning experience. That was the year Kennedy was shot. I got involved in trying to organize a case worker's union. Then, when I went back to graduate school,

I helped a fledgling group in Chicago called the Welfare Rights Organization in which we started advocating for welfare families. Then, when I went back to law school, I continued working with welfare and housing issues on the west side of Chicago. That was the year Martin Luther King came to Chicago [1965–1966].

In the sixties, you worked for the integration of Chicago's suburbs. Do you ever wonder if we have made any real progress in terms of integration since Martin Luther King's day?

The answer is yes and no. There has been some integration, but the situation is certainly worse for a lot of people. A small but important segment of the black population has had the opportunity to become part of the middle class, but, obviously, the bigger problems of poverty and discrimination and racism in American life are still very much with us.

There seems to be a move, especially among young blacks, towards separation, not integration. What are your thoughts on that development?

It's an inevitable development, especially among the young, who have the luxury of being angry at the injustices around them. That black anger has a militant and separatist aspect is predictable. Anger and disaffection among a significant sector of the population require a response; it's so obvious it's ridiculous. I find it astonishing today that people are so afraid to talk about race. One of the major developments in the sixties was that, as whites, we were forced to take account of racism. Blacks told white people that it was their problem and so go deal with it among yourselves. I agreed with that.

Society's problems must often be dealt with one to one as well as institutionally for real change to take place. When it comes to male-female relationships, how many men are willing to challenge things in their own households? How many dirty jokes among men get challenged? How many demeaning comments get challenged by men? Do you have the willingness to say something uncomfortable to people when they assume that "We are white. We can say this between each other." Or "We are both men. You are not going to tell on me."

When did you join SDS?

At the end of the summer of 1966, just after Dr. King left Chicago, I attended a meeting in which we discussed how we had organized the citywide rent strike on the west side. A couple of national SDS organizers were at the meeting, and they did what good organizers do: They took my phone number, called me the next day, and said we want you to come Uptown [the poor Appalachian neighborhood in Chicago] and work with us. [Laughs]

What did you know about SDS at the time?

I was beginning my third year of law school and admired SDS from a distance, but, actually, I didn't know much about the organization. It was '66 and '67 — the years the [Vietnam] war really escalated. SDS was interested in starting more community working-class draft-counseling programs. I did work in draft counseling in law school and later with SDS in Uptown.

As time passed, you quickly began to take more and more of a leadership role within SDS. Was there a lot of male chauvinism within SDS?

Oh, yes! There was sexism and discrimination within the movement.

But women did hold leadership positions.

Well, officially in the national office, there was just Jane Adams[7] and me. Of course, women in the SDS were major organizers, and we did do a lot of the work. They were leaders in the sense of being local and campus and community organizers and speakers, but it was always the men who were the officers and who held official positions and gave the big debate speeches.

How do you explain your rise to the top of the organization?

I don't really know. The escalation of the Vietnam War pushed many people forward in previously unimaginable ways. I didn't really have a plan laid out that said: This was what I was going to do within the SDS.

Were you involved with the first stirrings of the feminist movement? Were you having your consciousness raised?

At an SDS meeting in the fall of 1967 in Michigan, a group of women tried to make a presentation about women's issues and were hooted down. I can recall the auditorium vividly. It was packed with hundreds of people, and I was sitting in the very back on the top row on the steps. Pandemonium broke out in the auditorium because everybody began arguing and shouting at the person next to them about whether women's issues were legitimate political issues.

The women present were outraged. It was like the [Clarence] Thomas–[Anita] Hill hearings—an important moment for women. We went back to New York and formed a women's group. There were about fifteen of us. It was happening simultaneously around the country. Our women's group met every week, and it was amazing, really amazing! We talked about everything—from our own personal relationships to how we were brought up. It was an explosive process.

I wrote an article for *Ramparts* that year with another woman named Naomi Jaffe, who was a member of our group, which criticized a *Ramparts* glossy cover story of a photo of a large-breasted woman from the shoulders down. Our article was titled "Two Tits and No Head."

What was the point of your Ramparts *article?*

We attempted to analyze the impact of mass culture on women's lives and the view of women as sexual objects.

I read—I believe it was in Sale's history of SDS[8]—that women in SDS were thinking about starting their own organization. Was that true?

That may have happened in late 1969. There was talk about it, but SDS was falling apart by that time anyway. By '68, the treatment of women was becoming a bigger and bigger issue for more and more women, who were insisting on being respected and having equal status with men. But the old ways were entrenched.

Jane Adams told me that the camaraderie and solidarity among women in the movement cut across political lines. Would you agree with that?

Absolutely, and she and I are examples of that. We lived together for a year, even though we were on different edges of things, as were many other women in my group in New York. Things were splintering very quickly during the course of '68 and '69, and a number of people went their separate ways; but there was still a growing sense of solidarity among women.

I guess you see yourself as a feminist?

Oh yes, and living in a house of men. [Laughs]

[Laughs] Being a feminist, you must have watched the Hill-Thomas hearings with interest. What did you think of the whole episode? Did you begin to wonder if women had made any progress in the last twenty-five years?

Oh, women have made enormous progress. Hill's appearance in Washington was a matter of breaking down another door. What looked like a defeat for women was, in a bigger sense, a victory.

The ironies of history always seem to throw up heroes. She [Anita Hill] is certainly one of them. She really didn't want to sign up for the ride. She is Republican, ultraconservative, and has that choir girl look about her; but the confidence and dignity she showed in the situation was very telling. Maybe her lack of anger was harmful because Thomas was able to use anger so effectively. [Laughs]

And the white guilt trip.

But one of the things I liked was that it was like a mass "teach-in." You could talk to anybody that week [of the hearings]—cab drivers, doormen—about very fundamental issues of equality and power. Everybody had an opinion.

But what struck me was that so many women believed Thomas. How do you explain that?

I really don't know why, but in the black community, there was a powerful feeling she had betrayed a code that said, "Don't expose the black community to the white world." There was a stronger feeling among many black women and men that the issue of sexual harassment was secondary to racism and that they were impossible to separate. Leaders of the black churches disapproved of Hill coming forward.

But a year later, the polls suggest that both women and people generally had an overwhelming belief in her. It was a lot like the Gulf War. There was a TV-instant-poll kind of reaction, and the last person they heard was Thomas. But on reflection and with time, the people changed their minds and began to believe her.

Let's get back to the sixties where everything seemed to be getting out of control because of the way the [Vietnam] war was going. Did you come to the conclusion that violence was the way to go?

I don't think I ever came to that conclusion. I never thought violence was a good thing in a strategic sense. What happened was that I found the combination of militancy and the notion of direct action to be a very compelling strategy. We were trying to find ways to act that were nonviolent but more militant. I thought that people who were armchair radicals and said they followed Mao, Castro, and Ho Chi Minh but weren't ready to act on their beliefs were irrelevant and even destructive.

We saw the government escalate the war. Two hundred Americans and probably a thousand Indochinese, who didn't seem to count at all, were being killed each week in Vietnam. We saw the government kill Black Panther leaders right in front of our eyes.

The context of the late sixties was one of tremendous official government violence, and our attempt to respond to that in an appropriate way was called by everybody "violent"; but actually our behavior was temperate and restrained. Ours was a very decentralized and anarchistic movement, but with one or two exceptions; for over a decade, the militancy remained symbolic. We called it "propaganda of the deed."

Millions of people chanted "Off the pig," but that didn't mean they were going to go out and shoot a policeman in the head. The language was inflammatory on both sides, but the reality stayed in the realm of protest. If we compare the antiwar movement in the States with movements in England, France, Germany, Japan, and elsewhere, we see how restrained, temperate, and appropriate the American movement stayed. I reject the notion that we were violent. Of course, now we know the government was engaged in illegal acts of suppression and repression that only could be imagined at the time. [Laughs]

Have you had a chance to put in a freedom-of-information request and to get a look at your government files?

I've looked at bits and pieces. It costs an enormous amount of money to get the whole thing.

Based on what you examined, were your suspicions about the government true?

I was not arrested before 1969, but then, suddenly, I was arrested a number of times. This was a part of the government strategy to harass the movement. Our phones were tapped; we were followed. My sister's home was broken into. Dirty tricks were conducted in an attempt to turn people in the movement against each other, to promote splits, and to discredit spokespeople. But, of course, the attack on the black movement was much more harsh

and severe. The Chicago police's murder of Mark Clark and Fred Hampton
had a tremendous impact on us, certainly in terms of how we should respond
and what our moral and political obligation required.

Why did you decide to go underground?

Many different reasons. We did not want to spend a number of years in
courtrooms fighting the demonstration charges against us, and we wanted to
get away from the constant police and FBI surveillance and harassment. We
also decided to open up another front and force the government to devote
their resources to trying to find us, instead of killing Vietnamese people and
Black Liberation Movement leaders.

In retrospect, was that a realistic form of action, or does it seem naive now?

Both. It was realistic in the sense that we did catch the government by
surprise. It took them three full years to realize they were not going to catch
us using traditional methods. We certainly never expected it would develop
into a whole new mythology and outlaw culture. I don't think we recognized
at the time that going "underground" was the symbolic expression of extreme
defiance of U.S. authority and violent power. We and millions of others refused to be obedient and rejected the murder and aggression being conducted
by the U.S. in our names. Although there was just a hundred of us, we certainly
had the support of thousands of people who disagreed with many particular
things we said, but who did agree with the resistance.

We had great debates with others [in the movement] about how far to
carry militancy. The Berrigans, when they were underground, wrote us a series
of public letters in which they asked us what were the ethical edges of militancy. They also asked us to "remember what brought you into the movement."
A wonderful exchange of letters! They didn't think of us as pariahs. They
didn't say, "These are the people who are destroying a democratic movement."
It really wasn't like that at the time. People who never thought they would
throw rocks or fight back against the police did so in those extraordinary times.

When we went underground, we felt small and embattled; but remember,
two months later [after going underground], Kent State happened, and there
was this tremendous upheaval on campus, even without SDS or any structure
to support it. Then there was Jackson State . . . We were surprised that, even
though we were small, there was this bigger thing out there.

*There were many bombings during the first two years the Weather Underground
was underground.*

We only did a couple, and they were carefully done. They involved property and were not meant to harm anybody. They were symbolic and done so
that everyone would instantly recognize what was being said. It was "armed
propaganda." Sure, it was violent, and it's hard to justify twenty years later, but
it was extremely restrained and a highly appropriate response to the level of
violence being rained nationally and internationally.

Was the violence inevitable, given the continued escalation of the war?

I think so. It was appropriate, too. The people involved with it were overwhelmingly motivated by a desire to make the government accountable and listen to the people and to expose the hidden violence being conducted in our names.

I know some people in the movement thought a military coup might happen. Others thought a revolution would occur.

We certainly thought it was a revolutionary time.

And was the Weather Underground to be the vanguard of that revolution?

Yes. Ridiculously, we thought that for a time. For me, the major accomplishment of those times was the fact that, for twenty years, until the Gulf War, the antiwar movement and Black Liberation Movement inhibited the U.S. from directly intervening militarily in the Third World. That was a real victory, although we did not get the revolution we thought would happen.

Today, it's hard to remember how successfully the movement exposed the bankruptcy and hypocrisy of the U.S. leadership. It's going to be hard to build any confidence again in our leaders. The fact that Americans have turned to cynicism, rather than to anger and the determination to get something better in national life, to insist on participatory democracy, not passive democracy, to live among nations, to hold leaders accountable, is something I never would have expected.

But we are still fighting the Vietnam War. It's still with us.

Right. What Bill [Ayers][9] calls "the war to explain the war" is still going on. It's interesting that Bush touted the Gulf War as the final resting place of Vietnam. The military said we lost in Vietnam because they weren't allowed to finish the war. That's preposterous! The Vietnam War was militarily, legally, ethically, and morally flawed at the get go. The U.S. had no business invading Vietnam.

SDS failed to democratically reform America. Does that mean SDS is a failure?

I don't think so. We failed at our larger goals, but we were part of many long-lasting changes, and tens of thousands continue to organize for radical, democratic change. The charge that most sixties people joined the establishment and became sellouts is preposterous. Most people have stayed the course. Most people are trying to do work that is meaningful. Most people are trying to live lives that are whole. Most people are trying to live in harmony with their values. Most reject the dominant measure of success: money, power, and fame. Today, our work doesn't amount to a movement, because most of us are involved in single issues — law reform, environment, health care, education, political organizing. . . But this local work is part of the sixties legacy.

The Weather Underground dissolved in 1976 as a result of the end of the Vietnam War. What happened after that?

238 Sixties Radicals, Then and Now

The organization came apart quite bitterly over what to do next, as well as over the criticisms of me and other people in leadership. People made a lot of different choices. Most turned themselves in in '77 and '78. Some people decided to stay underground and pursue a strategy they called "armed struggle." At that point, Bill and I had our first child—Zayd—and I decided I needed a period to rethink what had happened and to figure out what my mistakes were. I just couldn't imagine turning myself in and "giving up." [Laughs]

What did Bill think?
Bill thought we should turn ourselves in, but he was really accommodating about my desire to think things through. He also liked the idea of devoting more time to being parents and to figuring out what to do next. I found it very useful for us to be very ordinary people with a kid and jobs and to kind of make our way back from a very political-oriented world to the "normal world." I waitressed and had babies. Bill was a baker and longshoreman and started doing day care more and more. We still saw a lot of political people and talked about a lot of issues with them. By the time Malik was born, it became clear that we wouldn't be spending the rest of our lives underground.

Other members of the Weather Underground made different decisions. Kathy Boudin was one. What are your thoughts about what happened to her? I believe the shootout occurred about a year after you surfaced.
Well, of course, we were devastated. There was nothing we could do to help Kathy, David Gilbert [her husband], or the other people who were arrested. We were friends of theirs. . . . It was awful.

How is Kathy Boudin doing?
She's an extraordinary person. She was sentenced to twenty years to life, which means she comes before a parole board about [the year] 2000. She has been in jail eleven and a half years. She's earned a masters degree in adult literacy and teaches incredibly creative classes in literacy. She's been a part of cranking up a program called ACE, which is the most advanced and developed AIDS program in the country. She's an indomitable organizer and a terrific person. So is David Gilbert, who is in much more difficult circumstances: a men's prison in upstate New York State. He's a tremendously ethical, decent person and remains an active intellectual.

Is his sentence twenty to life, too?
Sixty to life.

Do you still keep in touch with former SDS members?
Yes. When we moved to Chicago, we renewed our close friendship with many old friends, with whom we had differences in '69. We created a group during the Gulf War called "Women Against War," which included a wide array of people from the old days. We have so much in common.

Do you get nostalgic for the old movement days?

[Laughs] I try not to be. I don't like to live in the past. We laugh a lot when we get together. That's the best part. [Laughs] You won't make it through parenting or politics unless you have a healthy sense of humor.

What about the future?

I want to do everything, now that I'm past fifty. [Laughs] I still see myself as a radical, and I hope I'm a part of the future social movements. I want to take good care of my kids. I want to be a grandmother. I want to travel... I want to do everything.

Well, you have a lot of experience as a movement person. You've had success and failures.

Every movement in every historical era has to define itself. There is nothing more challenging and creative than a movement in which people's possibilities come to the fore. People emerge with remarkable creativity in art, music, literature expression, and new kinds of voices emerge. They are scary times, but absolutely intoxicating, heroic times. [Laughs]

16

Barry Melton

From Rock Musician to Activist Lawyer

> I like to think that San Francisco musicians were leaders in inculcating in musicians a sense of social responsibility. I hope we set a trend of giving something back. Watch MTV—an indicator of youth culture—and you will see musicians getting involved with causes and exhibiting a sense of social responsibility. Maybe that tradition is traceable back to San Francisco and the sixties.

In 1965 no one could have predicted that San Francisco would become the world's focal point for rock music. The local life-style was more beat than hip, and folk—not rock—was the dominant musical style. But in the late summer of 1965, the pioneers of San Francisco rock began to get their act together. By the late sixties, the scene was producing such famous and talented groups as Jefferson Airplane, The Grateful Dead, and Quick Silver Messenger Service.[1]

None of the groups emerging from the San Francisco musical scene, however, were more political than Country Joe and the Fish, which mixed humor, radical politics, sharp-witted satire, street theater, and folk, jug, and later psychedelic music into a distinctive sound. During the frenetic years of 1966 and 1967, when the Vietnam antiwar movement geared up and the counterculture took shape, the band became popular at protest rallies and love-ins, and its song "I-Feel-Like-I'm-Fixin'-to-Die Rag" became the antiwar movement's anthem.

Barry Melton and Country Joe McDonald started The Fish in 1965 as a loose-knit jug band, but, a year later, the group switched to electric instruments. The band appeared at the Monterey Pop Festival in 1967 and then at Woodstock the next year, where Country Joe got half a million young people to chant the group's famous "F-U-C-K" cheer before going into the group's most identifiable number, "I Feel-Like-I'm-Fixin'-To-Die Rag." The band continued to tour after Woodstock, but by 1969 the group had peaked. It got fewer bookings, especially after their arrest in Worcester, Massachusetts, for chanting the "F-U-C-K" cheer, which, according to the authorities, incited the crowd to lewd behavior.

Barry Melton (photo by the author).

When The Fish broke up in 1970, Country Joe McDonald continued to play professionally, but Barry Melton's life eventually took a far different turn: He took and passed the college equivalency test required by the State Bar of California and began studying law.

Born in New York City in 1947, Melton had always dreamed of being a lawyer. Melton grew up in California's San Fernando Valley before graduating from Van Nuys High School in 1965. At age 17, he enrolled at San Francisco State University but dropped out of college to play music and become a part of the exciting counterculture that was emerging in the San Francisco Bay area.

After his Fish experience, Melton launched a solo music career in the early seventies that eventually took him to Europe; but, in 1977, he began to pursue his dream of a law career in earnest. Five years later, he passed the California Bar Examination, becoming one of just a handful of self-taught lawyers in the state.

A full-time lawyer since 1982, Melton runs a solo law practice in San Francisco, which consists primarily of criminal, juvenile, and entertainment contract law. His pro-bono work on behalf of the poor earned him an Outstanding Lawyer in Public Service Award in 1985. With extensive experience working on juvenile delinquency cases, Melton is often invited to lecture at annual training sessions required of juvenile practitioners. He has also helped to establish a nonprofit recording studio at the Bay Area Opera House to be used by young people of the Bayview–Hunters Point Community. In his free time, the sixties radical continues to play music as lead guitar player for a group called the Dinosaurs. He is married with two children.

Our interview took place at Melton's San Francisco home, which he uses as an office. Dressed in a tie and conservative grey suit, Melton looked far removed from the radical sixties counterculture scene in which he was a major participant.

*   *   *

Let's start at the beginning. Where and when were you born?
I was born of humble origins in 1947 in a log cabin in New York City.

[Laughs] In a log cabin in Manhattan or Brooklyn?
[Laughs] It was Brooklyn. I don't have a lot of memories about Brooklyn because I was eight years old when my parents moved to California. I grew up in Southern California.

I understand from talking with your wife Barbara before our interview that you have a very political background.
My parents were left-wing people. They started persecuting left-wing people in the fifties, but in the thirties it wasn't unique to have a left-wing background. In the thirties, there were a million declared Communists in the U.S. and another three or four million who thought of themselves as Socialists. If you know your California history, you know a Socialist ran for governor. Many people thought he had won the popular vote, but it was ultimately rigged, so he was denied the office. That, of course, was Upton Sinclair.[2] My parents were a part of that left-wing movement in the thirties.

Did that background rub off on you?
Sure. I became politically aware at an early age because of the persecution my parents were subjected to in the McCarthy era.

What happened to them?
My father, who was a merchant seaman, lost the ability to pursue what he had been doing for twenty years. He had been making good money as a chief mate, but the stuff from the thirties spilled into the fifties, not because they were having Communist cell meetings in 1951 to plot the overthrow of the United States government, but because they were Communists and Socialists in 1938.

Historically, there had been an enormous depression in the thirties, and the Communists and Socialists militantly tried to move in and organize the working class, so to speak. The net result of that move on a progressive scale was the advent of Social Security and the rise of the labor unions as a powerful force in U.S. politics, although it's declining today. Social Security is socialism, even though that word is anathema to most Americans. Social Security is the concept that, if a worker becomes ill or disabled, then their government will take care of them. Welfare is a socialist concept, too...

We think of the Communists and Socialists as representing the extreme end of the political spectrum in this country, but after all, five million people in the thirties out of a total population of about one hundred and forty million considered themselves Communist or Socialist. They may have added up to ten percent of the population. Then you have the people who considered themselves Liberal Democrats. I'm sure a Liberal Democrat back then was much more liberal than one who calls himself that today. [Laughs]

In any case, the situation in the thirties gave birth to certain reforms. What happened was that the Democratic Party under Franklin Delano Roosevelt absorbed the growing dissatisfied mass of people into the Democratic Party. [Laughs] So when the Republicans make all those accusations about the Democrats, they are in part true. [Laughs]

That left-wing movement of the thirties was driven by folk music ... Woody Guthrie, Leadbelly, Joe Hill,[3] Pete Seeger... That folk tradition is the direct predecessor of the sixties' folk rock music. Bob Dylan modeled himself as a Woody Guthrie clone early in his career. The Byrds[4] first hit was "Turn, Turn, Turn," a Pete Seeger song. Country Joe and the Fish was on the record label that the Weavers[5] were on...

That's an interesting point. You are saying that the cultural roots of the sixties extended back to the thirties.

Yes. A part of the sixties, because the decade was so complex.

Were you exposed to music at an early age?

Absolutely! In fact, Woody Guthrie was a neighbor. I met the musical movers of the thirties era. That was my parents' music.

Did your parents encourage you to get into music?

[Laughs] I always tell people — and there is a lot of truth to it — that law is the profession I chose myself, but music was the one that my parents chose for me. One of the reasons I made a career change from musician to lawyer was because it was part of the liberating experience of growing up and getting away from what my parents wanted me to do.

So were you a reluctant musician?

Beginning at age five, I was trained on classical guitar. In fact, my mother would yell at me to stop playing and come inside and practice. So it wasn't exactly a matter of free will or choice. [Laughs] My parents decided I was going to be a musician and got me the best available instruments. They didn't have a lot of money, but they sacrificed a lot to make sure I could have music lessons. And they made me practice.

So I arrived in San Francisco in the early sixties at the time of the "guitar hero." Having been classically trained on the guitar gave me a tremendous advantage. Just think if my parents had decided I was going to be a saxophone player. [Laughs]

[Laughs] So are you saying it was easy to make the transition from classical to rock guitar?

I was a seventeen-year-old who had come to the Bay area to go to school. I had been playing musically with folk groups since I was fourteen, and I was familiar with the entire folk music idiom. So when I arrived in San Francisco, everybody was trying to finger pick the guitar, but I could play it fluently. I came into my own.

Why did you decide to come to San Francisco to go to school?

I came to study semantics with S.I. Hayakawa at San Francisco State.[6] Actually, all through high school, I had dreamed of being a lawyer and never remotely thought about having anything to do with music.

I came to San Francisco when the Bay area was right dab in the middle of a political and cultural revolution. I'm one of the best four or five guitar players in the entire area. Because of my background, I fit in well. I could talk left-wing politics with virtually anyone, and I could play guitar like nobody's business.

So you had no trouble breaking into the musical scene?

No. I became a part of the folk music scene. I was supposed to be in school, but here I was a seventeen-year-old kid on my own, and I could make money just by getting up on stage for thirty or forty minutes. It was a lot easier than working. [Laughs]

You see, I don't believe in the idea of talent or a predisposition toward music. I really don't. I really believe music is a language like French is a language. It can be learned. Certainly, people have talent in foreign languages, so they will become more silver-tongued than the less talented. But all of the really successful musicians I know started playing in early childhood. You will always speak it with an accent unless you learn to speak a language by a certain age. I don't know how much talent I have or could have had, but I learned to speak the language fluently.

At the same time, I was being motivated by the antiwar movement and had participated in the civil rights movement in the early sixties when I was in junior high. I took part in a sit-in of the Elementary Board of Education, had marched on a segregated restaurant, and had volunteered at the CORE [Congress of Racial Equality] headquarters in downtown L.A.

When did you get involved with the antiwar movement?

It was 1962 or '63 when Madame Nhu[7] came to L.A. I was involved in a demonstration outside her hotel.

So you were establishing yourself in the Bay area. How did the Country Joe and the Fish experience originate?

Joe and I met in Berkeley. He wanted to make a record that had a rock-jug band influence. He asked around: Who should play guitar? People said, "Barry Melton. He's one of the best around."

Joe called me. We cut the record before my eighteenth birthday . . . May 1965. Radio stations picked it up. The SDS had seen us play in San Francisco and offered us a tour of colleges in the Northwest. The SDS said it would help us to promote our music. Joe and I toured on a Greyhound bus as a duo [Country Joe and the Fish]. We sold some records.

What kind of response did you receive from the students?

Well, the SDS booked the tour, so I would say the tour went well. [Laughs] We played to small crowds at colleges like Lewis and Clark College in Oregon and the University of Washington at Seattle. . . We weren't playing rock music yet, but Joe and I did establish a rapport. When we got back to San Francisco [it was roughly the summer, fall of 1965], we began playing locally. Rock music seemed to be exploding in the Bay area, so I suggested to Joe that maybe we should get a rock band together. We put together an electric band, and by the end of 1965, we made a record that had tremendous local success.

What was your role in the band?

Well, I put the band together. [Laughs] Joe was the band's focus because he was the singer and principal song writer, but I was responsible, as much as anyone in the band, for its musical content and direction.

Someone wrote that Country Joe and the Fish was the first rock group to link people's music with people's politics.

I don't agree with that. Our band was just the lineal descendant of the groups from the thirties, such as the Weavers. We were a part of that tradition, although the Weavers were obviously not a rock band. We were familiar with them, and they were our heroes.

Did Country Joe have a significant impact in changing people's minds about the Vietnam War?

A small role, maybe. [Laughs] During that era, we were on the radio all the time, so I assume we had some effect on the consciousness of the period. I believe we caught the mood of the time, but I don't want to overstate our role.

[Laughs] Do you think you will make the history books?

Maybe as a footnote. I know that, if you play our music, it evokes a feeling for a particular period in American history. Maybe our music will survive as a musical artifact. Maybe twenty-five hundred years from now they will play our records in some history class, if they want to evoke the mood and feel of the sixties.

Were you influenced by some of the rock groups that were emerging at the time, say, for example, the Beatles and the Rolling Stones?

With all due respect for those two groups, they were pretty insipid. I'm not saying that the Beatles didn't mature into a marvelous musical group. But at the time Country Joe and the Fish were coming together, the Beatles were putting out garbage. Sure it was good popular music, but it didn't have any content. In the early sixties, I was a folk purist, and the Beatles and Rolling Stones were not the kind of groups I would listen to. They didn't receive any credibility as far as counterculture music was concerned until after Country Joe and the Fish was fully formed.

What impact did Country Joe and the Fish have on the emerging counterculture?
We were definitely a counterculture band, if not for our politics, then for the consciousness aspect of the music.

Was there a sense of community among the San Francisco rock bands in the sixties?
Yes, there was. We all knew each other before anybody was signed to a record contract. Many of us had played together, and we had a lot in common because of the emerging counterculture scene. But I believe the San Francisco music scene changed the music industry. San Francisco musicians staked out a position for artist's rights. We shared information among ourselves, which enabled groups to negotiate better deals with their record companies. This heralded an era in which musicians got a fairer share of what was going on.

Was there much competition between the rock groups?
Not really. I think the music field is much more competitive today because there are so many musicians trying to squeeze into the same space, and there is really not much room at the top. The music field was much more wide open in the sixties when I started in the recording industry. There was probably one album coming out each week. Today, there are five hundred. [Laughs]

It's been said that the San Francisco musicians had a sense of responsibility to the local community. Is that true?
I like to think that San Francisco musicians were leaders in inculcating in musicians a sense of social responsibility. I hope we set a trend of giving something back. Watch MTV[8] — an indicator of youth culture — and you will see musicians getting involved with causes and exhibiting a sense of social responsibility. Maybe that tradition is traceable back to San Francisco and the sixties.

How do you explain the longevity of such groups as The Grateful Dead and Jefferson Airplane, which in the seventies became transposed into the Jefferson Starship? In Los Angeles, there was Frank Zappa[9] until he died in 1993 of prostate cancer.
You can do it if you want to keep doing the same thing. You build equity by continuing to stay on the performance circuit. Those musicians are willing to do it, but it's a tough life.

Those groups were playing before Woodstock. Outside of the legend, what was the significance of that event?

It was the last. [Laughs] It killed the others off! [Laughs]

[Laughs] In what respect?

Well, Woodstock was the last in a series of large pop musical events, which ran from the time of the Monterey Pop Festival in 1967. After Woodstock, concerts were held in more structured settings, where the organizers and authorities could help keep count of people.

Why did they want to do that?

Because people saw the Woodstock movie, and they realized the various problems that come with crowd control: The roads were jammed . . . you had medical problems. . . . Communities became unwilling to be hosts for those kinds of events because they saw all the money that had to be spent. So Woodstock killed off large, unstructured rock concerts.

Was Woodstock the beginning of the end of the counterculture?

Oh, I don't know. Maybe in a symbolic way. But it did affect the music business. After Woodstock, mega pop musical festivals that had been planned were cancelled.

The sixties rock scene conjures up an image for many of drugs and wild sexuality. Is that a true picture of the counterculture?

Almost. [Laughs] Many of us were in our teens and early twenties and that is usually the wildest part of life. I think most of the real crazy things we do in life we do when we are about nineteen years old. If people are going to have multiple sex partners, that is the age they will have them. The age factor was a part of it. The other part is the time when it happened. Drugs were accepted. You won't find such a huge generational swing to drugs today as you had in the sixties because kids are more suspicious of drugs, as well as they should be.

I understand you advocated the use of LSD and believed it was an important part of the counterculture.

LSD had a phenomenal impact on San Francisco in the sixties. When the band formed in 1965, LSD was legal and you ran no legal risk if you carried it around and used it. LSD is a powerful drug! Being free and plentiful, acid had an enormous impact on the counterculture. It was less than cheap. Ask someone for a hit of acid, and they would give it to you. [Laughs]

What were your feelings when LSD was made illegal in 1966?

We thought it was unfair and an attempt to stifle the youth movement. But look! Not everything we did in the sixties was wholly sensible. Anyone with any kind of understanding realizes that LSD is not the panacea it was first thought to be. [Laughs] In fact, it's not good for everybody. I would not want to give it to a homicidal maniac. Nor do I believe it should be freely distributed.

So do you believe drugs should be legalized?

I don't really think that the country is spending its time effectively on the war on drugs, and I'm not so sure that this country could not be better off legalizing drugs for adults. Obviously, you got to have some of the prohibitions you have for alcohol. For example, you don't want people to drive a car around stoned, nor would you want people to maneuver airplanes stoned. Drugs like LSD effectively remove the taker from being able to take care of himself for at least a day and prevents him from doing anything effective for at least another couple of days.

So under what circumstances should drugs be legal? I believe that society wants the ability to save someone from themselves. As a criminal lawyer, I can tell you that some kids have been picked up by the cops and their parents had come to police headquarters, extremely relieved that their children were arrested. So I don't know if society would benefit by decriminalizing the whole drug problem.

But I do know that it's important that we begin looking at the drug problem as a national health problem, not a national crime problem. I don't know if we can make people criminals simply because they have a drug problem. I do know we are doing it wrong.

And doesn't doing it "wrong" mean that the so-called "war on drugs" is having a negative impact on civil liberties?

Yes! [Laughs] The entire system has to be overhauled when it comes to drugs because drugs don't belong in the criminal justice system. It belongs in the health system. I can spend hours talking about this subject, but let me say this: The criminal justice system should be front loaded, meaning that society should spend whatever it takes at the first manifestation of behavior. I believe the justice system is the most underfunded part of government today.

Where would you put the money?

Job programs for the kids for starters. The criminal justice system is draining society of its life blood. It's spending billions and billions of dollars on police, sheriffs, lawyers, jails. . . . I see firsthand the money being spent on the criminal courts. It's unbelievable! I'm telling you if we don't get down to the root causes—the ghetto—and provide alternatives and more opportunity, then the problem is going to continue to grow.

And what happens? If we don't solve the problem of the ghetto, does that mean we are going to have more and more law enforcement and less and less civil liberties?

Yes! It's already going on. When H. Ross Perot[10] was confronted with giving an answer to this problem, he said he would have the army conduct house to house searches. That was the way he would deal with the drug problem. People may say, "That's fine. It's not in my neighborhood." Everybody assumes that when Perot says that he means they are excluded.

That reminds me of what someone said about Nazi Germany. It went something like this: "First they came for the Communist. Then they came for the Jews and gypsies, and then they came for me . . ." That's the same principle working here, right?

It's frightening to think that people may be willing to give up their individual rights to cope with the problem.

But history shows that in stressful times societies have been willing to sacrifice freedom for security and order. Didn't Mussolini[11] make the trains run on time?

It's always what the authorities offer you. I don't care what the conservatives say. We are spending too much money . . . billions and billions . . . It's going into warehousing people, but the recidivism rate is so high! We are not doing anything for them. Incarcerated people should be learning how to fix computers. We should have the type of system where, if one gets ten years for a crime and doesn't do anything while in prison, then that person should spend ten years in prison. But if that person learns a trade, then he should be able to get out in four years. We should have an incentive-based system that has parole officers helping former inmates to find jobs. It's a lot cheaper than keeping people in a prison.

The scary thing is that we are creating a generation of disenfranchised young people who go to prison and come back unemployable, with a felony record. So they really haven't paid their debt to society. They pay that debt the rest of their lives.

That's scary because we are heading toward a revolution or, at the very least, a civil uprising. When an incident erupts like the Los Angeles riots that occurred after the Rodney King beating,[12] we get a glimmer of what our society will face and what the future holds if nothing is done to solve the problems.

Are your views on the criminal justice system widely shared by your colleagues?

I'm sure it's shared by a lot of people, especially in San Francisco. I live in a very liberal community.

Yet the people in power who make the decisions seem to be advocating the position that calls for building more and more prisons.

All over the country! But the people who end up in prison are extraordinarily and disproportionately people of color. We are beginning to see de facto apartheid in this country. The police presence in this city [San Francisco], for example, is located in minority neighborhoods. I'm just saying if we are going to spend all that money on the criminal justice system, let's spend it where it's going to do some good. The war on drugs costs so much money! If we abandoned it right now, we could cut the deficit and begin doing something to alleviate the problem.

So do you see any hope that there will be a change of strategy with [Bill] Clinton now in office?

One can only hope. Government moves so slowly in this country, so I don't think we will see a change until we reach crisis proportions. I guess the crisis will continue until we conclude that we can't afford it anymore. And we can't afford it! We can't keep building prisons to deal with our problems, just as we can't keep building hospitals to deal with AIDS. Are we going to keep allowing people to run around with unprotected sex and not teach them a goddamn thing about preventing the disease? We need hospitals, but the successful approach to the AIDS problem would involve passing out condoms.

Since the sixties, it seems that there has been little progress to alleviate some of the serious problems facing American society.

That's true on practically every front. It's demonstrably provable if you want to talk about not just the criminal justice but such things as air quality and the state of the oceans... They haven't done anything except get worse.

So what is the legacy of the sixties? Conservatives blame a lot of the problems we have today on the permissiveness and so-called narcissism of that period.

Oh, I don't believe that! There is plenty of blame to go around. I have very definite ideas about what the sixties did positively, what the sixties did negatively, and what the sixties tried to do but had no more impact than anything else.

Okay. Let's start with the positive.

The women's movement and the consciousness it raised about the roles played by the sexes began in the sixties and had a positive effect for women all over America. Women — and men, for that matter — owe a debt of gratitude for the reexamination of the relationship of the sexes that began in the sixties.

The sixties also heightened awareness of the ecology that affects every individual. People became aware of nutrition and conscious of what is being sprayed on their food. As a result, we are a more healthy country today.

The sixties counterculture led to the introduction in this country of Eastern thought and medical systems, such as acupuncture,[13] in this country. Today, alternative medicine is widely accepted and used in this country, and I think that's good.

But we learned an important lesson from the sixties. Science doesn't know everything. The sixties decade was one in which doctors would prescribe the most powerful antibiotics in the world to hold off infection. They were called "miracle drugs," and they were freely used. We were much less responsible about chemicals and how they affect health. Today, though, there are few doctors who would prescribe antibiotics unless they are sure the body can't fight infection. But, on the other hand, the drug problem and the chemical dependency problem we have today stems from the easy acceptance of drugs in the sixties.

That's a big negative, given that so many of our problems today seem connected to the drug problem.

Drugs became socially acceptable in the sixties as an entire generation defied the law.

So you wouldn't blame today's drug problems — say the inner city crack problem — on economics as a lot of other liberals do?

[Laughs] I don't know anybody who took crack in the sixties. [Laughs]

That's exactly the point —

The sixties made it socially acceptable to disobey the law and to use drugs and to openly advocate using drugs. It was done in mass so the authorities couldn't do anything about it. I think the sixties created a prevailing climate in which, if someone saw his neighbor sniffing cocaine from time to time, he would shrug and say, "Well, it's not bothering me."

So that is a major negative, and most things fall into the third category — things the sixties tried to do something about, but had no impact. Which is virtually everything that happened in the sixties. [Laughs]

[Laughs] That's kind of a summary dismissal.

Obviously, there was some impact, such as civil rights in the early sixties and the gay and lesbian movement in the late sixties. . . But most of the problems we tried to deal with in the sixties are still with us.

Could you give some examples?

Welfare, poverty, war. . . Look at the peace movement. What did it really accomplish? Has American policy really changed? Aren't we putting American lives on the line in disputes that don't concern us? The sixties counterculture tried to deemphasize materialism, but society today is more materialistic than ever. We, as a country, are still trying to decide how far we should go with free speech. . .

Yes you were involved with free speech in the sixties when you gave the Fish chant — "F-U-C-K" — and the authorities didn't like it. Recently, 2 Live Crew,[14] the rap group, got into trouble with the authorities over their use of language. Did you empathize with them?

Yes, I did. The rap groups[15] today, as groups like Country Joe and the Fish did in the sixties, are expressing their frustrations about the political landscape. I don't particularly like rap music that much, but the legacy of sixties protest music continues in the rap music. Rap musicians are my cultural descendants, if you will.

You ran for judge recently and lost. Does that mean Barry Melton has political aspirations?

That race may have cured me. [Laughs]

[Laughs] Why is that?

I owe a lot of money from that campaign, which I'm paying off every month.

So does one have to be rich to run for political office in this country and win?

What you have to do is spend a lot of time fundraising. You have to get on the phone and beg for money. One of the problems with our political system is that we force our representatives in the House and Senate to spend enormous amounts of time trying to raise money because they have to be money-generating machines in order to stay in office. It's possible your local congressman is spending thirty hours a week trying to raise money.

Do you have any ideas on how to reform the system?

We should undertake campaign reform. There are democratic countries that work perfectly well by modestly limiting the amount an elected representative spends. This gives all the politicians access to a public forum, and they don't need money to do it. It makes for a level playing field. Otherwise, you have a situation where Ross Perot can come in and distort the playing field and the national equation by spending wads of money. It isn't good for a democracy to have a system where only the wealthy can run.

By the way, did getting busted for marijuana possession in the sixties ever come back to haunt you professionally or politically?

No, because marijuana was decriminalized here in California in the mid-seventies. My bust was no big deal. All I had was a joint. Today, possessing a joint in California is a misdemeanor carrying a hundred dollar fine. Growing and selling marijuana is highly illegal in California today, but carrying it isn't.

You remain active in the community. What are some of the things you are doing?

Musically, I play my share of benefits. For example, I played for a benefit for the victims of the earthquake we had here recently. I play benefits for AIDS victims, for the food bank, and for the homeless. I work for the homeless advocacy program here in town, as well as Volunteer Legal Services. I give a lot of legal clinics, and I've never turned down anybody who has wanted legal service if they didn't have an alternative.

I believe strongly in community service. But one doesn't have to be a former sixties counterculture figure to be involved with the community. You have people who are presidents of the Lions Club and are active in their communities. [Laughs] It's just that some people have social responsibility and some don't.

What kind of music do the Dinosaurs play?

It's a sort of blues-folk-based music. We don't play past hits much. Mostly, we go on stage, jam and improvise. I play four or five times a month and go on the road for a week or two each year. I like that setup. I don't ever want to go on the road again for two-hundred-and-fifty days a year. I could never imagine doing that again!

I know musicians who have done that for the past thirty years. My hat is off to them. That is a tough existence to lead, particularly if you are making medium and not large bucks. [Laughs] It's rough if you have a family. You can't really take a seven-year-old kid on the road. It's not what I would like to do. And I know what they make — especially those who are working on the club circuit. They make as much as a lawyer who stays home. [Laughs]

[Laughs] You don't sound like a guy who gets nostalgic for the old days.

Not at all. I'm doing what's right for me at this time. I feel sorry for people whose identity is trapped into what they were doing twenty-five or thirty years ago when they were kids. I've changed. I hope it's for the better. There was a point in my life when I thought that, if you give LBJ some acid, he would come to his senses. Now I realize that, if we would have been able to give LBJ acid, he might have blown the goddamn world away! [Laughs] I know today that LSD is just a goddamn drug! We thought taking LSD was a way to reach enlightenment. But all it did was create a euphoric state for a while.

17

Peter Coyote

Hollywood Radical

> I think there is a lot left [of the sixties]. The counterculture
> helped create institutions that are everywhere today. You see it
> in the peace movement, the natural foods movement, the
> ecology movement, the women's movement, the civil rights
> movement . . . all these movements came to fruition in the six-
> ties... This legacy is much more enduring than the political
> ideology. That is the way change is manifested—by the way peo-
> ple live, not just by the way they talk. So I'm proud to be part
> and parcel of that.

Today, Peter Coyote is an established and accomplished actor who has appeared in such box office winners as *E.T., Jagged Edge,* and *Outrageous Fortune.* During the sixties, however, Coyote was a radical, a member of the
anarchistic Diggers and the Mime Troupe and heavily into the counterculture
and drug scene, so heavily into the drug scene, in fact, that he changed his sur-
name from Cohon as a result of a peyote vision.

Born the son of a well-to-do conservative family, Coyote spent much of
his childhood in Edgewood, New Jersey, and on a family farm in Pennsylvania.
But his youth was far from smooth. He constantly got into trouble and was
thrown out of several schools. In 1959, Mexican police busted him for possession of ten kilos of marijuana.

Coyote survived that run in with the law and went on to study at Grinnell
College in Iowa and then at San Francisco State University during the exciting
days of the sixties when the counterculture dominated the San Francisco
scene. He became a lead actor with the Mime Troupe and went on national
tour, performing in two controversial plays: first, *Minstrel Show* and then the
intense anti–Vietnam War drama *L'Amant Militaire.*

Burned out by the end of the second tour, Coyote joined the anarchistic
Diggers, a far-left group based in the Haight-Ashbury district, which wanted
to take the philosophy espoused by the counterculture to its ultimate limit.
Coyote subscribed to the Diggers program, which scorned money, provided
free medical care, performed radical guerrilla theater, started a free store

where goods could be had for the taking, and, despite the group's penchant for anonymity, became one of its most eloquent spokesmen.

But as Coyote later described the Digger experience in an interview in the eighties, "It was twenty-four-hours-a-day improvisatory acting designed to get people out of old ideas. It has the luminescence of a moth, ecstatically beautiful in the present; invisible to history. It released a lot of creative energy, but, unfortunately, a lot of this activity was fueled by a lot of drugs."[1]

So by the early seventies, the frenetic living of the sixties had almost killed the young rebel. He came down with a severe case of hepatitis and barely survived. Meanwhile, Coyote's father had died, leaving his mother heavily in debt. Coyote moved East to help his mother out. After selling the family farm to get her out of debt, Coyote returned to the San Francisco area to live out of his truck and teach acting in the ghetto schools.

In 1975, California Governor Jerry Brown appointed Coyote to the California Arts Council, and, for the next eight years, Coyote, as chairman of the group, fostered artistic activity, brought arts to the common man, and radically altered how the arts were funded in the state.

Despite his success in the political arena, Coyote decided he wanted to be a professional actor, even though he was camera shy and approaching 40 years of age. Coyote broke into Hollywood with appearances in a series of low-budget films and then appeared to get his break, landing the role of Keys in *E.T.*, one of the biggest grossing movies of all time. Despite appearances in more than 40 feature films and TV films and a reputation as "the thinking woman's sex symbol," Coyote has often been unemployed for long stretches and has even gone to Europe to find film work.

When not making movies, Coyote lives outside San Francisco in picturesque, but secluded, Mill Valley. Coyote's bungalow-style house is small but comfortably furnished and, for reasons that come out during our interview, is named Wild Dog Productions.

Coyote is an intensely private man, but he was open and friendly during the interview, revealing that he decided to talk to me after reading my *The Progressive* article about the plight of migrant peach workers in South Carolina.[2] Coyote still sees himself as a radical and keeps busy appearing at benefits for groups like the Mime Troupe and working and speaking out on behalf of Native American rights and environmental issues.

Coyote is approaching his mid–50s in age, but he looks remarkably youthful, with his wavy dark hair and lean features. He wore a conspicuously large gold earring in his left ear and was dressed casually in a plain blue sweat shirt, black jeans, and sneakers.

At 6 feet 2 inches tall, Coyote is a ball of sinewy but fluid movement. He lights up old-fashioned stogies, makes coffee, eats a spinach salad, and ends up washing dishes during our intense three-hour interview in which he gives blunt, but thoughtful and often unexpected, opinions on a variety of topics.

Peter Coyote (photo courtesy of Peter Coyote).

Recently, Coyote has had plenty of time to reflect, for he reveals that he has not had an acting role for 14 months.

*   *   *

You've been out of work for fourteen months? What have you been doing with yourself?
    I do what you do. I'm writing a book.

So you are using your time constructively.

Yes, I was a writer before I was an actor. I went to San Francisco State and got my Master's [in creative writing]. I've stayed a writer, although I do what I have to do to make money. But my first love is writing.

Are you a published author?

Yeah, but I don't write fiction. Two of the chapters from my book have been published in literary quarterlies. Over the years, I've had articles, usually on the subject of contemporary culture, published in different places. I've had an eight thousand-word article published in French *Vogue*.

What's your book about? Is it an autobiography?

It's not exactly an autobiography. It's called *The Free-Fall Chronicles* and takes a fair look at what I learned during the period from 1965 to 1975, when my life was dedicated to the pursuit of absolute freedom. I want other people to see what can be learned from my experience and what are the costs, for there are costs. Most everything I read about the period has been an apologia. "We were so young, so silly . . . blah, blah, blah." Or, "Weren't we all wonderful and romantic?" Both points of view are bullshit.

So what is a point of view that isn't bullshit?

My community was very left-wing, hard-edged, and radical, but we weren't trying to change the culture. We weren't ideological revolutionaries . . . Communists or Socialists. We were primarily artists who wanted to create a culture that was based on personal authenticity. It seemed to me that the capitalist and Communist models of what society should be were both exquisite machines for grinding up human beings and turning them into a citizen or a proletariat or some piece of bullshit I didn't want to be.

How did this disenchantment evolve?

I helped write a play for a radical theater company that won a big prize. I thought, "Jesus Christ. I'm writing a play, which is criticizing the middle class, and they are giving me a medal for it. Theater is not really a tool to make social change."

So a bunch of us evolved into the Diggers. We wanted to use our experiences as artists—our improvisation, our sense of imagination—to help us create lives that are beautiful and worth living. We wanted to live our lives as if the revolution was over and we had won. We wanted to set an example for other people to follow and to open the door in the culture that was available for them to walk through.

Let's back up a little. Why did you come to San Francisco? Was it to take creative writing at San Francisco State or was it because of the evolving counterculture?

Oh, no, there was no counterculture evolving in '64 when I came to San Francisco. As a matter of fact, at that time, there wasn't anything remotely like a counterculture in San Francisco. All there was, really, was the beginning of the Psychedelic Shop on Haight-Ashbury.

Were you political by the time you came to San Francisco?

Yes, I was. I was involved in the civil rights movement to some degree when I was young. I went on marches and demonstrated at Grinnell College in Iowa. My family was active, too. My mom was involved with the Urban League, the ACLU, and stuff like that.

Even though I was political, I never saw the connection between political beliefs and living them on a day-to-day basis until I got involved with the Mime Troupe.

What were some of the things you did in the Mime Troupe that got you thinking about the connection?

The Mime Troupe produced free plays in the park, outside where the people actually were. The fact that we did the plays for free was a political statement. We established a different relationship between the arts and the audience. We were all very good artists, and we tried to give a free show that had more elegance and class and finish than one they would have actually paid to see. Of course, we had to eat, so we passed the hat around afterward.

We acted out plays that dealt with things affecting people's lives — rent, taxes, arms control, and other issues of the day — and we talked about them in a very funny way. The plays we presented were written only after long and arduous debate and represented deep thought from a committed point of view that was democratic, egalitarian, and liberal. That was our point of view. We were saying, "Hey, here we are. This is what radicals are really like. This is what we sound like, taste like, smell like, think like. You make up your minds, but someone has got to put the ideas out."

Did people really listen to you?

Sure, they did. The Mime Troupe is famous. We traveled all over the country. People listened to us because we made our arguments with humor. If I give you a straight political rap, I don't know whether I have you or not. But if I sell it to you as a gag and you laugh, I know you've seen my point of view or you wouldn't have gotten the joke. We didn't bludgeon anyone over the head, but we were sharp, hard, and radical. That was why people believed us.

As the sixties progressed, did you get disillusioned with America like a lot of other people?

I am a little cynical, but that doesn't stop me from hoping for the best. Let me recall a fascinating experience I had. In 1962, during the Cuban Missile Crisis, a bunch of us in college were so freaked out by what we thought was going to be the end of the world that we dropped out of classes. We hustled up some money and bought two cars [a '48 Chevy and a '52 Ford] and went to Washington. We cut our hair, wore suits and ties, and picketed the White House on a three-day fast, protesting the resumption of nuclear testing.

[President John F.] Kennedy read about us in the newspaper and invited us into the White House. We were the first group in history to picket the White House and then be invited in. I was asked to be spokesman for the group. We met with McGeorge Bundy.[3]

At that time, I had actually thought those guys had not thought it out. The arrogance of the young, right? [Laughs] Bundy looked like a chameleon. His eyes were the coldest, most analytical I had ever seen in my young life. I changed my mind and said to myself, "This guy knows everything. This guy knows so much more than me that it is ridiculous. Nothing I say is going to change his mind. Neither am I going to affect anything by picketing in the streets and carrying a sign. I've got to do something else." That's when I began to think about culture as opposed to politics.

But it came out during the course of the sixties that the people in power like McGeorge Bundy didn't know a damn thing, especially when it came to Vietnam.

It's not that they are stupid. They are brilliant actually. But the government of the United States is run for the elite of the United States. All the elite cares about is making sure that the tax structure is in their favor, the factories are running, and they are making a lot of money. I wouldn't mind if the U.S. had an emperor who said this is my country and these are my subjects. I'm going to make it work for everyone. Yes, the rich might get a little less richer, but the poor are going to get a little less poorer, too.

When did you first become aware of Vietnam?
    When I was eighteen.

Because of the draft?
    Yes, that was about 1957, my senior year in high school. I applied as a conscientious objector and volunteered to be a medic. I went to the draft board and told them that I wasn't going to carry a gun and shoot somebody. I said I wanted to be a medic. They said no.

So what happened?
    I stayed in school and went to Grinnell College. I was planning to go on to graduate school to keep my student deferment, but I hated school. I said to myself, "I'm not going to stay in school to hide from the draft. This is bullshit. I told them what my principles were. Fuck 'em! I'll lie to them. If they're not going to let me be a medic, I'll tell them I'm a psychopath or a homosexual. I don't care." But eventually, they classified me as "Y," which meant that I had been psychologically deferred. This was probably 1963 or '64. I'm not good on chronology.

But you were ahead of your time. [Laughs] I read where you got busted for marijuana in Mexico in 1959. What happened there?
    I got involved with folk music and would go to folk festivals and play a little guitar. There was always a little grass around. I had known people who had

smoked marijuana all their lives, and so I tried it and liked it. I went to Mexico and thought I would bring some back home with me. I was basically an idiot. I threw it under the seat and tried to drive across the border. I just got pulled out of line, and they found it.

But I don't know if I was ahead of my time. I always thought that, when you believe in something, you just got to do it. It's funny how the media has this fucking term *activist*. Where I grew up, if a man didn't act on his beliefs, he was a hypocrite. Now the media has turned it around. Today, a man who does act out his beliefs is somehow out of the central fold—a little apart. He's not like you and me. That's bullshit! I've always believed in following my beliefs.

Today, if you had twenty kilos of marijuana and were trying to cross the Mexican border into the U.S., you would probably get twenty years in jail, given the current hard line on drugs. What's your views on the U.S.'s so-called war on drugs?

It's ridiculous! First of all, there is no human culture on earth that doesn't use something to alter its state of consciousness, whether it's fasting, prayer, music, coffee, nicotine, alcohol, tobacco, hashish, marijuana, mushrooms, peyote, meditation, Yahweh[4]... The desire to alter consciousness is universal. Trying to completely stop it is like trying to stop the tides.

So it seems to me that a line should be drawn—the line being those drugs that are the result of chemistry and those that aren't. Why waste your energy fighting drugs like peyote, marijuana, mushrooms, and mescaline? Doing those drugs doesn't make you a criminal.

It's hypocritical. The U.S. government subsidizes tobacco and alcohol, which are worse for a person. I think a hundred years from now, people are going to look at the drug policy we have in place as people today look at the religious beliefs of people who lived during the time of the Inquisition.

Do you think the U.S. will eventually come around to the point of view you have on drugs?

I don't know, but legalizing substances doesn't mean that they can't be regulated. Liquor is legal and is regulated. I, for one, believe drugs should be regulated. I don't believe for one minute that anyone should be able to get any drug anytime he wants. But I do believe the authorities shouldn't prosecute someone who takes drugs that are the equivalent of a cocktail or a cigarette or a cup of coffee. Why fight them? Instead, regulate the hard drugs and treat them as a medical problem, not a legal problem. The legal system is completely fucking clogged with people who only wanted to change their consciousness.

The U.S. has the highest incarceration rate in the world for a country not at war, largely because of its hard-line drug policy.

Yes, it costs about $10,000 a year to keep a prisoner in the joint. You can send them to Harvard for less than that. I can't believe it costs that much per person to run clinics and pay for psychiatrists. We have to make a decision as to what kind of culture we want to live in. Do we really want to live in a culture where it's illegal to pursue certain states of mind? What does that do to the rest of us? I'm not saying for one minute that crack isn't a disaster and a danger, but I will say that we have crack in this society because it is condoned.

How is that?

Kids in the black ghettos don't have ships and planes and don't run the borders. They just make up the middlemen who pass it out. We know who has had a hand in bringing the drugs to the ghetto. We know that George Bush was bringing it into the U.S. to get money to fund the Contras.

Yes, it's ironic that while the U.S. government talks tough about drugs, it has had a history of supporting the drug trade. It goes at least back to the CIA's drug trafficking during the Vietnam War.

Yes. Wasn't it funny that, during the Vietnam War, when our allies were opium growers, we had a heroin problem in the U.S.? And guess what!? When our allies in Latin America are coke smugglers, we have a coke problem. You don't have to be a rocket scientist to figure it out.

They call me a radical, but I'm not a gangster. I'm not using the U.S. Army to bring illegal substances into the U.S. that're going to ruin the lives of citizens. For what? To fight some ideological figment!

There is lot of shit going on that is just a smoke screen to distribute money. You can say, for instance, what Noam Chomsky says: that the governmental system of the United States is socialism and the Pentagon is the vehicle to distribute funds to the military industrial complex. The Cold War was the philosophical justification to do that.

I read where you were in rough shape in the early seventies largely because of your life-style. I believe you had hepatitis . . .

I had it three times. I made a lot of mistakes, but I also learned a lot. Unfortunately, because of my drug use and life-style, I am excluded today from public life. No guy like me can run for President of the U.S. Yes, I inhaled, I shot up, I sniffed it, I snorted it. I hope Clinton lied when he said he didn't inhale.

That's a sad commentary on American public life to say you hope Clinton lied.

But, really, I hope he lied. I find it much more disturbing if he couldn't figure out how to inhale. Besides, Al Gore admitted he smoked, and it didn't keep him from becoming vice-president.

What are some of the social causes you are involved with today?

I'm involved with the environment.

Just the environment in general or specific issues?

Well, almost any important environmental issue. My feeling is that we got to take care of the planet now because this is the only theater we have. Unfortunately, the indications are that the planet is dying, that the species are dying

... the salmon, the butterflies, the lizards, the birds... They are all dying. We are losing species faster than we did during the Ice Age.[5]

I want a place where my grandchildren can live without having to buy bottled watter or stay clothed in the sunshine. Being human means you live on a planet that is healthy and has a lot of species. A black panther in a zoo is not a black panther. It's a caged animal. A black panther that gets to act like a black panther is a black panther is a black panther. People who live in high-rise apartment buildings and go to work in an office all day are not human. Human beings have to be able to walk outdoors and play, hunt, and fish and be able to contemplate the mysteries of the universe. If people can't do that, they are not human beings.

You used the analogy of the black panther in a zoo. Are you involved with animal rights, too? Do you have strong views on that subject?

As a Buddhist, I have compassion for all living things, but animal rights is not a primary concern of mine.

But according to what I've read about you, you are involved in the rights of Native Americans.

That's my other primary concern. I'm one of the advisers to Leonard Peltier,[6] whom I've known for some twenty years. I'm familiar with his case. The history of the relationship of the United States and, to some extent, Canada with Native Americans has been one of genocide. We annihilated them! It's cultural blight on our history that we have to deal with. We are essentially the South Africans of the North American continent, the Afrikaners, as much as we are [like] the Medellín Cartel[7] [when we] brought drugs into China in the nineteenth century. That's our karma.

We are living a lie unless we apologize for what we have done to Native Americans and begin to change our policies to help diverse Native American cultures retain some health and integrity.

But haven't there been some encouraging developments as far as Native Americans are concerned? They do seem to be winning a lot of settlement claims.

That's still not the same thing as having a government policy that acknowledges the harm done to Native Americans in the past. The U.S. government has never honored its treaties with Native Americans or acknowledged the sovereignty of Indians, who have never been vanquished or defeated. It's not enough to make cash settlements or give them back some land so they can end up like the Navajos, who have leased their land to oil and gas companies so they can be like rich white people. The U.S. government has to deal with Native Americans as people.

The U.S. says it doesn't have any political prisoners, but do you consider Leonard Peltier a political prisoner?

Definitely. Leonard Peltier is a political prisoner. Geronimo Pratt[8] is a political prisoner. The U.S. has many political prisoners.

Peter Coyote (photo by the author).

What do you think are the chances that Leonard Peltier will ever be set free?

I have to believe they are good, that sometime, somehow — maybe now during Clinton's administration — people will begin to realize that the United States government completely falsified the evidence against this man. The first people they accused of the murder of the FBI agents were found innocent by an all-white jury. Then the prosecution plugged every hole in the first case and went and got somebody else. They falsified the data and committed perjury and acts that compelled the Canadian government to protest to the United Nations.

Why did the Canadian government do that?

The U.S. extradited Leonard from Canada using false affidavits. I've got a copy of the Canadian parliamentary motion protesting that action. Jesus said, "What you do to the least of me [*sic*], you do to me." What is done to one citizen like Leonard Peltier can happen to any of us, if we happen to be on the wrong side of the line.

Are you in contact with Leonard Peltier?

I talk to him twice a week.

How does he keep on going?

He has two options: either roll over and die or keep going. He's simply not a quitter. Besides, he also has a lot of people on the outside fighting for him.

Is he bitter about the system?

No, I don't see any bitterness in him. I find it amazing how the people that the government classifies as radicals are more disciplined and selfless and have a higher moral purpose and even greater gentility than the people they are fighting against. Go back in history to Sacco and Vanzetti and read what they said.[9] Their belief systems and ethics and morals were so high. Then go look at the Reagan administration. There were five hundred indictments! Five hundred indictments!

The prosecutor who got Leonard jailed called him a thug, but Leonard never referred to the judge as a thug. All he gave at his trial was an impassioned speech about what he did and why.

The Reagan administration may have been the most corrupt in U.S. history.

Yeah, so let's not delude ourselves. They just have the power. That's all. That's the basis on which they claim their righteousness. End of subject!

The Age of Reagan, in which we saw three conservative administrations in power, has ended. Do you think there will be any major change in policy with Clinton in office?

If I had stayed in politics, I would have been like him [Bill Clinton]. He has the ability to reconcile opposites. I'm happy that he has a real agenda to transform the United States. Whether he will be able to implement his agenda is another question. But I've already noted the NPR [National Public Radio] sniping at Clinton.

[Laughs] But conservative groups are always criticizing NPR for its supposedly "liberal bias."

Yeah, but NPR was never hard on Reagan, a guy who had to be shown cartoons in his cabinet briefings to understand the issues. I listened to the economic summit that Clinton organized. Clinton knew how to dot every "i" and cross every "t." He is a deep and educated guy, and the press is on him!

I heard some twit reporter last night talk about how it looks like Clinton will tax and spend. That reporter was using right-wing ideology in his analysis of Clinton's policies. Tax and spend! Nobody raised taxes higher than Reagan and Bush. Nobody! And it comes right from the middle class. Where does he spend it? On the Pentagon. When Clinton talks about tax and spend, he's talking about doing it for the people, not for the military industrial complex. In the face of the deficit the Republicans created, I can't see how they can stand up and open their mouths. I see Clinton as a person who is really trying to do something about the deficit problem.

Are there many actors in Hollywood who have political opinions like you and aren't afraid to express them?

Yes, there are a lot in Hollywood that talk like me. But there are people everywhere that talk like me. That is why the San Francisco Mime Troupe was so accepted during the sixties. People like to hear the straight goods. People know that this country is in a sorry state if NPR is the best we got. There is a lot of left-wing stuff out there. You can read *The Nation, The Village Voice,*

Mother Jones... I read them, but that doesn't mean those magazines are correct.

I got to stress that I believe people should get the widest possible variety of political ideas, programs, and policies so that they can make intelligent decisions. But they don't, and that's no accident. The media belong to the people who pay for it, and nothing is going to show up in the media that is antithetical to their interests.

I remember reading an article back in the mid-eighties in which the author said you were a star on the rise. But you have never quite made it big in Hollywood. How do you explain that? Does your outspokenness have anything to with it?

There can be two possible answers. For one, you can say it's a plot and that in the higher echelons of the studios, my name is on a blacklist. But I'll never know.

It could very well be. It happened during the McCarthy period. Your views aren't exactly mainstream.

Yes, blacklisting someone in Hollywood can be done a lot more skillfully these days. All someone has to say about me is, "You know, I heard Coyote is difficult to work with." I'm in trouble if that guy is a money man.

And what's the other possible explanation?

It could be that I've never been in a movie where my role was credited with making it work. That's what it really takes. Make somebody a lot of money, and you can work in Hollywood forever. There are guys out there — and I don't want to name names — who can't tie their shoelaces and talk at the same time, but they were in a movie that made a lot of money, so they work again and again.

Would Sylvester Stallone[10] be in that category?

You got to remember he's smart. He made *Rocky*. He acted and directed in it, and it made him a mega, mega star. I may not like his politics, but the guy did it.

Do you think Hollywood makes enough movies about the issues facing society today?

I don't think movies have to *always* be about contemporary issues, but *never*? Give me the name of a film out today that is about a contemporary social issue. That strikes me as curious. I can't read most of the scripts I get today. You pick the best of what you are offered, and so far the best I've been offered comes from Europe. I've been on the cover of every big magazine in Europe. I'm a big movie star in Europe. There, I get to play real complicated and interesting roles. I don't have to play a moron.

Given your success in Europe as compared to the U.S., why haven't you moved to Europe to live and work?

I'm an American. I like Europe and I get to go there a lot, but my children are here in the U.S., and I don't want to be an expatriate.

Being out of work for fourteen months, don't you get a little nervous that, one time, you might be out too long?
Yes, of course, I get nervous. I get on the phone and yell at my agent.

[Laughs] What does he do?
It's not his fault. He puts my name up for lots and lots of movies, but for some reason Hollywood likes the guy who is hot at the moment. What I'm doing now is writing scripts that I want to direct and sending them to Hollywood. Right now, I'm trying to raise the money for one of my movie scripts.

Will you be changing careers?
I like to think I'm adding a parallel track. The demographics of the movie industry are like fourteen to thirty-five. I'm fifty-two.

There are lot of actors in your age group who have a hard time finding work, aren't there? I think Donald Sutherland[11] is one of them.
Sutherland just got a role that I was up for. It was neck and neck. Donald's a wonderful actor. There are a lot of wonderful actors out there about whom one can ask: When was the last time I saw them in a movie? When was the last time you saw Elliot Gould[12] in a movie?

I can't remember. When we don't see actors like Gould, we assume they have retired or are taking it easy. But you're saying that's not the case. Many are actually looking for work.
Yes, but no one is hiring them! Look at Marlon Brando. Look at Meryl Streep,[13] who is one of our great, great actresses. Her movies don't make a lot of money, so she's not looked upon as a heavy hitter in Hollywood.

Do you have a lot of friends in Hollywood?
Yes, I do, and I have a good time there. My kids live here in Mill Valley, so that's why I live here. Hollywood is fun, but it's not the Sodom and Gomorrah that a lot of people think it is. The problem for me is that it's a company town, and I have a lot more interests than just the film business.

One of the interesting things I read about you was your work in the ghetto in the late 1970s. You must have learned a lot about some of the real serious social problems facing America.
Those problems are something I know about. I grew up around black people and, as I said, I have been politicized all my life. But I did get this job with CETA [Comprehensive Education and Training Act], and I taught acting in the ghetto schools. That was exciting, challenging, and very interesting; but then Jerry Brown [governor of California] appointed me to the state's art council, and I had the opportunity to shape educational policy. I thought I made a real contribution.

What were some of the things you did in terms of shaping educational policy?

We pointed out to people that the artist is a creative problem solver who can combine logic and intuition to help solve problems in a culture. When we sent artists into the schools, we weren't trying to "sensitize" the students to make them a part of the future audience for opera, the symphony, or ballet. We were trying to teach students creative problem solving, which they could apply to whatever aspect of their life they wanted to.

You can be a doctor, a lawyer, a plumber without ever having to use your intuition. You can learn to do any of those jobs by the book, but you will never learn how to be the best of anything without using your intuition. A bunch of artists created a film on teenage pregnancy for the Department of Health and Human Services that won five Emmies. It was created by young people for young people. Kids would come up with ideas for projects, and our artists would help them. Vandalism in the schools went down. Absenteeism went down. Teacher morale went up.

We were able to say to the powers that be, "Look we are not taking your tax dollars away and giving them to artists to be artists. They are performing useful services in the schools."

We weren't trying to stop opera, but we were saying you can't have two classes of people. You can't have a class of artists who receive money for nothing because the ruling elite thinks it's important. You are taking that money away from working stiffs who work hard. We wanted to show that the artists can work for society so that a father might say, "Well, I don't really care about opera, but they are teaching my kids to sing. So I am getting something from my tax dollars." He's not going to object to spending money on culture.

I was good at what I did. We raised the budget from $1 million to $14 million. No one in California had ever looked at the artistic community as a reservoir for creative problem solving in the state, such as helping to solve problems of self-esteem and discipline. We were successful at it.

It seems to me that you were applying your Digger experience to the problems of the schools. I see shades of radical theater and guerrilla theater . . .

And how to break down ideas and communicate them clearly and effectively and nonjudgmentally. Interestingly, I was supported by right-wing legislators after they realized I wasn't bullshitting. I didn't treat them like the enemy, and I didn't try to be ideological. We wouldn't lie to them. We admitted mistakes when we made them. I was the first person who went to the California state legislature who said, "You gave us $2 million to do this program last year, but it didn't work. But we learned A, B, and C from it, and if you give us that money again for the program, this time we know it will work.

They put a senator from San Diego on the arts council who had tried six times to abolish it. Within six months, he was my staunchest ally. He saw that we weren't bullshitting. We were playing fair and hard, and we were trying to make a difference. I remember one legislator — a real right-wing conservative —

who was on the finance committee. He overruled his own legislative analysts nineteen out of twenty-two times to get us through the committee. Then he voted against me, for the record, to protect his political ass. But we already had our appropriation. When I left my last finance hearing, all the senators were wearing hippie headbands. [Laughs]

What did you learn about yourself? For one thing, it must have been a tremendous confidence booster to deal with all those powerful politicians.

That was when I decided to go into movies. I learned I could talk to anyone. If I told the truth, never lied, and admitted every mistake, little by little, people would begin to trust me and I could find common ground with anyone. The experience with the arts council gave me the confidence to think, "Well, gee, I've always been curious about the movies and wanted to know what the industry was like. Let me give it a shot."

That's interesting because you were older as far as pursuing a Hollywood career. You weren't a young man in his twenties with stars in his eyes.

Remember, for ten years I had been on the far left, involved in an anarchist radical group, in which we did everything anonymously and never took money. I had kind of denied myself opportunity when I was a young man. I didn't get my Screen Actors Guild card until I was forty.

Why didn't you stay in education?

Jerry Brown offered me the opportunity to run the Department of Education, a $2,000,000,000 agency. But you know, it would have taken up the next ten years of my life. I came to the conclusion that politics was an illusionary thing. On the other hand, I thought that, as an artist, I could inspire people and give them ideas they could use. I was not suited for politics. I hated the fact that I would have had to always compromise with power.

Yeah, that must have been tough for a sixties idealist.

Yeah, I didn't want to knuckle under. I couldn't take it. There are people that do it and do it well, and I respect them, but it's not for me.

You must be a risk taker, though. Most people would have taken the safer road, especially when it offered a job with real power.

I don't consider myself a brave person. I have to push myself to do a lot of things. But I just had a hunch about Hollywood, a feeling that I would get lucky and do okay.

But you must be brave because I understand that you are camera shy. You wanted to be an actor, but the most important thing for an actor to be able to do is stand before a camera.

I don't like being the center of attention. There are people who like to cut the ribbon at the boat show, but I'm not like that. I'd much rather be behind the scenes, an advisor to a politician rather than a politician himself. But acting was something I knew how to do. Besides, I was getting older and had to make some money.

Of course, E.T. *was a movie that made you a familiar face. How did you get the role?*

Steven Spielberg[14] had seen me in the movie *Southern Comfort* and said this was the guy I want for the character Keys. I was hanging out with Steven at the time, and I told him, "I want to do the movie, but I don't want my character to be the bad guy." I didn't want my kids to grow up thinking science and adults were the enemy. Steven thought about it and agreed. He actually let me write that one scene in the hospital where I go to meet *E.T.* I did five drafts of that scene, and it was polished up and made better.

Spielberg didn't take offense at your point of view? After all, he's the famous director, and you were the up-and-coming actor.

Steven is the best. He makes his own movies. I've never worked for a kinder or more gentlemanly director, ever. He gave me complete access during the movie. I was hanging around his office, writing drafts, critiquing, and shooting my mouth off. I didn't have any idea that that was not how it was done. I thought to myself, "Boy, this is fun. It's just like hanging out with the guys." [Laughs] Everybody was great. I'm still a nobody, but then I was more of a nobody. I never have forgotten his generosity.

So he didn't mind your brashness?

I wasn't brash. I'm never brash. I was just being honestly inquisitive. But I've always been good at listening to people — taking their view into account. People like it when you hear what they have to say. I was having the time of my life. On the last night of the set, when we wrapped up shooting *E.T.*, Steven grabbed me and said, "I want to do a movie with you that has lots and lots of words. I love to hear you speak." [Laughs] [Shouts] I'm still waiting, Steven!

[Laughs] Well, you waited ten months after appearing in E.T. *before you got another role. Did that shock you?*

That blew my mind. The kids [actors in *E.T.*] were going off to meet the Queen, and Dee Wallace was getting her own TV series. I was thinking of creating a publicity campaign that would have shown my career was the only one to have floundered because of *E.T.* I couldn't believe it! I had been in three movies that made a half-billion dollars between them [*E.T.*, *Outrageous Fortune*, and *The Jagged Edge*]. I was out of work for nine months after *Outrageous Fortune* and ten months after *The Jagged Edge*. I never made another major movie since I made *Outrageous Fortune* in 1988.

People stop me on the street and say, "God, I love your acting ... blah, blah, blah." I don't know what it is. You got to ask a big studio executive what's going on.

You have been called "the thinking woman's sex symbol." Maybe the problem is that you come off as too intellectual on the screen.

Once upon a time, in the thirties and forties, enough people were going to the movies that you could make a movie like *Bringing Up Baby* or *Front Page*.[15] Now you don't have that two and a half percent of two hundred million people or something like that to make a sophisticated movie. So there are no "B" movie stars today. In another era, I could have been a Robert Ryan,[16] who worked all the time. But it doesn't bother me that I don't get the big films. It would be fun to make *Terminator*,[17] but I'm not really interested. It does bother me, however, that I don't get the little, interesting films. That's the part of the equation I don't understand.

Given the frustration you must feel at the way your career has been going, do you ever get nostalgic for the sixties?

I get nostalgic for the absolute synchronicity that existed between my political beliefs and my way of life. I was able to live in such a way that what I did for a living exactly reflected my political beliefs. Exactly! That is gone now. Today, I'm much less carefree. I have kids, and I have to attach myself to other people. That means I have to compromise. I guess the alternative is to not grow older. [Laughs]

[Laughs] Is the counterculture experience now a piece of Americana, or are parts of it still around today?

I think there is a lot left. The counterculture helped create institutions that are everywhere today. You see it in the peace movement, the natural foods movement, the ecology movement, the women's movement, the civil rights movement... All these movements came to fruition in the sixties. Acupuncturists are everywhere. Food co-ops are everywhere. Organic food is everywhere. Better restaurants are everywhere. People are agitating for better child care, mass transit, and environmental concerns. This legacy is much more enduring than political ideology. That is the way change is manifested— by the way people live, not just by the way they talk. So I'm proud to be part and parcel of that.

Do you feel lucky to have lived during the sixties and experienced so much?

Yes, I really do. I feel bad for kids today that have to worry about AIDS precisely at the time they are supposed to be experimenting sexually and finding out who they are. Today, they have to worry about crack and getting killed in a random shooting. The stakes seem to be much higher now.

Critics of the counterculture might argue that the breakdowns we see in today's society are the result of forces unleashed in the sixties.

It's easy to say, but I didn't urge anyone to sell crack and make money from drugs. Crack didn't come out of the psychedelic revolution. The psychedelic revolution was spiritual and transcendental. Crack comes out of disenfranchisement, when every option has been taken away from a people.

I never urged the president of the U.S. to take away the regulations from the savings and loans industry and bankrupt the fucking nation. So they sent a couple of guys—[Charles] Keating and [Michael] Milken—to jail as a symbol.[18] Milken serves twenty-four months and gets out with $500 million. No one I ever knew in the sixties was gimmicking the stockmarket. You can have the George Wills and the William Safires[19] and the other journalists who are the bagmen for the powers that be. They are bright men, but they are also like vacuum cleaner salesmen who say to you, "Buy my product, or you will die of dirt." I listen to free men and women who aren't beholden to anyone for their livelihood.

One final question—what about your future?

I want to keep working and to maintain my life so that it has some kind of integrity and thought to it. That's a tough job. My dad used to say to me, "Everybody has got to compromise, but a real man doesn't compromise more than he has to." So I will try to keep the compromises down.

18

Abbie Hoffman

An American Rebel

> Hello, I think this is Abbie Hoffman. Today, I was denied the right to vote in Bucks County. I don't know if I'm homeless or beyond homelessness. Wow! What a position for the old Jewish road warrior to be in, eh! But we've just begun to fight. You ain't seen nothing yet! Leave a message at the sound of the beep. We will get right back to you.
> — Recorded message on Abbie Hoffman's home phone.

Until his death in 1989, Abbie Hoffman was the embodiment of the American radical and a symbol of the activist sixties. In the sixties, Hoffman fought for civil rights, led protesters in opposition to the Vietnam War, and organized Americans into a political force to give them a more meaningful voice in the country's affairs. During the height of the protest movement in the late sixties, Hoffman made headlines with such zany tactics as throwing dollar bills on the floor of the New York Stock Exchange, trying to levitate the Pentagon, and referring to Julius Hoffman, the presiding judge during the trial of the Chicago Seven (Abbie was one of the defendants), as his illegitimate father.

Two decades later, Hoffman was still at it, tackling a host of environmental issues around the country, mobilizing opposition to American foreign policy in Central America, and helping young, inexperienced student activists organize the first national students' convention, held at Rutgers University in February (1988).

Meanwhile, Hoffman continued to be a thorn in the side of the establishment. He, along with 14 other activists, including former president Jimmy Carter's daughter Amy, were acquitted on April 15, 1987, by a Northhampton, Massachusetts, jury on a charge of trespassing on the University of Massachusetts campus in Amherst. Hoffman and his fellow defendants used the "necessity defense," proving successfully to the jury that their trespassing was justified, given decades of illegal recruiting by the CIA on America's campuses.

Hoffman, the author of the classic *Steal This Book* (Amereon Books, 1976),

272

had recently published *Steal This Urine Test* (reprint, Buccaneer Books, 1994),[1] which focused on two major issues facing America today — civil liberties and drug testing — and which the *Washington Post* called the most controversial to be published in the fall of 1988.

But for a period of nearly eight years, the high-profile Hoffman vanished. Still, after going underground in 1974 to avoid arrest on a cocaine trafficking charge, he managed to remain the activist. For example, he organized a successful campaign against the U.S. Army Corps of Engineers–proposed year-round barge canal for the Thousand Islands region. The governor of New York and New York Senator Daniel Moynihan lavishly praised the fugitive. Hoffman was even appointed to a federal water resources commission, which must be some kind of first. He resurfaced again in 1980, turned himself in, and spent nine months in jail.

Through it all, Hoffman remained the social activist wedded to causes and to the plight of the underdog, wherever they were. His last three arrests were in Bucks County, Pennsylvania, trying to save the Delaware River and fighting what the *New York Times* described as the longest running environmental battle in America: the Philadelphia Electric Company's attempt to build a nuclear plant.

When I interviewed Hoffman in November 1988, the activist was in the thick of a battle with local authorities to have his absentee ballot in a recent local election validated. The interview took place at Hoffman's home, a converted turkey shed located outside of New Hope, Pennsylvania.

It was midday when I showed up for the interview. I found Hoffman in the kitchen, cooking supper for his "running mate," the nickname he uses for his girlfriend, Johanna Lawrenson, his girlfriend and companion since his underground days. Hoffman was supposed to have had plastic surgery while underground, but he looked like Abbie Hoffman to me, except for a battered nose that gave him the appearance of a man that has been through some tough times. He said he had lost 20 pounds from recent fasting.

The shock of wiry hair was still there, a little grayer and sparser. Hoffman was as funny as ever. Even during the heavier parts of our conversation, he would see the humor. I guess to experience what he had gone through, one would need a good grasp of the absurd.

But little did I know that Hoffman had been diagnosed as a manic depressive in 1980. About five months after our interview, Hoffman was dead, an apparent suicide. While there was immediate speculation that Hoffman had been the victim of foul play, the coroner's report said that he swallowed 150 barbiturates with alcohol.

The death of the American legend stunned many. But during the course of our manic interview, I began to understand what one writer has called Hoffman's "wreckless brilliance."

*   *   *

I've got to get your name down on tape. I have to do that now because of that inter-view with Jerry Falwell[2] that a freelancer sold to Penthouse *a few years ago. He didn't have Falwell's permission.*

I fucked with Jerry Falwell. He's not such a macho guy. He's a warm, car-ing, loving guy. I know you're not going to believe it, but Jimmy Swaggart[3] has got the movie.

[Laughs] You're joking, of course.

No way. Mel Gibson[4] has signed to play me and Ned Beatty's[5] going to play Jerry Falwell. That's for sure. I know you don't want to talk about it, but the movie is there. Actually, I was going for Anal Roberts.[6] It's *anal,* isn't it [Laughs]—the guy that climbed the tower and said, "Send me $20 million or God will take my life"? [Laughs] How much do you think I'd get if I did an act like that. [Shouts] Send me $20,000,000 or God is going to take my life! [Laughs]

[Phone rings, Hoffman answers] Hello, what? I'm not going to watch foot-ball on the tube. I'm being interviewed. Make it quick, Jack! I couldn't get in on Syracuse. Did they win? I've got Notre Dame. [Hangs up]

You like to watch football?

No. Not really. But I like to play the point spreads. [Laughs]

But you do like battling the local authorities here in Bucks County over your right to vote?

It's incredible, man! Are they really going to deny me the right to vote, especially on the two hundred-year anniversary of the Constitution[7] that they are celebrating up in fucking Philadelphia? [Laughs] Even the winos have the right to vote in Bucks County.

Do you feel like you're going back in time to your activist days in the sixties?

It's like Mississippi was in the sixties. Here, in '82 and '83, the enemy was blowing up cars with dynamite. It's a heavy battle here.

You actually mean with dynamite?

Fucking-A! Right down the road there. The utility company [Philadelphia Electric Company] had a bunch of thugs working for them. I've never fought such a tough foe. Elected officials would have given up a long time ago. We had a referendum drive. In '82, '83, and '84, we kicked every fucking official out that opposed us.

Why are you taking on a utility company?

Utility companies are some of the most powerful corporations in Amer-ica. They don't play kosher. They would soon as fucking blow us away, just like what happened to [Karen] Silkwood.[8] It's not unusual in this country. I think it's Mark Twain[9] who said, "Whiskey is for drinking; water is for fighting over." [Laughs] There have always been water wars. It's like bullshit walks, money talks. It fucking swims with the utility companies. I've never seen a tougher foe.

Why are you involved with this particular issue?

I get about five or six requests a week from around the country to help people organize around an issue like a toxic dump or a polluted river. I'm involved with about eight cases right now. This project has a lot of intrigue. I came down here and started organizing. We stopped the bulldozers and had hundreds of people lying on the road you came down. I chained myself to the fence. The hard hats came by and start whacking me. [Laughs]

They don't like what I'm doing. It means jobs to them. We occupied the courthouse for three months. All kinds of street theater. You couldn't imagine! Meanwhile, the real estate values have skyrocketed so that the original people can't live here any more. But I'm still here. I pay $400 a month rent. [Points out the window] There's a $500,000 spread over there, and that one is about $700,000. They are wondering what I'm doing here. They think I'm some kind of eccentric millionaire. [Laughs]

The utility company said, "We'll build the pump anyway. Nobody stops the Philadelphia Electric Company." The judge who is ruling on this case, plays golf once a week at the fucking country club with the chairman of the board of the utility company, which owns the country club. Garb's his name. He's even got stock in the company!

How can the judge get away with that?

It's like any place. The powers that be make good speeches about how they like the birds, the fish, the environment; but when it comes right down to it, they fold their tents. They won't go against the judge. It's the same with the governor, the senators, the legislators. It's not a question of Democrat or Republican. They are all a part of the "good old boy" network, protecting the judge.

Do you have a particular strategy that you're using to fight the authorities?

They are not going to negotiate with us right out of the blue because they have all the power. You have to create what I call an eight hundred pound gorilla, or they won't negotiate. Get three hundred or four hundred people arrested, and demand individual jury trials. In a rural area, you can tie up a court system for three or four years, so you try to get the power structure to negotiate.

We are also using the necessity defense strategy. That's what we used at the CIA demonstration at the University of Massachusetts when we were arrested back in the spring [1987]. We commit a lesser crime, like trespassing. We go to the jury and admit we trespassed, but we say we were trespassing because of a bigger crime that has taken place. Every state allows the necessity defense. It's getting very fashionable to use in the movement, whether it's an environmental or antinuclear issue.

Let's talk about your new book, Steal This Urine Test. *I read it, and think it's one of the best books I have read on the subject.*

It's my best book, so go tell the *New York Times* why, after six weeks since the book came out, they haven't reviewed it yet?

I think it might be because you pointed out in your book that the liberal New York Times *drug-tests its employees. How the hell can they reconcile that?*

The *New York Times* published a list about a year ago of institutions that drug-tested their employees, and they didn't put themselves on it. There is no love lost between me and the *New York Times*. They fired Sidney Schanberg, my cousin, who wrote *The Killing Fields*.[10] After he came back from Cambodia and wrote the book, he took on New York's real estate interests like Donald Trump,[11] and the *Times* fired him.

They review every significant book nearly on the day it's published, but the *Times* has held up my review, although I'm not saying they might not eventually review it. If you don't get reviewed by the *New York Times*, even if they chop the hell out of it, the book becomes a nonevent for *Time, Newsweek*, the networks, and about two hundred newspapers around the country. That's how powerful the newspaper is.

What's scary is that what you call "the drug hysteria" is not just a product of the Right, but also of the Left. Doesn't that complicate things for activists like you who want to turn the tide against drug testing?

When I decided to write the book, my friends said, "Don't touch the subject. Let sleeping dogs lie." They said no one is really interested in a serious book about drug testing. [Laughs] I pointed out to them that thirty-five million people are being tested each year by means of a faulty test that is not accurate. Drug testing isn't a big deal? People are getting fired left and right because of it!

Yes, it makes for an uphill battle, but I knew the book had to be written. I came to this conclusion in the fall of '86 at the height of the hysteria. We had politicians challenging each other to urine tests, twelve-year-old kids turning in their parents, district attorneys pushing for strip searches in high school. Everybody has gotten on the bandwagon. It upsets me that even Jesse Jackson[12] has called for testing. It's what I call the National Party Line. The drug issue is like God versus Communism. There is no healthy debate going on in the country or Congress or the media. I'm convinced that within a year, the U.S. Supreme Court will ratify drug testing. The only opposing Supreme Court justice will be [William] Brennan.

But doesn't this country have a serious drug problem?

I'm asked that hundreds of times. [Laughs] What do you mean, Abbie!? There isn't a drug problem! Every country has a drug problem, but this is the only country that is dumb enough to think that what shows up in the urinals is going to have an effect on your job performance. That's one of the hoaxes.

What the public doesn't realize is that not only is drug testing unconstitutional, it's also dangerous. Information gathered during a drug test can be used for purposes other than for what it was collected. Say you are an epileptic and don't want your employers to know. They can find this out in a drug test and fire you! The drug test is more inaccurate than the lie detector test, which is now illegal in most states. The drug-testing companies even admit that their drug tests have an error margin of five percent.

Do you think that the drug hysteria has been manufactured by the Reagan administration as a bogus issue to take attention away from its inability to deal with the social and economic problems facing this country?

It's a conspiracy in fact. The Reagan clique organizes a "Just Say No" campaign and whips up the hysteria. They quickly leave government and go to work for corporations and consulting firms that make money starting drug-testing programs. They tell the corporations that the drug tests are accurate, which is bullshit. They say junkies are all over the place, which is nonsense. They say the government is not going to give them any contracts unless they get on the bandwagon.

It may be true, but no one seems to really care.

No one really cares because there is no worker solidarity in this country. It's the era of the shrinking middle class, the vanishing farmer, the demoralized work force. So people will gladly cut off their baby finger to keep a job. "Come, let's pull down our zippers for the gipper." Workers are lining up in droves to be tested!

Do you see any sign that resistance is forming, or will drug testing become as routine as punching a time clock?

The resistance to drug testing will come once people read my book and see how easy it is to get a lawyer and sue the company that tests you. In the past few months, there have been three cases of workers being fired because of urine testing. Let's take the case of Barbara Luck. She was three months pregnant and didn't want to take the test because she didn't want the company to know. Her company, the Southern Pacific Railway, which is in California, assumed she was using drugs, which is the way it is in one hundred percent of the cases, if you refuse. She was fired, but she went to court. Last week she won $485,000 in damages.

Chris Kelly, a Louisiana oil rigger, flunked the test. He proved in court that it was a false positive and won $125,000 in damages in court. Allan Pettigrew, who also worked for the Southern Pacific Railway, settled out of court for $125,000. There are now loads of workers winning $5,000 and $10,000 in compensation. Workers are going to learn that they don't even need the ACLU [American Civil Liberties Union], just a good lawyer, who gets a third of what you win in the lawsuit.

But not everybody is going to read your book. How is the word going to get out?

Yes, it's going to be difficult because the national media parrots the National Party Line.

So you're saying the press has been a good ally of the Reagan administration and the drug-testing industry on this issue?

Certainly. The press has compared the drug threat to the black plague of the Middle Ages, which killed two-thirds of Europe's population. Hell, last year, mortality statistics showed that no more than three thousand five hundred people died from illegal drugs in this country. Meanwhile, about five hundred thousand died from nicotine addiction and another one hundred and fifty thousand from alcoholism. Illegal drugs are the plague of the Middle Ages. [Laughs] But it's not just the press, it's the PTA [Parent-Teacher Association], the NCAA [National Collegiate Athletic Association]. . . If you believe in responsible drug education, you are fighting against a fundamentalist order that relies on blind faith. You are not going to win using science and common sense.

If this country, particularly its government, really cared about stopping drug abuse, it would stop the CIA from flying drugs into the country via Miami. Remember, the agency also flew heroin into Vietnam. In October of last year, at the height of the drug hysteria, Reagan signed into law the fifty-fifth antidrug bill in the last eighty years of enforcement history, which goes to show you how effective the other fifty-four were. [Laughs]

It's like about every two or three years, we have another bill. The latest bill allocated $3.96 billion for what Reagan called drug treatment and education. Three months later, he took away a billion dollars from the bill and recommended zero appropriations for drug treatment in fiscal 1988.

Telling a chronic drug addict to "Just Say No" is like telling a chronically depressed person to "Just cheer up." So Reagan's drug campaign is baloney. You have this Partnership for a Drug Free America. All it is is a front for the drug-testing industry.

Well then, what do you think should be done to combat drug addiction?

We should look to European programs of dispensing morphine to junkies because heroin addiction is a disease. We have to examine what went on in the nineteenth century when the drugs that are now illegal were legal and relationship of use and abuse was no greater than it is now with all the antidrug laws. We have to start talking about Alaska's experience in legalizing the possession of under four ounces [of marijuana] in your home. We have to look at why the press is putting down all these things or ignoring them.

How would you capsule the legacy of the Reagan administration?

It's a complete disaster. Look at civil liberties. We fought for decades to achieve our civil liberties, just to have them taken away by this administration. In the sixties and seventies, if you felt you were wrongly treated because of your sex, age, color of your skin, or whatever, you turned to the federal court system for a redress of your grievances. That's difficult to do now because Reagan appointees are taking over the court system. Reagan judges like Robert Bork or Douglas Ginsberg[13] hold one out of two positions on the federal court system now.

And, as for the U.S. Supreme Court, Reagan will get his judge, who among other things, will take away the woman's right to have control over her body. Meese has gone on record as saying his aim is to do away with the Miranda ruling.[14] Every month, some right gets taken away. As an activist in the sixties, I started off with capital punishment, the execution of Caryl Chessman in 1960.[15] By '72, capital punishment was viewed as cruel and unusual punishment. Now it's back again. So if the citizenry wants to protect its civil rights, it must be totally mobilized and aware.

Do you think those in the movement will reach a frustration level that will lead it to confrontational and even violent action like the country experienced in the sixties and early seventies?

I can see this frustration building now. The Alaska pipeline, for example, is sabotaged all the time. The workers are unorganized, but they are still committing sabotage. Right now, in our dispute with Philadelphia Electric Company, we have people who are saying that if the company wants to play dirty, they will play dirty. A big part of the reason that other countries are outproducing us is that our workers are angry, smoldering. Our society is deteriorating because there is no channel for this outrage. Workers are not taught how to organize and to use the system to change it.

Let's talk about your return from the underground. By your own admission, you are an egomaniac. When you went underground, was it hard being out of the spotlight?

I was very active underground.

Yes, the barge on the Thousand Islands . . .

That was just one of twelve battles I fought.

Tell me about some of your other battles.

I was in Guatemala in '76 helping earthquake victims. I almost got killed because I saw the generals stealing food that had been sent to Guatemala by the do-gooders in America from the victims. I was another person in Florida. Do you remember *Mary Hartman, Mary Hartman?*

Yesh, she was in Soap, *a real funny show.*

Louise Lassiter played Mary Hartman. She was in the class ahead of me in high school, so I've followed her career closely. *Soap* was a great show in a sea of sludge. [Laughs] When I was up north, I saw an episode from the show that was about lesbianism. I saw the same episode in Miami, and it had been censored. It was Public Broadcasting that censored it, too! So I organized a "Free Mary Hartman Committee." [Laughs] We got the station to admit that the program had been censored.

What other things were you involved with underground?

I don't want to get into all of them. It's still painful and personal. A book about my underground experiences is the last thing I'm going to write.

Somewhere, within three miles of this house, are three passports, six birth certificates, and $1,000 in cash. I'm still an activist. I haven't been "Big Chilled"[16] yet. [Laughs] Being an activist is still a dangerous occupation. I might be underground again by the time the interview comes out. [Laughs]

What did you learn about America while you were on the run?

I learned that, unless you are rich and famous, people don't listen very much to what you have to say. I would talk about Abbie Hoffman and the Chicago Seven trial with people, and they didn't care what my opinion was. [Laughs]

[Laughs] During your long career as an activist, did you ever feel your life was in danger?

Well, I've had my nose broken. The FBI had sixty-six thousand pages on me. I found this out through freedom-of-information requests. G. Gordon Liddy[17] made an offer to the Nixon administration to kidnap me. I've had my collarbone broken. My back has been dislocated twice by police. I've been shot at three times. At one time or another, I've been banned from entering eleven states. My father's customers were driven from his business, even though he was a Republican.

You got busted on a cocaine charge in '74. Were you really selling cocaine?

I got set up. I was there, but the New York City Red Squad had a lot to do with it.

But were you selling cocaine, or were you set up?

Well, it is possible that both occurred. I think that today in a court of law I would have gotten off like John DeLorean[18] did. But at the time in '73, there were circumstances that made it impossible to go to trial. For instance, you had [New York] Governor [Nelson] Rockefeller calling for the death penalty for a drug conviction.

Some of your critics said that your return from the underground just happened to coincide with the release of your autobiography, Soon to Be a Motion Picture.[19]

If that's the case, I'm a publisher's dream. [Laughs] I would risk life imprisonment for the publication of a book! The publisher held a news conference in their offices when it should have held it in the courthouse or in the streets. You got to remember that you are not talking to a Bill Cosby, or a Vanna White, or a Stephen King, who are making millions off their books.[20] I'm not making any money from my books.

You have been to Nicaragua five times recently and have brought groups over to that country. You're a Sandinista lover.[21] You make no bones about it.

[Points to the wall] Well, there's my picture of Danny Boy [Daniel Ortega].[22]

What about the human rights record of the Sandinistas? It hasn't been that good.
It's the most humane revolution in history, including this one.

You mean the American Revolution?
In the American Revolution, about fifteen percent of the people sided with the British. They were called Tories. They were thrown in jail, their newspapers closed. Many fled to Canada. Revolutions aren't exactly picnics. They are huge social upheavals. The Sandinistas haven't put their opponents against the wall and shot them. The first thing they did was to outlaw capital punishment. In Nicaragua, the most you can get for a crime is thirty years.

Yeah, but until recently, when the newspaper La Prensa *was allowed to publish again, the Sandinistas have silenced the press.*
The presses? Name one newspaper in Guatemala or El Salvador, and I'll give you a hundred dollars. They are supposed to be model democracies? Go ahead!

Good point.
The point is that you have focused on one little newspaper with a circulation of sixty thousand that gets money from the CIA. If you compare our country to what's happened to Nicaragua in the last six years, it would mean for the U.S. the equivalent of twenty-five million refugees, all its oil refineries blown up, enemy ships in its territorial waters, planes flying overhead. It would mean guerrillas in Canada and Mexico making daily incursions into our country. It would mean six or seven million dead.

Do you think we would allow a newspaper to open and support our enemy? Come on! It would be like a newspaper supporting Adolph Hitler. We wouldn't allow it to happen. During the Vietnam War, my friends and I were denied the right to speak. We were hounded by the FBI.

From reports, it looks like Nicaragua is preparing for an imminent U.S. invasion of their country. Do you think it will come?
Seventeen times the marines have invaded Nicaragua. Virtually throughout the 1920s, the marines occupied their country. I was in Nicaragua two years ago, staying in Ortega's house. He said to me that the Sandinistas had positive evidence that the marines are coming July 4 under the cover of our Independence Day celebration. It was July 1. Ortega said that the Sandinistas were mobilizing the whole country.

I was riding in a government truck with my best friend, and I said to him, "I tell you what I'm going to do when the marines come. I'm going to go to the first fucker that lands and start cussing him out in the most American language he has ever heard. [Laughs] Then I'm going to tell him to get his ass back to Omaha. You're going to get your ass shot off." [Laughs] The point is that we may think it's paranoia, but it's not. As one young Sandinista told me, "Americans have forgotten the history of our two countries, but we have to learn it. Our survival depends on it."

But what about the argument that the Sandinistas are exporting revolution to other Central American countries and are destabilizing the region?

America should start exporting free enterprise to other countries and stop supporting dictatorships. [Laughs] What threatens the Reagan administration is the independent model that Nicaragua represents to other Latin American countries. The Sandinistas lowered the country's illiteracy rate and got rid of major diseases. They've built hospitals in rural areas that didn't have them and were headed for economic independence, in that exports were equaling imports. The Nicaraguan model threatens the objectives of the Reagan administration in Latin America. There is no evidence they are shipping arms to guerrillas in El Salvador.

I noticed you referred to yourself as "the old Jewish road warrior" on your answering machine. Do you have a close affinity to your Jewish heritage?

Sure. My autobiography is very Jewish. But I identify more with Jewish dissidents in Russia than I do with B'nai B'rith or the American Jewish Congress here in the U.S. They are Reaganites; I'm a dissident. [Laughs] The Jews I identify with are the ones that say "Workers of the World Unite" [Karl Marx] or "Every guy wants to screw his mother" [Sigmund Freud] or "E = mc^2" [Albert Einstein]."[23] They are the Jews that wanted to change things. They didn't want to be assimilated. Unfortunately, most Jews are for assimilation.

Do you support the right of Palestinians to a homeland?

Yes, of course. I want social justice for everyone. It's the only safe path for a Jew to follow — to defend the underdog. Unfortunately, Jews are not doing it in Israel. The Israelies should be championing the cause of the Palestinians.

You are making your living giving speeches on campus. What kind of reception have you received?

When I speak on campus, fifty percent of the students expect me to be a woman. I call what's happening on campus the "dumbing of America." [Laughs] My favorite dumbism occurred a little while ago when I was talking at a very prominent eastern college about Martin Luther King and my experiences in the civil rights movement. One student got up and said, "What do you think we are — idiots? We know who Martin Luther King is and what civil rights was about. We study that all the time. Why don't you tell us about that other person. What was Malcolm Ten like?" [Long laughter]

[Laughs] What kind of reception do you get on campus?

Everyone I go, they cheer me.

Yes, but is that because you are a celebrity or because you have something to say?

I don't consider myself a celebrity. To be a celebrity means one is an airhead.

But if many students think you are a woman, how interested are they in what you have to say?

I have to be entertaining. Television demands it. Students expect it. I have to speak the language of popular culture. But if I go to Europe, I can speak the language of literature and use certain philosophical arguments and speak on a subject at length without having to throw in one-liners or the quick pun or always having to change subjects quickly.

Do you find that students have much interest in the sixties?

In the eighties, there is an awareness of a legacy from the sixties: that young people fought authority. I think a lot of students feel a little guilty about not doing anything about the system. CNN [Cable News Network] did a poll that asked sixteen- to twenty-year-olds what period in history would they like to live in. Overwhelmingly, they picked America in the sixties. It's not just the sex, drugs, and rock and roll. It's a feeling of being attached to history.

That students are starting to move again is the best kept secret in America. About ten thousand students have been arrested in three years protesting apartheid. Seventy-five schools have closed down CIA recruiting already. Next week, I'll be down at the University of Rhode Island with Amy Carter, moving again.

So do you think Amy Carter is the prototype of the new student activist?

No, but I like her as a person. She has good political instincts and savvy in terms of intergroup relations with her peers and the media. Not since the time of the Chicago Seven trial have I seen anyone as good with the press, even though she's only a nineteen-year-old. I wouldn't be surprised if she is the first woman president. You will see less of us together over the next few years because the press have made us an item. [Laughs] Of course, it's not true.

It seems like she gets a lot of support from her father.

I met both Jimmy and Rosalyn before I met Amy, and I like them both. After meeting Jimmy Carter,[24] I felt anyone could be president. [Laughs] It's mainly because of that Southern charm. He's supporting Amy, but he keeps saying she's shy and doesn't want the spotlight. But I hope her friends keep encouraging her to be more outspoken.

One last question: Do you ever get nostalgic for the sixties?

I think I get more nostalgic for the fifties because I was a teenager then. That's when I discovered sex. [Laughs] I don't get nostalgic like those characters in *The Big Chill.* I get nostalgic when I go to the campuses and realize how hard it is to grow up today. I'm sad for this generation. I think I know what I'm talking about because I spend so much time on campus.

This is a very nihilistic generation. They believe AIDS will get them or the polar ice cap will melt. They have about a dozen fantasies of how the world is going to end, the most common being a nuclear holocaust. I remember how much fun it was to be young.

But my God! The young people today are old. They talk like middle-class people: about their jobs, cars, and careers they don't have yet, and "how complex the world is." [Laughs] But we were young, foolish, reckless, wild, daring . . . and right. [Laughs]

Notes

Introduction

1. Goode, Stephen. *Affluent Revolutionaries: A Portrait of the New Left* (New York: New Viewpoints, 1974), p. 29.

2. SLATE, the popular title for an organization known as More Active Student Community, was organized at the University of California at Berkeley in 1957 by a group of student radicals who were inspired by the resistance of faculty members to enforced loyalty oaths. In 1959, SLATE won control of the Berkeley student government on a radical platform that called for abolition of loyalty oaths, capital punishment, and nuclear testing. It was the first time during the McCarthy era that a student government took such radical positions.

3. From an interview with Jane Adams, which is a part of this book.

4. Wood, James L. *New Left Ideology and Its Dimensions and Development* (Beverly Hills, CA: Sage Publications, 1975).

5. From an interview with Annie Popkin, feminist.

6. From an interview with Cleveland Sellers, which is a part of this book.

7. From an interview with Bill Ayers, which is a part of this book.

8. Morgan, Edward P. *The Sixties Experience: Hard Lessons About Modern America* (Philadelphia: Temple University Press, 1991).

Chapter 1. Paul Krassner

1. Steve Allen (1921–), American television writer and personality, was also master of ceremonies of the *Tonight Show*.

2. Harry Reasoner, a journalist, worked for CBS and became famous as reporter for CBS's *Sixty Minutes* television show.

3. Lenny Bruce, nightclub comedian and political satirist, was constantly in trouble with the authorities over his use of obscenities in his skits. John Lennon was a song writer and leading member of the enormously popular sixties rock group The Beatles.

4. Copeta, A. Craig. "The Itch Is Back," *Regardie's* (Oct. 1986), p. 146.

5. Ken Kesey is the author of the classic novel *One Flew Over the Cuckoo's Nest*, and one who in the sixties became a cultural legend as the leader of the counterculture group The Merry Pranksters.

6. Tammy Bakker, the wife of disgraced televangelist Jim Bakker (who served a prison term for fraud), is known for wearing a lot of makeup.

7. Spike Lee's movie *Malcolm X* (1992) starred Denzell Washington. This book includes an interview with Abbie Hoffman.

8. This book includes an interview with Dave Dellinger.

9. Krassner, Paul. *Confessions of a Raving, Unconfined Nut* (New York: Simon and Schuster, 1993).

10. Meryl Streep (1951–) is an American actress who won the 1979 Academy Award as best supporting actress in *Kramer Versus Kramer* (1979) and the 1982 Academy Award for best actress for her role in *Sophie's Choice* (1982).

11. Jackson Browne is a singer and song writer who has been active in antinuclear, environmental, and social causes.

12. In 1969, Charles Manson, and his cultist group, ritually murdered actress Sharon Tate, wife of film director Roman Polanski, and four others.

13. Their book is *Destructive Generation: Second Thoughts About the Sixties* (New York: Summit Books, 1990).

14. Bel Air is an affluent suburb of Los Angeles.

15. Comedian Mort Sahl (1927–) is credited with shaping political satire in the fifties.

Chapter 2. Cleveland Sellers

1. Lowery, Charles D., and John F. Marszalek. *Encyclopedia of African-American Civil Rights: From Emancipation to the Present* (Wesport, CT: Greenwood Press, 1992).

2. The Watts race riot took place in Watts, a small neighborhood in south-central Los Angeles, California, in August 1965. Thirty-nine people were killed, most of whom were black, and property damages was estimated at from $35 to $40 million. The Detroit (Michigan) race riot, which took place on July 23, 1967, was the worst of the many race riots to erupt in 1967. The National Guard shot 43 people, most of whom were black.

3. Jean Paul Sartre (1905–1980) was a French philosopher and leading exponent of the philosophy known as existentialism, which denied the existence of God and said man was alone in an empty universe. Bertrand Russell (1872–1970) was an influential British mathematician, philosopher, and social reformer who, in 1967, organized a War Crimes Tribunal to investigate charges that the United States was guilty of war crimes in Indochina.

4. Saul Alinsky has been described as one of the most colorful and controversial figures in American radicalism. His 1946 book *Reveille for Radicals* became a best-seller with its clarion call for a new kind of American democracy based on community-sponsored "people's organizations."

5. Director Spike Lee's movie *Malcolm X* appeared in 1992 and starred Denzell Washington.

6. In 1965, Dr. Martin Luther King, Jr., and the Southern Christian Leadership Conference (SCCC) organized the Selma-to-Montgomery march to dramatize the need for federal voter-registration laws. There were 770 people arrested.

7. Rosa Parks' arrest for refusing to relinquish her seat to a white man and move to the back of a Montgomery, Alabama, city bus sparked the Montgomery bus boycott, which lasted from December 1955 to December 1956. The boycott led to the integration of the city's bus system and encouraged the growing civil rights movement.

Chapter 3. Jane Adams

1. The Beat poets included Allen Ginsberg, Gary Snyder, and Lawrence Ferlinghetti.

2. In 1963 a Nuclear Test Ban Treaty prohibiting the explosion of nuclear devices in the atmosphere and underground was signed by the United States, Soviet Union, Great Britain, and more than 100 countries that were members of the United Nations.

3. Rosenwald schools were named for Julian Rosenwald (1862–1932), American merchant and philanthropist.

4. Sale, Kirkpatrick. *SDS* (New York: Random House, 1973).

5. George McGovern was the 1972 Democratic Party presidential nominee who lost in a landslide to Richard Nixon.

6. Libertarians oppose interference with the rights of the person and property and see the state as the main source of such interference.

7. John Wayne (1906–1979) was the extremely popular film actor who often played tough heroes. His films include *Stage Coach* (1939), *The Quiet Man* (1952), and *True Grit* (1969).

8. Ronald Davis (R.D.) Laing (1927–1989) was a Scottish psychologist who was critical of the psychiatry profession's use of medical models and helped inspire a skeptical anti-psychiatry movement.

Chapter 4. Dave Dellinger

1. The year 1992 was the 500th anniversary of Columbus's arrival in the New World.

2. The line begins Charles Dickens's novel, A Tale of Two Cities (1859). Dickens (1812–1870) was an English writer whose many other novels included David Copperfield (1850), Great Expectations (1861), and Oliver Twist (1838).

3. The Reverend Jesse Jackson (1941–   ) is an American civil rights leader, political activist, and Baptist minister.

4. Mohandas K. Gandhi (1869–1948) was an Indian political and spiritual leader who practiced nonviolence to lead India to independence from British rule.

5. Albert Camus (1913–1948) was a French writer and author of such books as The Stranger (New York: Knopf, 1946) and The Rebel (New York: Random House, 1956).

6. Thomas Hood (1799–1845) was an English poet noted for works such as "Song of the Shirt" and "Bridge of Sighs," which expressed his compassion for the poor and unfortunate.

7. Nicola Sacco and Bartolomeo Vanzetti were anarchists who were arrested in 1920 for the murder of a paymaster and his guard in South Braintree, Massachusetts. Supporters said the two were treated unfairly for their political beliefs, but they were executed on August 22, 1927. Their guilt or innocence has been debated ever since.

8. Joseph Campbell (1904–1987) was the world's foremost authority on mythology. Campbell began his career at Sarah Lawrence College where he taught for almost 40 years. He is the author of two classics: The Hero with a Thousand Faces and Masks of God.

9. Russian novelist Feodor Dostoyevsky (1821–1881) is a towering figure of world literature. He was exiled to prison in Siberia and later wrote The House of Dead (1862) about his experiences there.

10. Trotskyites are followers of Leon Trotsky (1879–1940), one of the leaders of the Russian Revolution, who in 1940 was murdered in Mexico, where he was living in exile.

11. Bayard Rustin (1912–1987) was considered a preeminent nonviolent strategist who helped shape and connect the civil rights and peace movements in the early sixties. After 1964, Rustin broke with his peace movement allies over U.S. foreign policy.

12. Founded in 1957, SANE (Committee for Sane Nuclear Policy) sought a comprehensive U.S.-Soviet nuclear test ban treaty. SANE has since merged with other organizations to form SANE/Freeze: Campaign for Global Security.

13. Bernard Fall was a U.S. journalist killed during the Vietnam War.

14. Gerald Ford, U.S. Congressman from Michigan, went on to become vice president in Richard Nixon's presidential administration and then president when Richard Nixon resigned on August 9, 1974.

15. Jane Fonda (1937–   ) is an American Academy Award winning actress who has starred in such box office successes as Klute (1971) and Coming Home (1977). The U.S. State Department censored her in 1972 for broadcasting on Hanoi radio an appeal to U.S. pilots to stop their bombing raids of North Vietnam.

16. Howard Zinn is best known as the author of A People's History of the U.S. (New York: Harper Collins, 1980).

17. The other Chicago Seven defendant was Rennie Davis.

Chapter 5. Bill Ayers

1. Like Neill's school, the Children's Community School allowed students to study subjects of their own choosing and at their own pace and involved parents in the operation of the school.

2. See Kirkpatrick, Sale. *SDS* (New York: Random House, 1970), p. 71.

3. Richard Daley, Jr., is the namesake and son of Richard Daley, who was mayor of Chicago during the memorable clash between police and demonstrators at the Democratic National Convention in August 1968.

4. The late Allan Bloom is the author of bestselling *The Closing of the American Mind* (New York: Simon and Schuster, 1988), a critique of liberal education.

5. See Heibroner, Robert. "Reflections: Economic Predictions," *The New Yorker*, (July 8, 1991), pp. 70–77.

6. A reference to the riots that occurred when a jury found the four police officers involved in the beating of Rodney King innocent.

7. The Shah of Iran was overthrown in 1979.

8. Jerry Brown, a former governor of California, was a candidate for the Democratic nomination for president.

9. William H. Rehnquist is chief justice of the United States.

10. Theo Bell and William Bennett are former U.S. secretaries of education.

11. President Bill Clinton appointed Richard Riley, former governor of South Carolina, as U.S. secretary of education in 1993.

12. Media mogul Chris Whittle has advocated the privatization of the country's public schools.

13. David Stockman was budget director during President Ronald Reagan's first term of office (1981–1985). In 1986 he wrote a book about his year in the Reagan administration titled *The Triumph of Politics: Why the Reagan Revolution Failed* (New York: Harper and Row, 1986).

14. Vladimir Ilyich Lenin (1870–1924) was a Russian revolutionary, Communist, a founder of Bolshevism, and a major force behind the founding of the USSR. Karl Marx (1818–1883) was a German social philosopher and revolutionary, who, with Friedrich Engels, helped found modern Communism and Socialism.

15. Henry David Thoreau (1817–1862) was an American writer and author of *Walden*. Mother Jones (1830–1930), whose real name was Mary Harris Jones, was prominent in union affairs for more than 50 years. Jane Addams (1860–1935) was an American social reformer who, along with Ellen Gates Starr, founded the Social Welfare Center in the slums of Chicago in 1889.

16. Bobby Sands was a member of the Provisional Irish Republican Army who, in 1981, went on a hunger strike and died in prison in Northern Ireland.

17. In its six years as a functioning clandestine organization, the Weather Underground claimed responsibility for about two dozen bombings. Only two of them—the bomb in the bathroom of the Capitol (1971) and the one in the bathroom of the Pentagon (1972)—did more than negligible damage.

18. *Born on the Fourth of July* (New York: McGraw-Hill, 1976) is the autobiography of Ron Kovic, Vietnam veteran and peace activist, whose wounds in the Vietnam War made him a paraplegic.

19. Their book is *Destructive Generation: Second Thought on the Sixties* (New York: Summit Books, 1990).

20. Julius and Ethel Rosenberg were executed in the summer of 1953 for "conspiracy to commit espionage" for the Soviet Union. They denied participation in a spy ring, and critics of the verdict say the evidence against the Rosenbergs was flimsy and circumstantial.

21. Maria Montessori (1870–1952) became internationally famous for designing an educational system for children that fostered intellectual growth and independence. Today, Montessori schools are located worldwide.

22. Carl Jung (1875–1961) was a Swiss psychologist and psychiatrist who developed the field of analytical psychology.

23. In 1983, U.S. troops overthrew a leftist regime on the tiny Caribbean Island of Grenada. In December 1989, President George Bush sent a 24,000-man military force to invade and occupy Panama and depose its government. Panamanian dictator Manuel Noriega was captured and returned to the U.S. for trial on drug charges.

Chapter 6. Warren Hinckle

1. Francis Ford Coppola (1939–) is an American film director, writer, and producer of such films as *Godfather I* and *II* (1972 and 1974) and *Apocalypse Now* (1979).

2. Hinckle, Warren, and William Turner. *Deadly Secrets: The CIA-Mafia War Against Castro and the Assassination of JFK* (New York: Thunder's Mouth Press, 1993).

3. Ambrose Bierce (1842–1914?) was an American writer who is most noted for his short story collections *(Midst of Things* and *Can Such Things Be?)*. He disappeared in Mexico in 1913.

4. The IRA stands for the Irish Republican Army, a nationalist organization dedicated to fighting for the unification of Ireland.

5. Immanuel Kant (1724–1804) was a German philosopher and one of the great figures in metaphysics who gained wide renown because of his teachings and writings.

6. Bill Graham is perhaps the most important rock promoter ever. He took over an operation known as the Fillmore, which became the cradle and then home of Bay Area bands in the sixties.

7. See interviews with Berg and Coyote in this book.

8. See interview with Rubin in this book.

9. New York: Summit Books, 1990.

Chapter 7. Peter Berg

1. See bibliography in this book for books that are written by Berg and explain his philosophy.

2. See note 1 above.

3. Rachel Carson (1907–1964) is the author of the classic book about the environment, *Silent Spring* (Boston: Houghton Mifflin, 1962).

4. An interview with Krassner appears in this book.

5. Donald Trump is a wealthy real estate developer who owns gambling casinos in Atlantic City, New Jersey, most notably Trump's Castle and Trump Plaza.

6. In July 1993, files that were to have been sealed until 2038 were opened by a public-records constitutional amendment passed by the Florida legislature in 1992. Those records revealed that the Johns committee, named for its chairman, the late Senator Charlie Johns, sought to root out homosexuals on college campuses and "Communists" in political organizations such as the NAACP. More than 100 teachers and administrators lost their jobs at schools because of the probe. As the records revealed, being different on a Florida campus could get a person labeled a homosexual.

7. Marlon Brando (1924–) starred in *The Wild One* (1953).

8. *Reefer* is a slang term for marijuana.

9. Mairowitz, David Zane. *The Radical Soap Opera: An Impression of the American Left* (London: Wildwood House, 1974).

10. Geoffrey Chaucer (1340–1400) was an English poet who was most famous for *The Canterbury Tales.*

11. In 1966, Rubin appeared before HUAC dressed as a revolutionary soldier.

12. An interview with Abbie Hoffman is included in this book.

13. Despite its liberal atmosphere, the Bay Area experienced racial tension and riots during the late sixties.

14. An allusion to Reformation leader Martin Luther (1483–1546), who on October 31, 1517, posted his famous *Ninety-Five Theses* on the door of the castle church in Wittenburg.

15. An interview with Peter Coyote appears in this book.

16. John Steinbeck, an American writer, was the author of such novels as *Of Mice and Men* (1937), *Cannery Row* (1945), and his classic *Grapes of Wrath* (1939).

17. The spring equinox occurs about March 21; the summer solstice is about June 22.

18. Gary Snyder was a Beat poet in the fifties who, along with Allen Ginsberg, Jack

Kerouac, and Michael McClure, helped introduce the Beat movement in literature to the public.

Chapter 8. Noam Chomsky

1. Thomas Paine (1737–1809) was an Anglo-American political theorist who wrote the pamphlet *Common Sense* and who played a prominent role in the American Revolution. Thomas Jefferson (1743–1826) was one of the founding fathers of American independence and third president of the U.S.

2. Eugene Debs (1885?–1926) was an American pacifist and Socialist leader who helped found the American Socialist Party and was its presidential candidate five times after 1900.

3. Founded in 1913, the Anti-Defamation League's stated purpose is to "stop the defamation of the Jewish people and to secure justice and fair treatment to all citizens alike."

4. In January 1968 in Boston, the U.S. Justice Department indicted Dr. Spock and four others on the charge of conspiracy to aid and abet the violation of the Selective Service Act. Spock and three of the others were found guilty as charged and given prison sentences and fines, which were appealed.

5. Arthur Schlesinger, Jr. (1917–   ), is an historian who served as an aide to President John F. Kennedy. In 1965, he published a study of Kennedy's White House years titled *A Thousand Days* (New York: Fawcett World, 1975), which won him the Pulitzer Prize.

6. In 1975, Sidney Schanberg (1934–   ) was one of the few Western correspondents to remain behind in the Cambodian capitol of Phnom Penh. The following year, Schanberg won the Pulitzer for reporting about events in Cambodia.

7. See Chomsky, Noam, and Edward S. Herman, *Manufacturing Consent: The Political Economy of the Mass Media* (New York: Pantheon Books, 1988).

8. Chomsky is actually referring to the 500th anniversary that took place in 1992 and marked Columbus's first voyage to the New World.

9. *Leave It to Beaver* was a popular television show in the 1950s.

10. Daniel Bell is the author of the book, *The End of Ideology: On the Exhaustion of Political Ideas in the Fifties* (New York: Free Press, 1965).

11. See note 10.

Chapter 9. Tim Leary

1. Pete Rose (1941–   ) is a former major league baseball player, famous for holding a major league record of hitting safely in 44 straight games and breaking Ty Cobb's major league record for most hits ever. Rose was nicknamed "Charlie Hustle."

2. Leary, Tim. *Flashbacks: A Personal and Cultural History* (Los Angeles: Jeremy P. Tarcher, 1990), p. 34.

3. George Bush was president of the United States from 1989 to 1992. Robert Bork was an unsuccessful Bush nominee for the U.S. Supreme Court. Pat Robertson is a well-known televangelist.

4. Mikhail Gorbachev (1931–   ) is former Soviet political leader who encouraged political change in Eastern Europe and helped end the Cold War through initiatives that led to a reduction in world tensions. He won the Nobel Peace Prize in 1990.

5. As a National Security Council staff member, Lt. Colonel Oliver North became involved in the Iran-Contra affair (see glossary).

6. Cary Grant (1904–1986) was an American film actor who appeared in such films as *Philadelphia Story* (1940) and *North by Northwest* (1959). Henry Luce (1898–1967) was an American publisher and founder of *Time* magazine. William F. Buckley, conservative

American editor and writer, founded the magazine *National Review* in 1955 and, since the sixties, has hosted the weekly public television show *Firing Line*.

7. Big Brother is the embodiment of the state in the British writer George Orwell's novel *1984*, which was published in 1949. Since then, the term *Big Brother* has been extended to mean any authoritarian or dictatorial leader.

8. American writer Mark Twain (pseudonym for Samuel Langhorne Clemens) wrote *Huckleberry Finn* (1884), the novel that is generally considered his masterpiece.

9. Captain Kirk and Captain Spock were characters in the sixties television show *Star Trek*, which has since gained a cult following.

Chapter 10. Philip Berrigan

1. Curtis, Richard. *The Berrigan Brothers: The Story of Daniel and Philip Berrigan* (New York: Hawthorne Books, 1974), p. 73.

2. The Paris Peace Accords of 1973 lead to the U.S. withdrawal from Vietnam.

3. Berrigan, Philip. "No Excuse for Ignoring Bloody Footprints in Snow." *National Catholic Reporter* (Oct. 11, 1991), p. 4.

4. Elizabeth McAlister, a former nun in the Order of the Sacred Heart, married Philip Berrigan in 1973. Like her husband, McAlister has been arrested for protests and demonstrations. In fact, she has served time for vandalizing a B-52 bomber.

5. On August 6, 1945, the Japanese city of Hiroshima was the target of the first atomic bomb. There were over 130,000 casualties and 90 percent of the city was leveled.

6. Somalia is a country in northeastern Africa that has suffered famine and civil war since the late 1980s. In 1992, the United States sent a military contingent to Somalia to help with relief operations of the International Red Cross and other nongovernmental agencies.

7. Howard Zinn is the author of *A People's History of the U.S.* (New York: HarperCollins, 1980).

Chapter 11. Anita Hoffman

1. Jezy, Marty. *Abbie Hoffman: American Rebel* (New Brunswick, N.J.: Rutgers University Press, 1992), p. 74.

2. Jezy, *op. cit.*, p. 72.

3. President John F. Kennedy wrote *Profiles in Courage* (New York: Harper & Row, 1964), an autobiographical account of his World War II experiences. Chester Bowles (1901–) has written *Africa's Challenge to America* (Berkeley: University of California Press, 1956) and *Ambassador's Report* (London: Collin's, 1954), among other works.

4. Students must pass the Graduate Record Examination, or GRE, to get accepted to most graduate school programs in the United States.

5. See the November/December 1988 issue of the *Utne Reader* for Krassner's article titled "A Message to Abbie Hoffman from His Old Pal Paul Krassner."

6. Abraham Maslow (1905–1978) was an American psychologist who believed that the human species has common and apparently unchanging psychological needs, which provide the framework for common human values.

7. Germaine Greer is an Australian writer and feminist who, with the publication of *The Female Eunuch* in 1971 (New York: McGraw-Hill), came to prominence as an international leader in the advancement of women's status.

8. *Steal This Book* was reprinted by Buccaneer Books in 1991.

9. Abbie Hoffman referred to Johanna Lawrenson, his companion underground, whom he called his running mate.

10. Jon Voight (1938–) is an American film actor who has appeared in such acclaimed movies as *Midnight Cowboy* (1969) and *Coming Home* (1977).

11. *Iron Curtain* — A phrase made popular by Sir Winston Churchill in the 1940s. The

phrase referred to the Soviet Union's isolation policy after World War II in which it set up trade barriers and rigid censorship that cut off the country and its Eastern Europe satellite countries from the rest of the world.

Chapter 12. Jerry Rubin

1. In the 1930s and '40s, Bud Abbott (1895–1974) and Lou Costello (1906–1959) were a popular comedy team who were famous for their comedy skit "Who's on First?"

2. A motorcycle gang based in Los Angeles with chapters throughout the world.

3. Big Brother is the embodiment of the state in British writer George Orwell's novel *1984* which was published in 1949. The term *Big Brother* has since been extended to include any authoritarian or dictatorial political leader.

4. *Yuppie* (Young Urban Professional), an expression originating in the early eighties, refers to a young, ambitious, and well-educated city dweller who has an affluent life-style and professional career.

5. Clarence Darrow (1857–1938) was the famous American lawyer who defended Eugene Debs and others in connection with the 1899 Pullman Strike and was involved in the famous Scopes Trial of 1925 in which he argued against the teaching of evolution in the public schools.

6. Groucho Marx (1895–1977) was one of the famous Marx Brothers, a comedy team who made such noted comedy films as *Duck Soup* (1933) and *Night at the Opera* (1935).

Chapter 13. Ericka Huggins

1. Hornsby, Alton, Jr. *Chronology of African American History* (Detroit: Gale Research, 1991), p. 165.

2. Carmichael, Stokely, and Charles V. Hamilton, *Black Power: The Politics of Liberation in America* (New York: Random House, 1967).

3. See Brown, Elaine. *A Taste for Power: A Black Woman's Party* (New York: Pantheon Books, 1992).

4. Bunchy Carter was the deputy minister of defense in the Black Panthers' Los Angeles chapter who, along with Ericka Huggins's husband, John, was killed on the UCLA campus.

5. See Hilliard, David, and Lewis Cole. *This Side of Glory: The Autobiography of David Hilliard and the Story of the Black Panther Party* (New York: Little, Brown, 1993).

6. See Bray, Rosemary. "A Black Panther's Long Journey," *New York Times Magazine* (Jan. 31, 1993), pp. 21+.

Chapter 14. Jim Fouratt

1. Duberman, Martin. *Stonewall* (New York: Dutton, 1993), p. xiv.

2. Numerous protests were made in the early sixties by peace activists who wanted to ban nuclear weapons.

3. Lee Strasberg was the artistic director of the Actor's Studio, a theater workshop in New York City, with a branch in Los Angeles, serving professional actors concerned with their growth. Actors from the workshop who have attained fame include Marlon Brando, Paul Newman, and Anne Bancroft.

4. After World War II, gay men and women started to organize several groups, one of which was the Mattachine Society. Organized in 1953 in a Los Angeles church, the Mattachine Society was not the first gay organization, but it served as an important foundation upon which the early gay rights movement could build and grow.

5. Andy Warhol (1928–1987) was an American artist, leading figure of the Pop Art movement, and founder of *Interview* magazine.

6. Outing is the controversial practice whereby gay activists publicly reveal the homosexuality of individuals, usually prominent, without their consent.

7. The North American Conference of Homophile Organizations (NACHO) was a national organization organized in the sixties to build a coalition from the many gay organizations. After a Chicago NACHO meeting in 1968, delegates from 26 organizations from all over the country adopted the radical slogan, "Gay Is Good."

8. "Chicago" refers to the Democratic National Convention in August 1968, the scene of violent confrontation between demonstrators and Chicago police.

9. Wounded Knee is a creek in South Dakota, which, in 1973, 200 members of the American Indian Movement occupied for 69 days and demanded a Senate investigation into the condition of American Indians.

10. Interviews with Krassner, Hoffman, and Rubin appear in this book.

11. Todd Gitlin is the author of *The Sixties: Years of Hope, Days of Rage* (New York: Bantam, 1967) and *The Whole World Is Watching: The Mass Media in the Making and Unmaking of the New Left* (Berkeley: University of California Press, 1980).

Chapter 15. Bernardine Dohrn

1. Van Gelder, Lindsy. "Bernardine Dohrn Is Weighed in the Balance and Found Heavy," *Esquire* (April 1970), p. 166.

2. Taken from program literature for the Children's Family Justice Center, Northwestern University.

3. Jane Addams (1860–1935) was an American social reformer who, along with her college roommate Ellen Gates Starr, founded the Social Welfare Center in the slums of Chicago in 1889.

4. Taken from program literature of the Children's Family Justice Center.

5. The United Nations Conference was held in Rio de Janeiro in 1992.

6. One hundred thirty-two years of French rule ended on July 3, 1962, when French President Charles de Gaulle proclaimed Algerian independence.

7. An interview with Jane Adams appears in this book.

8. Sale, Kirpatrick. *SDS* (New York: Random House, 1970).

9. An interview with Bill Ayers appears in this book.

Chapter 16. Barry Melton

1. Originally formed in the mid-sixties, the Jefferson Airplane became the most famous psychedelic band of the sixties era. They later became the Jefferson Starship. Founded in San Francisco in the sixties, Grateful Dead has proven itself to be one of rock music's most enduring bands. Founded in 1965, Quick Silver Messenger Service may be the best example of the San Francisco sound of the mid-sixties.

2. Upton Sinclair (1878–1968), American author and political figure, is best known for his novels advocating social reform. He ran for governor of California in 1934 as a Democrat with the slogan "EPIC—End Poverty in California." He lost the election after a savage campaign, but politicians eventually adopted many of his ideas.

3. The music of Leadbelly (1884–1949) led to the "rebirth" of blues and other black music. Joe Hill (1879–1915) was a Swedish-born musician and songwriter who popularized the goals of the American labor movement through his music; his real name was Joe Haggland.

4. The Byrds are the Los Angeles–based rock group that revolutionized the popular music scene with their unique blend of folk and rock styles. Their most famous recording is their version of Bob Dylan's "Mr. Tambourine Man."

5. The Weavers made some of the first folk recordings that became widely popular. Pete Seeger was a member of the Weavers from 1948–1957.

6. In addition to being a renowned expert on semantics, S.I. Hayakawa was president of San Francisco State College (now San Francisco State University). He gained fame in 1968 when, as acting president, he took firm measures to end student disturbances on his campus.

7. Madame Nhu was the wife of Ngo Dinh Nhu, who served as righthand man to his brother, South Vietnamese dictator Ngo Dinh Diem. Diem sent his sister-in-law Madame Nhu to the United States to rekindle support for his tottering regime. But Diem was overthrown in a coup in 1962.

8. MTV is a popular American pop-music-video cable television station.

9. As founder and the catalyst of the Mothers of Invention, which put out its first album in 1965, Frank Zappa helped make the band the premiere underground band in the America during the sixties era.

10. In 1992, Texas billionaire H. Ross Perot ran unsuccessfully for President on a third-party ticket, although he did garner the most votes ever by a third-party candidate.

11. Benito Mussolini (1883–1945) was the Fascist leader and dictator of Italy during World War II.

12. Rodney King was a motorist whom Los Angeles police beat in 1991. On April 17, 1993, two of the officers were convicted in a Los Angeles court of violating King's civil rights.

13. Acupuncture is a technique of medical treatment based on traditional Chinese medicine in which a number of very fine needles are inserted into a patient's skin at any of 800 specifically designated points.

14. 2 Live Crew is a rap group that, in the early nineties, was involved in controversy over their lyrics, which critics charged were offensive and demeaning to women. 2 Live Crew and its supporters protested what they saw as attempted censorship and suppression of artistic freedom.

15. Rap is a style of popular music developed by disk jockeys and urban blacks in the late seventies in which an insistent, recurring beat pattern provides counterpoint and background for rapid, slangy, and often boastful rhyming speech intoned by a vocalist or vocalists.

Chapter 17. Peter Coyote

1. Hurwitt, Robert. "Peter Coyote: Howling at Hollywood," *San Francisco Focus* (June 1986), p. 54.

2. See Chepesiuk, Ron. "Peonage for Peach Workers," *The Progressive* (Dec. 1992), pp. 22–25.

3. President Kennedy made McGeorge Bundy (1919–   ) special assistant for national security affairs in 1961. In that position, Bundy became one of President Kennedy's closest advisers.

4. *Yahweh* is the Hebrew name for God, and is the same word as "Jehovah."

5. Scientists have evidence of more than six Ice Ages going back more than three billion years.

6. Since 1975, Leonard Peltier, an American Indian Movement (AIM) leader, has been imprisoned for the murder of two FBI agents killed during an FBI attack against suspected AIM supporters at the South Dakota Pine Ridge Reservation. The 1975 battle with federal agents stemmed from the transfer of thousands of acres of the Pine Ridge Reservation, known to contain uranium and other minerals, to the federal government. Since Peltier's conviction, his supporters say evidence has surfaced to suggest that his trial was in violation of his due-process rights and was marked by intimidation of witnesses and distortion and suppression of evidence.

7. *Afrikaner* is a term used to describe those South African whites who are chiefly of Dutch (and some German and French) descent. The Medellín Cartel is a powerful drug cartel based in the Colombian city of Medellín.

8. Elmer Geronimo Pratt, deputy minister of defense in the Black Panthers' Los

Angeles chapter, is serving 18 years in jail because of run-ins with the law when he was a Black Panther.

9. In April 1920, anarchists Nicola Sacco and Bartolomeo Vanzetti were arrested for the murder of a paymaster and a guard in South Braintree, Massachusetts. Despite contradictory evidence, they were found guilty in July 1921 and sentenced to death. Their case became a cause célèbre and, after they were executed in 1927, debate on the case continued for years, and still does.

10. Sylvester Stallone (1946–) is an actor, writer, director, and producer most noted for his *Rocky* series (1976+) of movies.

11. Donald Sutherland (1935–), a Canadian actor, has starred in such films as *Klute* (1971) and *The Day of the Locust* (1975).

12. Elliot Gould (1938–) is an American actor who has starred in such films as *M*A*S*H* (1970) and *Ordinary People* (1980).

13. Meryl Streep, one of the world's most accomplished actresses, has starred in such films as *The Deer Hunter* (1978), *Sophie's Choice* (1982), and *Silkwood* (1983). Marlon Brando is also a distinguished American actor who has starred in such films as *A Streetcar Named Desire* (1951), *On the Waterfront* (1954), and *Mutiny on the Bounty* (1962).

14. Steven Spielberg (1947–) is a film director and producer of such blockbuster films as *Close Encounters of the Third Kind* (1977), *E.T.* (1982), *Jurassic Park* (1992), and *Schindler's List* (1993).

15. Directed by Howard Hawkes, *Bringing Up Baby* was made in 1938. *Front Page* was first made in 1930 and starred Pat O'Brien and Adolph Menjou. Howard Hawkes remade the movie in 1940 as *His Girl Friday*.

16. Robert Ryan (1899–1971) was a versatile American character actor who never seemed to get the film roles he deserved. His movies included *God's Little Acre* (1958) and *The Dirty Dozen* (1967).

17. *Terminator* (1991) stars Arnold Schwarzeneggar.

18. Michael Milken was a stockbroker and junk bond dealer who worked for the Wall Street stockbrokerage company of Burnham, Lambert, Drexel in the late eighties. Milken went to jail for insider trading. Charles Keating was a banker and former owner of Lincoln Savings and Loan Association, who, in the early nineties, was tried and convicted for investment fraud of his bank.

19. George Will and William Safire are conservative political columnists, Will with the *Washington Post Writer's Group* and Safire with the *New York Times*.

Chapter 18. Abbie Hoffman

1. Abbie Hoffman. *Steal This Urine Test* (Cutchoque, NY: Buccaneer Books, 1994).

2. Jerry Falwell is a prominent fundamentalist evangelist and the founder of the religious right political group, The Moral Majority.

3. Jimmy Swaggert was another prominent televangelist from Louisiana whose TV ministry ended as a result of his liaisons with prostitutes.

4. Mel Gibson (1956–) is an Australian leading actor who has appeared in such films as *The Year of Living Dangerously* (1983), *Mad Max III—Beyond Thunderdome* (1985), and the *Lethal Weapon* series.

5. Ned Beatty (1937–) is an American character actor who has appeared in such films as *Deliverance* (1972), *Nashville* (1975), and *The Big Easy* (1986).

6. A play on names. It's actually *Oral* Roberts, an evangelist and founder of Oral Roberts University in Tulsa, OK.

7. The U.S. Constitution went into effect when the ninth state, New Hampshire, ratified it on June 21, 1788.

8. Karen Silkwood was a woman who worked in a nuclear processing plant and

mysteriously died in an accident just before she was going to talk to a reporter about a safety problem at the plant. The 1983 movie *Silkwood,* starring Meryl Streep, dramatized her story.

9. Mark Twain (1835-1910) is the pen name for Samuel Langhorne Clemens. Twain was one of America's finest writers and author of such classics as *The Adventures of Huckleberry Finn* and *The Adventures of Tom Sawyer.*

10. In 1976, Sidney Schanberg (1934–) won the Pulitzer Prize for reporting about events in Cambodia in his book *The Killing Fields.*

11. Donald Trump is a wealthy real estate developer who owns gambling casinos in Atlantic City, New Jersey, and skyscrapers in New York City.

12. The Reverend Jesse Jackson (1941–) is an American civil rights leader, political activist, and Baptist minister.

13. Robert Bork and Douglas Ginsberg were unsuccessful Republican nominees to the U.S. Supreme Court in the 1980s.

14. Edwin Meese was attorney general during the Ronald Reagan presidential administration (1980-1988). The Miranda ruling refers to a case of *Miranda v. Arizona* in which the U.S. Supreme Court limited the power of police to question suspects. The court ruled in 1966 that what arrested persons say cannot be used against them unless they have been told they have the right to remain silent and other rights.

15. Caryl Chessman, a convicted rapist, was executed on May 3, 1960, at San Quentin Prison. It was the eighth time his execution had been scheduled over a period of 12 years. Evidence of his guilt was questionable, and his case had become a cause célèbre for opponents of capital punishment.

16. A reference to a 1983 movie *The Big Chill,* starring Tom Berenger and Glenn Close, in which university contemporaries from the sixties try to comfort each other after a death of a friend, while seemingly being nostalgic for the sixties.

17. G. Gordon Liddy was a former White House aide in the Nixon administration who directed the illegal entry into the Democratic National Headquarters in the Watergate complex in Washington, D.C. He was found guilty and sent to jail.

18. John DeLorean, the owner of the bankrupt DeLorean Motor Company, was caught in a government sting but was found innocent by a jury.

19. Abbie Hoffman, *Soon to Be a Motion Picture* (Cutchoque, NY: Buccaneer Books, 1994).

20. Bill Cosby (1937–) is a leading American actor, entertainer, and TV producer of the hugely popular *Cosby Show.* Stephen King (1947–) is a popular American writer of thrillers and horror stories, among others, *Carrie* (1974), *The Shining* (1977), and *Misery* (1987). Vanna White reveals the letters on the popular TV game show *Wheel of Fortune.*

21. Sandinistas are Nicaraguan rebels, named after Augusto César Sandino, who ousted dictator Anastasio Somoza Debayle in 1979 and set up a new government. The Sandinistas lost power in free elections, held in April 1990.

22. Ortega is a Sandinista who served as president of Nicaragua until the Sandinista defeat in 1990.

23. Karl Marx (1818-1883) was a German social philosopher and revolutionary who, with Frederick Engels, helped found modern socialism and Communism. Sigmund Freud (1856-1939) was a psychiatrist who was the founder of psychoanalysis. Albert Einstein (1879-1955) was an American theoretical physicist who is recognized as one of the greatest physicists of all time.

Bibliography

*The author found the following books
and articles useful in researching the interviews*

Books

Adam, Barry D. *The Rise of a Gay and Lesbian Movement*. Boston: Twayne Publishers, 1987.

Albert, Judith Clavir, and Steward Edward Albert, eds. *The Sixties Papers: Documents of a Rebellious Decade*. New York: Praeger, 1984.

Aya, Rodney, and Norman Miller. *The New American Revolution*. New York: Free Press, 1971.

Bane, Michael. *Who's Who in Rock and Roll*. New York: Everest House, 1981.

Berg, Peter, ed. *Reinhabiting a Separate Country: A Bioregional Anthology of Northern California*. San Francisco: Planet Drum Foundation, 1978.

_____, and George Tukel. *Renewable Energy and Bioregions: A New Context for Public Policy*. San Francisco: Planet Drum Foundation, 1980.

_____, Beryl Magikvy and Seth Zuckerman. *A Green City Program for the San Francisco Bay Area and Beyond*. San Francisco: Wingbow Press, Planet Drum Foundation, 1990.

Berrigan, Philip. *Widen the Prison Gates: Writings from Jails, April 1970–Dec. 1972*. New York: Simon and Schuster, 1973.

Brown, Elaine. *A Taste for Power: A Black Woman's Story*. New York: Pantheon Books, 1992.

Caute, David. *The Year of the Barricade: Journey Through 1968*. New York: Harper and Row, 1988.

Chafe, William H. *The Paradox of Change: American Women in the Twentieth Century*. New York: Oxford University Press, 1991.

Chomsky, Noam. *Deterring Democracy*. New York: Verso, 1991.

_____. *Manufacturing Dissent: The Political Economy of the Mass Media*. New York: Random House, 1988.

Cluster, Dick. *They Should Have Served That Cup of Coffee: Seven Radicals Remember the Sixties*. Boston: South End Press, 1979.

Collier, Peter, and David Horowitz. *Destructive Generation: Second Thoughts About the Sixties*. New York: Summit Books, 1990.

Curtis, Richard. *The Berrigan Brothers: The Story of Daniel and Philip Berrigan*. New York: Hawthorne Books, 1974.

Dass, Ram. *The Only Dance There Is*. Garden City, NY: Anchor Books, 1974.

_____, and Stephen Levine. *Grist for the Mill*. Santa Cruz, CA: Unity Press, 1977.

DeBenedetti, Charles. *Peace Heroes in the Twentieth Century*. Bloomington: Indiana University Press, 1986.

Dellinger, David. *From Yale to Jail: The Life Story of a Moral Dissenter*. New York: Pantheon Books, 1993.

_____. *More Power Than We Know: The People's Movement Towards Democracy*. Garden City, NY: Anchor Press, 1975.

_____. *Revolutionary Nonviolence: Essays by Dave Dellinger.* Indianapolis: Bobbs-Merrill, 1970.

Duberman, Martin. *Stonewall.* New York: Dutton, 1993.

Echols, Alice. *Daring to Be Bad: Radical Feminism in America, 1967–1975.* Minneapolis: University of Minnesota Press, 1989.

Eisen, Jonathan. *The Age of Rock: The Founders of the American Cultural Revolution.* New York: Vintage, 1970.

Gadlin, Howard, and Bertram E. Garskof, eds. *The Uptight Society.* Belmont, CA: Brooks Cole, 1970.

Gitlin, Todd. *The Sixties: Years of Hope, Days of Rage.* New York: Bantam Books, 1987.

_____. *The Whole World Is Watching: The Mass Media in the Making and Unmaking of the New Left.* Berkeley: University of California Press, 1980.

Goode, Stephen. *Affluent Revolutionaries: A Portrait of the New Left.* New York: Watts, 1974.

Gravy, Wavy. *Something Good for a Change.* New York: St. Martin's Press, 1992.

Hamalian, Leo, comp. *The Radical Vision: Essays for the Seventies.* New York: Crowell, 1970.

Hampton, Henry, and Steve Fayer. *Voices of Freedom: An Oral History of the Civil Rights Movement.* New York: Bantam Books, 1990.

Hayden, Tom. *Reunion: A Memoir.* New York: Random House, 1988.

Hayes, Harold, ed. *Smiling Through the Apocalypse: Esquire's History of the Sixties.* New York: McCall Publishing, 1970.

Helander, Brock. *The Rock Who's Who.* New York: Schirmer Books, 1982.

Hilliard, David, and Lewis Cole. *This Side of Glory: The Autobiography of David Hilliard and the Story of the Black Panther Party.* Boston: Little, Brown, 1993.

Hinckle, Warren. *Deadly Secrets: The CIA-Mafia War Against Castro and the Assassination of JFK.* New York: Thunder's Mouth Press, 1993.

_____. *If You Have a Lemon, Make Lemonade.* New York: W.W. Norton, 1974.

Hoffman, Abbie. *Soon to Be a Motion Picture.* Cutchoque, N.Y.: Buccaneer Books, 1994.

_____. *Steal This Urine Test.* New York: Penguin, 1987.

Hornsby, Alton. *African-American History: Significant Events and People from 1619 to the Present.* Detroit: Gale Research, 1991.

Howard, Gerald. *The Sixties: Art, Politics and Media of Our Most Explosive Decade.* New York: Paragon House, 1991.

Jezer, Marty. *Abbie Hoffman: American Rebel.* New Brunswick, NJ: Rutgers University Press, 1992.

Johnson, Michael L. *The New Journalism: The Underground Press, the Artists of Nonfiction and Changes in the Established Media.* Lawrence: The University Press of Kansas, 1971.

Krassner, Paul. *Best of the* Realist. New York: Running Press, 1984.

_____. *Confessions of a Raving, Unconfined Nut.* New York: Simon and Schuster, 1993.

_____. *How a Satirical Editor Became a Yippie Conspirator in Ten Easy Years.* New York: Putnam, 1971.

Leamer, Laurence. *The Paper Revolutionaries: The Rise of the Underground Press.* New York: Simon and Schuster, 1972.

Leary, Tim. *Flashbacks: A Personal and Cultural History.* Los Angeles: Jeremy P. Tarcher, 1990.

Lewis, Roser. *Outlaws of America: The Underground Press and Its Context.* London: Henrich Hanau, 1972.

Lipset, Seymour Martin, and Sheldon Wolin, eds. *The Berkeley Student Revolt.* Garden City, NY: Doubleday, 1965.

Lothstein, Arthur, comp. *"All We Are Saying": The Philosophy of the New Left.* New York: Putnam, 1971.

Lowery, Charles D., and John F. Marszazek. *Encyclopedia of African-American Civil Rights: From Emancipation to the Present.* New York: Greenwood Press, 1992.

Lucas, Anthony. *Don't Shoot — We Are Your Children.* New York: Random House, 1971.

Lyon, Danny. *Memories of the Southern Civil Rights Movement.* Chapel Hill: University of North Carolina Press, 1992.

Mairowitz, Davis Zane. *The Radical Soap Opera: An Impression of the American Left Since 1917.* London: Wildwood House, 1974.

Marcus, Eric. *Making History: The Struggle for Gay and Lesbian Equal Rights, An Oral History (1945-1990).* New York: HarperCollins, 1992.

The Marshall Cavendish Illustrated History of Popular Music. Freeport, NY: Marshall Cavendish, 1989.

Miller, James. *Democracy in the Streets: From Port Huron to the Siege of Chicago.* New York: Simon and Schuster, 1987.

Morgan, Edward P. *The Sixties Experience: Hard Lessons About America.* Philadelphia: Temple University Press, 1991.

Morrison, Joan, and Robert Morrison. *From Camelot to Kent State: The Sixties Experience in the Words of Those Who Lived It.* New York: Times Books, 1987.

Nelson, Jack, and Jack Bass. *The Orangeburg Massacre.* New York: World, 1970.

Obst, Lyunda Rosen. *The Sixties: The Decade Remembered Now, By the People Who Lived It Then.* New York: Rolling Stone Press, 1977.

Oglesby, Carl, comp. *The New Left Reader.* New York: Grove Press, 1969.

O'Neill, William L. *Coming Apart: An Informal History of America in the 1960s.* Chicago: Quadrangle Books, 1971.

Pareles, Jon, ed. *The Rolling Stone Encyclopedia of Rock and Roll.* New York: Rolling Stone Press, Summit Books, 1983.

Peck, Abe. *Uncovering the Sixties: The Life and Times of the Underground Press.* New York: Pantheon, 1985.

Peck, Jim, ed. *The Chomsky Reader.* New York: Pantheon, 1987.

Perry, Charles. *The Haight-Ashbury: A History.* New York: Random House, 1984.

Perry, Paul. *On the Bus: The Complete Guide to the Legendary Trip of Ken Kesey and the Merry Pranksters and the Birth of the Counterculture.* New York: Thunder's Mouth Press, 1990.

Powers, Thomas. *Diana: The Making of a Terrorist.* Boston: Houghton Mifflin, 1971.

Rossman, Michael. *Learning with a Teacher.* Bloomington, IN: The Delta Kappa Educational Foundation, 1973.

_____. *On Learning and Social Change.* New York: Random House, 1972.

_____. *The Wedding Within the War.* Garden City, NY: Doubleday, 1971.

Roszak, Theodore. *The Making of a Counterculture: Reflections on the Technocratic Society and Its Youthful Opposition.* Garden City, NY: Doubleday, 1969.

Rubin, Jerry. *Do It! Scenarios of the Revolution.* New York: Ballantine, 1970.

_____. *Growing Up at Thirty-Seven.* New York: Evans, 1976.

_____. *The War Between the Sheets.* New York: Marek, 1980.

Sale, Kirkpatrick. *SDS.* New York: Random House, 1970.

Santelli, Robert. *Sixties: A Listener's Guide.* Chicago: Contemporary Books, 1985.

Sargent, Lyman Tower. *New Left Thought: An Introduction.* Homewood, IL: Dorsey Press, 1972.

Sayre, Nora. *Sixties Going on Seventies.* New York: Arbor House, 1973.

Schachtman, Tom. *Decades of Shock: Dallas to Watergate, 1963-1974.* New York: Poseidon Press, 1983.

Sellers, Cleveland. *The River of No Return.* Jackson, MS, and London: University Press of Mississippi, 1990.

Sloan, Irving J. *Blacks in America, 1492-1970: A Chronology and Fact Book.* Dobbs Ferry, NY: Oceana Publications, 1971.

Stern, Jane. *Sixties People.* New York: Knopf, 1990.

Vickers, George. *The Formation of the New Left: The Early Years.* Lexington, MA: Lexington Books, 1975.

Weinstein, James. *Ambiguous Legacy: The Left in American Politics.* New York: Viewpoints, 1975.

Wolf, Leonard. *Voices from the Love Generation.* Boston: Little, Brown, 1968.
Woods, James L. *New Left Ideology: Its Dimension and Development.* Beverly Hills, CA: Sage Publications, 1975.
Zee, John Van Der, and Boyd Jacobson. *The Imagined City: San Francisco in the Minds of Its Writers.* San Francisco: A California Living Book, 1980.

Magazine, Newspaper, and Journal Articles

Askt, Daniel. "Freedom Is Still Rubin's Motto." *Los Angeles Times,* Jan. 21, 1992, 1D.
Ayers, William. "About Teaching and Teachers." *Harvard Educational Review,* Feb. 1986, 49–50.
_____. "The Activist Library." *The Nation,* Sept. 21, 1992, 294–95.
_____. "Are We Failing to Teach Teachers?" *Chicago Tribune,* Jan. 6, 1992, 18 (Section 1).
_____. "Chicago's Schools: The Real Work Can Get Underway." *Chicago Tribune,* Dec. 19, 1988, 19 (Section 1).
_____. "Distribute Resources Equitably." *Rethinking Schools,* Winter 1992–93, 13 and 15.
_____. "Local School Reform's Next Phase." *Chicago Tribune,* Jan. 11, 1990, 27.
_____. "Today Is a New Beginning." *Chicago Tribune,* Sept. 12, 1990, 19 (Section 1).
_____. "What Do 17-Year-Olds Know? A Critique of Recent Research." *The Education Digest,* April 1988, 27.
Berg, Peter. "Expanding Ecology—Renewing the Earth...." *Futures,* July 1991, 673–675.
Berrigan, Philip. "The Empire Lurches Downhill." *The Progressive,* March 1991, 18–20.
"Berrigan, Philip." *Current Biography,* 1976, 36–39.
Bray, Rosemary L. "A Black Panther's Journey." *New York Times Magazine,* Jan. 26, 1993, 21–26, 68, and 76.
Buckley, Stephen. "Berrigans Released While Appealing Contempt Term." *Washington Post,* March 28, 1992, 1D.
Chomsky, Noam. "The Masters of Mankind." *The Nation,* March 29, 1993, 412–416.
"Chomsky, Noam." *Current Biography,* 1970, 80–83.
Copeta, A. Craig. "The Itch Is Back: Paul Krassner's Return." *Regardies,* Oct. 1986, 146–154.
"Council Vote Deadlocked." *The New Hope Gazette,* Nov. 12, 1987, 1 and 8.
Editorial. "Children Abroad and at Home." *Washington Post,* Dec. 27, 1992, 6C.
_____. "Children Are Home Alone Every Day." *Chicago Tribune,* Jan. 5, 1993, 15 (Section 1).
_____. "Pardon Overdue Step Towards Reconciliation." *The State,* July 25, 1993, 2D.
_____. "These Children Can't Wait for Reform." *Chicago Tribune,* Jan. 22, 1993, 20 (Section 1).
Eichel, Henry. "Orangeburg-Riot Chapter Ends." *The State,* July 26, 1993, 1 and 6C.
_____. "South Carolina Pardons Man for Role in Riot." *The Charlotte Observer,* July 21, 1993, 1C.
Fitch B. "Forty-Eight Hours with the Berrigans." *Christian Century,* May 20, 1970, 643–646.
Gabriel, Joyce. "We All Pay for Their Suffering." *Atlanta Constitution,* Jan. 25, 1993, 11A.
Galloway, Paul. "Leary at 70: Mind-Boggling." *Chicago Tribune,* June 28, 1991, 1 (Section 5).
Geltman, M. "Berrigans Versus the United States." *National Review,* May 4, 1971, 470–474.
Gilboa, Netta. "Barry Melton Interview." *Gray Areas,* Spring 1993, 105–112.
Goldman, P., and G. Lubenow. "Keep the Faith." *Newsweek,* Sept. 5, 1977, 30.
Gray, D. "Acts of Witness." *New Yorker,* March 14, 1970, 44–46+.
Green, Charles. "Gay Rights: The New Frontier." *The Charlotte Observer,* April 17, 1993, 1C and 4C.
Hansen, Susan. "Four 'Plowshares Damage Battleship Missile Launchers." *National Catholic Reporter,* April 15, 1988, 2 and 5.
"Here Comes the Yippies." *Newsweek,* March 11, 1968, 68.
Hoffman, Abbie. "The Future Is Yours." *Harper's,* July 1987, 21 and 24.
"Hoffman, Abbie." *Current Biography,* 1981, 204–208.
"Hoffman Kicked Off Plane." (Rock Hill, SC) *Herald,* June 20, 1988, 5A.

Hinckle, Warren. "Ross Perot: Hero of the Counterculture." *New York Times*, July 10, 1992, 17A.

Isserman, Maurice. "He'd Rather Be Right." *The Nation*, June 14, 1993, 841–844.

Keerdoia, Eilleen. "Dave Dellinger's Life of Protest." *Newsweek*, July 11, 1983, 9.

Krassner, Paul. "The Diamond Ball." *Ramparts*, March 1968, 18–20.

————. "A Message to His Old Friend . . . from His Old Pal Paul Krassner." *Utne Reader*, Nov.–Dec. 1989, 113–115.

————. "The Milk-Moscone Case Revisited." *The Nation*, Jan. 14, 1984, 238–239+.

————. "Radical Philatelist." *Ramparts*, Jan. 1973, 41–43.

————. "Trial by Satire." *The Nation*, July 7, 1984, 4–5.

Lear, Patricia. "Rebel Without a Pause." *Chicago*, May 1993, 66–69, 96–99.

Leary, Timothy. "Tim Leary's Magic Bullet." *Psychology Today*, July 1983, 31+.

Levy, Shawn. "Leary of the Future." *American Film*, March 1991, 12.

Lopatkowa, Maria. "Give Children a Party." *World Press Review*, April 1993, 52.

Marshall, Steve. "Testy About Drugs: Activist's Book Looks at Drugs." *USA Today*, Oct. 6, 1987, 2A.

Martin, Douglas. "Jerry Rubin Is 50 (Yes, 50) Years Old." *New York Times*, July 16, 1988, 22A.

————. "Virtual Reality! Hallucination! Age of Aquarius!" *New York Times*, March 2, 1991, 25A.

Martinez, Al. "Peace on Parade." *Los Angeles Times*, May 9, 1991, 2B.

Miller, Jim. "Day-Glo Decade." *Newsweek*, July 11, 1983, 71–72.

Mitchell, Tammy. "Jerry Rubin." *Whole Life Magazine*, June 1986, 24–32.

Molnar, Alex. "Learning to Add." *The Charlotte Observer*, March 22, 1993, 9A.

Noble, Philip. "The Priest Who Stayed Out in the Cold." *New York Times Magazine*, June 28, 1970, 8–9+.

O'Kane, John. "Satirical Realism: Political Cabaret, Consciousness Expansion: An Interview with Paul Krassner." *Enclitic*, Spring 1989, 9–30.

Parshall, Gerald. "The Abbie and Amy Show," *U.S. News and World Report*, Dec. 8, 1986, 7.

Polskin, Howard. "Peter Coyote Doesn't Want to Play His Role Too Well." *TV Guide*, Oct. 24, 1987, 34–35.

Popkin, Annie. "An Early Moment in Women's Liberation: The Social Experience with Bread and Roses," *Radical America*, Jan.–Feb. 1988, 19–34.

Reynolds, Barbara. "We Should Be Debating Issues, Not Lives." *USA Today*, Nov. 10, 1987, 11A.

Roddy, J. "Case of the Jail-Bound Jesuit," *LOOK*, April 15, 1969, 63–65.

Rubin, Jerry. "Jerry Rubin Predicts Decade of Freedom." *USA Today*, Dec. 4, 1992, 10A.

Scroggins, Debra. "UNICEF Urges Global Crusade to Save Children." *Atlanta Constitution*, Dec. 17, 1992, 4A.

Scheff, David. "Timothy Leary Interview," *Rolling Stone*, Nov. 5, 1987, 228+.

Snider, Mike. "AIDS Top Killer or Young Adults in 64 Cities." *USA Today*, June 16, 1993, 1A.

"Stark Offering by Jerry Rubin." *The New York Times*, Aug. 18, 1986, 28N.

Stone, Judith. "Tune In, Turn On, Drop Out." *Discover*, June 1991, 32+.

"Timothy Leary: Getting High on High Tech." *Newsweek*, Dec. 22, 1986, 48.

Van Gelder, Lindsy. "Bernardine Dohrn Is Weighed in the Balance and Found Heavy." *Esquire*, April 1970, 164–170.

Waite, Bob. "Abbie Hoffman: Buck's Dollar a Year Dissident." *Delaware Valley Magazine*, Oct. 1987, 51–54.

Weiner, D. "Berrigan Back in Jail After Spilling Buckets of Blood." *New Times*, Aug. 7, 1978, 18.

Wills, Gary. "The Making of the Yippie Culture." *Esquire*, Nov. 1969, 135–138.

"Yippie for Money." *Newsweek*, Sept. 5, 1977, 29.

Young, Charles. "Noam Chomsky Anarchy in the U.S." *Rolling Stone*, May 28, 1992, 42–47.

Zintl, R.T. "New Rules for an Old Cast." *Time*, April 15, 1985, 52.

A Select Glossary

ACLU (American Civil Liberties Union) Established in 1920, a nonpartisan organization devoted to protecting basic rights set forth in the U.S. Constitution. The ACLU has supported nearly every major civil rights case since its founding.

Altamont rock concert At the 1969 festival in California, the Hell's Angels were hired as security but became involved with the stabbing death of a black man named Meredith Hunter right in front of stunned Rolling Stones singer Mick Jagger.

American Civil Liberties Union *see* **ACLU**

Baltimore Four Name given to Philip Berrigan and three associates who raided an inner-city draft board at the Customs House in Baltimore. Draft resistance to the Vietnam War took a new turn in October 1967 when they poured blood over the Selective Service records and then waited for authorities to come and arrest them. Philip Berrigan was later convicted.

Bay of Pigs invasion Unsuccessful invasion on April 17, 1961, by about 1,500 Cuban nationals who landed in Cuba in the Bahía de Cochinos (Bay of Pigs) in an effort to overthrow the Cuban Communist regime headed by Fidel Castro. It was supported by the United States, which brought strong criticism at home and abroad.

Beatles English rock musical group that in the sixties recorded numerous albums, toured widely, and dominated the pop music scene. The group, consisting of John Lennon, Paul McCartney, George Harrison, and Ringo Starr, disbanded in 1970.

Beatniks Members of the American Beat movement that originated in the 1950s and centered in the bohemian colonies of San Francisco's North Beach, California's Venice West, and New York City's Greenwich Village. The Beatniks expressed their alienation for mainstream society by adopting seedy clothes as well as the mannerisms and vocabulary of jazz musicians. The movement produced a number of outstanding writers, including Gary Snyder, Allen Ginsberg, and Lawrence Ferlinghetti. By about 1960, the movement began to fade.

Be-ins A celebration of the counterculture in which people did such things as play music, share food, chant, take drugs, wear outrageous clothes, and have a good time.

Berkeley Free Speech Movement (1964–1965) Began when the dean of students at the University of California at Berkeley issued a memorandum forbidding political solicitation on a 26-foot strip of sidewalk near the main entrance to the campus. Student groups, both liberal and conservative, banded together and formed the Free Speech Movement to protect their First Amendment rights, leading eventually to a general strike by students and closing of the campus.

Berrigan, Dan Peace activist and brother of Philip Berrigan; a member of the Baltimore Four.

303

Birmingham bombings Bombing of the Sixteenth Street Baptist Church in Birmingham, Alabama, on September 1, 1963, in which four young African American girls died.

Black Panther Party A militant African American political organization founded in Oakland, California, by Huey Newton and Bobby Seale. The party worked for black liberation but became involved in numerous clashes with police that led to deaths and arrests of party members. When another leader, Eldridge Cleaver, left the party in 1975, the Panthers were torn by rival factions. By the 1980s, the Black Panther Party had ceased to play an important role in the black liberation movement.

Black power Term first used by Stokely Carmichael, chairman of SNCC, on June 17, 1966, at a rally in Greenwood, Mississippi. He defined the term as "a call for black people in this country to unite, to recognize their heritage, and to build a sense of community." Carmichael angered many leaders and supporters of the civil rights movement. The press misinterpreted Carmichael's remarks as the condoning of violence against whites by blacks. But many young blacks in the civil rights movement adopted the slogan as a rallying cry for more aggressive action in the African American liberation struggle.

Boudin, Kathy A member of the Weather Underground who stayed underground after other members, such as Bill Ayers and Bernardine Dohrn, surfaced and turned themselves in. Then, on October 21, 1981, Boudin, along with other comrades, robbed a Brink's truck in Rockland County, north of New York City, and killed a guard and two police. Boudin and her associates were caught, tried, and convicted of robbery and murder. She received 20 years to life in prison.

Cambodian invasion In April 1970, U.S. and South Vietnamese troops thrust deep into Cambodia in an attempt to destroy the "sanctuaries" of the North Vietnamese from which men and matériel were being infiltrated into South Vietnam. By the end of 1971, war had engulfed most of Cambodia.

Carmichael, Stokely (1941–) Militant civil rights activist and chairman of SNCC, who changed the focus of the civil rights movement from integration and nonviolence to self-defense and black nationalism.

Carson, Rachel (1907–1964) American writer and marine biologist whose book *Silent Spring* (1962) was an influential study on the dangers of insecticides and helped to spark the modern environmental movement.

Castro, Fidel (1926–) Premier of Cuba since 1959, when he led a rebel force that overthrew Cuban dictator Fulgencia Batista.

Chaney, James; Andrew Goodman; and Michael Schwerner Three civil rights workers who, on June 21, 1964, the eve of the founding of the Freedom Summer project of 1964 in Mississippi, were arrested in Philadelphia, Mississippi, released from jail, abducted by Ku Klux Klansmen, and then murdered. Their bodies were found on August 4, 1964.

Chicago Seven In 1968 the U.S. Department of Justice indicted seven well-known radicals for crossing a state line in order to incite the Chicago riots that occurred at the August 1968 National Democratic Convention. There are interviews in this book with three of those accused of inciting the riots: Jerry Rubin, Dave Dellinger, and Abbie Hoffman.

Clark, Mark Member of the Illinois Black Panthers who, along with Fred Hampton, was killed by police on December 4, 1969. The police claimed the Panthers had instigated the shootout, but it soon became clear that the Panthers had fired, at most, a shot or two, while the police had riddled the walls with about 100 bullets.

Clark, Ramsey (1927–) Attorney general of the United States from 1967 to

1969, under President Lyndon B. Johnson, who has since been critical of many U.S. government policies.

Cleaver, Eldridge (1935–) Outspoken and controversial sixties black revolutionary and author of the classic *Soul on Ice,* who became minister of information in the Black Panther Party and a major architect of the party's program. The Black Panther Party fractionalized after Cleaver left it in 1975. Cleaver has since disavowed most of his radical past.

Coffin, William (1924–) Chaplain of Yale University in the sixties who played a prominent role in the anti–Vietnam War movement.

COFO *see* **Council of Federated Organizations**

COINTELPRO A controversial FBI program (COunter INTELligence PROgram) that activitists say had the objective of intimidating, disrupting, and ultimately destroying the New Left. An FBI memo made public in 1978 at hearings of the Senate Select Committee on Intelligence revealed that the purpose of the FBI campaign against the Black Panthers was to "prevent the rise of a black messiah who would unify and electrify the militant black movement."

Collier, Peter Editor of *Ramparts* magazine in the late sixties and coauthor, along with David Horowitz, of the book *Destructive Generation: Second Thoughts about the Sixties,* which depicts the legacy of the New Left and the sixties as being destructive and having negative consequences for American politics and culture today.

Communes Communities practicing common ownership of goods. Communes sprang up in the late sixties among various counterculture groups as well as gays and hippies.

Congress of Racial Equality (CORE) A civil rights organization, founded in 1942, which played a major role in the sixties civil rights movement. CORE organized Freedom Riders to test a Supreme Court ban on segregated interstate transportation and ultimately broke the back of Jim Crow. CORE later contributed to the 1964 Freedom Summer project and to the battle against racism and property in the urban ghettos.

Contras Refers to Nicaraguan guerrillas organized by the CIA to launch a war of attrition against the Sandinista government of Nicaragua.

CORE *see* **Congress of Racial Equality**

Council of Federated Organizations (COFO) Statewide organization of civil rights organizations in Mississippi. Robert Moses of SNCC and David Dennis of CORE spearheaded the formation of COFO in 1962. It disbanded soon after the Freedom Summer project of 1964 ended.

Counterculture The distinct culture that emerged in the mid-sixties from youth politics. Rejecting the values of mainstream America, members of the counterculture did such things as wear their hair long, eschew materialism, practice free love, live in communes, flock to rock festivals, practice Eastern mysticism, take drugs, and perform street theater.

Cuban Missile Crisis A major Cold War confrontation in 1962 between the United States and the Soviet Union. After the Bay of Pigs invasion, the Soviet Union began building missile launching sites in Cuba. After their construction was detected by U.S. reconnaissance flights, President John Kennedy demanded on October 22 that the Soviet Union withdraw the missiles. He immediately ordered a naval blockade of Cuba. On November 28, the Soviets agreed to dismantle the missile sites, and the crisis that brought the world to the brink of nuclear war ended.

Days of Rage Refers to four days in October 1968 in which 200 to 300 people, mainly students and exstudents, showed up at Lincoln Park in Chicago to "bring the war home." They smashed cars and windows and battled with police, who shot six of the fighters and wounded many others; 250 were arrested.

Debray, Regis French political thinker and author of *Revolution in the Revolution?*, which influenced New Left radicals. Debray believed that political and military leaders of a revolution should join and form a guerrilla group in the countryside rather than the city where Latin American communist parties traditionally focused. Debray later softened his stance and was an adviser to French Socialist President François Mitterrand.

Diggers An informal San Francisco-based group dedicated to nonviolent anarchy. Described as the conscience of the Haight (q.v.), the Diggers took their ideological roots from a seventeenth-century, anarchist, communal-farming group in Cromwellian England that were also known as the Diggers. The earlier group lived on wastelands scattered across the countryside and promoted the idea that the land should be free for all those who needed to use it. The modern day Diggers wanted everything to be free and worked to establish an entire economic network based on bartering and sharing rather than profit. For more information on the Diggers, see the interviews in this book with Peter Berg and Peter Coyote.

Dylan, Bob (1941–) American singer and composer whose songs captured the feeling of alienation of American youth in the sixties and became a profound influence on folk and rock music.

Economic Research Action Project (ERAP) An SDS program inspired by SNCC. In the summer of 1964, while many whites were going south to Mississippi, SDS recruited 100 or more students to work in the ghettos of Newark, Chicago, Cleveland, Philadelphia, and half a dozen other cities to organize an interracial movement of the poor. The next year, ERAP also tried to organize the Appalachian poor.

Ellison, Ralph (1914–1994) Black American writer who wrote the classic novel *Invisible Man* (Modern Library, 1963), which detailed the struggles of a nameless young black man in a hostile environment.

Fanon, Frantz (1925–1961) A West Indian from Martinique who became a political theorist, a leader of Algeria's struggle for independence from France, and posthumously influenced sixties radicals with his ideas about violent revolution.

Free Southern Theater Drama used to communicate the aims of the civil rights movement to the masses of black people in the rural South. The idea was conceived in the fall of 1965 by three civil rights workers: Gilbert Moses, a reporter from the *Mississippi Free Press*, and John O'Neal and Doris Derby of SNCC. During Freedom Summer of 1964, the Free Southern Theater conducted theater workshops for students from Tougaloo College and Jackson State College. By 1970, the Free Southern Theater had ceased to become a cultural arm of the civil rights movement.

Freedom Riders Led by CORE, more than 1,000 people, black and white, who rode buses into Southern states in 1961 to challenge segregation in the bus system. The Interstate Commerce Commisssion, as a result, was compelled to prohibit segregated accommodations on buses and in bus terminals.

Freedom Summer The summer of 1964 when approximately 1,000 mostly Northern white college students joined a cadre of predominantly African American civil rights activists in Mississippi. SNCC initiated the project and COFO supported it. Volunteers registered thousands of black voters and provided health and education services to black Mississippians.

Ginsberg, Allen (1926–) American poet of the Beat generation who remained active in the sixties as part of the antiwar movement and the counterculture. He is best known for his poem *Howl*, a long work attacking American values.

Goodman, Andrew *see* **Chaney, James**

Graham, Bill The most important rock promoter ever. He took over an operation in San Francisco, which became known as the Fillmore, the cradle and later home of Bay area bands in the sixties.

Grogan, Emmett A founding member of the Diggers and legendary sixties counterculture figure.

Guerrilla Theater (also called *street theater* because it was performed in the streets) Popular form of theater in the sixties. The skits were improvisational and provocative, and challenged the audience.

Guevara, Ernesto "Ché" (1928–1967) Argentine revolutionary leader who fought in the Cuban Revolution and became Cuban leader Fidel Castro's chief lieutenant. He served as minister of industry (1961–1965) and then left Cuba to foster revolutions in other Third World countries. He was executed after being captured in Bolivia in 1967.

Gulf of Tonkin Resolution A Congressional resolution granting war powers to President Lyndon Johnson. On August 4, 1964, President Johnson announced that the U.S. destroyers *Maddox* and *C. Turner* had been attacked in the Gulf of Tonkin, off the coast of North Vietnam. Some Americans doubted that the attack had occurred, but Johnson asked Congress for powers to "take all necessary measures to repel any armed attack against the force of the United States and to prevent further aggression." On August 7, Congress approved these powers in the Gulf of Tonkin Resolution. Johnson used the resolution as the legal basis for increased involvement in Vietnam. In March 1965, he sent a group of U.S. Marines to South Vietnam, the first American ground forces to enter the war. The original alleged attack has subsequently been proven fictitious.

Guthrie, Woodie (1912–1967) American folksinger and composer who wrote more than 1,000 songs, chiefly on social and political themes. Guthrie had a profound influence on younger performers like Bob Dylan. Musician Arlo Guthrie, composer and singer of the popular sixties song "Alice's Restaurant," is his son.

Haber, Al Activist and founding member of the SDS.

Haight-Ashbury Attractive and inexpensive area in San Francisco named for the intersection of these two streets near the Golden Gate Park that became famous during the 1967 Summer of Love when thousands of young people flocked to San Francisco to experience the counterculture. The Haight-Ashbury scene inspired the organization of counterculture communities across the country.

Hampton, Fred Member of the Illinois Black Panthers, who, along with Mark Clark, was killed by police on December 4, 1969. Police claimed the Panthers had instigated the shootout, but it soon became clear the Panthers had fired, at most, a shot or two, while the police had riddled the walls with about 100 bullets.

Harrisburg Seven A group of seven radicals (including Philip Berrigan, who was in jail at the time, and his wife Elizabeth), who were indicted for allegedly organizing an elaborate and bizarre plot to kidnap Henry Kissinger and to blow up heating tunnels in Washington's federal buildings. The jury failed to reach a verdict, but the Berrigans were found guilty of smuggling letters in and out of prison. The conviction was later appealed and reversed.

Hayden, Tom Author of the SDS's Port Huron Statement and a member of the Chicago Seven.

Hell's Angels Motorcyle gang based in California with chapters worldwide.

Hendrix, Jimi (1942–1970) Famous and innovative rock music guitarist who became a favorite of the counterculture. Hendrix died at age 27 of complications arising from a drug overdose.

Hilliard, David Former chief of staff of the Black Panther Party and author of *This Side of Glory: The Autobiography of David Hilliard and the Story of the Black Panther Party* (Little, Brown, 1993).

Hippies Members of the youth movement of the sixties and early seventies that started in the United States and spread to Canada, Great Britain, and many other countries. The hippies rejected the customs and traditions and style of mainstream middle-class society and tried to develop those of their own.

Ho Chi Minh (1890–1969) Vietnamese nationalist leader and president of North Vietnam (1954–1969). During the sixties, Ho led North Vietnam's struggle to defeat the U.S.-supported government of South Vietnam.

Hoffman, Julius Presiding judge at the trial of the Chicago Seven.

Holocaust Name given to the period (1933–1945) of persecution and extermination of European Jews and other minorities by Nazi Germany. Jews and others in Germany, as well as conquered countries, were systematically rounded up and sent to concentration camps. By the end of the war, an estimated six million victims of the Holocaust had perished.

Hoover, J. Edgar (1895–1972) Director of the Federal Bureau of Investigation (FBI) from 1924 to 1972. Hoover is a controversial historical figure, largely because he targeted alleged Communists after World War II and harassed civil rights leaders and left-wing dissenters in the sixties.

Horowitz, David *see* **Collier, Peter**

House Un-American Activities Committee (HUAC) A committee of the U.S. House of Representatives, created in 1948 to "investigate subversion and un–American propaganda that might be dangerous to American government as guaranteed by the Constitution." The HUAC became controversial durign the post–World War II Red Scare period when it tried to find Communist subversion in all aspects of American life and was severely criticized for its abuse of civil liberties.

Iran-Contragate Refers to the embarrassment faced by Ronald Reagan's presidential administration beginning in 1986 when it was revealed that while publicly denouncing Iran as a terrorist state, Reagan's administration, using Israel as an intermediary, had secretly sent weapons to Iran in exchange for money and American hostages, held by pro–Iranian fundamentalist forces in Lebanon. The profits from those arms sales to Iran were used to buy weapons for the Nicaraguan Contras in violation of law that prohibited U.S. aid to the Contras. An investigation followed.

Jackson State University On May 14, 1970, ten days after the shootings at Kent State, about 500 Jackson State University (Jackson, Mississippi) students protested the invasion of Cambodia. Police opened fire, killing two students and wounding 12 others.

Jim Crow laws Historically, the term used to describe the practice of legal and extralegal racial discrimination against African Americans.

Johnson, Lyndon Baines (1908–1973) President of the United States from 1963 to 1969. Sworn in after the assassination of John F. Kennedy on November 22, 1963, LBJ launched an ambitious economic and social welfare program to create what he called "The Great Society." However, his escalation of the Vietnam War led to huge demonstrations and angry domestic opposition. In March 1968, Johnson announced he would not run for reelection.

Joplin, Janis (1943–1970) White female blues singer generally recognized as the first female superstar of rock music. Her best known songs include "Me and Bobby McGee," "Mercedes Benz," and "Piece of My Heart." Joplin died of a drug overdose on October 4, 1970.

Kennedy, John Fitzgerald (1917–1963) President of the United States from

1961 to 1963, Kennedy was assassinated in Dallas on November 22, 1963. His domestic program, the "New Frontier," called for tax reform, federal aid to education, medical care for the aged under Social Security, and the extension of civil rights, but he also increased the number of U.S. advisers in Vietnam to 16,000.

Kent State The Ohio university at which four college students were shot and killed by National Guardsmen in 1970. When president Richard Nixon decided to invade Cambodia in late April, Kent State University in Ohio became one of 60 institutions that protested the move. On May 4, 1970, a National Guard contingent fired on a crowd of about 200 unarmed students. Four students were killed instantly, including two who were walking across campus to lunch. Nine others were injured. The shootings sparked a wave of student protest across the country that touched more than 530 universities.

King, Martin Luther, Jr. (1929–1968) Black American clergyman and civil rights leader who established the Southern Christian Leadership Conference in 1957 as a base for nonviolent protests, marchers, and demonstrations for black rights, such as the 1963 March on Washington and the 1965 voter-registration drive in Selma, Alabama. As civil rights activities became more militant in the sixties, Dr. King's leadership was challenged. In 1968, he was shot and killed in Memphis, Tennessee, while planning a multiracial "poor people's march" for national poverty legislation.

Kissinger, Henry (1923–) National security adviser to presidents Richard Nixon (1969–1974) and Gerald Ford (1974–1976) and U.S. secretary of state (1973–1975), who played a major role in formulating U.S. foreign policy.

Kunstler, William Radical lawyer and counsel for the Chicago Seven.

Lee, Herbert (1912–1961) An Amite County, Mississippi, farmer who, on September 25, 1961, was shot to death by state representative E.H. Hurst in Liberty, Mississippi. Hurst claimed he shot Lee in self-defense and was acquitted by a local jury.

LSD (lysergic acid diethylamide) A hallucinogenic and extremely potent drug that can cause physiological and behavioral changes, popular in the sixties among people who embraced the counterculture life-style.

McCarthy, Joe (1908–1957) United States senator from Wisconsin who achieved national prominence and power by his sensational but unsubstantiated accusations against those officials and citizens he termed "Communists." After the Senate "condemned" him in 1954, McCarthy's influence steadily declined.

Mailer, Norman (1923–) American writer and author of such books as *The Naked and the Dead* (Harper, Row, and World, 1948), *An American Dream* (Dial, 1964), and *The Executioner's Song* (Little, Brown, 1979). Mailer's book *The Armies of the Night* (New American Library, 1969), a journalistic account of the 1967 peace march on Washington, won him the Pulitzer Prize.

Malcolm X (1925–1965) Born Malcolm Little, a militant black American leader, a Muslim minister, and charismatic advocate of black separatism. He broke with Black Muslim leader Elijah Muhammed, and after a pilgrimmage to Mecca, he converted to orthodox Islam and founded the Organization of Afro-American Unity in 1964. While championing black nationalism, Malcolm also admitted the possibility of interracial brotherhood. In February 1965, he was assassinated in Harlem, New York, by Black Muslims. His *Autobiography of Malcolm X* (1964) is a classic of the sixties black liberation movement.

March on Washington On August 28, 1963, more than 250,000 people of all colors gathered between the Washington Monument and the Lincoln Memorial in Washington, D.C., for one of the seminal events in the history of the American civil rights movement. Dr. Martin Luther King, Jr., made his famous "I Have a

Dream" speech, an address that, in terms of its impact, has since been compared to Abraham Lincoln's Gettysburg Address.

Marijuana A relatively mild, nonaddictive drug with hallucinogenic properties, obtained from the flowering tops, stems, and leaves of the hemp plant. Marijuana was an integral part of the sixties culture and has been used medically to help relieve pain and nausea from cancer chemotherapy and in the treatment of glaucoma.

Mississippi Freedom Democratic Party (MFDP) The party organized during the summer of 1964 by SNCC and other participants of the 1964 Freedom Summer project, and designed to challenge the power of the Democratic Party. The MFDP tried to secure delegate representation at the national Democratic convention held at Atlantic City in August 1964, but Hubert Humphrey proposed a compromise calling for the regular white delegates to be seated if they swore loyalty to the national party and providing for the creation of two "at large" seats to be filled by members of the MFDP. The compromise broke down, and all but three of the party regulars walked out of the convention. When the entire MFDP delegation tried to take the seats of the party regulars, they were removed from the convention.

Morgan, Robin Journalist and leader in the women's liberation movement of the late sixties.

Motherfuckers An aggressive antiestablishment group, founded in 1967 on the Lower East Side of New York. The group's official name was "Up Against the Wall, Motherfucker," which was taken from a line in a poem of black poet LeRoi Jones. They performed street theater, practiced the martial arts, and urged hippies to interfere with the police when they were trying to make drug busts.

NAACP *see* **National Association for the Advancement of Colored People**

National Association for the Advancement of Colored People (NAACP) Founded in 1910, an organization of American blacks, with many white members, dedicated to ending racial equality and segregation. In the sixties, Black militant groups often accused the organization of passivity.

National Urban League *see* **Urban League**

New Left Group created in 1957 by young radicals who rejected the liberalism of the "old" Left because they felt it no longer met their needs. They opposed the power structure that they said robbed them of their freedom and individuality. In the sixties, peace and civil rights activists joined the New Left. Sociologist C. Wright Mills was credited with coining the phrase in the late fifties.

New Left Notes A publication of the SDS.

Newton, Huey Black militant and cofounder of the Black Panther Party.

Oughton, Diana Member of the radical Weather Underground (also: Weathermen) who, on March 6, 1970, was killed in an explosion in a Greenwich Village townhouse. Oughton and other members of the Weather Underground were manufacturing bombs when somone crossed the wrong wire, blowing up the house and igniting gas lines.

Parks, Rosa (1913–) A black woman who, on December 1, 1955, took a seat toward the front of a Montgomery, Alabama, city bus and refused to move to the back. She was arrested and jailed. She became a powerful protest symbol against segregation.

Pentagon Papers A top secret government study of U.S. military involvement in Indochina from 1945 to 1969. Their publication by the *New York Times* in 1971 led to debate about national security, freedom of the press, censorship, and civil liberties.

Progressive Labor A pro–Maoist faction of the SDS that tried to divert campus members of SDS away from campus politics and into a working-class movement.

Psychedelic drugs Mind-expanding drugs, such as LSD and marijuana, which alter consciousness.

Ramparts Radical sixties political magazine, published in San Francisco, which investigated U.S. government deception and skulduggery. For more information, see the interview in this book with Warren Hinckle.

Rap music A style of popular music, developed by disk jockeys and urban blacks in the late seventies, in which a recurring beat pattern provides the background and the counterpoint for rapid slang and often boastful rhyming patter glibly intoned by a vocalist or vocalists.

Rolling Stones English rock musical group that rose to prominence in the mid-sixties. The Stones' songs, which were mostly written by Mick Jagger and Keith Richards, include "Satisfaction," "Paint It Black," and "Sympathy for the Devil."

Savio, Mario Principal leader of the Berkeley Free Speech Movement.

Schlesinger, Arthur, Jr. (1917–) Historian and aide to President John Kennedy. In 1965, Schlesinger wrote a study of Kennedy's White House years titled *A Thousand Days*, which won him the Pulitzer Prize.

Schwerner, Michael *see* Chaney, James

SCLC *see* Southern Christian Leadership Conference

SDS *see* Students for a Democratic Society

Seale, Bobby Black militant, cofounder of the Black Panther Party, and a defendant in the trial of the Chicago Seven.

Seeger, Pete (1919–) American folk singer, musician, and composer who first gained fame in the 1940s singing about ordinary working people. Seeger's musical style and concern with social issues influenced Joan Baez and other folk singers from the sixties.

Sinclair, John Leader of the White Panther Party.

Sit-Ins Civil rights tactic used to desegregate eating establishments in the South, beginning in 1960. The sit-ins were met by physical violence and legal harassment, including massive jailings; but most restaurants eventually desegregated voluntarily, under court order or by legislation. The success of the sit-in strategy encouraged civil rights activists to use the method of nonviolent demonstration when discrimination persisted.

SNCC (Student Nonviolent Coordinating Committee) The civil rights organization that emerged in 1960 in the wake of the spontaneous student sit-in movement begun in Greensboro, North Carolina, when four black students sat in at a Woolworth's lunch counter that had refused to serve black people. SNCC played a key role in Freedom Summer, voter registration, Black Power, and other aspects of the civil right movement. SNCC became increasingly more militant as the decade progressed. For a discussion of SNCC history, see the interview with Cleveland Sellers in this book. The organization is no longer in existence.

Southern Christian Leadership Conference (SCLC) A civil rights organization founded in 1957 by Dr. Martin Luther King, Jr. Headquartered in Atlanta and composed largely of Southern black clergymen, the SCLC advocates nonviolent passive resistance as a means of securing equality for blacks. It sponsored the 1963 March on Washington.

Spock, Dr. Benjamin (1903–) American author, pediatrician, and peace activist whose book *Baby and Child Care* has sold more copies than almost any other book published in the United States. In 1967, Dr. Spock resigned his position as professor of child development at Case Western Reserve University in Cleveland,

Ohio, to devote his efforts full-time to the peace and antinuclear movements. He was the presidential candidate for the People's Party in 1972.

Student Nonviolent Coordinating Committee *see* **SNCC**

Students for a Democratic Society (SDS) An American radical student group founded in 1960 that was involved in the civil rights movement and the antiwar movement and tried to transform American society. With publication of its Port Huron statement in 1962, SDS declared the failure of the American political system to end poverty and exploitation and to achieve international peace and called for "participatory democracy" in which individuals could have a voice in decisions directly affecting their lives.

Teach-ins Informational sessions organized by antiwar activists to counteract government propaganda about the Vietnam War and to inform the American people about what was really happening in Southeast Asia. They began in 1965.

Tet Offensive North Vietnamese attack on South Vietnam in 1968 that discredited optimistic U.S. reports about how the war was going and led to increased domestic opposition to the war. (*Tet* is the three-day observation of the Vietnamese New Year that begins on the first new moon after January 20.)

Townhouse Explosion Explosion in a Greenwich Village townhouse in which three members of the Weather Underground (Diana Oughton, Terry Robbins, and Ted Gold) died on March 6, 1970. They and other members of the group (formerly: Weathermen) were manufacturing bombs when someone connected the wrong wire, blowing up the house and igniting the gas mains.

Urban League Group founded in 1910 that has local chapters in more than 100 cities and works to end racial discrimination and to increase the economic and political power of blacks and other minority groups in the United States.

Vietnam War A war between the government of South Vietnam, aided by the United States, and Communist insurgents, aided by North Vietnam. From 1961, the United States supplied troops to South Vietnam. By 1969, U.S. troops in South Vietnam numbered 550,000. The Americans pulled out in 1973, but the war continued until 1975 when North Vietnam launched their final offensive and routed the South Vietnamese army.

Watergate A series of scandals involving a break-in at the Democratic Party headquarters in the Watergate apartment building in July 1972 by agents of President Richard Nixon's reelection committee. An extensive cover-up led to a Senate investigation and, in August 1974, Richard Nixon became the first U.S. president to resign from office.

Weather Underground SDS faction (originally called *Weathermen*) that considered itself the vanguard of the revolution that would transform the United States. They believed in armed struggle, used sabotage as a tactic, and hoped that students, workers, and blacks would present a united front. Bernardine Dohrn and Bill Ayers were members of the organization.

Yippies Members of the Youth International Party. Abbie Hoffman, Jerry Rubin, Paul Krassner, Dick Gregory, and their friends declared themselves Yippies on December 31, 1967. Yippies advocated a blending of pot and politics, that is, a blending of the hippy and New Left philosophies. The Yippies and antiwar groups organized the massive demonstrations at the August 1968 National Democratic Convention. A violent confrontation ensued in which the police beat demonstrators as the demonstrators chanted, "the whole world is watching."

Yuppie (also Yuppy) An expression (based on an acronym: Young Urban Professional) originating in the early eighties that refers to a young, ambitious, and well-educated city dweller who has an affluent life-style and a professional career.

Index

A

Abbott, Bud 182
Abbott and Costello 182
ABC-TV 155, 208
Abortion 30, 68, 209, 220
Acid *see* LSD
ACLU 173, 179, 194, 258, 271
Acquired Immune Deficiency Syndrome *see* AIDS
ACT UP 212
Acting 213–14, 216, 221, 257, 268, 269
Actor's Studio 212, 214
Acupuncture 270
Adams, Dawn 72
Adams, Jane 56–73, 233
Addams, Jane 102
Africa 199
African Americans 34, 124–25, 127–29, 142, 171, 181, 200–4, 207–9, 217–18, 224, 226, 232–33, 236–37, 249, 262, 266
AIDS 19, 116, 198, 199–202, 221–22, 238, 250, 252, 270, 283
Alaska pipeline 279
Alcohol 248
Alcoholism 278
Alderson, West Virginia 84
Algeria 149–51, 170, 175–76
Algerian Revolution 231
Alinsky, Saul 149
Allen, Steve 25, 39
The Alliance for Survival 36
Altamont, California 69
Alternative medicine 250
Alternative press 25, 27, 35
American Jewish Congress 282
American Revolution 181–82, 188

American Scholar 168
Americans Before Columbus 76
Amite County, Mississippi 62
Anarchism 128
Ann Arbor, Michigan 101
Ann Arbor Draft Board 92
Antioch College, Ohio 56, 59–60, 72
Archivists 34
The Argonaut 108, 110
Arkansas 49, 109
Arts 267–68
Asia 199
Aspirin 152
Atlanta, Georgia 45
The Atlantic 112
Australia 123, 137
Ava, Illinois 59
Ayers, Bill 92–106, 224, 237–38
Ayers, Malik 99
Ayers, Zayd Shakur 93, 224
AZT 221

B

Baby boomers 190
Bakker, Tammy 28
Baltimore, Maryland 151, 165, 169, 171
Baltimore Four 158
Ban-the-Bomb demonstrations 212
Banks Street College of Education 93
Barnett, Ross 62
Bath houses 221
Bay of Pigs, Cuba 110
The Beatles 129, 173–74, 245–46
Beatniks 59, 214

Beatty, Ned 274
Be-ins 169, 174, 215
Bell, Theo 99
Bennett, William 99–100
Berg, Peter 114, 118–32
Berkeley, California 66, 70, 72,
    126–27, 188, 219
Bernstein, Carl 11
Berrigan, Daniel 86, 144, 159, 165,
    236
Berrigan, Philip 158–68, 236
The Bible 161–63, 168
Bierce, Ambrose 109
The Big Chill (movie) 283
Biodiversity 120
Bioregionalism 118–19, 121–23, 128,
    131
Bisexuals 200
Black Liberation 237
Black music 252
Black Panthers 55, 70, 105, 116–17,
    130, 149, 151, 166, 170, 175–77,
    198–99, 202–4, 207, 209–10, 218,
    235, 267
Black Plague 278
Black power 42, 52–53, 73, 203
Black separatism 207
Blacks see African Americans
Bloom, Allan 96
Bolivia 65
Bond, Julian 51
Bork, Robert 150, 278
Bottled water 180, 183, 185–86
Boudin, Kathy 258
Bowles, Chester 171
Brando, Marlon 125, 266
Brennan, William 276
Bringing Up Baby (movie) 270
Brooklyn, New York 25, 69, 242
Brooklyn College, New York 34
Brown, Elaine 203–4, 203, 209
Brown, Jerry 99, 255, 261, 268
Browne, Jackson 34
Bruce, Lenny 26, 32–33, 39–40
Buckley, William F. 153
Bucks County, Pennsylvania 273–
    74
Buddhism 83, 262
Bundy, McGeorge 259
Burlington, Vermont 78
Bush, George 29, 97–98, 134–36, 141,
    226, 229–30

C

Caffeine 142
California 120, 123, 184–85, 201–2,
    248, 266–67
Calvinism 129–30
Cambodia 140–41, 177, 276
Campbell, Joseph 83
Camus, Albert 81
Canada 87, 137, 281
Capital punishment 279
Capitalism 97–99, 110, 113, 122, 144,
    207
Carbondale 59–61, 65, 72
Carmichael, Stokeley 41–42, 55, 202
Carson, Rachel 120
Carter, Amy 272, 283
Carter, Bunchy 204
Carter, Jimmy 272, 283
Carter, Rosyln 283
Carthage, Mississippi 61
Castro, Fidel 108, 235
Caterpillar tractor 146
Catonsville, Maryland 159, 165
Censorship 30, 279
Central America 84, 143, 282
Central Intelligence Agency see CIA
Chaney, James 44, 61
Chaucer 127
Cheney State Teacher's College
    (Cheney, Pennsylvania) 202
Chessman, Caryl 279
Chicago, Illinois 26–27, 57, 65, 71,
    98, 103, 123, 125, 182, 199, 223–25,
    232, 236, 238
Chicago Public School System 95, 100
Chicago Seven 32, 59, 74–75, 86–89,
    175, 177, 179, 182, 272, 280, 283
Child care 270
Children's Community School 92, 101
Children's rights 224, 227–230
China 141, 174, 165, 262
Chomsky, Noam 133–46
CIA 32, 107, 109–111, 196, 261, 272,
    278, 281, 283
Cincinnati, Ohio 187
Civil liberties 194, 248, 273, 275–77
Civil rights 41–43, 44–55, 56–58,
    61–64, 68, 70, 73, 77, 84, 97, 101–2,
    125, 126, 129–30, 159, 171–72, 191,
    203, 207, 224, 229, 231, 244, 258,
    274, 279, 282

Clark, Mark 236
Clark, Ramsey 140
Cleaver, Eldrige 116, 149–51, 170, 175, 199, 218
Cleaver, Kathleen 175
Clinton, Bill 29, 80, 98–99, 109–10, 124, 134–36, 161, 164, 182, 221, 228–29, 249, 261, 263
CNN 283
Coca-Cola 97
Cocaine 170, 179, 280
Coffin, William Sloane 140
COINTELPRO 42, 45, 54–55, 198, 204, 210
Cold War 60, 75, 79, 162, 164, 180, 261
Cole, Larry 34
Cole, Michelle 34
Collier, Peter 37, 90, 105, 115–16
Colorado 220
Columbia, Maryland 139, 159
Columbia, South Carolina 44
Columbia University 171
Columbia University Teacher's College 93
Columbus, Christopher 75–76, 143
The Committee in Solidarity with the People of El Salvador 78
The Committee of Liaison with POWs 86
Committee of One Hundred Million Loyal Americans 212
Commonwealth Edison Company 92
Communists and Communism 102–3, 122, 138, 151–52, 154, 177, 213, 222, 242–43, 249, 257
Comprehensive Education and Training Act 266
Computers 147
Congress of Racial Equality *see* CORE
Connecticut 75
Conservatives and conservatism 136, 226, 250,
Contras 109
Cook County, Illinois 225, 226
Coppola, Frances Ford 108
CORE (Congress of Racial Equality) 61, 139, 244
Cosby, Bill 280
Costello, Lou 182
Counterculture 25–27, 30–31, 36, 38, 84, 114–115, 118–19, 129, 167, 169, 216, 224, 241–42, 246–47, 250–52, 254, 257, 270
Country Joe and the Fish 240, 243–46, 251
Coyote, Peter 114, 128, 254–71
Crack 48, 261, 270
Creative writing 257
Criminal justice system 248
Cromwell, Oliver 118
Crossings Program 199–200
Cuba 81, 108, 110, 187
Cuban Missile Crisis 258, 165
Cuernavaca, Mexico 149
Curry, Connie 51

D

Daley, Richard 27
Daley, Richard, Jr. 95
Danbury Correctional Institute 75
Danforth Fellowships 169
Darrow, Clarence 195
Dartmouth College 171
Dartmouth Review 171
Dasmann, Raymond F. 127
Davis, Rennie 86–87, 89, 127
Days of Rage 223
Death penalty 280
Debray, Regis 65
Dellinger, Dave 32, 74–91
DeLorean, John 280
Democratic National Convention (1968) 26, 41, 74, 182
Democratic Party 41, 52, 151–52, 243
Denmark, South Carolina 43–44, 48
Denmark Recreation Association 43
Denton, Michigan 127
The Depression 59, 137
Detroit, Michigan 62, 126
Dickens, Charles 77
Diggers 39, 114, 118–20, 126–32, 254, 257, 267
Disney, Walt 25
Dohrn, Bernardine 71, 92–93, 101, 223–39
"Doonesbury" (cartoon strip) 33
Dostoyevsky, Feodor 83, 91
Dover Club, San Francisco 109
Draft (military) 47, 66, 83, 92, 101, 133, 158, 165, 259

Draft resisters 140
Draft week 224
Drug smuggling 110
Drug testing 194, 273, 275–78
Drugs 48, 79, 89, 126, 147, 149,
    151–54, 167, 192–94, 204, 216–17,
    247–48, 250–53, 260–62, 276–78,
    280, 283; *see also* under name of
    drug
Duberman, Martin 211
Dylan, Bob 26, 69, 93, 208, 224, 243,
    293

E

Eastern Airlines 216
Eastern Europe 98
The Ecologist 123
Ecology 30, 74, 78–79, 99, 119–124,
    131–32, 223, 228–29, 235, 261–63,
    270, 272–73, 275, 279
Economic Research and Action Proj-
    ect *see* ERAP
Ecstasy (drug) 36
Edgewood, New Jersey 254
Education 92–97, 99–101, 106, 223,
    226, 267
Einstein, Albert 282
Eisenhower, Dwight D. 29, 138
El Salvador 81, 143, 281–82
Elections 251; of 1992 99; presiden-
    tial 1992 134
Ellison, Ralph 63
England 123, 141–42
Entrepreneurship 189–90, 192
Environment *see* Ecology
ERAP (Economic Research and Ac-
    tion Project) 70
Esquire 223
E.T. (movie) 269–70
Europe 137, 265–66
Exeter 95
Existentialism 59

F

Fall, Bernard 85
Falwell, Jerry 274
Family values 97, 226
Fanon, Frantz 49, 63, 198
Fasting 77

FBI (Federal Bureau of Investiga-
    tion) 27, 34, 42, 45–46, 54–55, 93,
    111, 139, 166, 177, 179, 198, 204,
    217, 236, 263, 280–81
Feminism 39, 57, 63, 66–67, 70–71,
    78, 128–29; *see also* Women's Rights
Florida 279
Flynt, Althea 38
Flynt, Larry 27, 38
Folk music 243–45, 259
Folsom Prison 150–51
Fonda, Jane 86
Food coops 270
Ford, Gerald 85
Fossil fuels 120
Foster care 228
Fouratt, Jim 211–22
Fox Network 39
France 235, 241
Free Southern Theatre 61
Free Speech Movement 126–27, 188,
    219, 251
The Free Store (New York City) 212
Freedom of Information Requests
    235
Freedom rides 41, 56, 159
Freedom Singers 61
Freedom Summer (1964) 41, 56, 64,
    172
Freud, Sigmund 179, 282
Froines, John 86
Front Page (movie) 270
Fuller, A. T. 82
Fundamentalism 106, 114, 129–30,
    153
Futique Inc. 149, 155

G

Gambling 274
Gandhi 81, 82
Gay Community Service Center 212
Gay Liberation Front 212, 219
Gay rights *see* Homosexuals; Les-
    bians
General Motors 113, 186, 189
Georgia 47
Germany 141, 168, 235
Gibson, Mel 274
Gilbert, David 238
Ginsberg, Allen 26, 31, 57, 153, 211

Ginsburg, Douglas 278
Gitlin, Todd 222
Glen Gardner, New Jersey 75
Goddard College 79
Goldhaft, Judy 128, 131
Goodman, Andrew 44, 46, 61
Gorbachev, Mikhail 151
Gore, Al 124, 261
Goucher College 109, 171
Gould, Elliott 266
Graham, Bill 114
Grant, Cary 153
Grateful Dead 240, 246
Greeks 127
Greenglass, David 105
Greensboro, North Carolina 41, 56
Greenwich, Connecticut 166
Greenwich Village, New York City 70, 93, 173, 211, 223
Greer, Germaine 178
Grenada 106
Grinnell College 254, 258–59
Grogan, Emmett 114, 128, 130
Guatemala 279, 281
Guerrilla Theater 87, 127–28, 182, 254
Guevara, Ernesto Ché 49, 65, 187
Gulf of Tonkin Resolution 85
Gulf War *see* Persian Gulf War
Guthrie, Woodie 60, 243

H

Haber, Al 72, 92
Haight–Ashbury District, San Francisco 114, 118, 126, 128–29, 131, 258
Hamilton, Charles 201
Hampton, Fred 198, 236
Harlem 83
Harmony Community 57–58, 62
Harper's magazine 112
Harris Poll 136
Harrisburg, Pennsylvania 154, 166
Hart, Jeffrey 171
Harvard University 42, 148–49, 151, 157, 234, 260
Hayakawa, S.I. 244
Hayden, Tom 86, 92
HBO 39

H.E.A.C. 212
Health care 187, 223, 227, 250
Health foods 183, 185–86
Health insurance 79
Heilbroner, Robert 98
Hell's Angels 69, 188
Hendrix, Jim 156, 208
Hepatitis 215, 255
Heroin 69, 152, 217
High definition television 180
Hill, Anita 67, 143, 181, 209, 233
Hill, Joe 243
Hilliard, David 204
Hinckle, Warren 107–17
Hippies 118–19, 129, 211, 215–16, 226
Hiroshima 160
Hitchcock, James 168
Hitler, Adolph 281
HIV virus 221
Ho Chi Minh 75, 85–86, 235
Hoffman, Abbie 25–26, 30–32, 36, 74, 86–89, 93, 113, 118, 127, 153, 169–79, 194–96, 206, 211, 215–17, 221, 229, 254–55, 264–65, 268–70, 272–84
Hoffman, Anita 169–81, 196, 222
Hoffman, Jack 176–77
Hoffman, Julius 272
Hollywood 25, 170, 221, 206, 254–55, 264–65, 268–69, 270
Holy Cross College 158
Home Box Office *see* HBO
Homeless 252
Homosexuals 14, 32, 78, 86, 116, 124, 129, 169, 180, 191, 200–1, 203–4, 211, 214, 216–18, 220–22, 251; *see also* Lesbians
Homophobia 129
Honduras 136
Hood, Thomas 82
Hoover, J. Edgar 42, 178, 217
Hope, Bob 36
Horowitz, David 37, 90, 105, 125–26
H.U.A.C. (House Unamerican Activities Committee) 105, 182
Huckleberry Finn (novel) 156
Huggins, Ericka 198–210
Huggins, John 199, 202, 204
Hull House 225
Human rights 281
Humphrey, Hubert 42
Hustler magazine 27, 38–39

I

India 164
Indians *see* Native Americans
Indigena 72
The Inquisition 260
Integration *see* Civil rights
Interactive technology 147–49,
    154–55, 180–81
Iowa 64
Iowa City, Iowa 65
IRA (Irish Republican Army) 109
Islam, Nation of 53
Israel 84, 81, 115, 138, 282
Italy 123

J

Jackson, Jesse 79, 276
Jackson, Mississippi 61
Jackson Council of Federated
    Organizations 61
Jackson County, Mississippi 68
Jackson State University 47, 236
Jagged Edge (movie) 254, 269
Jamaica 162
Japan 141, 154, 235; emperor of 141
Jefferson Airplane 240
Jefferson Starship 246
Jewish Anti-Defamation League
    138
Jews 34, 133, 137–139, 169, 171, 215,
    282
Jezer, Marty 177
Jim Crow 61, 63
Johns Hopkins University 164
Johns Hopkins University Applied
    Physics Laboratory 159
Johnson, Lyndon Baines 25, 34, 42,
    82, 140, 197, 229, 253
Jonah House 159, 161
Jones, Mother 102, 265
Joplin, Janis 208
Josephite Brothers 158–59, 164
Journalism 107, 110–12, 220
Jung, Carl 106
"Just Say No" Anti-Drug Campaign
Juvenile court 226
Juvenile delinquency 241–42
Juvenile justice 224–25

K

Kabul, Afghanistan 149
Kaminsky, Herschel 139–40
Kansas 64
Kant, Imammuel 112
Keating, Charles 107–8, 271
Kelly, Chris 277
Kelman, Scott 27
Kennedy, John F. 25, 27, 34–35, 38,
    60, 72, 82, 110, 138, 143, 171, 187,
    229, 236, 259
Kent State University 47–48, 236
Kesey, Ken 27, 31
King, Stephen 41, 50–51, 54, 159,
    217, 224, 232, 249, 280, 282
Kirk, Captain Jim 157
Kissinger, Henry 166
Knoxville, Tennessee 45
Koppel, Ted 220
Koreans 208
Kovic, Ron 105
Krassner, Paul 25–40, 89, 174, 176, 222
Ku Klux Klan 125
Kunstler, William 195

L

L.A. Weekly 149, 179
Labor 142, 146
Labor unions 103–4, 221, 242
Laing, R.D. 72
Lakehurst Academy, Chicago, Illinois
    100–1
Laos 140
Lapiner, Jane 128
Lassiter, Louise 279
Latin America 72, 142, 261, 199, 287
Latinos 203
Law enforcement 206, 223
Lawrensen, Johanna 179, 273
Lawsuits 183, 185
Lawyers 241, 243
Leadbelly 243
Leary, Rosemary 170, 175
Leary, Tim 31, 69, 147–57, 170, 175
Leave It to Beaver 44
Lebanon
Lee, Herbert 61
Lee, Spike 54
Leff, Sam 34

Lennon, John 26
Lesbian and Gay Community Service Center 212
Lesbians 218, 222, 251, 279; *see also* Homosexuals
Lewis and Clark College 245
Lewisburg Penitentiary 75, 166
Liberation 88
Liberation Press 75
Liberation theology 78
Libertarians 70, 143
Liberty House 169
Liddy, G. Gordon 280
Life magazine 34
Lincoln, Abraham 150
Lincoln, Nebraska 65
Lincoln University 201
Linden, Ann 128
Lions Club 252
Lorton, Virginia 159–60, 162
Los Angeles, California 27–28, 122, 128, 179, 183–85, 206
Los Angeles riots 98, 249
Los Angeles Times 35, 75, 204
Lou Grant 215
Louisiana 45
Love-ins 240
Loyola University 159
LSD 27, 32, 68–69, 89, 126, 132, 147, 149, 151–53, 170, 173, 247–48, 253
Luce, Henry 153

M

McAlister, Elizabeth 159–60, 167
McCarthy 73, 124, 213, 242
McDonald, Country Joe 240–41, 245
McDonald's restaurant 100
McGovern, George 68
McNair, Robert E. 42
Mad magazine 25
Mailer, Norman 26
Maine 161, 168
Mairovitz, David Zane 126
Malaysia 142
Malcolm X 30, 41, 49, 52–54, 224, 282
Male chauvinism 167
Manhattan 98
Manson, Charles 35, 38

Mao Tse-tung 174, 235
Maoists 65, 224
Marijuana 30, 36, 89–90, 149, 125, 160, 192–93, 252, 254, 259–60, 278
Marks, Mississippi 51
Married with Children 30
Marshall Plan 142
Martians 30
Marx, Groucho 26, 39, 196
Marx, Karl 102, 282
Marxism 199
Maryland 207
Maslow, Abraham 177
Mass media 136, 141, 144, 220–21, 260, 277–78, 283
Massachusetts Institute of Technology *see* MIT
Mattachine Society 214, 219
Medellín Cartel 262
Media *see* Mass media
Medicine 250
Meese, Edwin 279
Melton, Barry 240–53
Mexico 72, 126, 254–60, 281
Miami, Florida 278–79
Miami University (Oxford, Ohio) 223
Michigan State University 99, 107
Migrant workers 99, 107, 255
Military *see* U.S. Army
Milken, Michael 271
Mill Valley, California 255, 266
Mime troupe 118, 127–28, 254, 258, 264
Miranda ruling 279
Mississippi 41, 46–47, 53, 56, 61–64, 274
Mississippi Freedom Democratic Party 42, 63
Missouri 64
MIT 133, 145
MOBE 84
Montessori, Maria 106
Monterey Pop Festival 240, 247
Montgomery Bus Boycott 54
Morgan, Robin 175, 177
Moynihan, Daniel 273
MTV 246
Multilevel marketing 183, 185–86
Multimedia 170, 181
Murcutt, Billy 128
Music 125, 126, 249, 251–52; *see also* under type of music

N

NAACP (National Association for the Advancement of Colored People) 53, 203
Napalm 30, 35
Nashville, Tennessee 110, 264
National Association for the Advancement of Colored People *see* NAACP
National Catholic Reporter 112
National Collegiate Athletic Association *see* NCAA
National Committee for Independent Political Action 78
National Lampoon 33
National Lawyer's Guild 224
National Mobilization Committee to End the War in Vietnam 75
National Public Radio *see* NPR
National Student Association 107
Native American rights 74, 84
Native Americans 33, 119, 262
Navahos 262
Nazi Germany 69
Nazis 141, 249
NBC Television 155, 213
NCAA (National Collegiate Athletic Association) 278
Nebraska 64–65
"Necessity defense" strategy 272, 275
Neill, A.S. 92
New Haven, Connecticut 198, 202
New Hope, Pennsylvania 213
New Jersey 212, 254
New Left 37, 57, 103, 129, 133, 211–12, 214–15, 219
New Left Notes 66
The New Mary Tyler Moore Show 32
New Orleans 159
New York, New York 27–28, 57, 74, 84, 118, 121, 123, 125–26, 166, 169, 171–72, 174, 179, 183–84, 199–200, 211, 214–15, 221, 224, 242
New York City Red Squad 280
New York Review of Books 134
New York Stock Exchange 36, 272
New York Times 85, 106, 109–10, 113, 139, 141, 154, 204, 216, 220, 273, 276
New Yorker 98

Newark, New Jersey 83
Newburgh, New York 159
Newkirk, Allen Van 131
Newsweek 276
Newton, Huey P. 130, 150–51, 198, 201, 203
Nhu, Madame 244
Nicaragua 81, 84, 143, 280, 282
Nintendo 30, 154
Nixon, Richard 29, 69, 139–40, 149, 280
Noonan, Georgia 45
Norman, Oklahoma 69–70
North, Ollie 152
North American Bioregional Conference 119
North Beach, California 125
North Carolina 161, 168
North Vietnam 75, 85–86
Northhampton, Massachusetts 272
Northwestern University School of Law 224
Norway 227–28
Notre Dame University 274
NPR (National Public Radio) 137, 279
Nuclear disarmament 60, 74, 84, 164
Nuclear Test Ban Treaty 60
Nuclear war 165, 283
Nutrition 183, 185–86, 250

O

Oakland, California 204
Oakland Community Learning Center 204–5
Oklahoma 69
Omnitrition International 183, 187
O'Neal, John 61
Orangeburg, South Carolina 44
Orangeburg Massacre 42–48, 55
Organic food 270
Ortega, Daniel 280–81
Oughton, Diana 71, 93, 104
Outrageous Fortune (movie) 254, 270

P

Pacifism 74, 81
Palestinians 282

Panama 106
Parent-Teacher Association *see* PTA
Paris, France 176
Paris Peace Accords 159
Parks, Rosa 77
Partnership for a Drug Free America 278
Peace movement 79, 142–43, 251
Peacham, Vermont 75
Peltier, Leonard 262
Pennsylvania 254
Pentagon 36, 133, 135, 160, 169, 261, 264, 272
Pentagon Papers 142
Penthouse magazine 274
People magazine 35
People's Justice for Peace in America 75–76
Perot, H. Ross 137, 248, 252
Perrier water 183, 185
Persian Gulf War 29, 35, 73, 106, 143, 155, 208, 230, 234, 237–38
Pettigrew, Allen 277
Philadelphia, Mississippi 44, 54
Philadelphia Electric Company 273–75, 279
Phnom Penh 141
Pinkerton detectives 172
Planet Drum Foundation 118, 123, 131–32, 159
Plastic surgery 273
Police *see* Law enforcement
Political prisoners 262–63
Pornography 33–35, 38; *see also* Flynt, Larry; *Hustler* magazine
Port Huron, Michigan 57
Port Huron Statement 57
Portland, Oregon 123, 126
Poverty 251
Poverty program 224
POWs 86
Pratt, Geronimo 262
La Prensa (newspaper) 28
Presley, Elvis 124–25
Prisoners of War *see* POWs
Prisons 75, 83–84, 150–51, 157, 162–64, 166, 249–50, 262
The Progressive 255
Progressive Labor Party 65, 93, 224
Progressive Vermont Alliance 78
Psychedelic drugs *see* Drugs
Psychedelic shop 258

Psychedelics 69, 131, 180, 216
Psychologists 260
PTA (Parent-Teacher Association) 59, 278
Publishing 171–72
Puerto Rican independence 84
Puerto Ricans 200
Puget Sound 126
Puritanism 129

Q

Quayle, Dan 29
Queens, New York City 25, 169, 171
Quicksilver Messenger Service 240

R

Race relations 208–9
Racism 207, 209
Radicals, radicalism 81, 102–3, 115, 133–34, 137, 163, 211, 264, 229, 272
Rainbow Coalition 79
Raleigh, North Carolina 41
Ramparts magazine 105, 107, 110–14, 115, 117, 202, 233
Rap music 208, 251
Raskin, Marcus 140
Rasmussen, Howard 34
Reader's Digest 112
Reagan, Ronald 29, 31, 72, 97–98, 134–36, 143, 197, 226–27, 229, 264, 277–79, 282
Real estate 192–93
The Realist 25, 27, 33–35
Reasoner, Harry 25, 34
Reconstruction 62
Regardie's magazine 34
Rehnquist, William 99
Religion 83, 161, 163, 197
Republican Party 74, 150–52, 264–280
RESIST 1333 138
Restoration ecology 123
Revolutionary Youth Party 224
Rhino Records 212
Rhode Island 212
Richmond, Virginia 125
Riley, Richard 99
Riots 223
Roberts, Oral 274

Roberts, Terry 69–70, 72
Robertson, Pat 150
Robinson, Sis 84
Rock music 144, 240, 244–47, 283
Rockefeller, Nelson 280
Rolling Stone magazine 35
Rolling Stones 69, 114, 129, 156, 177, 245–46
Roman Catholicism 111–12, 148, 158–59, 161, 214, 217
Rome, Georgia 45
Ron Reagan (television show) 39
Roosevelt, Franklin Delano 110, 124, 137, 243
Rose, Pete 147
Rosenberg, Ethel 105
Rosenberg, Julius 105
Rostow, W.W. 82
ROTC 127
Rubin, Jerry 26, 31, 86–89, 113–15, 127, 171, 175–76, 182–97, 211, 222
Rubins, Reggie 51
Russell, Bertrand 49
Russia 75, 79, 98, 133, 154, 164–65, 167–68, 282
Rustin, Bayard 84
Rutgers University 272
Ryan, Robert 270

S

Sacco and Vanzetti 82, 264
Safire, William 271
Sale, Kirkpatrick 65, 235
Salisbury, Harrison 85
San Francisco, California 27–28, 33, 109, 113, 117, 120, 118–20, 123, 125, 126–28, 132, 143, 200, 219, 221, 240–41, 243–46, 255, 264
San Francisco Chronicle 108, 114, 117
San Francisco Examiner 108
San Francisco State University 241, 244, 254, 257
Sandinistas 280–82
Sanders, Bernie 78
Sands, Bobby 103
Santa Claus 182
Santa Fe, New Mexico 179
Sartre, Jean Paul 49
Saturday Night Live 33
Savio, Mario 188

Scanlon's Monthly 108, 113
Schanberg, Sidney 141, 276
Schlesinger, Arthur 140
Schwerner, Michael 44, 61
SCLC (Southern Christian Leadership Conference) 53, 224
Screen Actor's Guild 68
SDS (Students for a Democratic Society) 56–57, 65–66, 70–71, 92–93, 100–1, 103–5, 127, 129, 214, 232–33, 236–37, 245
Seale, Bobby 74, 89, 130–31, 198–99
Seattle, Washington 70, 123
Seattle Eight 88
Seeger, Pete 60, 243
Segregation 164
Sellers, Cleveland 41–55
Selma, Alabama 52, 54
Sex and sexuality 67, 109, 124, 173, 180, 217, 247, 270, 283
Sexism 30
Sexual harassment 180–81, 209, 233
Shah of Iran 98
Shakur, Zayd 224
Shanti Project 199–201
Shasta Region 119, 123
Shelley, Percy Bysshe 82
Silkwood, Karen 274
Simon and Shuster 39
Sinclair, John 177
Sinclair, Upton 242
Singer, Marcus 60
Sit-ins 56, 101, 125, 171–72
Slavery 151, 207
SNCC (Student Nonviolent Coordinating Committee) 41, 46, 49–57, 61, 63, 70, 84, 127, 159, 172, 216
Snyder, Gary 132
Soap 279
Social Security 242–43
Socialism 110, 112, 257
Socialist Party 59
Socialist Workers Party 64
Society of St. Joseph 158
Somalia 161, 163–64
Sophie's Choice (movie) 33
Sopin magazine 212
South Africa 100, 125
South America 123
South Carolina 47, 143, 255
South Carolina State Board of Education 43

South Carolina State College 42, 46
Southeast Asia 142
Southern, Terry 27
Southern Christian Leadership Conference *see* SCLC
Southern Comfort (movie) 269
Southern Illinois University 57, 60
Southern Pacific Railway 277
Soviet Union 151, 190, 229
Spain 123
Spielberg, Steven 269
Spock, Dr. Benjamin 133, 139–40
Springfield, Massachusetts 148
Spy magazine 33
Stalin, Joseph 106, 137
Stalinism 60
Stalinists 102, 105–6, 138
Stallone, Sylvester 265
Star Wars (missile system) 164
Steinbeck, John 12
Stockholm, Sweden 119
Stockman, David 99
Stonewall rebellion 211–12, 214, 216–17
Strasberg, Lee 213, 215
Streep, Meryl 33, 266
Student Nonviolent Coordinating Committee *see* SNCC
Student Peace Union 60, 64, 84
Students for a Democratic Society *see* SDS
Summerhill, England 92
Sutherland, Donald 266
Swaggart, Jimmy 274
Syracuse, New York 158
Syracuse University 274

T

Tallahassee Federal Corrections Institute 45
Tate, Saron 35
Teachers 95–97
Television, power of 113
Terre Haute, Indiana 45
Tet Offensive 140
Texas 119
Theological Seminary, New York City 74
Third World 93, 98, 142
Thomas, Clarence 67, 99, 181, 233
Thoreau, Henry David 102

Thorton, Mamma Mae 125
Thousands Island Region, New York 273, 279
Times Square 213
Townhouse explosion 70, 93
Trade Unions *see* Labor Unions
Trinity College, Connecticut 55
Trotskyites 65, 84
Trump, Donald 276
Turner, William 108
Twain, Mark 274
Two Harbors, Minnesota 158
2 Live Crew 251

U

Ukraine 153
UN Convention on Rights for Children 228
Underground Press 216
Unicorn News Service 221
Unitarian Church 59
United Front Against Fascism 70
United Nations 263
University of Alabama 148
University of California at Berkeley 148, 188
University of California at Los Angeles 204
University of Chicago 223, 231
University of Florida 124
University of Illinois at Chicago 93–94
University of Iowa 36
University of Massachusetts at Amherst 272, 275
University of Michigan 92, 101
University of North Carolina at Chapel Hill 50
University of North Carolina at Greensboro 42
University of Rhode Island 214, 283
University of San Francisco 112
University of Washington 245
Urban League 53, 258
Urbanization 121–22
US (Organization) 199, 204
U.S. Army 125–26, 220
U.S. Army Corps of Engineers 273
U.S. Congress 85
U.S. Constitution 274
U.S. Foreign Policy 134, 137

U.S. House of Representatives 188
U.S. Justice Department 30, 45, 139, 204
U.S. Postal Service 119
U.S. Supreme Court 28, 34, 38, 45, 165, 276, 279
USA Today (newspaper) 183, 185
USSR *see* Russia
Utility companies 273–75
Utne Reader 33, 176

V

Vancouver Island, British Columbia 123
Van Dong, Pham 85
Venice, California 27
Vermont College 79
Viet Report 107
Vietnam War 35, 37, 47, 51, 57, 64–66, 69, 74–75, 81, 84, 87, 90, 92–102, 105, 107, 112–14, 130, 133–34, 138–42, 144, 158–59, 161–62, 165–68, 169, 173–74, 188, 190, 192, 208, 211, 214, 220, 223–24, 230, 233, 235–36, 240, 244–45, 259, 261, 272, 278, 281
Village Voice 35, 173, 175, 264
Vogue 257
Voigt, Jon 179
Voting Rights Act (1965) 41

W

Waas, Murray 35
Wall Street 179, 195
Wall Street Stock Exchange 182
Wallace, Dee 269
Walton, Bobby 215
War on Drugs 100, 248–49, 266
Warhol, Andy 214
Washington, DC 75, 84, 127, 157, 162, 201, 204, 221
Washington, March on (1963) 41
Washington Post 111, 134, 220, 273
Watergate 38, 111
Watts riot 47–48, 52
Weather Underground 57, 70–71, 92–94, 104–6, 149, 170, 199, 210, 218–19, 221, 223–24, 236–38
Weavers 243, 245

Webster, Barbara 86
Weiner, Lee 86
Weiss, Cora 86
Welfare 179, 232, 251
West Coast Homophile Organization 216, 219
West Point 148, 157
Whitbey Island, Washington 126
White, Vanna 280
White House 160, 259
Whitefish Bay, Wisconsin 223
Whittle, Chris 99
Will, George 271
"Wilton North Report" (television show) 39
Women's Liberation *see* Feminism; Women's rights
Women's rights 84, 128–29, 169, 172–73, 175, 177, 179, 191, 209, 218, 229, 231, 233, 250
Woodstock Festival 240, 247
Woodward, Bob 111
Worcester, Massachusetts 158, 240
Wordsworth, William 82
World War II 69, 124, 141, 158, 164–65
World's Fair, Flushing Meadow, New York 172
Wounded Knee, South Dakota 221

X

Xavier University 159

Y

Yale University 74, 82–83, 147, 150, 202
Yeshiva University 169, 172
Yippies 26–27, 33, 86, 113, 170, 174–77, 195, 218
Yippy Party 37
Young People's Socialist League 65
Yugoslavia 98

Z

Zappa, Frank 246
Zinn, Howard 86, 166